Language Dynamics in the Early Modern Period

In the fifteenth and sixteenth centuries, the linguistic situation in Europe was one of remarkable fluidity. Latin, the great scholarly lingua franca of the medieval period, was beginning to crack as the tectonic plates shifted beneath it, but the vernaculars had not yet crystallised into the national languages that they would later become, and multilingualism was rife. Meanwhile, elsewhere in the world, languages were coming into contact with an intensity that they had never had before, influencing each other and throwing up all manner of hybrids and pidgins as peoples tried to communicate using the semiotic resources they had available. Of interest to linguists, literary scholars and historians, amongst others, this interdisciplinary volume explores the linguistic dynamics operating in Europe and beyond in the crucial centuries between 1400 and 1800. Assuming a state of individual, societal and functional multilingualism, when codeswitching was the norm, and languages themselves were fluid, unbounded and porous, it explores the shifting relationships that existed between various tongues in different geographical contexts, as well as some of the myths and theories that arose to make sense of them.

Karen Bennett is Associate Professor in Translation at NOVA University, Lisbon, and a researcher with the Centre for English, Translation and Anglo-Portuguese Studies (CETAPS), where she coordinates the Translationality strand.

Angelo Cattaneo is Researcher in History and Geography at CNR-National Research Council, Rome, and Research Associate of CHAM - Centre for the Humanities, NOVA University, Lisbon.

Multilingualism, Lingua Franca and Translation in the Early Modern Period
Series Editor: Karen Bennett (Universidade NOVA de Lisboa, Portugal)

The period 1400 to 1800 is a particularly interesting time in the history of modern language development, as languages and cultures came into contact like never before, throwing up new linguistic varieties, challenging established language philosophies, and stimulating all manner of translational processes.

This series explores these linguistic phenomena, and the efforts made to explore and transmit them through language codification and teaching, from a transdisciplinary perspective, bringing together scholars from cultural history, historical and missionary linguistics, palaeography, translation studies, literary studies and philosophy.

Language Dynamics in the Early Modern Period
Edited by Karen Bennett and Angelo Cattaneo

For more information about this series, please visit: https://www.routledge.com/Multilingualism-Lingua-Franca-and-Translation/book-series/MLFTEMP

Language Dynamics in the
Early Modern Period

Edited by Karen Bennett and
Angelo Cattaneo

NEW YORK AND LONDON

First published 2022
by Routledge
605 Third Avenue, New York, NY 10158

and by Routledge
4 Park Square, Milton Park, Abingdon, Oxon, OX14 4RN

Routledge is an imprint of the Taylor & Francis Group, an informa business

© 2022 selection and editorial matter, Karen Bennett and Angelo Cattaneo; individual chapters, the contributors

The right of Karen Bennett and Angelo Cattaneo to be identified as the authors of the editorial material, and of the authors for their individual chapters, has been asserted in accordance with sections 77 and 78 of the Copyright, Designs and Patents Act 1988.

With the exception of Chapter 3, no part of this book may be reprinted or reproduced or utilised in any form or by any electronic, mechanical, or other means, now known or hereafter invented, including photocopying and recording, or in any information storage or retrieval system, without permission in writing from the publishers.

Chapters 3 of this book is available for free in PDF format as Open Access from the individual product page at www.routledge.com. It has been made available under a Creative Commons Attribution-ShareAlike 4.0 International license.

Trademark notice: Product or corporate names may be trademarks or registered trademarks, and are used only for identification and explanation without intent to infringe.

Library of Congress Cataloging-in-Publication Data
A catalog record for this title has been requested

ISBN: 978-0-367-55214-5 (hbk)
ISBN: 978-0-367-55215-2 (pbk)
ISBN: 978-1-003-09244-5 (ebk)

DOI: 10.4324/9781003092445

Typeset in Sabon
by KnowledgeWorks Global Ltd.

The Open Access version of chapter 3 was funded by Univerza v Ljubljani.

This volume was prepared and produced with the collaboration of João Luís Lisboa (CHAM – Centre for the Humanities and DH – HIstory Department, Faculdade de Ciências Sociais e Humanas, FCSH, Universidade NOVA de Lisboa, 1069-061 Lisbon).

The project benefitted from the support of the Centre for the Humanities (CHAM, NOVA FCSH/UAc) through the strategic project sponsored by the Portuguese Foundation for Science and Technology (UIDB/04666/2020; UIDP/04666/2020).

It also received assistance from the Centre for English, Translation and Anglo-Portuguese Studies (CETAPS, NOVA FCSH).

Contents

List of Figures ix
List of Tables x
Foreword xi
Acknowledgements xiii

Introduction: The Great Upheaval – Multilingualism
and Lingua Francas in the Early Modern Period 1
KAREN BENNETT

PART I
Multilingualism and Its Discontents 19

1 Multilingual Events in Late Medieval Personal Documentary
   Texts from the Winchester Diocese Collection in 1400–1525 21
   DELIA SCHIPOR

2 Croatian Biblical Texts in the Early Modern Period: A
   Historical-Sociolinguistic Approach to Language Change 40
   VUK-TADIJA BARBARIĆ AND IVANA ETEROVIĆ

3 National Myths and Language Status in
   Early Modern Wales and Brittany 53
   OLIVER CURRIE

4 Bernardo de Aldrete's *Del origen:* Rejecting Multilingualism
   and Linguistic Essentialism in Early Modern Spain 74
   VICENTE LLEDÓ-GUILLEM

5 Multilingualism and Translation in the Early Modern
   Low Countries 89
   THEO HERMANS

viii Contents

PART II
The Defence of Latin   109

6   Should Latin Be Spoken? The Controversy between Sanctius
    Brocensis, Henry Jason and the Irish Jesuits of Salamanca   111
    EUSTAQUIO SÁNCHEZ SALOR

7   *Pro lingua Latina*: Girolamo Lagomarsini's Oration
    in Defence of Latin in Eighteenth-Century Italy   129
    JUAN MARÍA GÓMEZ GÓMEZ

8   Petropolis: The Place of Latin in Early Modern Russia   142
    BRIAN P. BENNETT

PART III
Pidgins, Jargons, Lingua Francas   167

9   On the Existence of a Mediterranean Lingua Franca
    and the Persistence of Language Myths   169
    JOSHUA BROWN

10 Immortal Passados: Early Modern England's Italianate
    Fencing Jargon on Page and Stage   190
    LAETITIA SANSONETTI

11 Linguistic Expression of Power and Subalternity
    in Peixoto's *Obra Nova de Língua Geral de Mina* (1741)   207
    CHRISTINA MÄRZHÄUSER AND ENRIQUE RODRIGUES-MOURA

12 "Long Time No See": The Use of Chinese Pidgin
    English as a Cultural Identity Symbol by the Canton
    Anglophone Trading Community   224
    ROGÉRIO MIGUEL PUGA

    Epilogue: Developing Historical Linguistic
    Awareness in a Multilingual World   242
    ANGELO CATTANEO

    Contributors   253
    Index   257

Figures

1.1 Distribution of texts in the bishops' registers of the Winchester Diocese collection (1400–1525) according to language   23
9.1 Title page of the *Dictionnaire de la langue franque ou petit mauresque* printed in Marseille in 1830   181
9.2 The first page of the *Dictionnaire de la langue franque ou petit mauresque* (1830) showing correspondences between French (left column) and the Mediterranean Lingua Franca (right column)   182
9.3 Taxonomy of Mediterranean Lingua Franca items listed in the *Dictionnaire de la langue franque ou petit mauresque* (1830)   183

Tables

1.1	Genres of personal documentary texts in the bishops' registers of the Winchester Diocese collection (1400–1525)	24
1.2	The Winchester Diocese collection – Bishops' registers at the Hampshire Record Office	39
9.1	A reproduction of Arends' (1998) corpus of primary documents containing evidence of the Mediterranean Lingua Franca (MLF)	174
9.2	Varieties other than Italo-Romance previously identified in MLF	178
9.3	Varieties of Italo-Romance previously identified in MLF	178

Foreword to the Series *Multilingualism, Lingua Franca and Translation in the Early Modern Period*

In the fifteenth and sixteenth centuries, the linguistic situation in Europe was one of remarkable fluidity. Latin, the great scholarly lingua franca of the medieval period, was beginning to crack as the tectonic plates shifted beneath it, but the vernaculars had not yet crystallised into the national languages that they would become a century later, and bi- or multilingualism was still rife. Through the influence of print capitalism, the dialects that occupied the informal space were starting to organise into broad fields of communication and exchange (Anderson, 2006: 37–46), though the boundaries between them were not yet clearly defined nor the links to territory fully established. Meanwhile, elsewhere in the world, languages were coming into contact with an intensity that they had never had before (Burke, 2004: 111–140), influencing each other and throwing up all manner of hybrids and pidgins as peoples tried to communicate using the semiotic resources they had available. New lingua francas emerged to serve particular purposes in different geographic regions or were imposed through conquest and settlement (Ostler, 2005: 323–516). And translation proliferated at the seams of such cultural encounters, undertaken for different reasons by a diverse demographic that included missionaries, scientists, traders, aristocrats, emigrés, refugees and renegades (Burke, 2007: 11–16).

This series, which has its origins in the *Host of Tongues* conference held in Lisbon in December 2018, brings together scholars from various disciplinary backgrounds (cultural history, historical linguistics, palaeography, translation studies, literary studies) to offer a broad survey of linguistic practices in the Early Modern period (1400 to 1800).

Each volume focuses on a different aspect of the theme: general language dynamics (Latin and the vernaculars, multilingualism, and other lingua francas); translation; and linguistics and language teaching.

Karen Bennett

References

Anderson, Benedict. *Imagined Communities: Reflections on the Origin and Spread of Nationalism*. Revised edition. London and New York: Verso, 2006.

Burke, Peter. *Languages and Communities in Early Modern Europe.* Cambridge and New York: Cambridge University Press, 2004.

Burke, Peter. 'Cultures of Translation in Early Modern Europe'. In *Cultural Translation in Early Modern Europe*, edited by P. Burke, Peter and R. Po-Chia Hsia, 7–38. Cambridge and New York: Cambridge University Press, 2007

Ostler, Nicholas. *Empires of the Word: A Language History of the World.* London: HarperCollins, 2005.

Acknowledgements

This volume had its origins in the international conference "*A host of tongues....*": *Multilingualism, Lingua Franca and Translation in the Early Modern Period*, held in Lisbon between 13th and 15th December 2018 with the support of the Centre for English, Translation and Anglo-Portuguese Studies (CETAPS) and the Centre for the Humanities (CHAM), both based in the School of Arts and Social Sciences at Nova University of Lisbon (FCSH NOVA), and the Centre for Studies in Letters (CEL) at the University of Trás-os-Montes and Alto Douro (UTAD). All are funded by the Fundação para a Ciência e a Tecnologia (FCT), the Portuguese national funding agency for science, research and technology.

The editors would like to thank FCSH NOVA for hosting the initial conference, all the delegates from around the world that made it such a resounding success and CETAPS and CHAM for their financial and logistic support. Thanks too to Catarina Barreiro Pereira (FCSH NOVA) for her invaluable assistance in the preparation of this volume.

Introduction
The Great Upheaval – Multilingualism and Lingua Francas in the Early Modern Period

Karen Bennett

At the beginning of the third decade of the twenty-first century, we are starting to feel the effects of what might prove to be the greatest linguistic shake-up in five hundred years. Contrary to the predictions made back in the nineties and 'noughties',[1] when English looked set to take over the world, we have not found ourselves in a linguistic monoculture dominated by the United States. Instead, provoked by unprecedented waves of migration, the effects of new technologies, and forms of linguistic 'jihad' that oppose 'Globish' on ideological or identity grounds,[2] International English has given way to what is now called the multi- or translingual paradigm (Jenkins, 2015; Pennycook, 2006, 2007; Canagarajah, 2013; Schneider, 2016) – a hermeneutic category that has already motivated a massive body of scholarship in different fields. English is still there 'in the mix' but it no longer operates on its own as an autonomous bounded entity. Instead, it comes in hybrid forms, blended or alternating with other linguistic codes in both life and art.[3] In ad-hoc contact situations where speakers of different tongues are thrown together and forced to communicate in whatever way they can, languages may be reduced to a set of 'mobile semiotic resources' that are transient, context-dependent and multi-semiotic (Blommaert, 2010) or replaced by new provisional codes consisting of fragments of different tongues – a practice now known as 'translanguaging' (Garcia and Wei, 2014).

Indeed, our whole notion of what constitutes a language has been thrown into disarray as we become aware that they are not, after all, watertight entities, territorially bounded, and the property of a restricted group of 'native speakers' with their own unique take upon the world. Philosophers such as Bakhtin (1981: 262–263) and Derrida (1985: 100) had already made the point, back in the 1980s, that all national languages contain bits of other languages in them, the result of centuries of mutual influence and translational processes. But it has taken up to now for this understanding to fully penetrate the ideological barriers that nation-states have erected to promote their own uniqueness and distinguish themselves from their neighbours. Makoni and Pennycook call this the 'disinvention of languages': the

DOI: 10.4324/9781003092445-1

acknowledgement that languages are 'social constructions, artifacts analogous to other constructions such as time' (2007: 1) and held in place by 'metadiscursive regimes' (Idem: 2).[4]

One of the results of this upheaval has been a reassessment of linguistic history in order to determine just when the 'monolingual mindset' took root. Most authors (e.g. Makoni and Pennycook, 2007; Yildiz, 2012; Schneider, 2016) indicate the late eighteenth and early nineteenth centuries as the crux, the moment when individual languages became identified with nation and territory.[5] Some point to German Romantic language philosophy, as manifested by Herder and Humboldt (Canagarajah, 2013: 20–24); others mention the French Revolution as the boundary consolidating the notion of the nation-state (Burke, 2004: 166). Before this, it is argued, identities were not constrained or configured by language in the way that they came to be later (Braunmüller and Ferraresi, 2003: 1), enabling a greater flexibility in the range of linguistic practices available to both individuals and cultures.

The implication is, therefore, that in the Early Modern period, *there was a state of individual, societal and functional multilingualism, when codeswitching was the norm and when languages themselves were more fluid, unbounded and porous*. Though most scholars agree that it was in this period that the seeds were sown of the nationalistic impulses that provided the conceptual framework through which language activity was processed in the coming centuries (Mignolo, 2012: 257; Burke, 2004: 160–162), multilingualism is seen by many as the natural state of affairs,[6] with something akin to 'translanguaging' practised routinely in intercultural 'contact zones' (Pratt 1991).

The aim of this first volume of the series *Multilingualism, Lingua Franca and Translation in the Early Modern Period* is to examine this hypothesis by taking a closer look at the linguistic dynamics operating in Europe and beyond in the centuries between 1400 and 1800. It is not the first exploration of the topic, of course. Significant scholarship about Early Modern multilingualism has already appeared in specialist volumes (e.g. Classen, 2016; Frijhoff *et al.*, 2017; Burke, 2004), as well as in works with a broader temporal framework (e.g. Braunmüller and Ferraresi, 2003; Braarvig and Geller, 2018; Pahta *et al.*, 2018) or narrower geographical one (e.g. Gilbert, 2014; Shearer, 2019). In addition, works about contemporary multilingualism often contain historical chapters (e.g. Edwards, 2004; Blommaert, 2010), just as works by historians may have chapters about language (Anderson, 2006). There are also specialised volumes focusing on particular aspects, such as multilingualism in the literary context (Delabastita and Hoenselaars, 2015) or resulting from exploration and settlement (Brownlees, 2020).

Consequently, this volume is not attempting to map out the 'ecology of languages' in the period – this has already been done comprehensively by Burke (2004) and others. Instead, we hope to examine the shifting relationships that existed between the various tongues vying for status as Latin, the great lingua franca of the Middle Ages, entered into decline, and to explore some of the myths and theories that circulated in order to sustain them. We are also interested in trying to gauge how people felt about the situation. Did they revel in multilingualism, showing off their skills with virtuosity and panache? Or was multilingualism a source of infelicity and angst, as suggested by Shearer (2019)? Or might it just have been seen as a pragmatic necessity and accepted as the inevitable consequence of the new political configuration that was emerging?

Let us begin by recalling what the situation was like in Europe and beyond at the end of the medieval period, before the invention of the printing press, the fall of Constantinople and Columbus's arrival in America – three events that would have a profound effect on the linguistic dynamics. In Europe, the classic picture of a continent united by a common lingua franca is somewhat simplistic. In many regions, Latin still held sway in the church, universities and schools, law courts and administration, but had already begun to give ground to the vernaculars in some domains: Dante and Chaucer were already producing major works of literature in their respective vernaculars, while Spanish had been promoted over Latin in many domains since Alfonso X in the thirteenth century. There was a complex relationship between the different vernaculars in some parts of Europe, with some, such as French and German, already at the centre of mini-'linguistic empires' (Burke 2004: 64). In the Iberian Peninsula, Arabic, Hebrew, Latin, Castilian, Catalan and a whole range of other Iberian languages, including Portuguese, jostled for status in the process of mutual enrichment (Classen, 2016: 9–10), while in central and eastern Europe, there was also a major clash and interaction of languages in the wake of massive migrational movements (idem).

Beyond Europe, we could see the presence of Greek in the remnants of the Byzantine Empire; Arabic in the Muslim world; Persian along the Silk Roads; and further to the East, a whole bevy of Indic, Sinitic and Dravidian languages. And we should also remember that the as-yet 'undiscovered' continents also had complex language networks of their own, which are only now starting to be mapped out.

As if the language situation in late medieval Europe were not complex enough, a series of events in the fifteenth century caused it to complexify even further. The invention of the printing press is, of course, absolutely fundamental in that it put pressure on the multiple dialects to cohere into a central standard, giving rise to what Anderson (2006) called the 'print languages', which then became the languages of the emergent nation-states, carried far afield in the quest for empire.[7] The fall of Constantinople in 1453 also brought important linguistic repercussions, as the migration of Greek-speaking scholars to Italy led to the rediscovery of lost Greek texts and the development of philological techniques with which to study them. The Reformation challenged the centrality of Latin in the church and made the translation of the Bible into one of its central pillars, giving a further boost to the vernaculars championed by the emergent middle classes. And then, of course, there was the 'discovery' of the New World, bringing Europeans into contact with peoples that spoke languages they had never heard before. The various attempts to dominate and civilise them produced a range of new language dynamics, not least the urge to codify and teach. Thus, there were both centrifugal and centripetal forces at work during this time, as Burke (2004: 102, 109) points out, the former leading to the breakup of the medieval lingua franca and the latter producing new centres in different parts of the globe.

All of this was accompanied by significant shifts in beliefs about language. The old medieval hierarchy, which accorded sacred status to the languages of the Bible and the cross,[8] as well as nationalistic myths tracing the origins of a particular language back to Aeneas or the sons of Noah[9] began to be challenged by more rational theories of language evolution and new forms of linguistic nationalism (Currie and Lledó-Guillem, this volume), while scholastic notions of a universal (i.e. God-given) grammar were sorely tested by the confrontation with the languages of the New World (Dürr, 2017: 75–76). This did not put an end to the notion of the perfect language, however. As Latin entered into decline, we see systematic quests for a new universal language to take its place (Eco, 1997).

The chapters in this volume, to a large extent, complicate the classic narrative of the gradual rise of vernaculars at the expense of Latin, revealing that these processes were not linear but instead were characterised by stops and starts, internal contradictions and backtracking. We see, for example, that although Latin was gradually being replaced by the vernaculars in domains such as official records/parish registers (Schipor), worship (Barbarić and Eterović) and scholarship (Gómez Gómez), it nevertheless had its defenders (Sánchez Salor, Gómez Gómez) and was even actively introduced into Russia as late as the eighteenth century to serve mostly scholarly and ceremonial purposes (B. Bennett). Should this be considered a conservative position or a progressive one? It is difficult to judge because the arguments used to defend it were no longer religious or reverent in nature but instead motivated by rational and practical concerns.

Also, as regards the rise of the vernaculars, this too was by no means linear. Some vernaculars, including ones which were thriving in the Medieval period, came to be increasingly threatened by hegemonic national languages (for example, the situation of Welsh in relation to English and Breton in relation to French, as discussed by Currie, and that of the various languages of the Iberian Peninsula in relation to Castilian, as recounted by Lledó-Guillem). There were even more complex processes at work in Croatia and the Low Countries, as described by Barbarić & Eterović, and Hermans, respectively.

There is also evidence of much language mixing, despite the centripetal effects of the printing press and growing nationalisms. In addition to hybrids produced by calquing vernacular structures onto Latin (such as the *sermo hispanolatinus*, described by Sánchez Salor), we see the developments of pidgins in contact zones to serve the needs of trade (e.g. the famous Mediterranean Lingua Franca, discussed by Brown, and Chinese Pidgin English in Canton and Macau discussed by Puga) or forced labour (as with the *língua geral da mina* in eighteenth-century Brazil, described by Märzhäuser and Rodrigues-Moura). There is even a case of mixing in Elizabethan courtly circles as Italian and other Continental languages blended with English to produce a 'theatrical' fencing jargon (Sansonetti).

All in all, the volume describes a linguistic panorama that has much in common with our own twenty-first-century situation: the breakdown of a near-global lingua franca into mutually incomprehensible tongues, combined with a drive to elevate a culturally pared-down version of it into a universal language of scholarship or administration;[10] the appearance of new political players on the world stage generating an interest in languages that had previously had only local or regional importance; and above all, the presence of multilingualism on all levels of society. In both contexts, these are the dynamics of transition, the turbulence that comes whenever there is a major reshuffling of power. Though the tumult will eventually subside as the forces settle into a new stability, this is beyond the scope of our concerns.

This volume, which contains contributions by linguists, philologists, literary scholars and cultural historians, is divided into three sections, each organised roughly chronologically. Part I, entitled *Multilingualism and its Discontents*, explores the theme of multilingualism from both an objective and a subjective/critical perspective. The first two papers, by linguists, use scientific methods to map out the actual linguistic situation in different parts of Europe during the period in question, while the second two are more concerned with attitudes, as revealed in language myths and other imaginative representations.

The first chapter, by **Delia Schipor**, presents the results of a systematic study to record the languages present in official documents (bishops' registers) in one small area of England right at the beginning of our period, from 1400 through to 1525. This is a snapshot of a society that is just beginning to emerge from the societal multilingualism that was such a marked feature of medieval England: then, as we know, officialdom conducted its affairs in Latin and French, while English was the spoken language of most of the population. Across the period in question, however, English began to make an appearance in personal documentary texts like statements and testaments, though almost always accompanied by Latin, in the form of margin notes or body text. It is this functional or documentary multilingualism that is the object of Schipor's attention. From a corpus of over five thousand individual texts, she records instances of multiple language use and analyses some of them in detail, with attention to phenomena such as visual markings and discourse organisation. She concludes that the use of English and French in personal documentary texts appears to be directly related to the moral and legal character of such documents, with the choice of one over the other being probably a matter of preference or social status. However, it is clear from the nature of the entries that, in this period, Latin was still regarded as the main language of record, which rather undermines the generalisation, present in many textbooks about the history of English, that English had already become the language of official documents by the fifteenth century.

With the next chapter, by **Vuk-Tadija Barbarić** and **Ivana Eterović**, we move to Croatia to focus on language change in the late fifteenth and sixteenth centuries, as manifested by bible translations. The linguistic situation in Croatia seems to have been extraordinarily complex in the medieval and early modern periods, with several languages, and indeed scripts, vying for supremacy in different domains. As elsewhere, Latin initially served an important role as the lingua franca of religion, administration, law, diplomacy and education, before giving way, in the liturgical sphere, to Old Church Slavonic in the ninth century. By the late medieval period, it was the regional variety of this *lingua sacra*, Croatian Church Slavonic, that was being used for the liturgy, with the Čakavian vernacular serving more practical religious needs. However, in the early sixteenth century, there is evidence that a new literary language – an amalgam of Croatian Church Slavonic and the Čakavian vernacular – was being used for the translation of religious texts, largely at the initiative of one individual, Šimun Kožičić Benja, the bishop of Modruš and Senj, who ran a printing press from his house at Rijeka. At the same time, the vernacular was itself gaining ground, largely thanks to the efforts of Croatian protestants, who translated biblical texts into it, in line with their counterparts in other European countries. Indeed, the authors conclude that it was probably when Croatian literary language varieties became open to horizontal translation (i.e. translation from other vernaculars as opposed to vertical translation from the more prestigious Latin or Croatian Church Slavonic) that the diglossia that was such a feature of the medieval landscape truly began to erode.

The next chapter deals not with the rise of the vernaculars in the face of a traditional lingua franca, but rather the struggles between rival vernaculars for prestige and status. **Oliver Currie** focuses on the fate of Welsh and Breton, as their powerful neighbours, English and French, expanded functionally and geographically, taking over domains of use from Latin and threatening to displace them following the formal annexation of their territories in the sixteenth century. Particular attention is given to the myths and pseudo-historical narratives that were used to explain national origins and assert language antiquity and language status. Hence, we learn that, until the sixteenth century, the Welsh and the Bretons both traced their origins to the Trojan military leader Brutus, great-grandson of Aeneas, who was believed to have settled first on the Island of Britain with a community of Trojan exiles, before spreading to northern France. However, in the second half of the sixteenth century, their national historical narratives diverged and began to draw closer to those of their larger neighbours. The reason for this in the case of Wales, Currie tells us, was primarily religious. English and Welsh Protestants sought to legitimise the new protestant Church of England by arguing that it represented a return to the pure Christian faith of the Early British Church, while in Catholic France, scholars preferred to trace the origins of both French and Breton back to ancient Gaulish, believed to have been brought into existence when God confused tongues at the Tower of Babel and brought to France by the sons of Noah. The religious divergence also seems to have had real implications for the survival of these subaltern vernaculars: the fact that the Bible was translated into Welsh in the sixteenth century stimulated the production of further literature in that language and allowed it to be used for religious worship, in church and at home. Currie is at pains to point out, however, that though the Bretons did not have a vernacular bible until the nineteenth century, there was also a flourishing print industry in that language, producing Catholic religious works such as catechisms, hymns, carols, hagiographies and religious instruction manuals.

Language myths also play a role in the next chapter, **Vicente Lledó-Guillem**'s study of Bernardo de Aldrete's 1606 text about the origins of Castilian. Aldrete is disputing the 'primitive Castilian' theory, according to which that language was one of the 72 languages that originated in Babel (supposedly brought to Spain by Noah's grandson Tubal before the Roman conquest of the Iberian Peninsula), arguing, in a thoroughly modern way, that Castilian is actually descended from Latin. What concerns Aldrete most, however, is the relationship between language and identity. Though he believes that monolingualism is the ideal state of humanity, he nevertheless rejects the idea of an essential or natural relationship between a language and the identity of the people(s) that speak it, and implies that human identities may be altered, transformed, and created by means of language. This, then, is the prelude for his proposal that Castilian has the qualities to succeed Latin as the language of the civilised world. Arguing not only that is it a living language that reflects the identity of the Hispanic people generally, but that it is also supported by a strong military power, Aldrete seems to be responding very pragmatically to the political circumstances of his day – the imminent expansion of Spanish power into Portugal, thanks to Philip II's inheritance of the Portuguese Crown.

Theo Hermans' chapter, which closes Part I, covers the period from 1550 to 1700 in the Low Countries, and is essentially a comprehensive survey of the complex linguistic phenomena encountered in that narrow spatiotemporal frame. The chapter takes its inspiration from Mary Louise Pratt's 1987 essay 'Linguistic utopias', which advocates a shift of perspective away from the 'linguistics of community' towards the linguistic operations that occur 'across lines of social differentiation' in the contact zones between different collectives, individuals and tongues (Pratt, 1987: 60). This switch of lens allows polyglossia and translation – which tend to be occluded in more traditional community-oriented accounts – to come into focus in a particularly striking manner. Hermans records cases of multilingualism on a range of different levels: *societal* (the region was as diverse linguistically in the sixteenth and seventeenth centuries as it is today, with Dutch, French, Latin, Spanish and Portuguese coming into contact on a regular basis, along with a host of other tongues operating in specific domains); *individual* (polyglots included merchants, diplomats, aristocrats, refugees, economic migrants, missionaries and academics, many of whom served as translators and interpreters, and/or authored multilingual works); and *textual* (in the form not only of works that incorporate different languages into their very fabric, but also parallel editions of same work in different languages). A particularly fruitful category Hermans introduces for the analysis of this complex world is that of the 'community of practice' (borrowed from Eckert and McConnell-Ginet, 1992), which yields yet another kind of multilingualism, as individuals pooled their linguistic resources in collaborative enterprises. We see this dynamic operating in the sphere of science (e.g. the monumental botanical work known as the *Hortus malabaricus*, compiled by a team of Indian and European botanists and medics at the initiative of Hendrik van Rheede tot Drakestein, and published in Amsterdam between 1678 and 1677), religion (e.g. the polyglot Bible, produced in Antwerp by scholars from all over Europe, brought together by Christopher Plantin in the years 1568–1572) and even theatre (as a well-organised 'creative industry' laboured to bring popular Spanish plays to the Amsterdam stage through a series of translational manoeuvres).

In the Low Countries, therefore, multilingualism does not seem to have been perceived in a particularly negative light. On the contrary, it both resulted from and contributed to the region's growing economic power, and appears to have been systematically milked by forward-thinking entrepreneurs as a source of further wealth and cultural prestige. This was not the case everywhere, however. In some other contexts, multilingualism is clearly a source of 'linguistic infelicity' (Shearer 2019), provoking a range of negative emotions from functional annoyance and frustration to a more existential nostalgia and regret.

Part II, *The Defence of Latin*, specifically looks at some late attempts to overcome this linguistic infelicity by reinvigorating or reinstating the lingua franca of medieval Europe. This is perhaps not entirely unexpected. For Peter Burke (2004: 43), Latin, during the Early Modern period, was 'a language in search of a community', in the sense that it 'expressed and contributed to the cohesion of two international communities, in particular, the Catholic Church and the Republic of Letters'. Many people seem to have viewed with alarm the prospect of the disintegration of these two communities, as the different vernaculars staked their claims to become the languages of religion and scholarship, as well as of statehood and administration. Hence, it was not surprising that, in addition to the various seventeenth-century attempts to create new universal languages to take its place,[11] Latin itself became the object of renewed attention.

However, we should recall that, by this time, Latin was by no means a single unified tongue. Instead, there were various Latins with considerable differences between them. For our purposes, we might list four: Classical Latin (the literate Latin used in the late Roman Republic and Empire by the great authors and orators such as Cicero); Vulgar Latin (the demotic oral form of the language that had coexisted with Classical Latin, eventually giving rise to the Romance languages); Medieval Scholastic Latin (the version of the language used as a lingua franca of knowledge and culture in the Medieval period); and the New Latin, developed in Renaissance Italy in the fourteenth and fifteenth centuries as a result of the increased interest in Classical civilisation.[12] The three chapters that make up this section of the book concern various attempts to negotiate the role and form that Latin would take in the period under examination.

Eustaquio Sánchez Salor's chapter examines from close-up one facet of the sixteenth-century dispute about what constituted correct Latin. His paper concerns a controversy between the Spanish humanist Francisco Sánchez de las Brozas (otherwise known as El Brocense or Sanctius) and an Irishman called Henry Jason (who was exiled in Salamanca to escape Elizabeth I's persecution of Catholics) on the subject of whether Latin should or should not be spoken. Despite firmly believing in the importance of a Latin education, Sanctius refused Jason's request to use Latin rather than Castilian in his Rhetoric classes on the grounds that Latin was defiled by being spoken. His response took the form of an extensive tract (which would eventually become Paradox II of the 4th Book of *Minerva*, 1592) attacking the contemporary practice of calquing structures and lexis from Spanish onto the Latin tongue. Jason responded with an equally extensive document (the *Disquisitio Responsoria*) in which he insisted that, although spoken Latin was not the most elegant form of Latin, it could be decent enough and did not have to the debased *sermo hispanolatinus* that Sanctius so despised. The controversy culminated in the publication in 1611, by the Irish Jesuits of Salamanca, of a manual called the *Ianua linguarum* ('Gateway of Languages'), which taught the Latin forms of the most common terms and phrases in Castilian. Representing a new and less demanding concept of linguistic elegance, this manual, and the various others that followed it, effectively confirmed the value of Latin as a practical tool for use in the contemporary world, above and beyond its consecrated role as the vehicle for Classical and humanistic learning. The fact that this dispute was roughly contemporaneous with Aldrete's text on Castilian provides interesting testimony about the shifting relationship between these languages in Iberia at the turn of the sixteenth and seventeenth centuries.

With the next chapter, by **Juan María Gómez Gómez**, we move forward in time to Italy in the eighteenth century, when Latin was in serious decline due to the influence of Rationalist thought. In the sphere of education, reformist pedagogues were arguing that education should offer training in citizenship and proposed the inclusion of more practical subjects to the detriment of the traditional Humanities curriculum. In this context, Latin began to be viewed as retrograde and an obstacle to progress, and efforts were made to introduce the vernacular into primary and middle education, as had already happened in other parts of Europe. Modern pedagogues argued that mastery of Latin was necessary only for those destined to become members of the intellectual elites, and that young people whose future lay in agriculture, crafts or trade would be better served by a vernacular education. It was in this context that Girolamo Lagomarsini presented a series of seven lectures in Florence in which he defended not only the traditional humanist curriculum, but also the use of Latin. However, in the oration specifically devoted to the latter (*Pro lingua Latina,* delivered 1736), he does not employ the old tropes about the inherent perfection of the traditional tongue (in fact, he expressly states that no language is innately superior to any other as regards its expressive power) but instead, invokes distinctly modern arguments of utility. The fact that Latin already has an extensive community of speakers is mentioned, as is the benefit of having an international lingua franca of knowledge: works written in the vernaculars will be read only by the speakers of those languages, he argues, and will therefore be condemned to obscurity. Finally, he makes the point that serious scholarship will benefit from the dignity that Latin has acquired after so many centuries of use, a position that is not very far from that of the encyclopaedists Jean le Rond D'Alembert and Nicolas Beauzée, who proposed recovering Latin as a universal philosophical language to operate alongside the vernaculars in its highly specialised domain.[13]

These arguments intersect with some of those being invoked in Russia at around the same time, as described by **Brian Bennett** in his chapter. Here, we see again Latin being recruited to serve as a language of science and ceremonials. This was even more remarkable given the famous ignorance in Russia of Classical languages, as remarked by travellers to the realm in the sixteenth and seventeenth centuries. Bennett's chapter traces how Latin in Russia passed from being a 'rare linguistic commodity...restricted to doctors and diplomats' to the language of the lecture hall, used in the Imperial Academy of Sciences in St Petersburg and other educational establishments, and for ceremonial purposes. This transformation of Russia's linguistic culture is associated above all with Peter the Great (r. 1682–1785), who believed that knowledge of Western European languages would be essential for the new modern empire he was projecting. Latin, despite being in decline in most of Western Europe by this time, was presented in Russia (in a landmark text entitled *A Treasury of Slavonic*, published in 1704 by Fedor Polikarpov) as the most widely used language around the world for civil and educational matters. This ultimately led to a 'momentous bifurcation' in Russian cultural history as a new script (the Latinate civil script) began to compete with traditional Cyrillic in much the same way as the new westernised capital of St Petersburg was now competing with byzantine Moscow.

Latin was of course not the only lingua franca in operation in the Early Modern globalised world. There were also others: *koinés*, like Arabic, which had overspilled the boundaries of its immediate community with the military conquests of the seventh to ninth centuries and was now spoken across a vast territory; or Persian, which was a prestige language across much of Asia for centuries, most notably in Mughal India; other *lingua sacra*,[14] like Sanskrit or Old Church Slavonic (already mentioned in the chapters by Bárbarić & Eterović, and B. Bennett); as well as pidgins or linguistic blends forged at the interface of cultures to serve a pragmatic need.[15] The final section of this book, Part III: *Pidgins, Jargons, Lingua Franca*, focuses on this kind of linguistic phenomena in order to examine what light they shed on the whole notion of how languages were conceptualised in this all-important moment of transition prior to the crystallisation of the national tongues.

The first chapter of the section, by **Joshua Brown**, looks at the original Lingua Franca, the mythical trading language used around the Mediterranean basin between the late medieval and early modern periods.[16] The term 'lingua franca' actually derives from the 'language of the Franks' (the name given by Arabs to all the people of western Europe), and does not, therefore, evoke 'the language of free trade', as analogies with terms like *porto franco* (freeport) might suggest (Salverda, 2018: 32). This Mediterranean Lingua Franca (MLF) seems to have contained elements of various Romance languages, mixed with Arabic, but there was so much spatial and temporal variation in the use of the term (Salverda 2018: 37) that doubts persist as to whether it could actually be considered a coherent 'language' at all. Joshua Brown's unique contribution to the ongoing debate about this mysterious tongue is to focus on the metadiscourse that emerged about it from the nineteenth century onwards and to frame this within the nationalistic concerns of the day. His chapter analyses one of the best-known documents relating to the Mediterranean Lingua Franca – the *Dictionnaire de la langue franque ou petit mauresque* of 1830. By classifying the data recorded in the *Dictionnaire* in an alternative way, Brown suggests that most of the recorded forms are actually very similar to standard Italian, thus undermining the hypothesis that MLF could be considered a separate language variety. Indeed, the myth that arose about it is probably more interesting for what it says about the language philosophy that inspired the *Dictionnaire* (i.e. the drive to codify unrecorded language varieties on the model of the by-now-circumscribed national tongues) than about the actual Lingua Franca itself, which is likely to have been an ad-hoc pidgin that took different forms in different times and places, with very little internal coherence.

Laetitia Sansonetti's chapter is an account of a quite different kind of language mixing, the development of a fencing jargon in England in the first half of the sixteenth century through the systematic incorporation of terms from Italian and other European languages. A series of books about the art published in the 1590s, combined with the establishment of fencing schools in London by Italian teachers, led to the influx of Italian fencing terms into English, and Sansonetti begins her piece by analysing the various strategies used for their importation. However, there is also evidence that the fencing jargon borrowed features from different Continental languages (Spanish and French, as well as Italian). By analysing a series of dramatic works in which fencing terminology plays a key role (and it is significant that fencing schools were located in the same part of London as the theatres), she observes that the Italianate fencing jargon acted as a sort of 'theatrical lingua franca' that was both a 'cypher testing (and enlarging) the audience's knowledge of current fashions' and a 'code pointing to affectation, an index of irony'. The discussion is framed within the language politics of the day, in which classical Latin still held sway as the prestige language at the top of the linguistic hierarchy, but where English was progressively gaining ground. The Italian words used in fencing treatises and bandied about on stages thus reveal the essentially 'multilingual' nature of English itself, and serve to delineate multilingual communities by marking the boundaries of an in-crowd, those that were able to understand them.

From the courtly circles of Elizabethan England, we pass to a very different world, the slave society of Vila Rica (today Ouro Preto) in eighteenth-century Brazil. The *língua geral da Mina* (LGM), described here by **Christina Märzhäuser** and **Enrique Rodrigues-Moura**, is not the Tupi-based *língua geral* established by the Jesuits, which became the main language spoken in colonial Brazil in the seventeenth and eighteenth centuries. Rather, this *língua geral* was the African language Fon, brought to Brazil by the slaves that worked the gold mines of Minas Gerais, and of which vestiges still remain in the languages used by certain Afro-Brazilian religious communities today. Märzhäuser and Rodrigues-Moura centre their analysis on a 1741 manuscript by a Portuguese clerk, António da Costa Peixoto, who lived and worked in the Vila Rica region. His *Obra Nova de Língua Geral de Mina* ('New work on the general language of Mina') – essentially a glossary of terms supplemented by short dialogues in LGM with translations to Portuguese – is interesting not only linguistically, but also because of what it reveals about the society in which it was used. From the discussion of this manuscript, we learn, for example, that some slaves managed to buy their freedom and engage in petty trade, enjoying an unexpected degree of agency in their relationships with the Europeans in the town. Indeed, the very fact that Peixoto took the trouble to learn this African language – and that he recommends that his fellow Europeans do the same in the interests of social peace – suggests that Gayatri Spivak's famous question 'Can the subaltern speak?' (Spivak, 1994) deserves an affirmative answer in this particular case.

The volume closes with an account of another trading language, China Pidgin English (CPE), in the chapter by **Rogério Miguel Puga**. Like the Mediterranean Lingua Franca, this seems to have been something of an eighteenth- or nineteenth-century construct, in this case serving an ideological purpose as a manifestation of social and colonial hierarchies. It was clearly a contact language which merged to serve the ad-hoc needs of trade, and was first spoken by the traders, servants, hawkers and prostitutes that had contact with the British and American merchants operating in the Pearl River Delta. However, when those Anglophone traders were joined by their wives and children, this predominantly male trading language gradually spread to the domestic space, becoming part of the family heritage and shared memory. In this chapter, Puga examines some of the textual representations of CPE made in the eighteenth century by Anglophones in the Canton factories and Macau homes in the form of travel narratives, diaries, letter and memoirs, supplemented by newspaper reports, and official records and chronicles. He concludes that CPE was effectively constructed in these documents as a form of linguistic chinoiserie, analogous to the chinaware, furniture and other commodities that those traders and their families later took back home as souvenirs and signs of their cosmopolitanism. In the texts analysed, the Chinese are represented as comic performers communicating and interacting with foreigners in 'broken' English – an effect that allowed these traders and their families to claim cultural superiority through a process of linguistic Othering. Curiously, though, once these westerners had returned home, CPE words and expressions (like 'savvy', 'no can do', or 'long time no see') acquired a quite different charge as exoticised markers of status, power and wealth, eventually spreading to become part of the soundscapes of cities like London, New York, Boston and Philadelphia.

Taken together, then, these chapters reveal a very complex picture of linguistic relations in the Early Modern period. Multilingualism was clearly rife, but it seems to have been viewed in contrasting ways in different contexts. For some, it was a decidedly negative state of affairs, representing the Babel-like breakdown of idealised communities, whether religious or scholarly. For others, it meant freedom from the yoke of a dominant language, the opportunity to affirm a national or regional identity in a new linguistic marketplace, or a mark of sophistication and cosmopolitanism. For yet others, it was a pragmatic necessity involving something akin to the 'translanguaging' that has become such a feature of our own times. Although the seeds of linguistic nationalism were clearly sown in the period under consideration, we would have to wait another couple of centuries before the 'monolingual mindset' truly became established in Europe, with ideological repercussions throughout the rest of the world.

Notes

1. See, for example, the literature on English as a Global/International Language (e.g. Crystal, 1997; Modiano, 1999; Graddol, 1999) or as Lingua Franca (Jenkins, 2007; Seidlhofer, 2011).
2. See Barber (1992), who described the situation of the day in terms of a cosmic struggle between the 'centrifugal whirlwind' of 'Jihad' (shorthand for the tribalism resulting from the identity demands of increasingly narrow community groupings) and the 'centripetal black hole' of 'McWorld' (i.e. the forces of globalisation). The terms were then applied to the English language by Mary Snell-Hornby (1999).
3. In addition to postcolonial and diaspora literatures, which have long made linguistic hybridity central to their concerns, multilingualism now frequently features in films (e.g. Iñárritu's *Babel* of 2006) and popular music genres like hip-hop (c.f. Pennycook, 2007: 1–5; Canagarajah, 2013: 2–4; Alim et al., 2009). See Yildiz (2012: 3) for more examples.
4. Above all, this involved the development of an ideology according to which languages were perceived as 'separate and enumerable categories', a form of essentialism that fed into the Eurocentric project of codifying and delineating in order to control and govern (Makoni and Pennycook, 2007: 2).
5. This 'monolingual mindset' was then artificially created as policies were put in place to ensure that a single language variety would become the locus of patriotic sentiment and collective identity. The national tongue was artificially demarcated from its neighbours and sustained by a range of social and semiotic processes, such as the development of national literatures and literacy programmes, and the marginalisation of inconvenient language practices (Makoni and Pennycook, 2007: 1–4). See also Yildiz (2012), Hajek and Slaughter (2015).
6. This claim is made particularly forcefully by Canagarajah and Liyanage (2012) and Braunmüller and Ferraresi (2003: 1–7).
7. This was not always as simple a process as Anderson suggests. Burke (2004: 93) points out, for example, that in Iberia the printing press arrived in various cities simultaneously, leading as much to 'chaos' and competition as to uniformity.
8. Hebrew, Latin and Greek were believed to have been written on the cross (Eco, 1997: 15).

9. The first of these represents a calque of the Roman national origin myth as told in Virgil's *Aeneid* (see Currie, this volume) while the second, which tells of how the descendants of Noah spread out into many lands after the Flood, was adopted by many Christian peoples including the Castilians (see Lledó-Guillem this volume) and even the Christianized Amerindians (Pratt, 1991).
10. See Wright (2004) for an overview of the arguments concerning the similarities between Latin and English.
11. For example, by Francis Lodwick (1652), George Dalgarno (1661) and John Wilkins (1668) in England, and Liebniz (1679) in Germany (Eco, 1997).
12. See Leonhardt (2013), Ostler (2009), Janson (2004) and Waquet (2001) for book-length explorations of the long career of the Latin language. For more on its role as a lingua franca and lingua sacra, see also Ostler (2005: Ch. 8 & 9; 2011: Ch.6), Bennett (2017: Ch. 3), Gordin (2015: Ch. 1); Salverda (2018), amongst others.
13. The historian of science, Michael Gordin has also suggested that Latin's status as a scientific language at this time rested precisely on the contrast it made with the use of the vernaculars in other contexts: 'the more specialized scholarship became, the more unvernacular Latin had to be' (2015: 35).
14. See Bennett (2017: 1–20) and Salverda (2018) on the specific characteristics of *lingua sacra*.
15. For more on lingua francas in general, see Ostler (2011) and Braarvig and Geller (2018). On Sanskrit, the definitive work is by Pollock (2006).
16. The precise dates are difficult to establish. Salverda (2018: 23) mentions that, though the first written reference to it dates from the fifteenth century, it may have been around much earlier, since 'some form of late Vulgar Latin, in contact with Arabic, was...around in North Africa by the time the Crusades began'.

References

Alim, H. S., Ibrahim, A. and Pennycook, A., eds. (2009). *Global Linguistic Flows: Hip Hop Cultures, Youth Identities, and the Politics of Language.* New York: Routledge.

Anderson, B. (2006). *Imagined Communities: Reflections on the Origin and Spread of Nationalism.* Revised edition. London and New York: Verso.

Bakhtin, M. (1981). The Dialogic Imagination: Four Essays. Eds. M. Holquist; Trans. M Holquist and C. Emerson. University of Texas Press Slavic Series, No. 1. Austin: University of Texas Press.

Barber, B. (1992). Jihad vs. McWorld. *The Atlantic*, March. Available at https://www.theatlantic.com/magazine/archive/1992/03/jihad-vs-mcworld/303882/. [Accessed 1 May 2021].

Bennett, B. (2017). *Sacred Languages of the World: An Introduction.* Hoboken, NJ: Wiley.

Blommaert, J. (2010). *The Sociolinguistics of Globalization.* Cambridge: Cambridge University Press.

Braarvig, J. and Geller, M. J., eds. (2018). *Studies in Multilingualism, Lingua Franca and Lingua Sacra.* Berlin: Max Planck Institute for the History of Science.

Braunmüller, K. and Ferraresi, G., eds. (2003). *Aspects of Multilingualism in European Language History*. Amsterdam and Philadelphia: J. Benjamins.

Brownlees, N., ed. (2020). *The Language of Discovery, Exploration and Settlement*. Newcastle: Cambridge Scholars.

Burke, P. (2004). *Languages and Communities in Early Modern Europe*. Cambridge and New York: Cambridge University Press.

Canagarajah, S. (2013). *Translingual Practice: Global Englishes and Cosmopolitan Relations*. Milton Park, Abingdon, Oxon and New York: Routledge.

Canagarajah, S. and Liyanage, I. (2012). Lessons from Pre-Colonial Multilingualism. In: M. Martin-Jones, A. Blackledge and A. Creese, eds., *The Routledge Handbook of Multilingualism*, pp. 49–65. London and New York: Routledge.

Classen, A., ed. (2016). *Multilingualism in the Middle Ages and Early Modern Age: Communication and Miscommunication in the Premodern World*. Berlin and Boston: De Gruyter.

Crystal, D. (1997) *English as a Global Language*. Cambridge, UK and New York: Cambridge University Press.

Dalgarno, G. (1661), George Dalgarno on Universal Language: The Art of Signs (1661). In: D. Cram and J. Maat, eds. *The Deaf and Dumb Man's Tutor (1680), and the Unpublished Papers*. Oxford: Oxford University Press. 2001

Delabastita, D. and Hoenselaars, A. J., eds. (2015). *Multilingualism in the Drama of Shakespeare and His Contemporaries*. Amsterdam and Philadelphia: John Benjamins.

Derrida, J. (1985). *The Ear of the Other: Otobiography, Transference, Translation*. Eds. C. McDonald; Trans. P. Kamuf. New York: Schocken Books.

Dürr, R. (2017). Reflection on Language in Christian Mission: The Significance of Communication in the Linguistic Concepts of José de Acosta SJ and Antonio Ruiz de Montoya SJ. In: A. Flüchter and R. Wirbster, eds., *Translating Catechisms, Translating Cultures: The Expansion of Catholicism in the Early Modern World*, pp. 50–91. Leiden and Boston: Brill.

Eckert, P. and McConnell-Ginet, S. (1992) Think Practically and Look Locally: Language and Gender as Community-Based Practice. *Annual Review of Anthropology*, 21, pp. 461–490.

Eco, U. (1997). *The Search for the Perfect Language*. London: Fontana.

Edwards, V. (2004). *Multilingualism in the English-Speaking World: Pedigree of Nations*. Malden, MA: Blackwell.

Frijhoff, W., Escalle, M. and Sanchez-Summerer, K., eds. (2017). *Multilingualism, Nationhood, and Cultural Identity: Northern Europe, 16th-19th Centuries*. Amsterdam: Amsterdam University Press.

Garcia, O. and Wei, L. (2014). *Translanguaging: Language, Bilingualism and Education*. Basingstoke and New York: Palgrave Macmillan.

Gilbert, C. M. (2014). *The Politics of Language in the Western Mediterranean c.1492-c.1669: Multilingual Institutions and the Status of Arabic in Early Modern Spain*. PhD dissertation. Los Angeles: University of California.

Gordin, M. D. (2015). *Scientific Babel: How Science Was Done before and after Global English*. Chicago and London: The University of Chicago Press.

Graddol, D. (1999). The Decline of the Native Speaker. In: D. Graddol and U. H. Meinhof, eds., *English in a Changing World (AILA Review)*, Vol 13, pp. 57–68. Amsterdam and Philadelphia: John Benjamins.

Hajek, J. and Slaughter, Y. eds. (2015). *Challenging the Monolingual Mindset*. Bristol and Buffalo: Multilingual Matters.
Janson, T. (2004). *A Natural History of Latin*. Trans. M. D. Sørensen and N. Vincent. Oxford and New York: Oxford University Press.
Jenkins, J. (2007) *English as a Lingua Franca: Attitude and Identity*. Oxford: Oxford University Press.
Jenkins, J. (2015). Repositioning English and Multilingualism in English as a Lingua Franca. *English in Practice*, 2(3), pp. 49–85.
Leonhardt, J. (2013). *Latin: Story of a World Language*. Trans. K. Kronenberg. Cambridge, MA and London: The Belknap Press of Harvard University Press.
Liebniz, G. (c. 1679). On the General Characteristic. In L. Loemker, ed. *Philosophical Papers and Letters*. Alphen aan den Rijn and Philadelphia: Kluwer Academic Publisher.
Lodwick, F. (1652). *The Ground-Work, of a New Perfect Language*. Menson (Yorks): Scolar P. 1968.
Makoni, S. and Pennycook, A. eds. (2007). *Disinventing and Reconstituting Languages*. Clevedon and Buffalo: Multilingual Matters.
Mignolo, W. (2012) *Local Histories/Global Designs: Coloniality, Subaltern Knowledges, and Border Thinking*. Princeton, NJ: Princeton University Press.
Modiano, M. (1999). International English in the global village. *English Today*. 15(2), pp. 22–28.
Ostler, N. (2005). *Empires of the World: A Language History of the World*. London: HarperCollins.
Ostler, N. (2009). *Ad Infinitum: A Biography of Latin*. New York: Walker and Co.
Ostler, N. (2011). *The Last Lingua Franca: The Rise and Fall of World Languages*. London and New York: Penguin.
Pahta, P., Skaffari, J. and Wright, L. eds. (2018). *Multilingual Practices in Language History: English and Beyond*. Boston: De Gruyter Mouton.
Pennycook, A. (2006). The Myth of English as an International Language. In: S. Makoni and A. Pennycook, eds., *Disinventing and Reconstituting Language*. Clevedon and Tonawanda, NY: Multilingual Matters, pp. 90–115.
Pennycook, A. (2007). *Global Englishes and Transcultural Flows*. London and New York: Routledge.
Pollock, S. (2006). *The Language of the Gods in the World of Men: Sanskrit, Culture, and Power in Premodern India*. Berkeley: University of California Press.
Pratt, M. L. (1987). Linguistic Utopias. In: N. Farb, D. Attridge, A. Durant and C. MacCabe, eds., *The Linguistics of Writing. Arguments between Language and Literature*. New York: Methuen, pp. 48–66.
Pratt, M. L. (1991). Arts of the Contact Zone. *Profession*, 91, pp. 33–40.
Salverda, R. (2018). Empires and their Languages: Reflections on the History and the Linguistics of Lingua Franca and Lingua Sacra. In: J. E. Braarvig and M. J. Geller, eds., *Multilingualism, Lingua Franca and Lingua Sacra*. Berlin: Max Planck Institute for the History of Science, pp. 13–78.
Schneider, E. (2016). Hybrid Englishes: An Exploratory Survey. *World Englishes*, 35(3), pp. 339–354.
Seidlhofer, B. (2011). *Understanding English as a Lingua Franca*. Oxford: Oxford University Press.

Shearer, E. (2019). *Multilingualism, Language Trouble, and Linguistic Infelicity in Early Modern English Writing, 1550-1642*. PhD dissertation, University of Michigan.

Snell-Hornby, M. (1999). Communicating in the Global Village: On Language, Translation and Cultural Identity. In C. Scäffner, ed., *Translation in the Global Village*. Clevedon, UK and Buffalo: Multilingual Matters, pp. 103–120.

Spivak, G. (1994). Can the subaltern speak? In P. Williams and L. Chrisman, eds., *Colonial Discourse and Post-Colonial Theory. A Reader*. New York: Columbia UP, pp. 66–111.

Waquet, F. (2001). *Latin: Or the Empire of a Sign*. Trans. John Howe. London and New York: Verso.

Wilkins, J. (1668). *An Essay towards a Real Character and a Philosophical Language*. London: Royal Society.

Wright, R. (2004). Latin and English as World Languages. *English Today*, 20(4), pp. 3–13.

Yildiz, Y. (2012). *Beyond the Mother Tongue: The Postmonolingual Condition*. New York: Fordham University Press.

Part I
Multilingualism and Its Discontents

1 Multilingual Events in Late Medieval Personal Documentary Texts from the Winchester Diocese Collection in 1400–1525

Delia Schipor

Introduction

The linguistic situation in late medieval England was characterised by societal multilingualism, meaning that Latin, French and English were used within one society. While English was the spoken language of the majority of the English population, Latin and French were used in official documents for different purposes. Textbooks on the history of English commonly present English as the language of official documents in England starting from the fifteenth century (Barber *et al.*, 2009; Millward and Hayes, 2010: 147–149). According to Stenroos (2020: 40–41), this is based on an earlier claim made by Samuels (1963: 71), who noted that from 1430 English was regularly used in government documents. However, according to Dodd (2012), Latin was still the main language of the Privy Seal during the fifteenth century.

Similarly, Schipor (2018) found that in the period 1400–1525 Latin was the main language of official writing in manorial, local government and episcopal administration in Winchester and the surrounding areas. This is based on findings from her doctoral study, which investigated 7,070 texts from three collections: the Jervoise family, the Winchester city archives and the Winchester Diocese.[1] Of these texts, 6,847 were written in Latin (Schipor, 2018: 102), which is the dominant language in all of the three collections. However, the same study indicates that in this period, personal documentary texts, such as statements and testaments, were increasingly written in one of the vernaculars, namely English and, very rarely, French. In these texts, the vernaculars are almost always accompanied by Latin, resulting in the use of more than one language within a single text. The aim of the present study is to investigate the types and functions of such instances of multiple language use.

This chapter discusses multiple language use in personal documentary texts recorded in 12 bishops' registers from the Winchester Diocese collection in the period 1400–1525 (Appendix, Table 1.2). The registers cover this period almost entirely, with a gap of 22 years corresponding to the second part of the register of Henry Beaufort, which has either

DOI: 10.4324/9781003092445-3

been lost or destroyed.[2] These registers contain 5,359 texts,[3] which represent 76% of the total number of texts collected and analysed in Schipor (2018).

Digital images of all the texts dated to 1400–1525 were collected from the three collections mentioned above. This was carried out in compliance with the archive's copyright regulations. All of the texts were carefully examined and then registered into a database that contains both linguistic and extralinguistic information. To be more specific, the following details were noted: languages used, place and date of text production, text type, domain, and persons mentioned. For the aim of the present study, the instances of multiple language use in personal documentary texts were identified and a selection of multilingual events were thereafter analysed in detail from a sociolinguistic and philo-pragmatic perspective.

The chapter first presents an overview of the data, including clarifications regarding the types of texts constituting the material. The theoretical framework is then presented and explained. The following section contains an in-depth discussion of the types and functions of multiple language use in a selection of texts. Directly quoted examples from manuscripts are provided in italics and underlining is used to signal the presence of contractions in the manuscript. The ~ sign indicates the final-word flourishes in the original and the & sign represents various manuscript abbreviations for "and". The final section of the chapter is dedicated to conclusions.

The tables and figures in this chapter have been produced by the present author, based on her doctoral study.[4]

Materials

The texts here studied have survived as copies recorded in bishops' registers. According to Smith (1981: ix), the main distinctive feature of a bishop's register is the record of appointments of clergy to benefices. This would include material related to the appointment of parish clergy to rectories and vicarages, of chaplains to chantries and hospitals and of higher clergy to dignities and canonries in cathedral and collegiate churches. Coupled with these entries are the exchanges of livings, resignations and deprivations of incumbents, appointments of coadjutors, inquiries about the causes of vacancies and rights of patronage, and a host of similar business relating to benefices and the parochial clergy. Jacob (1953: 3) describes a bishop's register as the official record of his administration. The two most salient characteristics of such a register are the eclectic character of contents and the extensive coverage across time (Jacob, 1953: 3).

The texts found in bishops' registers may generally be referred to as documentary texts. Documentary texts are related to specific situations, places, persons and dates and have pragmatic functions, for example, they disseminate information, convey decisions and record transactions (Bergstrøm, 2017: 46). Even when the time and place of text production are not mentioned explicitly, they may often be inferred from references to specific persons and historical events. Of the 5,359 texts in the 12 bishops' registers, 66% represent memoranda documenting a variety of parochial and episcopal business. Other frequent categories of texts are conveyances, directives, statements and correspondence. Such texts contain information about the socio-economic and legal-administrative aspects of daily life in late medieval England, thus facilitating a socio-pragmatic study of multilingualism.

The registers contain 5,288 texts in Latin, 23 in English and 48 written in more than one language (Figure 1.1). The Latin texts form a mega genre on the basis of their shared characteristics. Although they represent different categories, they have similar topics, such as the employment and retirement of clergy. They also represent top-down communication from the bishops and their representatives, addressed to members of the lower levels of ecclesiastical hierarchy. Such texts are largely monolingual, with the exception of English and French proper names and place names.

Of the 48 texts written in more than one language, three show the use of French together with Latin. It may be noted that French, as opposed to English, is always accompanied by Latin in the register texts. One of the

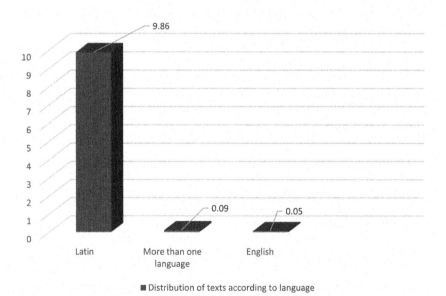

Figure 1.1 Distribution of texts in the bishops' registers of the Winchester Diocese collection (1400–1525) according to language

Source: © Delia Schipor

Table 1.1 Genres of personal documentary texts in the bishops' registers of the Winchester Diocese collection (1400–1525)

	English	French	Latin	Multilingual events
Abjurations	7	0	0	4 – English, Latin
Allegiances	0	0	0	1 – Latin, French; 1 – English, Latin
Juraments	0	0	0	1 – French, Latin; 1 – English, Latin
Testamentary texts	12	0	41	25 – English, Latin
Total	19	0	41	33

Source: © Delia Schipor

three texts with French and Latin is an assignation of pensions, representing the only instance where this text type shows the use of French in the registers (Schipor, 2018: 217). The remaining two texts with French and Latin are statements (Table 1.1).

The 23 texts written in English represent testamentary texts and abjurations. In 45 texts, English is used together with Latin in various text types, such as testaments, abjurations, agreements, court proceedings, and religious rules. The two languages are used in different ways and proportions across the text types. In the religious rule, for example, Latin is used to refer to the names of the prayers in the English body text (Schipor, 2018: 178–179). In some of the court proceedings, English and Latin appear to be used in almost equal proportions. By contrast, in abjurations and testaments, Latin is most commonly used in marginal and text-final notes (see examples 1 and 6).

Of the 48 texts, 33 are personal documentary texts, belonging to seven of the 12 bishops' registers (see Appendix, Table 1.2). Documentary texts written in the first person are here referred to as personal documentary texts. There are four types of personal documentary texts in the material here studied: abjurations, allegiances, juraments and testamentary texts (Table 1.1). Abjurations, allegiances and juraments are legally binding statements, while testamentary texts are conveyances concerning transactions of a spiritual and material nature (Schipor, 2018: 9). Abjurations represent renunciations of religious beliefs, given on oath, usually in an ecclesiastical court. Allegiances are statements of service and loyalty to a sovereign or feudal lord. Juraments are oaths made on entering an office or monastic rule.

The term *testamentary texts* is used to refer to wills and testaments collectively, based on their similarities. Traditionally, the main difference between the two text types is that wills typically cover unmovable goods, while testaments refer to movable goods, spiritual matters, funeral arrangements and alms. However, this distinction is often blurred. For example, certain fifteenth-century female testators from St Albans refer to their testaments as "wills", even when they bequeath movable goods (Schiølde, 2019: 57).

There are several similarities between statements and testamentary texts in terms of structure and form. First of all, they are written in the first person. Secondly, they begin with the name of the person making the statement or testamentary text, often accompanied by a formulaic opening phrase. In the case of abjurations and testaments, for example, this is almost always represented by the divine invocation *In the name of God amen* or its Latin equivalent *In dei nomine amen* in testaments. Wills, on the other hand, usually begin with the standard phrase *This is my last will*. Thirdly, statements and testamentary texts commonly end with providing contextual information such as the date, place and names of witnesses.

Another important aspect shared by statements and testamentary texts is that they are in some ways closely connected to oral statements. For example, defendants would read aloud or repeat their abjurations in court, depending on their level of literacy (Stretton, 1998: 31–33). The copies of abjurations found in bishops' registers would most likely have been made after this stage. Testamentary texts were generally drawn on the basis of dictation or information provided orally by testators when they were not written by the testators themselves (Wright, 2015: 36). The resulting documents were thereafter proved by a probate court and recorded in a bishop's register after validation (Schipor, 2018: 157).

The complex nature of textual processing results in structural and linguistic multi-layering. The process of copying documentary texts in large volumes such as bishops' registers has led to the occurrence of textual elements which were most likely not found in the previous versions of the documents. In certain cases, elements such as titles, headings and marginalia are written in a different language than the copied text. The lasting character of episcopal collections allowed the different scribes who accessed them to insert their own notes at different points in time (Schipor, 2018: 161), which contributes to the visual complexity of the manuscript page. The study of multiple language use in this context requires a tailored theoretical framework that accounts for the visual fluidity of historical manuscripts.

Theoretical framework

Studies of multilingualism have traditionally employed the term *code-switching*, which may be defined as the "change from one language to another within one act of communication" (Schendl, 2000: 77). This concept was initially used for investigating multilingualism in spoken communication and thereafter commonly adopted in studies of written communication, including historical texts. While code-switching may be successfully applied to certain instances of multilingualism in manuscripts, attempting to employ it for all types of multiple language use may prove challenging. Written language is less linear than spoken language in the sense that its permanence allows for alternating sequences of reading and writing. In other words, different visual elements of texts may not necessarily be read or written in a specific order, especially when they have different pragmatic functions. For example, a reader with limited time may look first at the title of a text and then at the concluding paragraph to find the needed information. Similarly, a scribe may copy a text and return to it at a later stage to add marginal notes. In such contexts, it may be problematic to establish where and if switching occurs.

Pahta *et al.* (2017: 11–12) have previously noted that studies of historical multilingualism may benefit from the adoption of a general term, such as *multilingual practices*, to cover all types of multiple language use. In the present study, multilingual practices are understood as general practices of scribes and readers in interaction with multilingual texts, which result in the creation of *multilingual events* (Schipor, 2018: 44). Multilingual events are constituted by the presence of stretches in different languages within a single text across the manuscript page. A *stretch* is here understood as a continuous sequence in one language within a single text/element. In this study, only stretches longer than one word, which are not proper names are taken into consideration, with the exception of marginalia (Schipor, 2018: 45), which typically contain single or very few words and in some cases may consist solely of personal names or place names. There are two main reasons for this principle of selection. Firstly, one-word instances of another language may be considered borrowings, while sequences longer than one word may be classified as multiple language use (Ingham *et al.*, 2016). Secondly, proper names given in a different language constitute specialised multilingual events, which may be referred to as *onomastic multilingual events*. Such events seem to be exponentially more frequent than other types of multilingual events in documentary texts (Schipor, 2018: 147) and thus merit an investigation dedicated exclusively to them.

Multilingual events may be classified based on four main aspects: visual and syntactic structure, level of expectedness, content and visual marking. In terms of visual structure, multilingual events may occur *intra-* or *inter-elementally*, that is, within one element or between elements. An *element* is an integral part of a text which is visually separated from other parts of the same text. Such elements may vary in length and may be written in one or more languages. An inter-elemental multilingual event would be, for example, the use of Latin in a title preceding an English body text. An intra-elemental multilingual event would be the alternation between English and Latin within a body text. Such multilingual events may be termed code-switching as defined above. Syntactically, intra-elemental multilingual events may occur *intra-* or *inter-sententially* (Myers-Scotton, 1993), that is to say, within a sentence or between sentences. For example, the insertion of the Latin phrase *et multes alijs* "and many others" at the end of a list of witnesses in a testamentary text would be an intra-sentential multilingual event (see example 2). An example of an inter-sentential multilingual event with English and Latin is found in the abjuration of Court Lamporte (see example 5).

According to the level of expectedness, multilingual events may be classified as: *formulaic, customary* and *free* (Schipor, 2018: 45). Formulaic multilingual events are constituted with set phrases which occur in the same language across time and text types. Two examples of set phrases are the Latin phrases *In dei nomine amen* and *et multes alijs*, typically written in Latin in both Latin and English texts. Even when the English equivalents of these phrases are used, they show precisely the same wording, respectively: "In the name of God amen" and "and many others". Customary multilingual events occur when certain pieces of information or elements generally appear in a certain language, but the choice of words and extent of multilingual input may vary. For instance, dates are usually given in Latin – or both Latin and English – even in English texts. However, in some texts, they appear as running text, while in others, they are written in a combination of nominal phrases and Roman numerals. Marginal notes indicating the functions of the texts they accompany may also be classified as customary since this may be considered common practice in large collections like bishops' registers (Schipor, 2018: 257). Multilingual events which are neither formulaic nor customary may be classified as free.

Based on their content, multilingual events may be classified as *parallel* and *complementary* (Sebba, 2012: 14–15). Parallelism occurs when the same information is provided in different languages, while complementarity is the result of providing distinct details in different languages. For example, using Latin to provide novel contextual information at the end of an English text constitutes a complementary multilingual event.

Scholars have suggested that the alternation of languages in the same text is often accompanied by variation in its layout (Piller, 2001: 161–162; Sebba, 2012: 173; Kaislaniemi, 2017: 165–166). The present study accounts for several layout features, such as size, colour and position on the page. Based on the combined use of such features, stretches in different languages may be visually marked up, down, or confused. A stretch may be marked up by a larger and more formal script, its central position on the page, as well as red ink, rubrication, embossing and underlining. Conversely, a stretch may be marked down by a smaller and less formal script, as well as its position at the bottom of the page. Alternatively, the different languages employed in a text may show no visual marking in relation to each other. In other cases, the marking may be confused. This is the case of a text-final note in Latin, found at the end of a town rule of Winchester written in English. The Latin note reads:

Example 1: Explicit hic totum pro Christo da michi potum
Everything ends here, for Christ's sake give me a drink.

This scribal comment is placed under the English body text, towards the bottom of the parchment roll. The English body text is written in a script that may be classified as Cursiva Mixed, while the Latin note is written in a script resembling Textualis, which may be perceived as more formal. However, the Latin note is written in a smaller-size script than the English body text. Therefore, the Latin stretch may be classified as marked down from the English body text based on position and size but marked up according to the style of the script. Although intricate, the choice of visual marking here may not be accidental. This is a customary scribal comment, indicating the scribe's esteemed profession and – most likely – his ability to write Latin (Schipor, 2018: 207). It is, in other words, an instance of the scribe's voice, textually less significant than the lengthy town rule preceding it but not less authoritative. Although the classification of multilingual events according to visual cues may be complex, it is required for a holistic understanding of the functions of such events.

The framework presented in this section facilitates the classification of different types of multiple language use in documentary texts, which may be used to analyse and discuss the functions of multilingual events based on their type.

Multilingual events in personal documentary texts

The analysis of multilingual events is structured on the basis of their type and function rather than the type of text they belong to. This is because the four types of personal documentary texts investigated here (Table 1.1) are represented unequally in the material. The most frequent type is the testamentary text, which accounts for more than two-thirds of the 33 texts. However, the shared characteristics of these texts allow the thematic discussion of the functions of multilingual events based on their grouping across the text types.

A detailed investigation of every multilingual event in the material is beyond the scope of this chapter. The personal documentary texts collectively show all of the types of multilingual events presented in the previous section, but some types are more frequently represented than others. For example, there are multiple instances of formulaic events in various texts and one instance of free multilingual events, found in a testamentary text (see example 6). This discussion addresses both frequent and infrequent types of events in order to present a complex overview of the various functions they perform.

Three languages are used in these documentary texts: English, French and Latin. French appears only in two of the texts studied here, an allegiance and a jurament. This reflects the findings presented in Schipor (2018), where only 20 out of 7,070 texts employ French, and its use is limited to the first quarter of the fifteenth century (Schipor, 2018: 102, 253–254).

The two vernaculars, English and French, are quantitatively dominant in the personal documentary texts with multilingual events, except for the allegiances where Latin and the vernaculars seem to be employed in almost equal proportions. Latin is generally used in marginalia, text-final notes, as well as introductory and closing phrases.

Text type and formulaicity

All of the 33 personal documentary texts are to some extent characterised by formulaicity, in the sense that they use very similar or identical phrases which appear to be text-type specific. In certain cases, such phrases are given in a different language, which creates formulaic multilingual events. This is often the case of testaments written in English which begin with the divine invocation in Latin. For example, the testament of Hugh Vaghan, dated to 1517, is written in English and begins with the Latin divine invocation *Jn dei nomine amen*. This constitutes an inter-sentential switch between Latin and English which acts as a discourse structuring device, indicating the beginning of a testament. Abjurations begin with the same invocation, *Jn the name of god amen*. However, in the 11 abjurations found in the bishops' registers, this introductory phrase is always in English.

Another Latin formulaic phrase, *et multes alijs* "and many others", is typically used in testaments, abjurations and allegiances, when presenting lists of witnesses. In the testament of Edmond Atkynson, dated to 1513, the use of Latin constitutes an intra-sentential switch from English:

> Example 2: *witnesse to the same Mr Thomas Crokwell~ Curate of Sainct margarette parish in Sowthwerk Raynold newington~ and Richard Atkynson~ et multes alijs.*

Latin is here used to indicate that some of the witnesses to the transaction remain unnamed, so the resulting multilingual event may be classified as complementary. At the same time, the Latin phrase marks the end of the list and of the testament itself, so it has a discourse organising function. This phrase is used in precisely the same manner in the allegiance of Richard Tystede, dated to 1402. By contrast, in the abjuration of Jsabelle Gartrygge, the same Latin phrase is used in a longer stretch of Latin text, where it seems to completely replace the list of witnesses (see example 4). In other words, this set phrase seems to have various pragmatic functions in different contexts and may not always form multilingual events.

In the testament of Richard Mathewe, dated to 1515, there is an intra-sentential switch from Latin to English with the Latin discourse marker *Jn primis* "Firstly", which introduces the testator's first bequest, namely the conveyance of his soul to God. In other testaments, such as that of Henry Bodill, dated to 1511–1515, the same discourse function is carried out in English. The two texts belong to the same register and are written in the same hand, so the alternating choice of English and Latin in such discourse markers appears to be a matter of preference rather than a pragmatic function.

All of the personal documentary texts representing statements – the jurament, allegiances and abjurations – contain the rhetorical formula "so help me God" or variations thereof. An example of this is found in the abjuration of Court Lamporte (see example 5). A slightly different version is found in the jurament of Agnes Burton, dated to 1449:

Example 3: *si dieux me eide & sez seintz*
If God help me and his saints.

The English and French allegiances contain an almost identical phrase. Although these formulae are without exception written in the language of the respective statement, they are followed by Latin interventions in certain cases, such as Lamporte's abjuration and the allegiance of Richard Tystede (see section "Multi-layered voices" below).

Intra-elemental multilingual events of a formulaic nature appear to mainly carry out discourse organising functions in personal documentary texts. Although the same formulae are used across texts, they may be used in English or Latin in English texts, with different pragmatic functions. However, they never appear in English in Latin texts.

Navigation by marginalia

The vast majority of texts recorded in bishops' registers, including personal documentary texts, contain marginal notes which mainly present the function of the texts and the names of the persons concerned. The marginalia in bishops' registers are generally in Latin, but the frequent use of abbreviations may represent a challenge in drawing distinctions between languages.

Whenever Latin marginal notes accompany English or French body texts, they form inter-elemental multilingual events. An example is found in the jurament of Agnes Burton, most likely given after she was elected abbess of St Mary's monastery. The body text of the jurament is accompanied by a marginal note represented by the nominal phrase *tenor cedule intercluse*, meaning "contents [of the] enclosed document". Both "tenor" and "cedule" are of Latin origin and refer to, respectively, "contents" and "document, piece of writing". They would be borrowed into French and possibly into English, but it is difficult to determine whether they represent established loanwords into English at the time of text production. "Intercluse" is the feminine plural of the past participle form of the Latin verb "interclūdĕre", meaning "to shut up, enclose, confine within bounds". The absence of prepositions and articles indicates that this marginal note is written in Latin rather than in French or English. This represents a complementary multilingual event since the Latin stretch provides additional information. In this case, the marginal note does not indicate the function of the text, but it gives insight into the context of text production, indicating that the jurament it accompanies was copied from another document.

A similar multilingual event is found in a jurament for the rule of St Paul the hermit, containing a vow of chastity. This text may be dated to 1470–1486 based on the text immediately following it on the register page (Schipor, 2018: 178). The jurament starts with *J.N.*, which may be read as both "In nomen" and "In Name", and continues in English. This may indicate that it represents a pre-composed text used by different prospective hermits taking their oath upon entering the respective rule. The marginal note which accompanies the jurament reads *Professio her~mite* "profession of hermit", which may be read in English, French or Latin, and may thus be considered an inter-elemental multilingual event.

The testament of Hugh Vaghan, dated to 1517, contains a marginal note in Latin reading *testam~ hugonis vagham* "testament [of] Hugh Vagham", which is apparently written in a different hand and possibly added after the body text of the testament was copied. Other similar notes are: *testamentu~ henr~ Bodill, Johannis Farre testum~, testm~ Agnetes Wyght and Testm~ Johannis Lovestede*. The various abbreviations of the word "testament" enable its reading as English, Latin or French. However, the latinisation of first names prompts the reader to classify such notes as Latin, especially since the same names are not latinised in the corresponding English body texts. These marginal notes facilitate searches through the voluminous register books by indicating the function of texts and the names of the testators. In other words, marginalia perform a navigational function (Birke and Christ, 2013).

The will of Henry Bodill, written in English, is also accompanied by a Latin marginal note, reading *vltima vo^{tas} eiusdem* "last will of the same". The note states the function of the text but not the name of the person concerned. Instead, it performs an indexical function by using "eiusdem" to refer to Bodill's name, which was mentioned in the preceding marginal note found a few lines above on the same register page. The physical proximity of Bodill's testament and will – and their corresponding marginalia – eliminates the need to mention his name twice in the margin. Given the size of registers, the use of such indexical marginal notes in similar contexts would have saved time without cancelling their usefulness.

Since most of the marginalia in registers is in Latin, this conventional practice appears to have expanded to English body texts

(Schipor, 2018: 161). Scribes producing bishops' registers did not have time to translate vernacular texts into Latin and there was no requirement to do so. Producing Latin marginalia for English body texts required no additional effort and was convenient for both producers and users of registers, who would have been trained in Latin. The use of Latin may have had the pragmatic function of enhancing the navigational character of marginal notes, especially in a context where Latin, especially the system of Latin abbreviations, was expected and familiar to fifteenth-century scribes producing and handling such documents.

The multilingual events with Latin marginalia may be classified as inter-elemental and parallel since the Latin notes typically indicate the functions of texts, which are easily inferred from the English body texts. The events may further be classified as customary since the marginal notes in Latin with a navigational function are generally expected in registers.

Multi-layered voices

The process of copying personal documentary texts in bishops' registers has resulted in the multi-layering of "voices", revealed by the presence of multilingual events. This is visible in cases where statements and testamentary texts were given in one of the vernaculars, then copied in registers, and supplemented with scribal comments in Latin. This occurs in all of the four types of personal documentary texts investigated in various ways.

The four abjurations which contain multilingual events are written in English, with Latin towards the end, to present details such as the date, place and witnesses to the oath. For example, the abjuration of Jsabelle Gartrygge, dated to 1491, contains the following multilingual event:

> Example 4: *J putto my signe & fecit signum Cruces Cora~ Magistro Canc~ & multes Alijs in Capella de Fromonde Jnfra Coll~ beate marie virginis prope winton~ ij^{do} die Mens~ Septembris A° domini Millesimo CCCCxC^{mo} Primo.*
> I put my signature and [she] made the sign of the cross in the presence of the master chancellor and many others in the chapel of Fromond of the College of St Mary the Virgin in Winchester the second day of September 1491.

After the abjurer renounces her witchcraft practices and makes the solemn oath to avoid relapsing, she indicates signing her declaration. At this point, the voice of the scribe takes over in the third person – indicated by the Latin verb *fecit* – to provide contextual details and describe the non-verbal gesture of the defendant. The transition from the voice of the abjurer to the voice of the clerk is thus accompanied by an

Late Medieval Multilingual Events 33

inter-sentential switch from English to Latin. This multilingual event is not visually marked, except for the fact that the date is written in darker ink, which may indicate that the scribe changed the ink or inserted the date at a later stage. The text of the abjuration was most likely composed in advance by a clerk, then read aloud or repeated by Gartrygge in an official setting. The date and place of the solemn oath were probably unknown when the declaration was prepared, meaning that these details were added at the hearing. The fact that the scribe added them in Latin rather than English indicates that Latin was perceived as the language of record.

The abjuration of Court Lamporte, dated to 1493–1501, has a similar structure, but the scribal intervention at the end does not provide information about the date and place of the oath:

> *Example 5: also god me help and thes holy eu*a*ngelist*es *& oscu-*
> *latus est libru*m *And in to the witnesse therof to my p*r*esent*
> *abiuracon*n *J put to my signe et fecit signu~ cruc*es
> also God help me and these holy evangelists and the book is kissed
> And to the witness thereof to this my present abjuration I put my signature and [he] made the sign of the cross.

In this example, there are two switches from English to Latin, where Latin is used to describe the non-verbal behaviour of the abjurer. The alternation of languages coincides with shifting between voices, as indicated by the first-person verbs in the English stretches and third-person verbs in the shorter Latin ones. If the abjuration was prepared in advance, the gestures presented in Latin – kissing the Bible and making the sign of the cross – probably had a prescriptive function and would have been translated to the defendant as he was guided through the process of renunciation.

In the allegiance of Walter Mymes, the contextual information is provided in Latin at the beginning of the English statement. In other words, the text of the allegiance is prefaced by a scribal comment indicating that Mymes sworn allegiance to the prior of Southwark on 3 November 1473 at the prior's residence in Southwark. The two sections are written in the same hand. Although they are separated by an empty line, there is a curly bracket on the right-hand margin which links them, indicating that they form a single entry. This entry is also accompanied by a marginal note in Latin: *For*u *iura*ti *homagiu~ facientis* "oath of homage made publicly", which indicates the function of the text. The presence of Latin thus creates a visual-linguistic frame around the vernacular in the register.

The allegiance of Richard Tystede, delivered in 1401, is written in Latin and French in almost equal proportions. The beginning and the end of the register text are in Latin, while the statement itself is in

French, so first, there is an inter-sentential switch from Latin to French, followed by a switch in the opposite direction at the end of the statement. The Latin introduction provides the name of the person who makes the allegiance, *Ricardus Tystede*, as well as the date and place of the event. The allegiance ends with the standard formula: *si dieux me aide & touz ses seintz* "may God and all his saints help me", which is followed by the names of some of the witnesses, in Latin. The switch from Latin to French is accompanied by a change of footing. To be more specific, there is a transition from the extra-linguistic details of the event provided in the third person to the allegiance itself in the first person. The scribe signals that the allegiance is given in Tystede's own words by using the Latin phrase *sub hac forma verborum* "under the form" which is followed by the statement in French. Although the scribe would have had the competence to produce the whole register entry in Latin, he preserved the original statement in French. This is very similar to what occurs in abjurations: Latin is used to provide extra-textual information, while the statement is given in English. Equally important, the scribe would have been able to produce the whole entry in French, but he preferred to use Latin as the contextual frame for the French statement.

There is an instance of scribal comment at the end of the will of John Saynctjohn, dated to 1512, which contains an inter-sentential switch from English to Latin. After providing the list of witnesses, the scribe inserts a Latin note indicating that the testament of the same person was recorded on a preceding folio:

Example 6: No*ta que* testa*mentum* iste*is* defuncti scribitur in fo prox~ preceden~
Note that the testament of the defunct is written on the immediately preceding folio.

In most cases where the will and testament are not part of the same text, the separate texts usually appear in the register in succession, so they are in physical proximity. In this case, however, the two texts – the will and the testament of John Saynctjohn – are interspersed with other testamentary texts. The pragmatic function of this multilingual event is navigational because it informs the reader that the register also contains the testament of John Saynctjohn, written on the previous folio. Based on the level of expectedness, this is a free multilingual event since the scribe seems to have chosen the wording at his own convenience. Notes with similar content may have been commonly used at the time, but this is the only instance of a free event with a navigational function in the set of 7,070 texts investigated in Schipor (2018).

All of the multilingual events where the juxtaposition of Latin and the vernaculars indicate the multi-layering of manuscript voices may be classified as intra-elemental because they are found within the same visual element, namely the body text. In terms of content, they may all be classified as complementary since they add new information to the register copies. Further, the events signal the change of footing between scribe and abjurer, testator or liegeman, depending on the text in question. Except for the note in Saynctjohn's will, these multilingual events perform the pragmatic function of presenting the spatio-temporal context of the statements or transactions they refer to. At the same time, they create Latin frames around the vernaculars, which indicates that Latin was perceived as the main language of record in bishops' registers.

Visual marking

Certain types of multilingual events seem to have a greater tendency to be visually marked than others. However, the presence of marking does not seem to be triggered by the introduction of a different language within a certain text. To be more specific, marginal notes, for example, are intrinsically marked down by position since they are placed in the margins, surrounding the central space occupied by body texts. Wherever visual marking is present, it seems to be the result of various practices.

The intra-elemental multilingual events with a discourse organising function are not visually marked consistently. In some of the English testamentary texts, the divine invocations in Latin are marked up by size and a more formal script. This occurs, for instance, in the testament of Robert Palling and Thomasyn Dalacourt, both dated to 1511. However, in other English testaments, such as that of Richard Mathewe, the Latin invocation is not visually marked. The same testament also contains a Latin discourse marker (see section "Text type and formulaicity" above) which lacks visual marking. Such varying practices of visual marking are also visible in Latin testaments. For example, while the testament of Robert Bassett, dated to 1516, contains a visually marked invocation, the testament of Johannes Harix, dated to 1517, does not. This indicates that visual marking was part of the variation which largely characterised late medieval documentary texts from England.

The note added at the end of Saynctjohn's will is preceded by a virgule, which separates the English stretch from the Latin one. Although it may seem that the virgule indicates the introduction of a different language, it is, in fact, also used in monolingual texts in order to distinguish between different parts of the same text (Schipor, 2018: 198, 256–257).

The intra-elemental multilingual events with Latin framing are generally not visually marked, except for Myme's allegiance, where the Latin intervention is placed above the English statement, with an empty line between the two stretches. There is then another visual feature, resembling a curly bracket, indicating that they are to be considered a single entry.

In terms of visual features, some register texts show an interesting characteristic. The texts found in the second part of the register of

Richard Fox all contain decorations referred to as the twisted-ribbon decorative style by Kennedy (2014: 147–152). This is represented by minutely decorated initials, typically containing profiles of bearded male faces, with a frowning or sad countenance, in some cases also adorned by drops of tears. In the context of episcopal administration, such serious facial expressions may be considered adequate. Such an adorned letter is the capital "p" at the beginning of a probate note following the will of John Lovestede, dated to 1506–1511. Such tragic facial expressions are especially appropriate in the context of testamentary texts, which deal with the demise of souls and their funeral arrangements. Perhaps more importantly, such decorations may function as layout organising devices. Together with empty lines, they may be used to locate the beginning of a new entry. On the whole, the presence of visual marking seems to be related more to organising the discourse or layout of texts rather than the introduction of another language.

Conclusion

The use of English and French in personal documentary texts appears to be directly related to the oral and legal character of such documents. Abjurations, for example, were legally binding, meaning that if the abjurers did not respect their oath, they would most likely be sentenced to death. The statements were legally valid only if the abjurers could be held accountable for them, which implied they had to be in a language they understood. The other types of personal documents also had legal value, which may explain the use of the vernaculars. Interestingly, French was used only in two of the 33 texts, an allegiance and a jurament, both dated to the beginning of the fifteenth century. Selecting French rather than English in these particular situations may have been a matter of preference or social status. The restricted use of French and prevalence of English seems to indicate a shift to English in personal documentary texts.

Documentary texts of a personal nature found in bishops' registers contain multilingual events with, on the one hand, English and Latin and, on the other hand, French and Latin. The language of the original statements was preserved when recording the corresponding texts in the register, which leads to the occurrence of multilingual events consisting of Latin and one of the two vernaculars. This indicates that Latin was perceived as the main language of record, together with the fact that the overwhelming majority of texts in Schipor (2018) are in Latin.

As far as the types of multilingual events are concerned, personal documentary texts recorded in registers contain both inter- and intra-elemental multilingual events. These multilingual events serve various functions: they act as discourse organising devices, guide the reader through the register, make reference to the context of text production and provide extra-textual information about the social context in which the personal statements were given.

The functions of multilingual events seem to correlate with their types. To be more specific, inter-elemental multilingual events mainly have a navigational function and may sometimes provide insight into the context of text production. On the other hand, intra-elemental multilingual events with discourse markers mainly have an organisational function while also facilitating the recognition of various types of texts. Intra-elemental multilingual events with Latin framing provide contextual details, while at the same time indicating that this information is given by a different person than the one making the statement. However, both inter- and intra-elemental multilingual events seem to be used to transfer the vernaculars to the conventional framework of bishops' registers, which were written in Latin.

As far as the visual aspect of personal documentary texts is concerned, visual marking does not seem to be triggered by the occurrence of multilingual events. Although certain multilingual events are visually marked, this may result from their nature, as is the case of marginalia, or may be triggered by the discourse markers constituting the respective events.

The present study has investigated the use of multilingual events in personal documentary texts by employing a framework designed specifically for an integrated analysis of pragmatic functions and visual features. The use of Latin to frame the vernaculars, together with previous research, situates Latin as the language of record in fifteenth-century England. As English was becoming increasingly more common in personal documentary texts, multilingual events seem to have held a significant pragmatic role for facilitating the navigation of texts and registers and allowing for the multi-layering of voices on the manuscript page. The study of historical multilingual events might further benefit from investigations of visual features extended to various text types and formats.

Notes

1. The doctoral thesis is titled *A Study of Multilingualism in the Late Medieval Material of the Hampshire Record Office*, and was completed in 2018.
2. Special thanks to archivist Adrienne Allen from the Hampshire Record Office for this information.
3. A *text* is here understood as a "discourse unit which is coherent in terms of content and visually distinct" (Schipor, 2018: 6). In this sense, different texts are units of information which are coherent on their own and separated visually by empty lines or different sheets of paper or parchment. However, visually separated units on a page may represent a coherent text based on their content.

References

Barber, C., Beal, J. C. and Shaw, P. A. (2009). *The English Language: A Historical Introduction* (2nd ed.). Cambridge: Cambridge University Press.

Bergstrøm, G. (2017). *Yeuen at Cavmbrigg': A Study of Medieval English Documents of Cambridge*. PhD Thesis, University of Stavanger.

Birke, D. and Christ, B. (2013). Paratext and Digitized Narrative: Mapping the Field. *Narrative*, 21(1), pp. 65–87.

Dodd, G. (2012). Trilingualism in the Medieval English Bureaucracy: The Use – and Disuse – of Languages in the Fifteenth-Century Privy Seal Office. *Journal of British Studies*, 51(2), pp. 253–283.

Ingham, R., Sylvester, L. and Marcus, I. (2016). Loans and Code-Switches in Medieval English Text Types. Paper presented at Historical Sociolinguistics and Socio-Cultural Change, University of Helsinki, 11 March.

Jacob, E. F. (1953). *The Medieval Registers of Canterbury and York: Some Points of Comparison*. London: St. Anthony's Press.

Kaislaniemi, S. (2017). Code-Switching, Script-switching and Typeface-Switching in Early Modern English Manuscript Letters and Printed Tracts. In: M. Peikola, A. Mäkilähde, H. Salmi, M. L. Varila and J. Skaffari, eds., *Verbal and Visual Communication in Early English Texts*. Turnhout: Brepols, pp. 165–200.

Kennedy, K. E. (2014). *The Courtly and Commercial Art of the Wycliffite Bible*. Turnhout: Brepols.

Millward, C. and Hayes, M. (2010). *A Biography of the English Language* (3rd ed.). Boston: Wadsworth.

Myers-Scotton, C. (1993). *Duelling Languages: Grammatical Structure in Codeswitching*. Oxford: Clarendon.

Pahta, P., Skaffari, J. and Wright, L., eds. (2017). *Multilingual Practices in Language History: English and Beyond*. Berlin: De Gruyter Mouton.

Piller, I. (2001). Identity Constructions in Multilingual Advertising. *Language in Society*, 30, pp. 153–186.

Samuels, M. L. (1963). Some Applications of Middle English Dialectology. *English Studies*, 44, pp. 81–94. Reprinted in: Laing, M., ed. (1989). *Middle English Dialectology: Essays on Some Principles and Problems*. Aberdeen: Aberdeen University Press, pp. 64–80.

Schendl, H. (2000). Linguistic Aspects of Code-Switching in Medieval English Texts. In: D. A. Trotter, ed., *Multilingualism in Later Medieval Britain*. Cambridge: D.S. Brewer, pp. 77–92.

Schiølde, J. K. (2019). *To Almyghtty God et cetera: An Edition of Medieval Testamentary Texts of Women from St Albans*. MA thesis, University of Stavanger.

Schipor, D. (2018). *A Study of Multilingualism in the Late Medieval Material of the Hampshire Record Office*. PhD thesis, University of Stavanger.

Sebba, M. (2012). Researching and Theorising Multilingual Texts. In M. Sebba, S. Mahootian and C. Jonsson, eds., *Language Mixing and Code-Switching in Writing Approaches to Mixed-Language Written Discourse*. London & New York: Routledge, pp. 1–26.

Smith, D. M. (1981). *Guide to Bishops' Registers of England and Wales: A Survey from the Middle Ages to the Abolition of Episcopacy in 1646*. London: Butler & Tanner.

Stenroos, M. (2020). The "Vernacularisation" and "Standardisation" of Local Administrative Writing in Late and Post-Medieval England. In: L. Wright, ed., *The Multilingual Origins of Standard English*. Berlin: De Gruyter Mouton, pp. 39–85.

Stretton, T. (1998). *Women Waging Law in Elizabethan England*. Cambridge: Cambridge University Press.

Wright, L. (2015). On Medieval Wills and the Rise of Written Monolingual English. In: J. Calle-Martin and J. C. Conde-Silvestre, eds., *Approaches to Middle English: Variation, Contact and Change*. Oxford: Peter Lang, pp. 35–54.

Appendix

Table 1.2 The Winchester Diocese collection – Bishops' registers at the Hampshire Record Office

Register	Date	Multilingual personal documentary texts	Archive reference no.
William of Wykeham, Part I	1367–1404	No	21M65/A1/10
William of Wykeham, Part II	1367–1404	Yes	21M65/A1/11
Henry Beaufort, Part I	1405–1425	No	21M65/A1/12
William Waynflete, Part I	1447–1470	Yes	21M65/A1/13
William Waynflete, Part II	1470–1486	Yes	21M65/A1/14
Peter Courtney	1486–1492	Yes	21M65/A1/15
Thomas Langton	1493–1501	Yes	21M65/A1/16
Richard Fox, Part 1	1501–1504	No	21M65/A1/17
Richard Fox, Part 2	1506–1511	Yes	21M65/A1/18
Richard Fox, Part 3	1511–1515	Yes	21M65/A1/19
Richard Fox, Part 4	1518–1522	No	21M65/A1/20
Richard Fox, Part 5	1522–1534	No	21M65/A1/21

Source: © Delia Schipor

2 Croatian Biblical Texts in the Early Modern Period
A Historical-Sociolinguistic Approach to Language Change[1]

Vuk-Tadija Barbarić and Ivana Eterović

Introduction

Historical sociolinguistics has only recently been recognised as a promising theoretical and methodological framework in Croatian philology, especially when it comes to Medieval and Early Modern Croatian literacy, where this approach is still rather underdeveloped (Peti-Stantić, 2008; Hoyt, 2012; Kapetanović, 2015; Schubert, 2016; Barbarić, 2017). Multilingualism and diglossia were introduced as key concepts in previous historical sociolinguistic research on the history of Croatian literary language,[2] mostly applied to Medieval Croatian Glagolitic literacy (Mihaljević, 2010). New findings on the genesis and formation of the oldest Croatian lectionaries, however, have drawn attention towards the need to introduce a more calibrated sociolinguistic scheme (Barbarić, 2017).

Due to their long continuity and overall stability as a text genre, as well as their conservative language, translations of biblical texts can clearly show possible changes in attitudes towards the language of literacy. It was for this reason that Croatian translations of biblical texts from the late fifteenth and the sixteenth century in their historical and linguistic context were chosen as the subject of this chapter. The research on Croatian translations of biblical texts throughout this long period traces biblical passages in three different text types: liturgical books (missals and breviaries), paraliturgical books (lectionaries) and Bible translations.[3] No Croatian translation of the entire Bible has been preserved, although archival records and historical sources point to several Bibles that might have existed in the Middle Ages and the Early Modern period.[4]

Our attention will be directed here towards the macro-level, applying a descriptive historical sociolinguistic analysis; we will address the factors that influenced the choice of literary language variety by slightly reformulating one of Joshua Fishman's central questions in his analysis of societal multilingualism (1965) – Who uses what literary language variety with whom, and when, in Early Modern Croatian literacy?

DOI: 10.4324/9781003092445-4

The language(s) of the liturgy in Medieval and Early Modern Croatian literacy

The Medieval and Early Modern Croatian language community was essentially multilingual. As was generally the case throughout Western Europe during the Middle Ages, Latin was the only written language of Early Medieval Croatian literacy and served as a *lingua franca*, being the language of religion, administration, law, diplomacy and education. Its first attestations are found on epigraphic monuments dating from the ninth century; during the following centuries, its use gradually expanded, leading to further diversification of the functions and text genres for which it was used (Hercigonja, 2006: 21–31, 39–57, 113–197).

However, Latin was not the only language of the liturgy in Medieval Croatia. In the early 860s, the Slavic liturgy came into existence when Ss. Constantine-Cyril and Methodius, Byzantine missionaries from Thessaloniki, invented the Slavic letters (Glagolitic script) and translated the most important liturgical books into the Slavic language for the purpose of the Christian mission among the Slavs in Great Moravia, thereby laying a common foundation of literary tradition for all the Slavic world. The language of these first Slavic translations, whose base was an East South Slavic dialect spoken in the native city of Cyril and Methodius, is usually termed Old Church Slavonic. Other than Latin, Greek and Hebrew, it was the only language that gained the Pope's official approval (granted in the late 860s) to be used as the language of liturgy in the Roman Church (Verkholantsev, 2014: 19–26).

After Methodius's death, their disciples were forced to flee from Moravia and Pannonia. Spreading across the Slavic world, they continued to disseminate the Slavonic liturgy. It is during the late ninth or early tenth century that they probably reached the Croatian historical lands. However, in the late eleventh or early twelfth century, Old Church Slavonic began to differentiate into separate regional varieties. The same period also marked the earliest appearance of Croatian Church Slavonic,[5] which remained the most prestigious Slavic language variety in Croatia until the sixteenth century, as will be elaborated in the following sections.

Slavic language varieties in Medieval Croatian literacy: the emergence of diglossia

The language of Medieval Croatian literacy consisted of different but genetically related Slavic varieties that were functionally distinguished and engaged in complementary distribution. Croatian Church Slavonic was the superposed variety, whose prestige and authority were primarily derived from the fact that it was the language of religion. These Slavic language varieties differed not only in function and prestige but also in literary heritage, acquisition, standardisation, stability, phonology, grammar and vocabulary.[6] Taking into consideration the status of the Croatian Church Slavonic, the existence of two stages in Medieval Croatian literacy was proposed.[7]

The first stage, which dates from the eleventh to the fourteenth century, was characterised by a diglossic[8] distribution between Croatian Church Slavonic and the Čakavian[9] vernacular (Hercigonja, 2006: 76, 78; Mihaljević, 2010: 230).[10] Croatian Church Slavonic was the literary language of liturgical and non-liturgical texts, while the Čakavian vernacular was used only to satisfy everyday, practical needs, such as in legal documents or epigraphic monuments, as well as in colophons, rubrics and marginal notes in codices.[11]

The second stage, which dates from the second half of the fourteenth century to the sixteenth century, is characterised by a triglossic distribution between Croatian Church Slavonic, a Croatian Church Slavonic–Čakavian amalgam and the (Čakavian) vernacular (Hercigonja, 2006: 83; Mihaljević, 2010: 231).[12] Croatian Church Slavonic was used for liturgical texts, the Croatian Church Slavonic – Čakavian amalgam for literary texts, and the (Čakavian) vernacular for legal texts.

This sociolinguistic scheme has been primarily applied to the Glagolitic constituent of Medieval and Early Modern Croatian literacy, but it is very important to note that Croatian literacy consists of three different scripts, as well as different variants of these three scripts, which poses some problems to the above-mentioned scheme. In addition to the Glagolitic Croatian texts, Croatian texts were also written in the Latin and Cyrillic scripts (Hercigonja, 2006). Within the Glagolitic sphere, the appearance of different types of the Glagolitic script matches the appearance of different types of literary language varieties: uncial is used for Croatian Church Slavonic (liturgical texts), cursive is used for Čakavian vernacular (legal texts) and semi-uncial and bookish cursive were used for the Croatian Church Slavonic – Čakavian amalgam (Žagar, 2009: 154–187). The only place where all of these variants could appear simultaneously, regardless of the text type or function, was in graffiti (Fučić, 1982).

Moreover, Croatian philology still awaits a more systematic and detailed elaboration of how certain texts in different scripts fit into the diglossic/triglossic framework. One of the newly suggested supplements has been proposed by Vuk-Tadija Barbarić, who, following his research on the genesis and formation of the oldest Croatian lectionaries, added a fourth functional domain, which he calls paraliturgical, which includes Latin-script and Cyrillic lectionaries from the fourteenth to the sixteenth century (2017). It should also be noted that, despite some Kajkavian and Štokavian traces in the texts from the Glagolitic sphere, their vernacular is based on Čakavian, while the vernacular in the texts from the Latin-script and Cyrillic sphere can be based on either the Čakavian or the Štokavian dialect group.

Future investigations on this topic will also have to consider the question of whether texts written in different scripts belong to the same sociolinguistic complex, as it has been suggested by some of the previous researchers. For example, Andrew Roy Corin suggested that Late Medieval and Early Renaissance Croatian literacy consisted of two entirely different sociolinguistic complexes, cultures, spheres or structures, which were essentially distinct, but could in some cases overlap (Corin 1993: 161–166). According to this scheme, the former can be termed Glagolitic and the latter Latinic. Within the Glagolitic sociolinguistic complex, texts of biblical content were written in Croatian Church Slavonic and in the Glagolitic script, while within the Latinic complex, they were written in the vernacular and in the Latin script. There was no real competition between a missal and a lectionary in the Middle Ages because they were not part of the same sociolinguistic complex: missals were never composed in the vernacular, nor were lectionaries composed in Croatian Church Slavonic (Corin 1993: 161, 164).[13]

Despite the proposed terms, the crucial difference between these two sociolinguistic cultures was no script or language, but rather "the *set of relationships between language varieties in the community*" (Corin, 1993: 163). Moreover, one should not think of them as two isolated spheres or separated geographic regions, but rather as two different structures that "existed most often in separate locations" (Corin, 1993: 165). Corin sees the Glagolitic complex as being characterised by Croatian Church Slavonic – vernacular diglossia, while the Latinic complex was characterised by Latin – Čakavian bilingualism, which – as presented in the previous paragraphs – is only partly true (1993: 162).[14] As the history of the Croatian literary language shows, these two sociolinguistic complexes, if they ever existed at all, were constantly communicating and overlapping, finally dissolving into one single sociolinguistic complex in the Early Modern period. One should not forget that the bearers of these sociolinguistic complexes were very often the same. Although the above-mentioned hypothesis about the existence of different sociolinguistic complexes in Medieval and Early Modern Croatian literacy has not been further tested and elaborated, it remains very interesting and poses some new challenges to historical sociolinguistic approaches.

Slavic language varieties in Early Modern Croatian literacy: the disintegration of diglossia

In the sixteenth century, the high status of Croatian Church Slavonic finally collapsed and lost the competition with the Croatian vernaculars.[15] This period is therefore characterised by bilingualism between Croatian Church Slavonic and Croatian vernacular (Mihaljević, 2010: 231). According to Charles Ferguson, the disappearance of diglossia is typically caused by three trends: "(a) more widespread literacy (whether for economic, ideological or other reasons), (b) broader communication among different regional and social segments of the community (e.g. for economic, administrative, military, or ideological reasons), (c) desire for a full-fledged standard 'national' language as an attribute of autonomy or of sovereignty"[16] (1959: 338). These trends can result (a) in the adoption of the high variety, (b) the adoption of the low variety or (c) the adoption of a modified, mixed variety (Ferguson 1959: 338). Ferguson's scenario of the breakdown of diglossia bears remarkable similarity to the Croatian literary language situation in the sixteenth century, where we witness the existence of all three of these concepts of literary language in liturgical texts, which represented the most conservative genre.

The adoption of the high variety

The language of Croatian Glagolitic liturgical books (missals and breviaries) published at the turn of the fifteenth century into the sixteenth commonly points to a situation of triglossia maintenance, i.e. the maintenance of Croatian Church Slavonic as the most prestigious type of literary language, but with an adapted and altered norm.[17] Even today, these codices find themselves in the shadow of their more well-known predecessors. This can be seen as a consequence of the fact that the history of the Croatian literary language is still predominantly understood in monolithic terms, as well as in terms of the traditional conception of literary language history, where a strong accent is placed on the search for the earliest historical traces of the national language. Although a shift can be noted among contemporary Croatian philologists towards a polyphonic rather than a monolithic conception of literary language history, and though Early Modern Croatian literacy has moved significantly from the periphery to the centre of philological interest, knowledge about the language of these codices is still insufficient.

Among them, we can mention the example of three missals published at the turn of the fifteenth century into the sixteenth: *Misal po zakonu rimskoga dvora* [*Missal According to the Law of the Roman Court*], 1483; *Senjski misal* [*Senj Missal*], 1494; and *Misal Pavla Modrušanina* [*Missal of Pavao Modrušanin*], 1528. It is indicative that these three missals show great mutual similarity, which testifies to the amount of prestige still associated with Croatian Church Slavonic in the Early Modern period. In spite of the fact that each shows certain vernacular innovations, most of them are sporadic as they are not considered to be acceptable from the point of view of the Croatian Church Slavonic norm.[18]

The adoption of a mixed variety

In the 1530s, Šimun Kožičić Benja, the bishop of Modruš and Senj, initiated a brief but intense period of printing activity in his house in Rijeka, where in only two years, six Glagolitic books were published: *Oficii rimski* [*Roman Office*] (1530), *Psaltir* [*Psalter*] (1530), *Knižice krsta* [*Little*

Books of Cross] (1531), *Od bitiê redovničkoga knjižice* [Little Books of Being a Monk] (1531), *Knižice odъ žitiê rimskihъ arhierêovъ i cesarovъ* [Little Books of Lives of Roman Bishops and Emperors] (1531) and *Misal hruacki* [Croatian Missal] (1531). Croatian Missal was surely the crucial publishing project and remained the most voluminous edition of Benja's printing house. Kožičić expressed his discontent with the language of Croatian liturgical books (written in Croatian Church Slavonic) and advocates that they be revised, primarily at the textological level. In his opinion, the liturgical books deviated too much from the Latin template; therefore, he collated the text of the missal in accordance with the Latin model, most likely editing his *Croatian Missal* in accordance with a Latin missal which was in use around the same time (Žagar, 2015).

Traditional Croatian philology failed to capture the essence of Kožičić's literary language due to the still predominant comparative approach, shaped in the nineteenth century during the very foundation of Slavic philology as an independent discipline. According to the traditional comparative method, the crucial criterion for the determination of a text type is the prevalence of either Croatian Church Slavonic or Čakavian elements. However, even though it is an undeniable fact that Kožičić's concept consists of a certain mixture of these two linguistic systems, it clearly does not meet the criteria of the text function and thus falls out of the triglossic sociolinguistic scheme of Early Modern Croatian literacy. Specifically, in the editions published in his printing house, Kožičić inaugurated and implemented a unique and specific concept of the literary language, both in liturgical and non-liturgical texts, regardless of the text function (Holjevac, 2012; Žagar, 2015). On the phonological and lexical levels, he brings the language of his editions closer to the vernacular, while on the morphological and syntactic levels, it wears more traditional, Croatian Church Slavonic clothing. Therefore, it can be concluded that the breakdown of diglossia has already set in by the first half of the sixteenth century.[19]

The adoption of the low variety

The written vernacular as the language of translations of biblical texts first arose in the Latinic sphere and can be traced back to the fourteenth century, when the genesis of Croatian lectionaries began.

As has recently been shown by Barbarić (2017), Croatian vernacular lectionaries most probably emerged under the influence of Italian vernacular lectionaries and Bible translations. Furthermore, Barbarić applied a distinction originally introduced by Gianfranco Folena (1991) between horizontal and vertical translation to explain the heterogenous nature of Croatian lectionaries on both the textual and the linguistic levels. To put it quite simply, in this case, horizontal translation means translation from one vernacular to another, i.e. between languages of the same or comparable prestige in their communities, e.g. between Italian and Croatian (Čakavian). On the other hand, there are two kinds of vertical translations associated with these lectionaries – from Croatian Church Slavonic to the vernacular and from Latin to the vernacular. It is quite obvious that this is a translation from a language of higher prestige to one of lower prestige.[20]

The most important Croatian lectionary is *Bernardinov lekcionar* [*Bernardin's Lectionary*] (or *Lekcionar Bernardina Splićanina* [*The Lectionary of Bernardin Splićanin*]). Printed in 1495, it formed a foundation for the entire handwritten and printed lectionary production of the sixteenth century. As textual witnesses show, this Čakavian lectionary was frequently copied in the sixteenth century[21] but was also adopted and adapted in Štokavian communities, where not only its language was changed, but its Latin script was changed to the Cyrillic script.[22] This can also be considered an instance of horizontal translation that happened between Croatian Medieval communities. *Bernardin's Lectionary* left its mark on Croatian translations of biblical texts throughout later centuries as well (on Štokavian as well as on Kajkavian translations).

In the Glagolitic sphere, the adoption of the vernacular in all text types, including the translation of the Bible, was explicitly stated by Croatian Protestants in the forewords of their editions printed in Urach from 1561 to 1564. The first Croatian integral translation of the New Testament appeared at the beginning of the second half of the sixteenth century (1562–1563). It was published in two editions: Glagolitic and Cyrillic. From Primož Trubar's foreword to the first Slovenian translation and Stipan Konzul's and Antun Dalmatin's foreword to the first Croatian translation, we learn that they consulted many other works while translating, including German, Latin, Italian and Czech bibles, in addition to a Croatian book recently printed, they say, in Venice (we now know that this was *Bernardin's Lectionary*, 1543 edition, as indeed had already been noted at the end of the nineteenth century [Barbarić and Eterović, 2020]). Clearly, Folena's distinction between horizontal and vertical translation could be applied here as well.

By choosing the vernacular for the basis of the literary language, Croatian Protestants were in line with their European counterparts. However, in the case of Croatia, the use of the vernacular in the liturgy was not new. In the sixteenth century, there had already existed a five-century-long (at least) Croatian Church Slavonic tradition that Croatian Protestants were loathed to part with. However, although the basis of their translation of the New Testament was *Bernardin's Lectionary*, they subjected the text of this lectionary to a thorough revision. The first step was a textological revision using Erasmus's and Luther's Bibles as alternative sources[23]; the second step was a linguistic revision according to the chosen conception of the literary language. Those passages that deviated more from Erasmus's Bible and Luther's Bible were translated anew, and many of the regional language features of the *Bernardin's Lectionary* were changed towards more general ones, which were often closer to the Croatian Church Slavonic norm (Čupković, 2013; Barbarić and Eterović, 2020). Instead of a radical deviation from the traditional language of the liturgy, it seems that these Croatian Protestants could not escape tradition to quite the extent that they had initially planned.

Conclusion

Clearly, many questions remain concerning the language situation in Medieval and Early Modern Croatia. In this chapter, we have shown that the emergence and disintegration of diglossia can be observed through the analysis of a single text type – translations of biblical texts – over a period of two centuries. In this case, biblical texts from the late fifteenth and the sixteenth century proved to be mirrors of a quite complex language situation. This obviously shows that the diglossic framework cannot be easily rejected. At the very least, it continues to explain certain aspects of the Croatian historical literary language situation despite the fact that many texts tend to escape straightforward classification in this regard.

Finally, we can conclude that the first step towards the disintegration of diglossia was made at the very moment when Croatian literary language varieties became open to horizontal translation. As we have indicated earlier for vernacular lectionaries, this most probably occurred as early as the fourteenth century. However, only with the benefits of the printing press did this process accelerate until it became unstoppable. We have pointed to the fact that even the high variety exhibited sporadic vernacular innovations, while this was obvious on the phonological and lexical levels of Kožičić's mixed variety. On the other hand, the low variety openly and freely recognised even the authority of biblical passages written in foreign vernacular languages.

Notes

1. This chapter was produced with support from the Croatian Science Foundation under the project *The language of the Urach Protestant press editions within context of the sixteenth century literary language guidelines*, grant number HRZZ-IP-2014-09-6415.
2. The application of these concepts has proven to be not just fruitful but also successful in research on the history of Slavic languages in general, e.g. the Medieval and Early Modern Russian (Hüttl-Folter, 1978; Worth, 1978; Uspenskij, 2002), Serbian (Grković-Mejdžor, 2007) or Slovak language situations (Lauersdorf, 2002, 2003, 2010).
3. Biblical readings can also be found in Early Modern Croatian postils: three editions printed by Croatian Protestants in Urach and Regensburg in Glagolitic (1562), Cyrillic (1563) and Latin script (1568), as well as the

one published by Antun Vramec (1586). These editions will remain out of our focus in this chapter since this text type cannot be traced back to the fifteenth century.
4. In historical sources, the existence of a Slavic Bible is mentioned in Zadar in the late fourteenth century, as well as in Omišalj (Krk) and Cres in the fifteenth and sixteenth centuries (Bučar, 1910: 112; Fancev, 1916: 154–156; Hercigonja, 2006: 265). According to Primož Trubar, in the first half of the sixteenth century, a small scriptorium in Ozalj was organised by prince Bernardin Frankopan with the task of translating the Bible into Croatian, but the results of this project remain unknown (Hercigonja, 2006: 222).
5. On the Croatian Church Slavonic norm, see Mihaljević and Reinhart (2005).
6. The difference between the various Slavic language varieties of Medieval Croatian literacy on all these levels has been elaborated in detail by Lozić Knezović and Galić Kakkonen (2010) and Mihaljević (2010). However, Corin (1993: 166–167) gave fair warning to a possible misreading of Ferguson's original characterisation of diglossia. He emphasised that Ferguson's features were designed only as tools for identifying a diglossic situation without being properly defined; thus, any approach that merely checks off each of Ferguson's features can lead to an overly simplistic description.
7. The "bipolarity" of literary language (Croatian Church Slavonic in liturgical and Čakavian vernacular in non-liturgical texts) in Medieval Croatian literacy, as well as the existence of a third variety (Čakavian – Church Slavonic in literary texts) was already noted by Croatian philologists in the nineteenth and twentieth centuries (Valjavec, 1892: XIII; Hamm, 1963: 54; Nazor, 1963: 68–69; Hercigonja, 1983; Damjanović, 1984, 2008), but it is only at the turn of the last two centuries that the historical sociolinguistic lenses were put on (Corin, 1993; Mihaljević, 2010; Lozić Knezović and Galić Kakkonen, 2010).
8. The term *diglossia* was first introduced by Charles Ferguson in 1959 and defined as follows: "DIGLOSSIA is a relatively stable language situation in which, in addition to the primary dialects of the language (which may include a standard or regional standards), there is a very divergent, highly codified (often grammatically more complex) superposed variety, the vehicle of a large and respected body of written literature, either of an earlier period or in another speech community, which is learned largely by formal education and is used for most written and formal spoken purposes but is not used by any sector of the community for ordinary conversation" (1959: 336).
9. There are three groups of dialects in Croatia: Čakavian, Štokavian and Kajkavian. From the early centuries, almost exclusively Čakavian texts are preserved; however, in sociolinguistic terms they are all on the same, vernacular level, and for the purposes of this chapter there will be little necessity to distinguish between them.
10. Recently, Snow (2013) called for a more precise definition of diglossia, one which would distinguish between three sub-categories of diglossia. In this framework, Medieval and Early Modern Croatian literacy falls within the sub-category of traditional diglossia, where Croatian Church Slavonic as an ancient sacred language served as the high variety. According to Snow, this sub-category is the prototypical manifestation of diglossia, involving "a pre-modern civilisation or empire in which a large geographic region with many L vernaculars is bound together by, among other things,

a shared H language" (2013: 62). The command of Croatian Church Slavonic was limited to a small elite group, while the vast majority of the population knew only the Croatian vernacular. Despite the differences between Croatian dialects at that time, there was general agreement upon the domains of the high and low varieties within the Croatian (literary) language community.

11. It seems that the possibility of applying this concept to the language situation in the Croatian Medieval period was first examined by Peter Rehder (1981). However, he sees the complementary distribution between Croatian Church Slavonic and the written (Čakavian) vernacular only as a tendency that does meet some of the criteria stipulated by Charles Ferguson, but he generally believes that it was never fully established as diglossia in the real sense of the word. The applicability of the diglossia framework to Croatian Medieval literacy has also recently been put into question by Kapetanović (2017). Attempting to provide a more convincing explanation of the complex (socio)linguistic situation in the Croatian Middle Ages, Kapetanović has suggested the introduction of the concept of three registers, supposedly inherited from ancient rhetoric and poetics (2017: 83–84). We find it doubtful or, at the very least, unconvincing that this model could replace the diglossia framework. As we will show here, the diglossic model still remains a quite useful framework to describe the Croatian Medieval language situation.

12. The designation *Čakavian* is put here in brackets to point out that – although the basis of this literary language variety remains Čakavian – Kajkavian and Štokavian elements are beginning to enter at a very slow pace.

13. The oldest vernacular missal (manuscript in Latin script) dates to the end of the sixteenth century (Giannelli and Graciotti, 2003).

14. As Corin himself noted, he did not take into account the role of Italian literacy in Late Medieval – Early Modern Dalmatia (1993: 162). However, new research on the genesis and formation of the oldest Croatian lectionaries calls for an active inclusion of Italian in the proposed scheme (Barbarić, 2017).

15. Corin assumes that the breakdown of diglossia began "no later than the sixteenth century, and probably already in the fifteenth" (1993: 161), while Milan Mihaljević places it in the mid-sixteenth century (2010: 231).

16. In other words, as Dan Snow puts it, "Traditional diglossia is born in pre-modern societies that have not undergone the changes generally associated with modernisation, such as the rise of publishing and print culture, promotion of mass literacy and education, secularisation of society and government, the rise of a nation-state form of political structure, and promotion of a national language" (2013: 63).

17. Two stages in the development of the Croatian Church Slavonic norm can be distinguished during the Middle Ages: the older one present mostly in fragments from the twelfth to the thirteenth century, and the younger one attested in the so-called golden age of Croatian Glagolism in the fourteenth and fifteenth centuries. They differ more or less on all language levels.

18. Corin stresses the need to determine whether vernacular features truly had non-normative status within Croatian Church Slavonic or whether they were acceptable as inherent variation (1993: 160–161).

19. Corin points out that the Glagolitic and the Latinic sociolinguistic complexes could intersect "in just such environments, in which the traditions and achievements of both literacies were known, and in the work of those

individuals who had mastered, and even participated in, both systems of literacy," where "we would expect especially intense stylistic (both linguistic and literary) experimentation and innovation" (1993: 165). Although Corin does not seem to be familiar with the life and work of Šimun Kožičić Benja, the initiator of the Glagolitic printing house in Rijeka (1530–1531), it is exactly Kožičić who gives an excellent example of the experimentation and innovation that Corin refers to, by promoting a mixed, modified variety of the literary language.
20. However, for horizontal translation, Folena made another claim – that between the languages in question there exists a cultural appeal ("forte affinità culturale") and that they are similar in structure (Folena, 1991: 12–13, 75, 78). This claim was made as a result of his interest in Romance languages, but it is essentially obsolete, as the distinction between vertical and horizontal translation can successfully be applied at least in any community that experienced the Renaissance. In the Croatian case, the cultural appeal goes in one way, and there is no obvious structural similarity between Romance and Slavic languages, yet horizontal and vertical translations can be distinguished. As this leaves us with prestige as a key factor, it becomes clear that the distinction is sociolinguistic in nature. Folena's terminology has also entered English textbooks on translation studies. Bassnet (2002: 59), for example, claims that "[t]he distinction between *horizontal* and *vertical* translation is helpful in that it shows how translation could be linked to two coexistent but different literary systems" (see also Barbarić, 2017: 143–146). For Barbarić, this distinction was useful in explaining why the oldest Croatian vernacular lectionaries do not firmly adhere to Latin or Croatian Church Slavonic missals.
21. It was also reprinted twice, in 1543 and in 1586 (all editions were printed in Venice).
22. Namely in the area around the city of Dubrovnik, as two remaining handwritten lectionaries witness. One of them is today held outside Croatia, in Leipzig (Barbarić, 2012: 2–4). In the only preserved Latin script manuscript from Dubrovnik (*Ranjina Lectionary*, beginning of the sixteenth century), the text from *Bernardin's Lectionary* was merely copied, not adapted.
23. The most recent research (Barbarić, 2021) suggests that Croatian Protestants relied somewhat more on Erasmus's Bible.

References

Barbarić, V.-T. (2012). Nove spoznaje o *Lajpciškom lekcionaru*. Rasprave Instituta za hrvatski jezik i jezikoslovlje, 38(1), pp. 1–18.

Barbarić, V.-T. (2017). *Nastajanje i jezično oblikovanje hrvatskih lekcionara*. Zagreb: Institut za hrvatski jezik i jezikoslovlje.

Barbarić, V.-T. (2021). Mogu li nam (i kako) onimi pomoći u tekstološkoj raščlambi protestantskoga Novog testamenta. In: I. Eterović and M. Žagar, eds., *Jezik hrvatskih protestantskih izdanja u kontekstu hrvatskih i europskih književnojezičnih koncepcija XVI. stoljeća*. Zagreb: Hrvatska sveučilišna naklada – Staroslavenski institut, pp. 11–23.

Barbarić, V.-T. and Eterović, I. (2020). O utjecaju lekcionara na hrvatski protestantski prijevod *Novoga zavjeta*. In: T. Kuštović and M. Žagar, eds., *Stumačeno pravo i razumno: Studije o jeziku knjiga hrvatskih protestanata 16. stoljeća*. Zagreb: Hrvatska sveučilišna naklada – Adventističko teološko visoko učilište, pp. 511–528.

Bassnet, S. (2002). *Translation Studies*. Third edition. London and New York: Routledge.
Bučar, F. (1910). *Povijest hrvatske protestantske književnosti za reformacije*. Zagreb: Matica hrvatska.
Corin, A. R. (1993). Variation and Norm in Croatian Church Slavonic. *Slovo*, 41–43, pp. 155–196.
Čupković, G. (2013). Prilog proučavanju inojezičnih izvora hrvatskoga reformacijskoga prijevoda Novoga testamenta. *Croatica et Slavica Iadertina*, 9(1), pp. 137–144.
Damjanović, S. (1984). *Tragom jezika hrvatskih glagoljaša*. Zagreb: Hrvatsko filološko društvo.
Damjanović, S. (2008). *Jezik hrvatskih glagoljaša*. Zagreb: Matica hrvatska.
Fancev, F. (1916). Jezik hrvatskih protestantskih pisaca 16. vijeka: Prilog historičkoj gramatici jezika hrvatskoga ili srpskoga. *Rad JAZU*, 212, pp. 147–225; 214, pp. 1–112.
Ferguson, C. A. (1959). Diglossia. *Word*, 15, pp. 325–340.
Fishman, J. A. (1965). Who Speaks What Language to Whom and When? *La Linguistique*, 1(2), pp. 67–88.
Folena, G. (1991). *Volgarizzare e tradurre*. Torino: Einaudi.
Fučić, B. (1982). *Glagoljski natpisi*. Zagreb: Jugoslavenska akademija znanosti i umjetnosti.
Giannelli, C. and Graciotti, S. (2003). *Il messale croato-raguseo (Neofiti 55) della Biblioteca apostolica vaticana*. Cittá del Vaticano: Biblioteca apostolica vaticana.
Grković-Mejdžor, J. (2007). Diglosija u starosrpskoj pismenosti. In: Grković-Mejdžor, J., ed., *Spisi iz istorijske lingvistike*. Sremski Karlovci – Novi Sad: Izdavačka knjižarnica Zorana Stojanovića, pp. 443–459.
Hamm, J. (1963). Hrvatski tip crkvenoslavenskog jezika. *Slovo*, 13, pp. 43–67.
Hercigonja, E. (1983). *Nad iskonom hrvatske knjige: Rasprave o hrvatskoglagoljskom srednjovjekovlju*. Zagreb: Sveučilišna naklada Liber.
Hercigonja, E. (2006). *Tropismena i trojezična kultura hrvatskoga srednjovjekovlja*. Zagreb: Matica hrvatska.
Holjevac, S. (2012). *Prilog analizi jezika Kožičićevih glagoljskih knjiga*: Od bitija redovničkoga knjižice. *Fluminensia*, 24(1), pp. 185–199.
Hoyt, A. D. (2012). *A Historical-Sociolinguistic Analysis of the Written Correspondence of Vjekoslav Spinčić*. Dissertation. Zagreb: Filozofski fakultet Sveučilišta u Zagrebu.
Hüttl-Folter, G. (1978). Diglossija v drevnej Rusi. *Wiener slavistisches Jahrbuch*, 24, pp. 108–123.
Kapetanović, A. (2015). Reflections of Church Slavonic-Croatian Diglossia on the Baška Tablet: A New Contribution Concerning Its Language and Linguistic Layers. *Zeitschrift für Slawistik*, 60(3), pp. 335–365.
Kapetanović, A. (2017). Languages and Their Registers in Medieval Croatian Culture. *Studia Ceranea: Journal of the Waldemar Ceran Research Centre for the History and Culture of the Mediterranean Area and South-East Europe*, 7, pp. 79–98.
Lauersdorf, M. R. (2002). Slovak Standard Language Development in the 15th–18th Centuries: A Diglossia Approach. In: L. A. Janda, S. Franks and R. Feldstein, eds., *Where One's Tongue Rules Well: A Festschrift for Charles E. Townsend*. Bloomington, IN: Slavica Publishers, pp. 245–264.

Lauersdorf, M. R. (2003). Protestant Language Use in 17th Century Slovakia in a Diglossia Framework. In: P. Žeňuch, ed., *Život slova v dejinách a jazykových vzťahoch: Na sedemdesiatiny profesora Jána Doruľu*. Bratislava: Slavistický kabinet SAV, pp. 49–60.

Lauersdorf, M. R. (2010). *The Morphology of 16th-Century Slovak Administrative-Legal Texts and the Question of Diglossia in Pre-Codification Slovakia*. München and Berlin: Verlag Otto Sagner.

Lozić Knezović, K. and Galić Kakkonen, G. (2010). Odnos crkvenoslavenskoga jezika i govornoga jezika u hrvatskome srednjovjekovlju. *Croatian Studies Review*, 6, pp. 211–226.

Mihaljević, M. (2010). Položaj crkvenoslavenskoga jezika u hrvatskoj srednjovjekovnoj kulturi. In: I. Velev, A. Girevski, Lj. Makarijoska, I. Piperkoski and K. Mokrova, eds., *Zbornik na trudovi od Megjunarodniot naučen sobir "Sveti Naum Ohridski i slovenskata duhovna, kulturna i pismena tradicija" (organiziran po povod 1100-godišninata od smrtta na sv. Naum Ohridski)*. Skoplje: Univerzitet "Sv. Kiril i Metodij," pp. 229–238.

Mihaljević, M. and Reinhart, J. (2005). The Croatian Redaction: Language and Literature. *Incontri Linguistici*, 28, pp. 31–82.

Nazor, A. (1963). Jezični kriteriji pri određivanju donje granice crkvenoslavenskog jezika u hrvatskoglagoljskim tekstovima. *Slovo*, 13, pp. 68–86.

Peti-Stantić, A. (2008). *Jezik naš i/ili njihov: Vježbe iz poredbene povijesti južnoslavenskih standardizacijskih procesa*. Zagreb: Srednja Europa.

Rehder, P. (1981). The Concept of the Norm and the Literary Language among the Glagoljaši. In: G. Stone and D. Worth, eds., *The Formation of the Slavonic Literary Languages*. Columbus, OH: Slavica Publishers Inc., pp. 183–191.

Schubert, B. (2016). *U suton kajkavskoga književnog jezika: Povijesnosociolingvistička analiza jezika Ivana Krizmanića*. Zagreb: Srednja Europa.

Snow, D. (2013). Revisiting Ferguson's Defining Cases of Diglossia. *Journal of Multilingual and Multicultural Development*, 34(1), pp. 61–76.

Uspenskij, B. A. (2002). *Istorija russkogo literaturnogo jazyka (XI–XVII vv.)*. Moskva: Aspekt Press.

Verkholantsev, J. (2014). *The Slavic Letters of St. Jerome. The History of the Legend and Its Legacy, or, How the Translator of the Vulgate Became an Apostle of the Slavs*. DeKalb, IL: Northern Illinois Press.

Worth, D. S. (1978). On "Diglossia" in Medieval Russia. *Die Welt der Slaven*, 23(2), pp. 371–393.

Žagar, M. (2009). Hrvatska pisma u srednjem vijeku. In: A. Bičanić, ed., *Povijest hrvatskoga jezika 1: Srednji vijek*. Zagreb: Croatica, pp. 107–219.

Žagar, M., ed. (2015). *Jezik Misala hruackoga. Studije o jeziku Misala Šimuna Kožičića Benje (1531)*. Zagreb: Hrvatska sveučilišna naklada.

3 National Myths and Language Status in Early Modern Wales and Brittany

Oliver Currie

Introduction: conflict and contradiction in the use of historical narratives

The early modern period saw the expansion of powerful European kingdoms such as England and France first into neighbouring kingdoms and then beyond the shores of Europe through a process of global colonisation.[1] The hegemonic vernacular languages of these kingdoms, English and French, also expanded both functionally, taking over domains of use from Latin, and geographically, displacing the vernacular languages of the subjugated territories at least initially as the language of administration and to an extent as the language of the political and landowning elite, if not of the wider population.

This paper explores how the cultural interchange, language contact and linguistic conflict which arose as a result of the imperial expansion of the English and French kingdoms into neighbouring territories is reflected in contemporary ideologies of national origins, language antiquity and language status. I focus in particular on how the use of national myths or (pseudo-)historical narratives[2] in early modern Britain and France reveals *conflicts* and *contradictions* between the perspectives of the dominant nations, England and France, and those of two subordinate nations, Wales and Brittany, formally annexed by their larger neighbours in the 16th century, Wales by England and Brittany by France. I examine in turn how the use of the (pseudo-)historical narratives impinged on the status of Welsh and Breton, the indigenous vernacular languages of Wales and Brittany, respectively. In focusing on *conflicts* and *contradictions* in the use of national pseudo-historical narratives, I am referring to three phenomena:

a Conflicts and contradictions between versions of the same pseudo-historical narrative as used by different cultures which were in contact with each other, specifically between dominant and subordinate cultures. Different religious faiths (Catholic vs. Protestant) as well as cultures shared the same or similar national historical narratives;

DOI: 10.4324/9781003092445-5

This chapter has been made available under a CC-BY-SA license.

    insofar as the different cultures were in conflict or in competition, such as English and Welsh on the one hand, and Breton and French, on the other, the way a national narrative was used by one culture could contradict or undermine the way it was used by another culture.
- b Internal contradictions, tensions or inconsistencies within individual pseudo-historical narratives.
- c Contradictions or mismatches between myth or ideology and reality, specifically between ideological perceptions of language status implicit in a pseudo-historical narrative and sociolinguistic reality.

Previous scholarship has tended to focus either on the religious dimension of conflicts in the use of historical narratives, such as how during the Reformation, Protestant and Catholic polemicists each sought to appropriate Church history to legitimise their own faith while undermining that of their religious opponents (Williams, 1967: 19–54; Heal, 2005; Kewes, 2006; Oates, 2012), or on the political/cultural dimension, such as the use of historical narratives in the development of national identity and nationalism (Bradshaw, 1996, 1998; Roberts, 1998; Nice, 2009). Here, I seek to focus on the linguistic dimension, on the one hand examining the role of national vernacular languages in national historical narratives themselves, in particular how the narratives reflect changes in the status of vernacular languages in the early modern period (e.g. the development and promotion of vernacular languages, the functional expansion of vernacular languages at the expense of Latin especially in religious worship, the association of vernacular languages with national identity at a time of increasing nationalism as well as changing ideas on language origins and antiquity), and on the other hand exploring the relationship between the ideological status of vernacular languages in national historical narratives and their actual political, cultural, sociolinguistic status. The English, Welsh, French and Breton national historical narratives all came to be revised in the 16th century, reflecting these wider contemporary political, religious and cultural changes. In the following section, I present a brief overview of the narratives and how they changed in the 16th century before discussing the points of conflict and contradiction in the use of the narratives and their implications for the status of the indigenous vernacular languages, first in Wales and then in Brittany.

Revision of national historical narratives in the 16th century

Until the 16th century, both Wales and Brittany had the same national origin story (the "medieval British national origin myth"), reflecting the actual shared history of the two nations, with the Bretons of Brittany descended from Britons, also ancestors of the Welsh, who emigrated from the Isle of Britain to Brittany from the fourth to the sixth centuries (Guy, 2014). The Welsh and Breton languages are also closely related as Brythonic sister languages. According to the medieval British national origin myth, the Britons traced their origin to the Trojan military leader Brutus, great grandson of Aeneas, who settled the Island of Britain, then only inhabited by a few giants, with a community of Trojan exiles (Geoffrey of Monmouth, 2007: 20–29; Le Duc and Sterckx, 1972 [early 15th century]: 26–29). The Britons came to rule the whole Island of Britain and, in turn, settled Brittany. The Trojan origin of the British was calqued on the Roman national origin myth in Virgil's *Aeneid* and was also, significantly, shared by the medieval French national origin story, which in its earliest attested version traced the origin of the French to an eponymous mythical ancestor Francion, the son of Friga, brother of Aeneas, who fled Troy and eventually settled in what is now France (Beaune, 1985: 19–54; Rio, 2000: 27–32).

In the second half of the 16th century, the Welsh and Breton national historical narratives diverged and began to draw closer to those of their larger neighbours, the English and the French, respectively. The key factor underlying the revision of the English and Welsh national historical narratives was religious: the English Reformation. English Protestant apologists such as James Pilkington (1563/1842: 510–515), John Jewel (1567: 492), John Foxe (1563/2011: 32) and Matthew Parker (1568: ii–v) sought to legitimise the new protestant Church of England against accusations by Catholics that it was a new-fangled religion by arguing that it represented a return to the pure Christian faith of the Early Church, specifically the early British Church, while Roman Catholicism was a corruption (Heal, 2005; Oates, 2012; Williams, 1967). Here the conflict and contradiction in the use of national historical narratives centres on the appropriation of history. The English version of the narrative effectively appropriated Welsh history since the early British Church was the church of the ancestors of the Welsh, the ancient Britons, and predated the settlement of the English, who moreover were still pagan at the time of their conquest of the Island of Britain. Richard Davies, in turn, also recast the Welsh national historical narrative in Protestant terms in his preface to the 1567 Welsh translation of the New Testament (Davies, 1567/1967), acknowledging the spiritual leadership of the Church of England and the political supremacy of the English monarchy in Wales. However, at the same time, Davies re-appropriates the early British Church as a part of Welsh history and cultural heritage, and in so doing, at least implicitly subverts aspects of the English narrative. Language and specifically the status of the Welsh language is central to this story. Davies' narrative was a powerful apology for the Welsh language as the marker of Welsh identity and as the vehicle of the Christian worship in Wales, past, present and future, just as much as it was an apology for the

Protestant Church itself. Davies' narrative was influential in Wales and contributed to a cultural context, together with the Welsh Bible translation, in which the Welsh language could flourish despite the increasing dominance of English.

In the case of France and Brittany, it was the story of national origins itself that was revised. In the 16th century, French then Breton scholars began to trace their national origins to the ancient Gauls (or Celts) rather than to the Trojans. This shift in the quest for ancestry reflected two wider trends in contemporary European thought: the questioning of the Trojan tradition on the grounds that it was not attested in rediscovered classical sources (Beaune, 1985: 26–27) and the desire to trace national and linguistic origins ultimately to Biblical sources, specifically to the generations of Noah and the first emergence of differentiated languages following the confusion of tongues at the Tower of Babel (Genesis 10–11). The rediscovery of the ancient Gauls also enabled French scholars to develop a distinctively French national origin story and, therefore, one with more nationalistic potential since the previous Trojan-centred narrative was shared with other nations (the Germans and English as well as the Welsh and Bretons). The linguistic dimension of the Breton national historical narrative is particularly interesting as it is this which sets it apart from and at odds with the French national historical narrative. The Breton chronicler Bertrand d'Argentré (1582) and after him 17th and 18th century Breton grammarians and scholars (Maunoir, 1659; de Rostrenen, 1732, 1738; Le Pelletier, 1752; Pezron, 1703) claimed that Breton was the same language as the ancient Gaulish language, which in turn was believed to be one of the ancient, original languages of the generations of Noah – specifically the language of Gomer, the son of Japheth and grandson of Noah – which came into existence by Divine creation following the confusion of tongues at the Tower of Babel.[3] French, on the hand, was considered to be a more recent language, created by Man through the mixture of Latin, Germanic and Gaulish. Through their language, the Bretons thus had a stronger claim to Gaulish ancestry than the French, whose connection with the ancient Gauls was only historical and territorial. So, in the case of France and Brittany, the conflict and contradiction in the use of national historical narratives lie in the paradox of status: despite its prestigious historical pedigree (according to contemporary language ideology, antiquity was a supreme marker of prestige), Breton now had a low sociolinguistic status, subordinate to French. French was the official language of the French state, the regional administration of Brittany, as well as the predominant language of learning, letters and scholarship in the Breton speaking western half of Brittany. In section 4, I explore how this paradox is reflected in contemporary Breton sources and whether Breton's historical pedigree had an impact on its status as a living language.

National historical narratives and the status of the Welsh language

Historical context

At the time of the Act of Union of England and Wales in 1536, Wales was overall a strongly monolingual Welsh-speaking nation and remained largely so throughout the early modern period (Jenkins *et al.*, 1997). However, following the Union of England and Wales, there was a real possibility of the complete anglicisation of Wales. Since King Edward I of England's conquest of Wales in the 13th century, Wales had ceased to be independent and had been part of the crown dominion of England, without being fully integrated into the Kingdom of England. The Act of Union formally made Wales an integral part of the Kingdom of England, establishing legal and administrative uniformity throughout England and Wales. English law was established as the only applicable law throughout England and Wales and English became the official language of the law and administration. Welshmen were only able to hold public office in Wales if they spoke English and risked the forfeiture of their function for using Welsh (Roberts, 1989: 28). Although the use of English in the law and administration may not have immediately and directly affected the everyday life of most Welsh speakers, the adoption of English as an official language encouraged the anglicisation of the native Welsh upper classes. However, the effect of the 1549 Act of Uniformity, which adopted the English Book of Common Prayer as the sole legal form of worship, was potentially more wide-reaching, as it established English as the language of worship in the new Protestant Church of England (Roberts, 1989: 50).

Nevertheless, there was little opposition to the Union with England. In the words of Bradshaw (1996: 47), "the annexation of Wales 'as a very member and joint of the English realm' not only failed to elicit the slightest whimper of protest from the Welsh but [...] came to be eulogised by their literati as a benevolence". At the same time, Wales maintained a strong sense of national identity and indeed paradoxically, as Peter Roberts (1998: 8) remarked, "Wales and Welsh identity emerged from the imperial programme of the Tudors strengthened rather than undermined". Various factors seem to have contributed to the acceptance by the Welsh of the Union with England, on the one hand, and the maintenance of a distinctive Welsh national identity, on the other. First, under the Act of Union, the Welsh became equal citizens of the Kingdom of England with the English; previously, in parts of Wales (the so-called Englishries, areas settled by English and Anglo-Norman immigrants), the Welsh had been treated as foreigners in their own country. Second, the English royal house of Tudor (comprising five monarchs, Henry VII, Henry VIII, Edward VI, Mary and Elizabeth I spanning the period from

1485 to 1603) had Welsh origins. The Tudor union of England and Wales could therefore be interpreted in terms of the Welsh national historical narrative as a rebirth of the old (and glorious) kingdom of Britain when the British, the ancestors of the Welsh, had possession of (the whole) of the Island of Britain. Third, a renewed Welsh national identity developed following the Union with England, based on the Protestant faith and the Welsh language and enabled crucially by the translation of the Bible and liturgy into Welsh: the Book of Common Prayer, Psalms and New Testament in 1567 followed by the whole Bible in 1588.

The tension between the acceptance of the union with England and the re-assertion of a distinctive Welsh identity in opposition to England is apparent in Richard Davies' use and adaptation of the Welsh national historical narrative in his preface to the 1567 Welsh translation of the New Testament, known as the *Epistol at y Cembru* ("Address to the Welsh Nation"). First, I outline the medieval Welsh national historical narrative as it existed prior to Davies' *Address to the Welsh Nation* per Geoffrey of Monmouth, then how British history was used by English protestant apologists and finally how Richard Davies in turn revised the Welsh narrative.

Who are the inheritors of the glorious British past? Ambiguity in the medieval British national historical narrative

The traditional Welsh national historical narrative was based on Geoffrey of Monmouth's *Historia Regum Britanniae* ("History of the Kings of Britain"), dated to the first half of the 12th century (Geoffrey of Monmouth, 2007). This work was translated into Welsh (commonly known as *Brut y Brenhinedd*) and the Welsh translation is attested in numerous manuscripts (approximately 60), the earliest dating from the 13th century (Roberts, 1984: xxiv). The key elements of this narrative pertinent to our discussion here are:

- Britain was converted to Christianity during the reign of Lucius son of Coillus (*Lles fab Coel* in Welsh), who wrote to Pope Eleutherius requesting instruction in the Christian religion. The Pope sent Fagan and Duvian to instruct him and Lucius was converted, with the people of the Island of Britain following suit. In their wars with the English, the Welsh are portrayed as Christians fighting against the pagan English, who were only converted much later to Christianity in the time of Pope Gregory.
- The Britons experienced an era of glory under King Arthur, who not only won many victories in the wars with the English but also conquered Gaul.
- Brittany (Armorica) was settled by Britons from the Island of Britain, led by Maximianus and Conan Meriadoc, turning Armorica into a

"second Britain"; Britons replaced the indigenous population and the British language came to prevail there.
- The Britons used to have possession of the whole of the Island of Britain, but the English settled there and obtained through conquest from the Britons most of the Island of Britain, the part that came to be known as England ("Loegria"). The Britons were ultimately forced to retreat to Wales and Cornwall.
- Geoffrey of Monmouth's narrative concludes (2007: 280–281) with a contrast between the past glory of the Britons and the present state of decline of their descendants, the Welsh. He notes that "as their culture ebbed, they were no longer called Britons, but Welsh" ("Barbarie etiam irrepente, iam non vocabantur Britones sed Gualenses"), while in contrast, the English acted more wisely and thus came to rule most of the Island of Britain. Moreover, the Welsh are described as "unworthy successors of the noble Britons" who "never again recovered mastery of the whole island" ("Degenerati autem a Britannica nobilitate Gualenses numquam postea monarchiam insulae recuperaverunt").

The concept of "Britain", as is apparent even in Geoffrey of Monmouth's narrative, is a double-edged sword. On the one hand, "Britain" could be seen from a linguistic and cultural perspective as the expression of a distinctly Welsh identity, since the Welsh were the descendants of the Britons and spoke the same language; from this perspective, the Welsh were the inheritors of the history of Britain. On the other hand, Britain could be seen as reflecting the political and territorial reality, where the English occupied the majority of the island and controlled also those parts, Wales and Cornwall, still occupied by the Britons. From this second perspective, the English could appropriate British history as their own, as though by virtue of becoming political masters of the territory of the island of Britain, they had inherited the whole history of Britain, even that which predated their presence on the island (Currie, 2016: 154–155).

16th century Protestant adaptation of the British national historical narrative

The story of the early conversion of the British to Christianity was useful to English Protestant apologists in the 16th century who sought to defend the new Protestant Church of England from accusations by Catholic apologists that it was a newly invented religion without authority or historical legitimacy. Two arguments were critical for the Protestant apologists: first, that the British had been converted early to Christianity, so had the pure faith of the Early Church before it became corrupted by the addition of extraneous practices characteristic of the

Catholic Church (e.g. celibacy of priests, cult of the Virgin Mary), and second, that the British acquired Christianity directly from an apostle of Christ, Joseph of Arimathea,[4] rather than from Papist Rome. The English protestant apologists drew on various sources, typically Classical historians and Church fathers – Geoffrey of Monmouth was not as central for them as he was in Wales and Brittany. One consequence of emphasising the roots of the Church of England in the early British Church was the undermining of the role played by St Augustine of Canterbury, traditionally credited with converting the English to Christianity from the end of the sixth century (Williams, 1967: 215). Augustine, once the saviour of the English, is now attacked for bringing heretical practices to Britain as well as for being complicit in the massacre of thousands of Christians (in particular British monks at Bangor on Dee) as, for example, by Jewel in his *Defence of the Apologie of the Churche of Englande* (Jewel, 1567: 492). It is important to stress that the way the history of the British Church is used by English apologists is not uniform – there are differences in detail and emphasis – but generally, they do not acknowledge potential contradictions in their narrative, in particular the fact that English were first pagan when the British were already Christian and the fact that the Welsh may have a competing claim on the history of the British Church which could undermine the English one. Foxe is an exception in stating "the Saxones being then infidels, with Hengistus their kinge, subdued the Britans by fraudulent murder, & inuaded their land" (Foxe, 1563/2011: 32).

Richard Davies's *Address to the Welsh nation* gives the historical narrative a particularly Welsh dimension, with the Welsh language playing a central role. First, Davies emphasises that the British, ancestors of the Welsh, had been converted to Christianity at the time of the Early Church directly by a disciple of Christ, Joseph of Arimathea, before the Roman Church had become corrupted. Centuries later, the Welsh had the corrupt Roman Catholic faith imposed upon them by force by the English (Anglo-Saxons), after being conquered by the English. Davies argued that the Christian faith which Saint Augustine of Canterbury brought to England at the end of the sixth century was already corrupt, meaning that the English (who were converted to Christianity later than the Welsh) acquired from the beginning a corrupt form of Christianity. Davies further emphasised how ingrained Christianity had become in Welsh culture, citing current Welsh proverbs (e.g. *A Duw a digon: heb Dduw heb ddim* "God is plenty: without God there is nothing", Davies 1967: 31-33) and giving several quotations from earlier Welsh poetry, which, he argued, encapsulated the Christian message. Davies further asserted that the Welsh had also had the Bible in their own language (he refers to a Welsh version of the five Books of Moses he remembered seeing as a boy), but that the manuscripts which contained the Welsh Bible along with many other precious manuscripts had been destroyed in the wars with the English. So, Davies concluded, the Welsh had been privileged by God in comparison with other nations in being converted so early to Christianity, then suffered a dramatic fall from grace in losing their pure faith, but now had been presented with a unique chance of redemption with the printed translation of the New Testament in their own language and the pure Protestant faith of the Church of England. At the same time, Davies acknowledges the spiritual hegemony of the Church of England and expresses gratitude to the Queen of England and the Bishops of the Church of England for granting the Welsh the opportunity to have the Bible again in their own language. Davies's message is overtly a justification of the new Protestant faith of the Church of England for a Welsh audience with the aim of winning over priests and laity attached to the traditional Roman Catholic faith. However, at the same time, Davies' specifically Welsh narrative at least implicitly subverts the English historical justification of the Church of England.

It would be misleading and over simplistic, however, to seek to present a black and white picture of English cultural appropriation and oppression, on the one hand, and Welsh resistance, on the other. While Davies appears to subvert the English narrative with his Welsh one, he and his fellow (and principal) translator of the 1567 New Testament, William Salesbury, were also an important source of antiquarian information on the British Church for the English Protestant apologists and corresponded with Archbishop Matthew Parker (Roberts, 1998: 28–29; Williams, 1953). Further, the translation of the Bible into Welsh was enabled by a 1563 Act of the English parliament, which was passed both as a result of lobbying on the Welsh side and support from key English figures such as William Cecil, Lord Burghley, chief advisor to Queen Elizabeth I (Roberts, 1996: 130).

Significance for the status of the Welsh language

The development of national historical narratives in 16th century England and Wales provides an additional insight into the cultural interchange and tensions between the two nations at a time of major political and religious change. It is also pertinent to consider whether the use of the English and Welsh national historical narratives and the apparent conflicts and contradictions between them may have had a wider significance or impact the beyond learned circles where they were expounded and debated. I would argue that the Davies' historical narrative did have a wider impact beyond learned circles: it came to be particularly influential in Wales, contributing to the positive reception of the translation of the Bible into Welsh as well as to a renewed national identity based upon the Protestant faith and the Welsh language (Price, 2019: 190–191). The 1567 Welsh New Testament (Salesbury, 1567), in which Davies' *Address to the Welsh nation* appeared, was superseded by another (complete)

Bible translation only 21 years later. However, Davies' narrative lived on, became the received version of Welsh church history and continued to be influential in Wales for at least the next two to three centuries. Aspects of Davies' narrative and the underlying British national historical narrative based on Geoffrey of Monmouth's *History of the Kings of Britain* were reproduced or retold in historical and religious treatises – such as Charles Edwards' *Y Ffydd Ddi-ffvant* (Edwards, 1677) and Theophilus Evans' *Drych y Prif Oesoedd* (Evans, 1716/1961), both of which had a wide circulation – as well as in popular drama such as 18th century interludes (Owen, 1734/5; Parry, 1737).

The translation of the Bible into Welsh was also a pivotal moment for the development of the Welsh language. It is widely recognised that, had the Bible not been translated into Welsh, the survival of Welsh as a literary and indeed community language could have been threatened. The 16th century translation of the Bible into Welsh, made possible by a 1563 Act of the English parliament, also appeared to go against the grain of contemporary political developments. The 1536 and 1543 Acts of Union as well as the 1549 Act of Uniformity suggested a trend of political and cultural assimilation of Wales into England, while the translation of the Bible into Welsh, on the other hand, was a major step in maintaining Welsh cultural distinctiveness. The translation of the Bible into Welsh further encouraged the development of a new, abundant (predominantly) religious literature in Welsh, both original and translated, in particular popular works of practical religious instruction as well as more learned treatises and polemical works. The availability of popular printed works, including a portable version of the Bible from 1630, as well as regular religious worship in Welsh both in church and at home, also encouraged wider literacy despite the lack of formal education in Welsh (Ó Ciosáin, 2013: 15).

National historical narratives and status of the Breton language in Brittany

Historical context

The linguistic situation in 16th century Brittany was significantly different from that of Wales. Whereas 16th century Wales was a largely monolingual Welsh-speaking nation, Brittany was only partially Breton-speaking. Even before the union with France (formal legal union took place in 1532, though effective union had occurred in 1491 with the marriage of Anne, duchess of Brittany, to king Charles VIII of France), French had become the official language of Brittany, reflecting a wider pattern of the expansion of standard or the "King's" French throughout the regions of France (Lodge, 1993: 119–133). Since the early Middle Ages, when Breton retreated from most of Eastern Brittany, Brittany had been divided into two distinct cultural halves: a Breton-speaking West (Lower Brittany) and a Romance-speaking[5] East (Upper Brittany). The ducal capitals of Brittany, Rennes and Nantes, were both in the East. While Lower Brittany remained until well into the second half of the 19th century a very largely monolingual Breton-speaking nation (Broudig, 1995: 55), the consequences of this early retreat of Breton were profound. In a trilingual society, Breton was at the bottom of the linguistic hierarchy, below both Latin and French; Breton remained predominantly a language of oral communication and the proportion of written material from Brittany up to the 18th century in Breton was minuscule compared to that in Latin and French (Guyonvarc'h, 1997) and Breton literature, in general, came to be a peripheral literature dependent to varying degrees on the French cultural sphere (Blanchard and Thomas, 2014: 14–21). The chronicles where the Breton national historical narrative is presented are also written in French (Le Baud, 1638; Argentré, 1582; Bouchart, 1514/1986) or Latin (Le Duc and Sterckx, early 15th century/1972), with none in Breton. However, it is significant that even for French-speaking chroniclers from Upper Brittany (such as Argentré and Le Baud), who represented the majority of Breton historiographers (Kerhervé, 1997: 247), the Breton language was regarded as central to Breton identity and as a key factor which differentiated Brittany from France (Rio, 2000: 142).

The medieval British national origin myth connected Brittany historically, culturally and linguistically to Britain and emphasised its distinctness from France – while it was still an independent duchy – both ethnically, as its population was believed to be descended from Britons as opposed to Gauls or Franks, and crucially, linguistically, as the Bretons spoke a different language from the French. The *Chronicon Briocense*, for example, states that the Bretons preserved the language of the ancient Trojans, while the French, who also had ultimate Trojan origins, became mixed with the Gauls and adopted the language of the Franks (Le Duc and Sterckx, early 15th century/1972: 74). Following the revision of both the Breton and French national origin myths in the 16th century, the Breton origin myth became aligned with the French one at least in terms of ethnic origins, as the ancient Gauls were recognised as the ancestors of both nations; Brittany's historical ties with Britain – now the Kingdom of England and a major rival to France – and equally the grounds for a potential English claim to Brittany were thus weakened. The crucial role of language in keeping Brittany distinct from France was, however, maintained in the revised Breton national origin myth.

Reinvention of the Breton and French origin legends

The first Breton scholar to revise the Breton national historical narrative was Bertrand d'Argentré in his 1582 *Histoire de Bretaigne* (Argentré, 1582; Rio, 2000: 184–214). Argentré attacks Geoffrey of Monmouth's

Brutus/Trojan origin story as well as the notion that Brittany was settled by Britons from the Isle of Britain and instead argues that the Bretons are descended from the ancient Gauls, who then settled in Britain and brought their language to the island. Argentré further argues that the Bretons alone in Gaul/France have maintained the language of the ancient Gauls, as Brittany was the part of Gaul least overrun by foreign invaders, whether Romans or Franks, whereas elsewhere in Gaul, the language of the Romans prevailed, which ultimately developed into Romance ("romande") under the influence of the Francs. Interestingly, Argentré notes the exception of the Romance-speaking eastern part of Brittany "neighbouring France which through the effect of trade and proximity changed language some centuries ago, though originally the language was one and the same [i.e. Breton]" (my translation of Argentré, 1582: 38). Argentré also notes that the Welsh are the survivors of the Gauls in the Isle of Britain, that they still speak the British language ("langage breton") and that the Welsh and Bretons can still understand one an other.

The Gaulish origin myth was already well established in France prior to the publication of the first edition of Argentré's history of Brittany in 1582, with writers such as Jean Lemaire de Belges (1882 [1512]), Guillaume Postel (1552), Guillaume du Bellay (1556), Jean Picard (1556), Robert Céneau (1557) and François Hotman (1574), amongst others, tracing the origins of the French nation back to the Ancient Gauls. The key elements of the French Gaulish origin myth involved demonstrating the antiquity of the Gauls, rehabilitating their reputation as a glorious but forgotten civilisation older than ancient Rome and establishing the French as their descendants and inheritors of their glorious past. According to Dubois' detailed study of the development of the "Gaulish/Celtic" origin myth in 16th century France (Dubois, 1972), the revision of national origin myths reflected a broader nationalist trend: a shift from an essentially common origin legend centred on Rome (and Troy) to particular national origin legends for individual nations to set themselves apart from and raise themselves above their neighbours and rivals. In the French case, as Dubois has argued, identifying with the ancient Gauls served both as a form of cultural decolonisation vis-à-vis Greece and Rome and, at a time of French imperial expansionism, of justifying France's current greatness by projecting it into the past: "la celtomanie de cette époque, au temps des entreprises impérialistes de François Ier et de Henri II, fait chercher dans le passé un fondement à la grandeur présente" (Dubois, 1972: 28).

The French national myth, in general, seems to have emphasised historical and territorial rather than linguistic continuity with the ancient Gauls; language does not on the whole have a prominent role in the French sources (Postel, 1552; Picard, 1556; Du Bellay, 1556). Fauchet, for example, who does mention the Gaulish language in his treatise on the origin of the French language and poetry, states that Gaulish became extinct and that French, or more accurately "Romance" ("Romand"), derives primarily from Latin (Fauchet, 1581: 12–13). Hotman (1574: 21) and Taillepied (1585: 84b) even suggest that Breton-speaking Bretons ("Bretons bretonnants") are the linguistic descendants of the ancient Gauls, having alone retained their language.

Significance for the status of the Breton language

The identification of the Breton language with Gaulish presented a curious paradox: according to the Breton national myth, Breton was considered to be a particularly ancient language and thus had a historical pedigree superior even to that of French, despite being a low-status language with no official recognition or support. I sought to investigate two questions: is this paradox reflected in early modern works dealing with the Breton language and did the ideological prestige conferred upon Breton have any impact on its actual status and development?

While the first Breton source of the revised national myth was a historical work – Bertrand d'Argentré's (1582) chronicle – later sources, all in French,[6] are works specifically devoted to the Breton language: Julien Maunoir's *Sacré Collège de Jesus* including a Breton grammar, dictionary and catechism (1659), Grégoire de Rostrenen's Breton dictionary (1732) and grammar (1738), Abbé Pezron's treatise on the antiquity of the Breton or Celtic language (1703) and Dom Louis Le Pelletier's Breton etymological dictionary (1716/1975, 1752). An antiquarian interest in Breton may have encouraged the codification of the language and emergence of a Breton grammatical and lexicographical tradition in the 17th and 18th centuries (Hincks, 1995) since, in the prefaces, the authors justify the fact they are publishing works on Breton in part because of its historical and etymological interest. However, the main motivation for Maunoir and Grégoire's grammars and dictionaries seems to have been religious: to facilitate Catholic missionary work in Breton-speaking Brittany by providing grammars and dictionaries to help priests to learn Breton and preach and catechise in the language. This religious motivation is stated explicitly in the prefaces to Maunoir's grammar and Rostrenen's dictionary and grammar, and is reflected in the long title of Grégoire's dictionary. Both Maunoir and Grégoire were in fact themselves priests, Maunoir a Jesuit, Grégoire a Capucin. Maunoir's historical justification of the Breton language is indeed at one with his religious justification. He argues that Breton is the same language as the ancient Gaulish language and that Gaulish was, in turn, one of the original languages of the generations of Noah which came into existence following the confusion of tongues at the Tower of Babel (Maunoir, 1659: 10–16; Pezron, 1703: 183–184; Rostrenen, 1732: i–ii). Breton was thus a more ancient language than French and had a superior divine pedigree since it was one of the original languages created by God, whereas French was a derived language created by Man – a mixture of corrupt Latin, Germanic and Gaulish (Maunoir, 1659: 13).

The tension between Breton's antiquarian pedigree and its contemporary sociolinguistic status is not reflected explicitly in Maunoir's preface but is in the later works by Grégoire and Le Pelletier. Grégoire uses the antiquity of Breton to justify publishing his grammar against the potential objection that it is too late to codify a *"dying* language" (Rostrenen 1738: vi), and argues that it is worthwhile, indeed necessary, to conserve a language which survives in only two small corners of France and England, since it provides etymologies for countless words as well as personal and place names in languages across Europe (1738: ix). Grégoire further counters the objection to conserving and cultivating Breton on the grounds that linguistic uniformity would be desirable for France (and beyond) by arguing that if the Romans with all their power and cultural predominance could not achieve linguistic uniformity, no monarch can, so each nation should speak and preserve its mother tongue, both to maintain community cohesion and to fulfil divine will (1738: x). Grégoire's arguments were, in fact, lifted from Davies's defence of the Welsh language in the preface to his Welsh grammar (Davies, 1621/1968), which Grégoire used as a model, so do not provide unambiguous direct testimony of Breton's sociolinguistic status, though Grégoire seems to have found them relevant and to have adapted them to the French and Breton context.

The starkest expression of the tension between Breton's historical pedigree and its sociolinguistic status is found in the preface to Le Pelletier's (manuscript) Breton etymological dictionary, which, unlike Maunoir and Grégoire's works, focuses on the antiquarian interest of the language – in particular for French scholars – rather than on its practical codification or use. Le Pelletier extols the glorious past of Breton, but contrasts this with its current lowly, indeed threatened status as a living language, denigrating its speakers in the process and implying that a language without the trappings of official status (like French) is not a fully developed language:

> Je l'ai trouvée si respectable pour son antiquité, si belle pour sa simplicité, si douce à l'oreille, et si sonnante par l'accent et la délicatesse de la prononciation, et surtout si noble par son origine et ses alliances, que j'ai continué mon travail avec plaisir, autant pour assurer à notre France une langue mère si ancienne et étendue, que pour répondre aux vœux des savants [...] que deviendra une pauvre Langue abandonnée au caprice et à la rusticité d'une populace ignorante et grossière; sans prince qui l'honnore, sans Academie qui la deffende de la corruption, sans inscriptions, sans actes publics, sans Auteurs ni livres anciens. [...] une langue ainsi dépourvüe de tout

ce qui peut la faire passer à la posterité, ne peut manquer de périr pour toujours, si on vient à cesser de la parler. Et cela ne peut beaucoup tarder, Le François étant déjà la langue vulgaire non seulement dans les villes, mais aussi dans les bourgs, bourgades, passages et auberges [...].

(Le Pelletier, 1716/1975: Preface 2–3)

I found it [Breton] so honourable on account its antiquity, so elegant in its simplicity, so pleasant to the ear as well so melodious in its accent and subtleness of pronunciation and above all so noble in its origin and lineage that I continued my labours with pleasure, both to reveal this ancient and once widely-spoken ancestral language to our French nation and to respond to scholars' requests. [...] what is to become, though, of a language abandoned to the whim and coarseness of an ignorant and uncultivated folk, without a prince to honour it, without an Academy to defend it from corruption, without inscriptions, without public acts, without writers or ancient books. [...] a language thus bereft of all that is needed to ensure it is passed on to posterity cannot but be condemned to oblivion if it ceases to be spoken. Such a fate cannot indeed be far off: French is already the vernacular language not only of the towns, but also of the townships, villages, alleyways and inns [...] (My translation)

The promotion of French as the sole official language of the French nation at the expense of regional languages intensified during the early modern period, especially from the 17th century as the French kingdom further expanded and annexed non-French speaking areas on its borders such as Alsace, Béarn and Roussillon (Van Goethem, 1989). Notwithstanding its lack of official status, however, Breton continued to thrive throughout the early modern period both as the spoken vernacular of Lower Brittany and as a language of religious worship. Indeed, despite the fact that Breton was not the official language of religious worship (in contrast to Protestant Wales) and that there was not a complete Breton Bible translation until the 19th century (again in contrast to Wales), there was an active printing industry for practical religious works such as catechisms, hymns, carols, saints' lives and religious instruction manuals as well as a flourishing (predominantly religious) popular theatre (Roudaut, 1997). The Breton Saints' Lives (*Buhez an Sent*) was particularly popular and widely distributed, and its importance in Breton-speaking Brittany has been compared to that of the Welsh Bible in Wales (Le Menn, 1990: 508–510). The apparent widespread use of Breton practical religious works, as indicated in a study by Le Menn (1990: 508) of an 18th century printer's records, which revealed a large inventory of Breton language religious books and relatively high annual sales volumes, in turn suggests a potentially higher literacy in Breton amongst the ordinary population than might have been expected given the lack of formal education in the language.

Breton's perceived superior historical pedigree compared to French did not alter its subordinate sociolinguistic status to French as a living language. The reappropriation of Breton history by Breton scholars to reclaim the antiquity language's antiquity did, nevertheless, seem to reflect a reaffirmation of and pride in the continued existence of the Breton language; for the strongest advocates of Breton amongst them, priests such as Maunoir and Grégoire, who sought to codify the language and actively promoted its use in worship, its value was more than simply symbolic and antiquarian.

Conclusion

The linguistic dimension of early modern national historical narratives is significant not just because the revision of the narratives coincided with rising nationalism and the promotion and expansion of national vernacular languages, but also because language was becoming an increasingly important badge of national identity and instrument of nationalism itself, in particular with the increasing identification of the nation state with a single national vernacular language. A key rationale for the revision of national historical narratives in the 16th century, as Dubois (1972: 28) has argued, was individual nations' quest for unique historical origins, in the place of a previously common origin story centred on ancient Rome and Latin culture, in order to reaffirm a distinct cultural identity and historical pedigree, as a well as potentially to justify their current political greatness or imperial ambitions. However, because early modern European nation-states like the kingdoms of England and France were, in fact, multinational and multilingual, we find similar, revised early modern national historical narratives also shared by different nations but within the same state.

In the case of England, a Protestant national historical narrative was shared by the English and Welsh, with both claiming religious continuity with the early British Church; in the case of France, both the French and the Bretons traced their origins to the ancient Gauls. The sharing of similar national historical narratives necessarily entailed conflicts and contradictions between the perspectives of the dominant nations England and France, on the one hand, and those of the subordinate nations, Wales and Brittany, on the other. The English Protestants claimed to have inherited the true and pure faith of the early British Church, but from the Welsh perspective, the early British Church was the church only of the ancestors of the Welsh, who identified themselves as the real descendants of the ancient Britons as they spoke the same language as them. The French claimed the ancient Gauls as their ancestors, but the Bretons had, in their version of the narrative, a stronger claim to continuity with the ancient Gauls, as they, unlike the French, had preserved their language. So while the subordinate nations of Wales and Brittany enjoyed pre-eminence in their perceived antiquity, demonstrated by means of language, the English and French enjoyed political predominance, which enabled them to lay claim to and effectively appropriate the history of the territory which they controlled. Welsh and Breton writers, in turn, channelled the historical pedigree of their cultures and languages to promote the active use of their vernacular languages – in particular for religious worship – at a time of increasing dominance of the national official languages, English and French. The tension between the dominant and subordinate nations' appropriation and reappropriation of history in national historical narratives thus had a significance beyond that of antiquarian debate and impinged on the actual status of the vernaculars in competition.

Notes

1. I acknowledge the financial support of the Slovenian Research Agency (research core funding No. P6-0265).
2. I use the term "*pseudo*-historical" as opposed to simply "historical" narratives here to indicate that the narratives typically combine both history and myth. While there was a keen debate in the 16th and 17th centuries over the historicity of national origin stories (Williams, 1967; Kewes, 2006; Oates, 2012; Heal, 2005), my focus here is on how these narratives were used, not on their veracity.
3. Welsh scholars, notably John Davies in the preface to his 1621 grammar of the Welsh language (Davies, 1621/1968), also adopted the Gomer/Japheth myth. This chapter focuses on the use of church history, specifically the antiquity and authenticity of the British Church in the Welsh (and English) national historical narratives rather than on the antiquity of the Welsh language. See Davies (2000) for a discussion of the development of language antiquity myths in early modern Wales.
4. The conversion of the Britons by Joseph of Arimathea, earlier than the one by King Lucius in Geoffrey of Monmouth, is a later addition to the narrative (Heal, 2005: 605; Oates, 2012: 141; Davies, 1567/1967: 18).
5. I am using the term "Romance-speaking" to include both French and Gallo, the langue d'oïl variety traditionally spoken in Upper Brittany.
6. Maunoir (1659) includes a catechism in Breton, but the preface with his apology of the Breton language is in French, as is his Breton grammar.

References

Argentré, B. d' (1582). *L'Histoire de Bretaigne*. Paris: chez Jacques du Pvys.
Beaune, C. (1985). *Naissance de la nation France*. Paris: Editions Gallimard.
Blanchard, N. and Thomas, M. (2014). Prologue: Qu'est-ce qu'une périphérie littéraire? In: N. Blanchard and M. Thomas, eds. *Des littératures périphériques*. Rennes: Presses Universitaires de Rennes, pp. 11–24.
Bouchart, A. (1986). *Grandes croniques de Bretaigne*. Edited by M-L. Auger, G. Jeanneau and B. Guenéez. Paris: Centre national de la recherche scientifique. (Original work published 1514.)

Bradshaw, B. (1996). The Tudor Reformation and Revolution in Wales and Ireland: The Origins of the British Problem. In: B. Bradshaw and J. Morrill, eds. *The British Problem, c. 1534–1707. State Formation in the Atlantic Archipelago*. London: Macmillan Education, pp. 39–65.

Bradshaw, B. (1998). The English Reformation and Identity Formation in Wales and Ireland. In: B. Bradshaw and P. Roberts, eds. *British Consciousness and Identity. The Making of Britain, 1533–1707*. Cambridge: Cambridge University Press, pp. 43–111.

Broudig, F. (1995). *La pratique du breton: de l'Ancien Régime à nos jours*. Rennes: Presses Universitaires de Rennes.

Céneau, R. (1557). *Gallica Historia*. Paris: Apud Galeotum a Prato.

Currie, O. (2016). The Sixteenth-century Bible Translations and the Development of Welsh Literary Prose Style. *Translation Studies*, 9(2), 152–167.

Davies, R. (1967). Testament Newydd 1567. Richard can rat DYW Episcop Menew, yn damuno adnewyddiat yr hen ffydd catholic a gollaun Evangel Christ ir Cembru oll, yn enwedic i bop map eneid dyn o vewn ey Escopawt. In: G. H. Hughes, ed. *Rhagymadroddion 1547–1659*. Caerdydd: Gwasg Prifysgol Cymru, pp. 17–43. (Original work published 1567.)

Davies, J. (1968). *Antiquae Linguae Britannicae Rudimenta 1621*. Menston: The Scholar Press Limited. (Original work published 1621.)

Davies, C. (2000). *Adfeilion Babel: Agweddau ar Syniadaeth Ieithyddol y Ddeunawfed Ganrif*. Caerdydd: Gwasg Prifysgol Cymru.

Du Bellay, G. (1556). *Epitome De L'Antiqvite Des Gavles Et De France*. Paris: Sertenas.

Dubois, C.G. (1972). *Celtes et Gaulois au XVIe siècle: le développement littéraire d'un mythe nationaliste*. Paris: Librairie philosophique J. Vrin.

Edwards, C. (1677). *Y Ffydd Ddi-ffvant sef, Hanes y Ffydd Gristianogol, a'i Rhinwedd*. 3rd ed. Rhydychen: Hen. Hall.

Evans, T. (1961). *Drych y Prif Oesoedd: yn ôl yr Argraffiad Cyntaf, 1716*. Edited by G. H. Hughes. Caerdydd: Gwasg Prifysgol Cymru. (Original work published 1716.)

Fauchet, C. (1581). *Recueil de l'origine de la langue et poesie françoise, ryme et romans*. Paris: M. Patisson.

Foxe, J. (2011). *The Unabridged Acts and Monuments Online or TAMO (1563 Edition)*. Sheffield: The Digital Humanities Institute. Available at: http//www.dhi.ac.uk/foxe. [Accessed 3 Nov. 2018]. (Original work published 1563.)

Geoffrey of Monmouth. (2007). *The History of the Kings of Britain: An Edition and Translation of De gestis Britonum (Historia regum Britanniae)*. Latin text edited by M. D. Reeve and translated by N. Wright. Woodbridge: Boydell Press.

Guy, B. (2014). The Breton migration: A new synthesis. *Zeitschrift für celtische Philologie*, 61(1), 101–156.

Guyonvarc'h, C. (1997). Du moyen breton au breton moderne: langue et littérature. In: J. Balcou and Y. Le Gallo, eds. *Histoire littéraire et culturelle de la Bretagne*. Paris: Champion, pp. 193–210.

Heal, F. (2005). What Can King Lucius Do for You? The Reformation and the Early English Church. *English Historical Review*, 120, 593–614.

Hincks, R. (1995). *I Gadw Mamiaith Mor Hen: Cyflwyniad i Ddechreuadau Ysgolheictod Llydaweg*. Llandysul: Gomer.

Hotman, F. (1574). *La Gavle francoise de François Hotoman Jurisconsulte. Nouuellement traduite de latin en francois.* Cologne: H. Bertulphe.

Jenkins, G. H., Suggett, R. and White, E. M. (1997). Yr Iaith Gymraeg yn y Gymru Fodern Gynnar. In: G. H. Jenkins, ed. *Y Gymraeg yn ei Disgleirdeb. Yr Iaith Gymraeg cyn y Chwyldro Diwydianol.* Caerdydd: Gwasg Prifysgol Cymru, pp. 45–119.

Jewel, J. (1567). *A defence of the Apologie of the Churche of Englande conteininge an answeare to a certaine booke lately set foorthe by M. Hardinge, and entituled, A confutation of &c. By Iohn Iewel Bishop of Sarisburie.* London: By Henry VVykes.

Kerhervé, J. (1997). La naissance de l'histoire en Bretagne: milieu XVe-fin XVIe siècle. In: J. Balcou and Y. Le Gallo, eds. *Histoire littéraire et culturelle de la Bretagne.* Paris: Champion, pp. 246–271.

Kewes, P. (2006). History and its Uses. In: P. Kewes, ed. *The Uses of History in Early Modern England.* San Marino, California: Huntingdon Library, pp. 1–30.

Le Baud, P. (1638). *Histoire de Bretagne, avec les chroniques des maisons de Vitré, et de Laval.* Edited by P. d'Hozier. Paris: Chez Gervais Alliot.

Le Duc, G., and Sterckx, C. (1972). *Chronicon Briocense: Chronique de Saint-Brieuc (fin XIVe siècle) éditée et traduite d'après les manuscrits BN 6003 – BN 8899.* Rennes: Imprimerie Simon. (Original manuscript dated to the early 15th century.)

Le Menn, G. (1990). Langue et culture bretonnes. In: M. Simon, Y. Pelletier, G. Le Menn and R. Chauvet, eds. *Histoire générale de la Bretagne et des Bretons. Tome II. Culture et mentalités bretonnes.* Paris: Nouvelle Librairie de France, pp. 465–577.

Le Pelletier, L. (1752). *Dictionnaire étymologique de la langue bretonne ou l'on voit son antiquité son affinité avec les anciennes langues, l'explication de plusieurs passages de l'Écriture Sainte, et des auteurs profanes, avec l'étymologie de plusieurs mots des autres langues par Dom Louis Le Pelletier.* Edited and with a preface by Ch. Taillandier. Paris: François Delaguette.

Le Pelletier, L. (1975). *Dictionnaire de la langue Bretonne.* Vol. 4. Rennes: Bibl. Municipale. (Original manuscript dated 1716.)

Lemaire de Belges, J. (1882 [1512]). *Oeuvres de Jean Lemaire de Belges. Premier livre.* Edited by J. Stecher. Louvain: J. Lefever.

Lodge, R. A. (1993). *French: From Dialect to Standard.* London: Routledge.

Maunoir, J. (1659). *Le Sacré College de Iesvs divise en cinq classes, ov on enseigne en Langue Armorique les Leçons Chrestiennes avec les 3 clefs pour y entrer, vn Dictiõnaire, une Grammaire & Syntaxe en même Langue.* Quimper: Jean Hardouyn.

Nice, J. (2009). *Sacred History and National Identity: Comparisons between Early Modern Wales and Brittany.* London: Pickering & Chatto.

Ó Ciosáin, N. (2013). The Print Cultures of the Celtic Languages, 1700–1900. *Cultural and Social History,* 10(3), 347–367.

Oates, R. (2012). Elizabethan Histories of English Christian Origins. In: K. E. van Liere, S. Ditchfield and H. Louthan, eds. *Sacred History: Uses of the Christian Past in the Renaissance World.* Oxford: Oxford University Press, pp. 165–185.

Owen, M. (1734/5). *Enterliwt Ynghylch Cronicl y Cymry er Amser Brutus hyd at Sior y 3ydd.* Manuscript, NLW 833B, National Library of Wales, Aberystwyth.

Parker, M. (1568). *The. holie. Bible. conteynyng the olde Testament and the newe.* London: Richarde Lugge.

Parry, R. (1737). *Enterlute neu chwaryddiaeth Ar Destun Odiaethol yn dangos pa Drigolion a fu'n Preswulo yn y Deyrnas hon cyn dyfod Cymru na Saeson erioed iw Meddiannu o wnaethuriad R. P.* Manuscript, NLW 833B, National Library of Wales, Aberystwyth.

Pezron, P. (1703). *L'Antiquité de la Nation et de la Langue Celtique ou Gauloise.* Paris: P. Marchand.

Picard, J. (1556). *De prisca Celtopaedia, libri qvinqve.* Parisiis: Ex typographia M. Dauîdis.

Pilkington, J. (1842). The Burning of St Paul's Church: Confutation of an Addition. In: J. Scholefield, ed. *The Works of James Pilkington, B.D., Lord Bishop of Durham.* Cambridge: The Parker Society, pp. 497–616. (Original work published 1563.)

Postel, G. (1552). *L'Histoire mémorable des expéditions depuys le déluge faictes par les Gauloys ou Françoys. A la fin est l'Apologie de la Gaule contre les malevoles escripvains.* Paris: Sebastian Nivelle.

Price, A. (2019). Welsh Humanism after 1536. In: G. Evans and H. Fulton, eds. *The Cambridge History of Welsh Literature.* Cambridge: Cambridge University Press, pp. 176–193.

Rio, J. (2000). *Mythes fondateurs de la Bretagne: aux origines de la celtomanie.* Rennes: Editions Ouest-France.

Roberts, B. F. (1984). *Brut y Brenhinedd.* Dublin: Dublin Institute for Advanced Studies.

Roberts, P. (1989). The Welsh language, English Law and Tudor Legislation. *Transactions of the Honourable Society of Cymmrodorion*, 1989, 19–75.

Roberts, P. (1996). The English Crown, the Principality of Wales and the Council in the Marches, 1534–1641. In: B. Bradshaw and J. Morrill, eds. *The British Problem, c. 1534–1707. State Formation in the Atlantic Archipelago.* Basingstoke: Macmillan Education, pp. 118–146.

Roberts, P. (1998). Tudor Wales, National Identity and the British Inheritance. In: B. Bradshaw and P. Roberts, eds. *British Consciousness and Identity: The Making of Britain, 1533–1707.* Cambridge: Cambridge University Press, pp. 8–42.

Rostrenen, G. de(1732). *Dictionnaire François-Celtique ou François-Breton nécessaire à tous ceux qui veulent apprendre et à traduire le François en Celtique, ou en langage Breton, pour Prêcher, Catechiser, & Confesser, selon les differens Dialectes de chaque Diocese; utile & curieux pour s'instruire à fond de la Langue Bretonne, & pour trouver l'éthymologie de plusieurs mots François et Bretons, de noms propres de Villes, & de Maisons.* Rennes: Julien Vatar.

Rostrenen, G. de (1738). *Grammaire Françoise-Celtique ou Françoise-Bretonne, qui contient tout ce qui est nécessaire pour apprendre par les Règles la Langue Celtique, ou Bretonne.* Rennes: Julien Vatar.

Roudaut, F. (1997). La littérature religieuse en breton. In: J. Balcou and Y. Le Gallo, eds. *Histoire littéraire et culturelle de la Bretagne.* Vol. 1. Paris: Champion, pp. 231–244.

Salesbury, W. (1567). *Testament Newydd ein arglwydd Jesu Christ.* London: Henry Denham.

Taillepied, N. (1585). *Histoire de l'Estat et Republique des Druides, Eubages, Sarronides, Bardes, Vacies, anciens François.* Paris: Iean Parant.

Van Goethem, H. (1989). La politique des langues en France, 1620–1804. *Revue du Nord*, 71, 437–460.

Williams, G. (1953). *Bywyd ac Amserau'r Esgob Richard Davies.* Caerdydd: Gwasg Prifysgol Cymru.

Williams, G. (1967). *Welsh Reformation Essays.* Cardiff: University of Wales Press.

4 Bernardo de Aldrete's *Del origen*

Rejecting Multilingualism and Linguistic Essentialism in Early Modern Spain

Vicente Lledó-Guillem

Del origen y principio de la lengua castellana ò romance que oi se usa en España (*On the origin and beginning of the Castilian or Romance language that is used in Spain nowadays*) (1606) by the Andalusian canon Bernardo de Aldrete (1565–1645) has been considered an important landmark in the historiography of the Spanish language from a historical-grammar point of view (Nieto Jiménez, 1975: 33; Lledó-Guillem, 2010: 1–2).[1] At the same time, *Del origen* is an important example of a metalinguistic text that can help us understand the *Zeitgeist* in Early Modern Spain. While in recent years special attention has been paid to certain ideological and political aspects of Aldrete's work,[2] there is still a need to analyse and contextualise *Del origen* even further by adopting a glottopolitical approach in which historicity is considered

> as a dynamic interaction between language phenomena and a multilayered context that includes social conditions simultaneous with the phenomena themselves as well as other language phenomena – previous or subsequent – of which the one under study may be a reformulation, reinterpretation or precedent.
>
> (Del Valle, 2013: 18)

One of the main objectives of *Del origen* consisted of demonstrating that Castilian[3] descended from Latin and that it had therefore not been one of the 72 languages that originated in Babel. In other words, Aldrete is disputing the "primitive Castilian" theory of origin, according to which it had been brought to Spain by Noah's grandson Tubal before the Roman conquest of the Iberian Peninsula.[4] In my study, I will argue that, by opposing this theory, *Del origen* focuses on the relationship between language and identity and implies that there are negative, positive and neutral associations as regards the link between the two. In addition to rejecting the idea of an essential or natural relationship between a language and the identity it represents and warning the reader of the dangers of a language ideology based on this belief,[5] Aldrete argues that monolingualism is the ideal state of humanity. Moreover, while every

DOI: 10.4324/9781003092445-6

single language may potentially become the language of the civilised world, Castilian is the best candidate for the role since it is superior not only to Latin but even to the common human language that existed before Babel. This is partly because it is a living mother tongue that represents a clear identity – Hispania (an identity that is not permanent but variable, as demonstrated by the language's origin and its subsequent expansion). Most importantly, though, the Castilian language is supported by a strong military power.

Multilingualism and the negative associations between language and identity: Babel and Iberia

The divine punishment meted out at the Tower of Babel constitutes the basis of Aldrete's rejection of multilingualism and linguistic essentialism. By linguistic essentialism I refer to the belief that a language is by nature associated with a permanent identity. As this supposed natural association between language and identity would become an important ideological aspect in the construction of centralised states in Early Modern Europe, we may identify linguistic essentialism with linguistic nationalism.[6]

In the biblical episode of the Tower of Babel, a dichotomy is set up between monolingualism and multilingualism that is later applied to other contexts in time and space by means of a semiotic process that linguistic anthropologists call "fractal recursivity".[7] In this case, the dichotomy of monolingualism versus multilingualism in the world is projected onto the Iberian Peninsula. According to Aldrete's text, this produces different results, and by focusing on the author's descriptions we may infer that these results may be negative, positive or neutral. With regards to negative linguistic outcomes, Aldrete analyses two examples in his work, the most destructive of which is obviously the origin of multilingualism itself: Babel. The other negative instance that is discussed extensively is the transformation of a supposedly monolingual Iberia into a multilingual Hispania after the arrival of the "Moors". In both cases we witness the birth and reinforcement of linguistic nationalism or essentialism.

In the "prologue" of *Del origen* Aldrete describes the origin of multilingualism:

> Mankind received through Divine Grace two blessings that are the most ancient, extremely useful and of high nobility: reason and its interpreter: language. With the former, man was made similar to God and with the latter, God allowed mankind to have the company of other human beings by means of communication and human contact. Both were extremely valuable gifts that deserved enormous gratitude. Yet mankind showed a lack of gratitude when humans became too ambitious and started to build that magnificent tower

that brought with it a well-deserved confusion of languages. This linguistic diversity gave rise to a division of the will and energy of those who did not share the same language, which brought with it hatred and wars, since those who used a different language were also considered different by nature.

(Aldrete, 1606/1975: ii)[8]

Linguistic essentialism is one of the consequences of the divine punishment of multilingualism and it is harmful to humankind. Aldrete highlights the dichotomy between an initial monolingualism that made possible the construction of the tower and a multilingualism that led to the division of humanity into different groups. The expression "different by nature" shows that the impossibility of returning to a monolingual society was reinforced ideologically by the conviction that linguistic differentiation responded to a natural division of humanity that needed to be maintained. In other words, in time humanity forgot that multilingualism had been a divine punishment and naturalised the idea that their different languages made humans different by nature, even insisting that these linguistic essences needed to be protected.

The opposition to linguistic essentialism or linguistic nationalism was especially important at the beginning of the seventeenth century when Bernardo de Aldrete published *Del origen*. King Philip III (r. 1598–1621) had inherited both the Spanish and Portuguese possessions from his father, King Philip II (r. 1556–1598), who became King of Portugal in 1580 after the death of Henry II of the House of Aviz (r. 1578–1580) without descendants. Amidst a tense debate about how to organise the Spanish Empire between those who supported a centralist position in which Castile would play a dominant role versus a more federal approach,[9] *Del origen* explains why there are different Romance languages spoken in the Iberian Peninsula:

After Latin became the common language in the whole Hispania, when the Goths arrived, they founded a new kingdom and spoilt and corrupted the language. As a result, the Romance language was born and became the common language in the whole of Hispania until the arrival of the Moors, who introduced the Arabic language in their territories. Christians eliminated Arabic and brought back the Castilian or Romance language while they recovered the territories that the Moors had previously occupied. It was introduced in Aragon, Navarre, Galicia, Old and New Castile, Extremadura, Andalusia and the Kingdoms of Murcia and Granada [...]. As far as the conquest of the Principality of Catalonia is concerned, the Hispanic people received help from the French and this is the beginning of the Counts of Barcelona. For this reason, the Romance language got mixed up with French and, as a result, we have that language that is very similar and not very different from the *langue d'oc*, or language of Narbonne, where the latter is supposed to have been born [...] In Portugal there is another different language, which is, no doubt, the result of a mixture with the French language. The French language arrived with the French community that came with Henry I, Count of Portugal, when Alfonso VI gave that kingdom to his daughter Teresa as a dowry [...] I know that others believe that Portuguese is a different language because of the communication with Galicia, where the ancient language seems to be the same as Portuguese. According to them, the language must have expanded because of the proximity and because the conquest started there [in Galicia]. It can be added that the language changed in Galicia because that is where the Suebi established their kingdom leading to the corruption of the Latin language. However, I support the first version [the mixture with the French language] because if the Galician language had been the same as Portuguese, it is not logical that it has been kept in Portugal and not in Galicia.

(Aldrete, 1606/1975: 164–166)[10]

This passage narrates how a monolingual Hispania was transformed into a multilingual political and geographical space due to the Muslim invasion. The dichotomy of monolingualism versus multilingualism described in the episode of the punishment of Babel is placed in a different context in order to explain the Iberian linguistic differences by means of the semiotic process known as fractal recursivity explained above. Thus, multilingualism is presented as resulting from human disaster: multilingualism in Babel was the consequence of divine punishment, whereas in medieval Iberia, it was the outcome of the "Moorish" invasion.

The negative aspect of multilingualism is clearly highlighted by both narratives in which an intense disaster brings with it the loss of a common language. In Babel the common language was the original language used by humanity whereas, with regards to the Iberian Peninsula, the common language was the Romance language, which is clearly identified with Castilian. According to the text, the common Romance language was the result of the corruption of Latin under the Visigoths. The identification of this Romance language with Castilian is very significant since it emphasises that Castilian was the common language of communication in Iberia. We can infer that, for Aldrete, Castilian is important as an instrument of communication rather than a marker of an identity.

This dichotomy is reminiscent of Woolard's (2007) distinction between authenticity and anonymity in language. According to this, an anonymous language is the language of everyone (and, at the same time, of no one in particular), while authentic languages display a more intimate relationship with their respective communities.[11] Aldrete is clearly subscribing to the Neogothic thesis, initiated by Ximénez de Rada in the thirteenth century and reinforced in the fifteenth century by Rodrigo

Sánchez de Arévalo (1404–1470) in his *Compendiosa historia Hispanica* (*Brief Hispanic History*) (Arévalo, 1470), which holds that only the Crown of Castile was entitled to reclaim the Visigothic inheritance (Nadal and Prats, 1996: 335–336; Lledó-Guillem, 2018: 129–130). By using the word "Romance", Aldrete indicates that this was effectively the language of everyone and no one, common all over Hispania. However, when the word "Castilian" is used as a synonym of "Romance", the connotations are rather different, especially when the author provides a list of the areas of Hispania where this language has spread following the Christian occupation of Islamic territories. The implication is that, while this Romance language was the common anonymous language of Iberia at the time of the Visigoths, it has only been preserved in its purity by the Castilians and, consequently, shows a degree of authenticity that needs to be highlighted. This does not prevent it from again becoming the common anonymous language of the Iberian Peninsula (and eventually, the whole Spanish Empire, and the world), as indicated in Aldrete's statement that "those who are conquered receive the language of the conquerors, who have used weapons and soldiers" (Aldrete, 1606/1975: 138).[12]

The passage explains that Portuguese and Catalan result from the mixture of the natural Hispanic language (associated with Castilian) with French due to political and historical circumstances. In the case of Catalan, the language does not have a clearly defined identity, since it is very close to the language of the south of France known as Occitan or *langue d'oc*. In fact, the description of the relationship between Catalan and the *langue d'oc* is quite ambiguous since, previously, Aldrete had indicated that "the language of the Catalans has some elements of the *langue d'oc*" (Aldrete, 1606/1975: 143).[13] These statements can be interpreted either as Catalan being the result of a double "mixture" of Castilian with French and *langue d'oc* or as Catalan not being a separate language from the *langue d'oc*.[14] These linguistic "mixtures" took place, he insists, once the Visigothic Kingdom in Spain fell after the Muslim occupation.

However, there is some linguistic information that could undermine Aldrete's linguistic approach: the existence of Basque and Galician. As far as Basque is concerned, Aldrete simply erases it and does not acknowledge its presence on the seventeenth-century linguistic map of the Iberian Peninsula.[15] Yet he does mention it later in the context of the 72 languages that had supposedly originated in Babel: Basque is believed by some scholars to be one of these (he says), brought to Hispania by Tubal and used as the general language in Iberia, until the arrival of other nations led to its retreat (Aldrete, 1606/1975: 227–228). At this point, Aldrete presumably refers to Basque because it can oppose the "primitive Castilian" theory.

With regards to Galician, Aldrete first uses the semiotic process of erasure but later provides an explanation to make sure that its difference from Portuguese is highlighted. In the passage quoted above, Aldrete mentions that one of the areas into which Castilian has entered is Galicia. This implies that, after the Christian occupation, Galicia is a Castilian-speaking area (meaning that the presence of a different language is completely erased). However, once the Portuguese language is described as the result of a "mixture" of Castilian and French due to political circumstances, the Galician language becomes an ideological issue that cannot be erased so easily. Aldrete explains that Portuguese and Galician are two different languages, since the origin of Galician lies in the presence of the Germanic Suebi in the area. Nevertheless, the existence of Galician does not undermine Aldrete's linguistic ideology because, by highlighting its antiquity as well as its independence from Portuguese, *Del origen* implies that Galician is in the process of being substituted by Castilian, which spread into the area more recently.

Consequently, according to Aldrete, the existence of languages such as Portuguese, Catalan and Galician in the Iberian Peninsula illustrate the negative aspect of multilingualism, much as occurred in Babel after the divine punishment. Claiming that these languages correspond to different identities would support a harmful language ideology that started in Babel and associate different languages with different natures. In the Iberian case, these languages are the result of "mixtures" that have destroyed the original Castilian monolingualism that existed during the Visigothic monarchy before the arrival of the "Moors".

The creation of new identities by means of language: Positive aspects

However, it is also possible to infer that in *Del origen* the association between language and identity is not always viewed negatively, as long as it is perfectly clear that this relationship is not essential, eternal and immutable. Aldrete shows that new identities can be created by means of language, especially when a language is powerful enough to absorb and eliminate other languages after conquering the peoples who use them. This way, the association between language and identity can be used to support the pursuit of a monolingual humankind.

The best example of this phenomenon was the expansion of the Latin language, which had the honour of appearing on the cross where Christ was crucified and expanded Christianity around the world. Thus, Latin united different kingdoms and helped correct the linguistic diversity that started in Babel (Aldrete, 1606/1975: 2–3). However, Latin was also important because it proved that language can create new political identities, as we can observe in the city of Emporiae in northeastern Spain. Aldrete's description reflects a language ideology in which human identities are not constant but may be altered, transformed and created by means of language. Thus, language precedes the identity or identities that are associated with it. According to Aldrete, when the Romans conquered Emporiae a new identity was created. Aldrete bases his opinion on an inscription on a stone that might have been written in Emporiae after the Roman occupation. While Aldrete warns the reader that the authenticity of the stone has been called into question, he indicates that, regardless of its authenticity or not, the inscription describes a linguistic and political fact that is undeniable: the Latin language created a bigger community and identity in the city of Emporiae:

> The inscription indicates that the Greeks in the area of Emporiae built a temple in honor of Diana of Ephesus during that century. They neither abandoned the Greek language nor learned the language of Hispania, but later adopted the customs, language, law, and government of the Romans [...] The inscription distinguishes the ancient Hispanic language from the Roman one and states that they had not received the former. On the contrary, as they had lived in Hispania for so long, they considered themselves natives of the land and had kept their Greek language. However, they had to receive and adopt the Latin language as their only language and subjected themselves to the Roman laws and government [...] Those who became part of the Roman Empire had to adopt the Roman customs, language and laws [...] Titus Livius explains it better when he describes how Cato came to Hispania and indicates that, at that time, there were two peoples: the Greeks and the Hispanic population, which were divided by walls [...] Having defeated Pompey's sons, Cesar brought Roman inhabitants and thus the whole city was united. Soon after, the Hispanic population became Roman citizens followed by the Greeks [...] Having all become Roman citizens, they adopted the Latin language. And the Greeks had not adopted the natural language of their homeland, Hispania, after so many years living there. It can be assumed that they had settled in Hispania two hundred years earlier, since from the time of Cato, who found them divided, until Julius Cesar, when they united, more than one hundred and fifty years had gone by. Therefore, they were entitled to consider Hispania their homeland.
> (Aldrete, 1606/1975: 93–94)[16]

With the help of the inscription, Aldrete explains that Greeks established themselves in Emporiae 200 years before the Romans settled in the city under Julius Cesar. Before the Roman settlement, they ended up considering Hispania their homeland but never abandoned their Greek language nor adopted the "natural" language of the native Hispanic population who were their neighbours. A wall separated them until the Romans arrived and united the native Hispanic population and the Greeks, who by then considered themselves Hispanic. The Romans established a common law and, most importantly, a common language: Latin. The Latin language was, therefore, the force that demolished a material and symbolic wall that separated the two peoples.

This description responds to a particular way of approaching human linguistic diversity. The idea of an impregnable wall that remained untouched for two hundred years reminds us of Gottfried Wilhelm Leibniz's (1646–1716) concept of the monads, a "metaphysical picture" which "saw reality as a whole of independent entities, each of which expresses the entire universe and represents it from its own particular 'viewpoint'" (Cassirer, 1968: 51).[17] In this case, we are talking about monads without windows (Hina, 1986: 15) or separated by walls, since they are not supposed to be in contact with each other and need to preserve their own identity and independence.

It could be argued that the city of Emporiae actually represents the organisation of the entire world. We find two different groups with their own language divided by a wall. Each group behaves, at least linguistically, as if theirs were the only universe that existed. There is no contact until another group, the Romans, with a different language, appears. The Romans are described as a powerful force that conquers Emporiae and imposes the Latin language. The wall is demolished, at least linguistically, because both the native Hispanic group and the Greeks, who consider themselves Hispanic, accept the Latin language. We may infer that this linguistic substitution opposes the monadic conception of the universe because the Romans unite two isolated monads: the native Hispanic group and the Hispanic Greeks. However, this is not quite the case because, in fact, one of the languages, Latin, has occupied and absorbed two other independent languages. In Aldrete's description, there is no reference whatsoever to any change in the Latin language. Consequently, it is possible to assume that Latin has simply expanded its reach, eliminating the other two languages.

We can also infer that this description constitutes a linguistic project that can be applied to the entire world: an independent group may potentially absorb all the other linguistic communities without itself being transformed, ultimately creating a monolingual humankind. It could be argued that, following the Roman model, this might be achieved through military force. This would be coherent with Aldrete's statement mentioned above that "those who are conquered receive the language of the conquerors, who have used weapons and soldiers" (Aldrete 1606/1975: 138).[18] In fact, the Roman Empire demonstrated that it is possible to return to a pre-Babelian monolingual world in which a powerful group imposes a common language on the rest of the groups.

Another example of this ideology of windowless monads, in which one language may take over others without itself being transformed, appears when Aldrete describes how, in the fourth century, after the emperors Valentinian and Gratian fought and defeated the Germans, a German girl called Bissula became the servant of Consul Ausonius Galus. Galus indicated that while the girl had intense blue eyes and blonde hair, her Latin accent was so perfect that she seemed to have been born in Latium (Aldrete

1606/1975: 79–80).[19] This is Aldrete's goal when he considers the Latin linguistic expansion as a good model in the quest for a monolingual world.

The creation of neutral linguistic identities: The Visigoths and the birth of a unified Hispanic Romance

As we have seen, Aldrete intended to demonstrate that Castilian descended from Latin and was not, therefore, one of the 72 languages that were created by divine punishment at Babel. Furthermore, he considers it to be the best candidate to follow the Latin linguistic legacy and expand its dominion all over the world. The main problem is that Castilian is the result of a linguistic "mixture" between Latin and the Gothic language, i.e. the Germanic language of the Visigoths. Yet in Aldrete's narrative it is possible to deduce that, thanks to this linguistic "mixture", a new exclusive Hispanic identity has been created. This language is far more valuable than both Latin and even the original language used by humanity before Babel because it is authentic enough to be the native language of a certain group of people and powerful enough to expand and become anonymous. Consequently, Aldrete's defence of Castilian is based largely on the importance of military power.

Aldrete explains that the appearance of new empires has important consequences. Thus, "while the Roman Empire lasted the Latin language was maintained, but once the Empire collapsed the language was corrupted and changed. From the Latin ashes and ruins a new language was born" (Aldrete, 1606/1975: 151).[20] He indicates that the Goths tried to learn Latin, but they lacked linguistic skills and ended up corrupting it, which gave rise to Castilian (Aldrete, 1606/1975: 151). Later, he introduces the element of linguistic "mixture" and states that, after fighting against the Romans in Hispania,

> the Barbarians had rejected any kind of weapon and had started using the plough. They showed affection and gave presents to the Romans who had stayed as companions and friends, to such an extent that some Romans preferred to live with the Barbarians and be poor and free rather than suffering distress with their own people [...] This friendship lead to the mixture of their languages [...] Consequently, it can be argued that the arrival of the Barbarians caused the birth of the Castilian language.
> (Aldrete 1606/1975: 156)[21]

This passage implies that the Castilian language became the common language of the Hispanic monarchy created under the Visigoths, which lasted until the Muslim arrival in 711 A.D. In fact, Aldrete explains that Castilian started being used by ordinary people until it soon became the language of everybody (Aldrete, 1606/1975: 158). As we indicated above, this narrative places Castilian above the other languages of the Iberian Peninsula such as Catalan and Portuguese according to the criterion of linguistic "mixture".

However, Castilian is also the result of a "mixture" – to a lesser degree than Catalan or Portuguese, but still a "mixed" language – as Latin became Castilian after being corrupted by the Gothic language. In fact, its degree of "mixture" was similar to Galician since, as Aldrete had previously indicated, Galician was supposed to have been born from the "mixture" of Latin with the language of the Suebi. How could Aldrete demonstrate that Castilian was as important or even more valuable than Latin?

I believe it is possible to argue that, in Aldrete's narrative, the dichotomy between Latin and Castilian is transformed into the opposition between Castilian and the mixed Iberian languages: Portuguese and Catalan.[22] The temporal context is different: Castilian plays the role of Latin, French corresponds to the Gothic language, and Portuguese and Catalan would be the results of harmful linguistic "mixtures". In the Hispanic context, after the arrival of the Muslims, Castilian has become the new Latin, and with the description of the origins of Portuguese and Catalan, Castilian appears as the "pure" language despite its problematic origin. Galician may have had a similar degree of "mixture" as Castilian, but Galician could not play the role of Latin.

In addition, by reading *Del origen* we may infer that Castilian has given rise to a new identity that did not exist with Latin. Latin had been the language of an empire, but it was never the exclusive language of Hispania. With the birth of Castilian, Hispania has a common language that represents only the Hispanic population. From this point of view, it can be argued that Aldrete considers Castilian as an authentic language because of its Hispanic or Iberian exclusivity. Latin has, by this time, been forgotten as a native language. It can be studied but it is not transmitted from generation to generation. Castilian descended from Latin but there is no return since Latin cannot become a mother tongue again. In Iberia, however, there is the possibility of returning to the original and pure Hispanic language – Castilian – provided that Portuguese and Catalan speakers align themselves with this objective and use Castilian again. In fact, Aldrete indicates that this is happening already, despite some administrative difficulties (such as the use of Catalan in the courts of Catalonia and the Kingdom of Valencia, which is delaying the inevitable process of language substitution) (Aldrete, 1606/1975: 100).[23]

We can also infer that the ancient common language of humanity before Babel would not be superior to Castilian as the world language because it was no longer a living mother tongue. However, the main reason relates to Aldrete's idea that "those who are conquered receive the language of the conquerors, who have used weapons and soldiers" (Aldrete 1606/1975: 138).[24] This statement suggests that any single language can become the most important linguistic force in the world as long as it has the support of a strong army. Moreover, Aldrete's reference to "the language of the conquerors" favours the notion of a constant linguistic struggle in which languages compete with one another without losing their integrity. In other words, languages should not be "contaminated" by the languages with which they come into contact. A language should simply conquer and substitute the language of the conquered population, as we saw in Aldrete's description of Bissula, who spoke Latin like a native despite her Germanic origins. When Aldrete writes *Del origen*, Castilian is the dominant language in the Spanish Empire and it is supported by a very powerful army.

In Aldrete, therefore, we find indirect support for the idea that, in the end, the value of all languages is arbitrary, since it is with military force that Castilian can finally become the heir of the Latin language, perhaps even going further and bringing a return to a monolingual world that was lost after Babel. Aldrete's main objective might have been to demonstrate that Castilian descended from Latin (contesting the theory of "primitive Castilian") and that it was now the purest and most authentic language of Iberia without being associated with a permanent identity. Nonetheless, the underlying message of his work was that Castilian deserved to become the dominant language of a monolingual world mainly because of the military might that supported the authentic and anonymous language of a unified Hispania.

Notes

1. *Del origen* is "considered to be the very first history of the [Castilian] language" (Rojinsky, 2007: 299).
2. See Binotti (1995, 2000, 2012), Woolard (2004, 2013) and Lledó-Guillem (2010, 2015, 2018: 130–197).
3. Also known as Spanish since the sixteenth century (Alonso, 1938: 84).
4. See Binotti (1995).
5. By language ideology, I refer to "a group of explicit or implicit ideas about language that are the result of a concrete political, social, and cultural context. Such ideas about language become naturalised by being presented as eternal, immutable, and valid for every time period and geographical area" (Lledó-Guillem, 2015: 192) and (Lledó-Guillem, 2018: 8). See also Del Valle (2007: 19–20) and Gal (2006: 15).
6. See Lledó-Guillem (2015: 192) and Lledó-Guillem (2018: 14). Woolard explains that while nationalism as a political belief appears at the end of the eighteenth century, certain European circles shared a community conscience in the sixteenth and seventeenth centuries (Woolard, 2004: 64).
7. Fractal recursivity consists of "the projection of an opposition, salient at some level of relationship onto some other level" (Irvine and Gal, 2000: 38).
8. Recibio el hombre de la Diuina mano dos beneficios en antigüedad natural los primeros, en vtilidad ricos, en nobleza ilustres, la razon i la lengua su interprete, con el primero le hizo semejante a si, i con el segundo, que tuuiesse compañia con los otros hombres mediante la comunicacion, i trato; ambos dones soberanos dignos de todo agradecimiento. El qual faltò leuantandose el hombre à maiores, començando aquella soberuia

torre, que merecio por justo castigo la confusion delas lenguas. Dela diuersidad dellas nacio la diuision, enagenandose los animos i voluntades delos que en la habla no eran conformes, i de aqui se siguieron los odios i guerras, estimando como por diuersa naturaleza alos que en la lengua eran diferentes (Aldrete, 1606/1975: ii). Unless otherwise indicated, all the translations into English are mine.

9. As John Huxtable Elliott explains, this debate became particularly intense in the second half of the sixteenth century. On the one hand, the centralist position was supported by the noble houses of Zapata and Álvarez de Toledo with the Duke of Alba, Fernando Álvarez de Toledo (1507–1582), as the most important representative. On the other hand, the federalist approach was advocated by Ruy Gómez, prince of Éboli (1516–1573), the Valencian Furió Ceriol (1527–1592) and the Aragonese Antonio Pérez (1540–1611) (Elliott, 1990: 260).

10. Porque auiendose admitido en toda España la lengua Latina de la suerte, que emos dicho, i con la venida de los Godos, i nueuo Reino, que fundaron, estragadose i corrompido, el Romance, que della nacio, fue vulgar en toda España hasta la venida de los Moros, que en su señorio introduxeron la Arauiga. Laqual fueron los Christianos desterrando en los lugares, que recobrauan del poder, i usurpación de los Moros, i tornauan a introduzir la Castellana, o Romance. I assi fue admitida en Aragon, Nauarra, i Galizia, como en Castilla la vieja, i nueua Estremadura, Andaluzia, Reinos de Murcia, i Granada. [...] En Cataluña, para la conquista de aquel principado, se aiudaron los Españoles del socorro de Francia, i se dio principio a los Condes de Barcelona, por la qual causa el Romance se mescló con la lengua Francesa, de que resultò a quella lengua mui semejante, i poco diferente de la de Lenguadoc, o Narbonense, de donde a quella tiene parte de su origen [...] En Portugal ai otra lengua diuersa de la Castellana, que sin duda tiene mescla de la Francesa. Pego se les de los Franceses, que truxo consigo Don Henrrique primero Conde de Portugal. Quando Don Alonso el sexto Emperador de España le dio a quel estado en dote con Doña Teresa su hija [...] Bien se, que otros atribuien lo particular de aquella lengua ala comunicación de Galizia, donde la antigua parece la misma que la Portuguesa, i la vecindad, i auerse desde alli començado la conquista, fue la causa de dilatarse la lengua. A que se pueden añidir, que en Galizia variò la lengua, por auer puesto en ella su reino los Sueuos, i assi fue causa de que la Latina se corrompiesse en aquella forma. Pero tengo por mas cierto lo primero. Pues no ai razon, para que en Portugal se aia conseruado assi, i en Galizia no, si fue la de Galizia la misma, que la Portuguesa (Aldrete, 1606/1975: 164–166).

11. (Woolard, 2007: 133). Authentic languages would not be the best candidates to become global or anonymous languages (Woolard, 2007: 131) since "the quality of authenticity has a tendency to become not just characteristic of but even the special preserve of minority speakers themselves" (Woolard, 2016: 24). See Lledó-Guillem (2018: 13–14).

12. "Los vencidos reciben la lengua de los vencedores, rindiendola con las armas, i personas" (Aldrete, 1606/1975: 138). Peter Burke has emphasised the importance of Aldrete's statement as well as the association between language and empire (Burke, 2004: 21–22). See also Rojinsky (2010).

13. "Lo que los Catalanes adquirieron, su lengua tambien, que tiene parte dela de Lenguadoc" (Aldrete, 1606/1975: 143).

14. See Lledó-Guillem (2010: 4) and Lledó-Guillem (2015: 199). With regards to the political and ideological linguistic relationship between Catalan and Occitan in the Middle Ages and the Early Modern Period, see Lledó-Guillem (2018).

15. Irvine and Gal define erasure as "the process in which ideology, in simplifying the sociolinguistic field, renders some persons or activities (or sociolinguistic phenomena) invisible. Facts that are inconsistent with the ideological scheme either go unnoticed or get explained away" (Irvine and Gal, 2000: 38–39).
16. En ella se dize, que los pueblos de Empurias Griegos hizieron aquel templo a Diana de Epheso en aquel siglo, que ni dejada la lengua Griega, ni aprendida la de su tierra España se reduxeron a las costumbres, lengua, derecho, i señorio de los Romanos [...] Distingue la lengua Española antigua de la Romana, i dize que no la auian recibido, sino antes conseruado la propia Griega, conser ia naturales de España auiendo tantos años, que en ella biuian, i vuieron derecibir la lengua Latina, reduziendo se a ella, i a las leyes i sujecion de los Romanos [...] El que se sujetaua al imperio Romano, las costumbres, lengua, i leies auia derecibir [...] Tito Liuio lo dize mejor tratando de quando Caton vino a España, i dize, que estonces eran dos pueblos vno de Griegos, i otro de Españoles diuididos con sus murallas [...] Cesar después de vencidos los hijos de Pompeio añidio vecinos Romanos, con que todos se hizieron vn cuerpo, i a los Españoles primero, i después a los Griegos se los concedio, que fuessen ciudadanos Romanos [...] Con ser ciudadanos Romanos recibieron la lengua Latina, i no auian recibido la natural de su patria España en tantos años, como auia, que estauan en ella, que serian mas que doscientos, a loque se puede conjecturar, pues desde Caton, que los hallo diuididos, hasta Iulio Cesar, en cuio tiempo se juntaron corrieron mas de ciento i cinquenta años, assi podían con razon llamar a España Patria suia. (Aldrete, 1606/1975: 93–94).
17. See Lledó-Guillem (2013: 83–84), Lledó-Guillem (2015: 196) and Lledó-Guillem (2018: 194).
18. See note 12.
19. See Lledó-Guillem (2015: 198).
20. "La mudança de nueuos imperios los causa tambien en la lengua, que mientras se conservò el Romano, perseuerò ella, i acabado se estragò, i mudò, haziendose de sus ceniças, i ruinas otra" (Aldrete, 1606/1975: 151).
21. "Los barbaros abominando las armas, se auian aplicado a los arados, i acariciauan i regalauan a los Romanos, que auian quedado como compañeros i amigos, i se hallauan algunos Romanos, que querian mas entre los barbaros tener vna libertad pobre, que sufrir, i pasar entre los suios congoja [...] conesta amistad hizieron la mescla de lengua, que emos dicho [...] De lo qual con llaneza conocemos auer començado la lengua Castellana" (Aldrete, 1606/1975: 156).
22. This could be interpreted as an example of fractal recursivity. See note 7.
23. See Lledó-Guillem (2015: 200).
24. See note 12.

References

Primary sources

Aldrete, B. de. (1606/1975). *Del origen y principio de la lengua castellana ò romance que oi se usa en España*. Lidio Nieto Jiménez, ed., 2 Vol. Madrid: Consejo Superior de Investigaciones Científicas.

Arévalo, R. S. de. (1470). *Compendiosa historia Hispanica*. Rome: Ulrich Han.

Secondary sources

Alonso, A. (1938). *Castellano, español, idioma nacional. Historia espiritual de tres nombres.* Buenos Aires: Facultad de Filosofía y Letras de la Universidad de Buenos Aires-Instituto de Buenos Aires.

Binotti, L. (1995). *La teoría del "Castellano Primitivo": nacionalismo y reflexión lingüística en el Renacimiento español.* Munster: Nodus.

Binotti, L. (2000). "La lengua compañera del imperio". Observaciones sobre el desarrollo de un discurso de colonialismo lingüístico en el Renacimiento español. In: O. Zwartjes, ed., *Las gramáticas misionera de tradición hispánica (siglos XVI–XVII).* Amsterdam and Atlanta: Rodopi, pp. 259–287.

Binotti, L. (2012). *Cultural, Capital, Language and National Identity in Imperial Spain.* Woodbridge, Suffolk, UK/Rochester, NY: Tamesis.

Burke, P. (2004). *Language and Communities in Early Modern Europe.* Cambridge, UK: Cambridge University Press.

Cassirer, E. (1968). Giovanni Pico della Mirandola. In: Paul Oskar Kristeller and Philip P. Wiener, eds., *Renaissance Essays: From the Journal of the History of Ideas.* New York: Harper & Row, pp. 11–60.

Del Valle, J. (2007). Glotopolítica, ideología y discurso. In: J. Del Valle, ed., *La lengua, ¿patria común?: Ideas e ideologías del español.* Frankfurt am Main and Madrid: Vervuert-Iberoamericana, pp. 13–29.

Del Valle, J. (2013). Language, Politics and History: An Introductory Essay. In: J. Del Valle, ed., *A Political History of Spanish: The Making of a Language.* Cambridge: Cambridge University Press, pp. 3–20.

Gal, S. (2006). Migration, Minorities and Multilingualism: Language Ideologies in Europe. In: C. Mar-Molinero and P. Stevenson, eds., *Language Ideologies, Policies and Practices. Language and the Future of Europe.* New York: Palgrave MacMillan, pp. 13–27.

Hina, H. (1986). *Castilla y Cataluña en el debate cultural 1714–1939. Historia de las relaciones ideológicas catalano-castellanas.* Translated by Ricard Wilshusen. Barcelona: Península.

Irvine, J. T. and Gal, S. (2000). Language Ideology and Linguistic Differentiation. In: P. V. Kroskrity, ed., *Regimes of Language: Ideologies, Polities, and Identities.* Santa Fe, NM: School of American Research Press, pp. 35–83.

Lledó-Guillem, V. (2010). ¿Compañera o rebelde? La lengua y el imperio según Bernardo de Aldrete. *Bulletin of Hispanic Studies*, 87(1), pp. 1–15.

Lledó-Guillem, V. (2013). Jorge de Montemayor traduce a Ausiàs March: la creación de un mito barroco. In: V. J. Escartí, ed., *Escribir y persistir. Estudios sobre la literatura en catalán desde la Edad Media a la Renaixença.* Vol. 2. Buenos Aires, Argentina and Los Angeles, CA: Argus-a, pp. 68–92. Available at: http://doczz.es/doc/4976199/escribir-y-persistir—argus-a [Accessed 25 April 2019].

Lledó-Guillem, V. (2015). La obra de Bernardo de Aldrete en el contexto catalanohablante: imperialismo frente a nacionalismo lingüístico. *Hispanic Research Journal*, 16(3), pp. 191–207.

Lledó-Guillem, V. (2018). *The Making of Catalan Linguistic Identity in Medieval and Early Modern Times.* Cham, Switzerland: Palgrave Macmillan.

Nadal, J. M. and Prats, M. (1996). *Història de la llengua catalana 2. El segle XV.* Barcelona: Edicions 62.

Nieto Jiménez, L., ed. (1975). *Del origen y principio de la lengua castellana ò romance que oi se usa en España*. Vol 2. Madrid: Consejo Superior de Investigaciones Científicas.

Rojinsky, D. (2007). Teaching nationalism, imperialism and Romance philology. *La Corónica*, 35(2), pp. 293–301.

Rojinsky, D. (2010). *Companion to Empire: A Genealogy of the Written Word in Spain and New Spain, C. 550–1550*. Amsterdam: Rodopi.

Woolard, K. A. (2004). Is the past a foreign country?: Time, language origins, and the nation in early modern Spain. *Journal of Linguistic Anthropology*, 14(1), pp. 57–80.

Woolard, K. A. (2007). La autoridad lingüística del español y las ideologías de la autenticidad y el anonimato. In: J. Del Valle, ed., *La lengua, ¿patria común? Ideas e ideologías del español*. Madrid and Frankfurt: Iberoamericana-Vervuert, pp. 129–142.

Woolard, K. A. (2013). The seventeenth-century debate over the origins of Spanish. In: J. Del Valle, ed., *A Political History of Spanish: The Making of a Language*. New York: Cambridge University Press, pp. 61–76.

Woolard, K. A. (2016). *Singular and Plural: Ideologies of Linguistic Authority in 21st Century Catalonia*. New York: Oxford University Press.

5 Multilingualism and Translation in the Early Modern Low Countries

Theo Hermans

Introduction

The following pages celebrate the multiple languages of the Early Modern Low Countries and their interface with translation. The focus is on roughly the period from 1550 to 1700 and on pluralities: not just multiple languages and varieties of translational interaction but also geographical multiplicities and temporal shifts. In Early Modern times – or today, for that matter – the Low Countries (plural) were neither a politically unified nor a monolingual territory, and the sixteenth century differed significantly from the seventeenth, when the Dutch Republic could boast a global presence that needs to be taken into account.

The considerations that follow take their cue from Mary Louise Pratt's 1987 essay 'Linguistic Utopias', in which she suggested moving away from what she called a 'linguistics of community', with its emphasis on language as a shared patrimony, on standard languages and on individual languages as discrete, homogenous entities. Instead, she recommended paying attention to 'the operation of language across lines of social differentiation' and on 'modes and zones of contact' between different collectives, individuals and tongues, together with the power differentials these contacts entail (Pratt, 1987: 60). Adjusting the focus in this way will enable us to see polyglossia and translation in action. Another concept that will prove useful is that of 'communities of practice', understood as 'groups working together in some mutually beneficial endeavour' (Eckert and McConnell-Ginet, 1992: 464), which in our case will involve temporary cooperation between individuals across linguistic and other divides for a particular purpose.

I will trace the occurrence of multilingualism at the level of society, individuals and texts, following Rainier Grutman's threefold division in the *Routledge Encyclopedia of Translation Studies* (Grutman, 2009: 182). These levels are, of course, interdependent and fluid, but they provide a structure. The main argument will be that the linguistic diversity of the Low Countries correlates with a variety of social, economic, cultural and scientific interactions, but that it also invites reflection on the nature and manifestations of multilingualism. I will suggest that, at the level of individuals and texts, it is possible to stretch the notion of multilingualism by considering extended, distributed or cooperative forms of it, enabling the idea of multilingualism as socially produced rather than as an inherent quality or property.

First, however, it may be good to provide some basic historical orientation regarding the Low Countries in the Early Modern period. Here is a very quick and crude sketch. The area comprises roughly the contemporary Netherlands and Belgium, a small but economically prosperous territory. Even in Early Modern times it was a highly urbanised part of the world, with a high literacy rate. In the seventeenth century about half the population in the province of Holland lived in towns, and more books were being bought there per inhabitant than anywhere else in Europe (Prak, 2018: 16–17; Helmers, 2018: 130; Pettegree and Der Weduwen 2019: 12). In the sixteenth century the economic and cultural centres of gravity in the Low Countries were the metropolitan cities of Antwerp and Brussels in what is now Belgium. In the early seventeenth century the centre shifted northwards, to Amsterdam in particular. The watershed occurred in the decade or so before 1600 and the shift was sealed within a generation. While for most of the sixteenth century the Low Countries had been a motley collection of provinces under Habsburg dynastic rule, in the 1560s an armed rebellion broke out against the – by then Spanish – Habsburg overlords. The rebellion, known as the Revolt of the Netherlands, engulfed all of the Low Countries and was partly political, directed against the centralising policies of the Habsburgs, and partly religious, against the Habsburg suppression of Protestantism. The war reached a stalemate in the late 1580s and resulted in a territorial division that turned out to be permanent. The southern areas were brought back under Habsburg control and became known as the Spanish Netherlands, while the north, bolstered by an influx of Protestant refugees from the south, saw the creation of an independent Dutch Republic under the princes of Orange-Nassau. The south was subsequently transformed into a bastion of the Counter-Reformation. The Republic in the north saw spectacular economic growth, a relatively tolerant intellectual climate, and the emergence of an overseas trading empire spearheaded by the powerful United East India Company (Vereenigde Oostindische Compagnie, or VOC) and the West India Company (Westindische Compagnie, or WIC).

Society

A number of languages were in use in the Early Modern Low Countries, although their prevalence varied across space, time, gender and social class. For our purposes, the most important languages were Dutch, French, Latin, Spanish and Portuguese.

Dutch, the native tongue of the overwhelming majority of the population, retained strong regional and dialectal variations. Its written form began to show signs of standardisation from the mid-sixteenth century onwards, due in large part to publishers eager to sell books across the territory. The language gradually gained prestige as an intellectual vehicle, especially in the Republic, where its promotion to the status of national language received a boost from the Bible translation of 1637 known as the States Bible, a joint venture by the highest political authority, the States General, and the official Calvinist church.

By far the most important source languages for translation into Dutch were Latin and French. Latin, here as elsewhere in Europe, remained the preserve of the intellectual and social elite. Employed primarily as a written language, it possessed cultural prestige and international reach, but in the course of the seventeenth century it lost ground to both Dutch and French. French had always been spoken in the southernmost provinces bordering on France and was widely used in metropolitan areas as the language of commerce. In 1570s Antwerp, for instance, 85% of schoolteachers taught French as well as Dutch in so-called French schools, which catered for the practical needs of the merchant class (Frijhoff, 2010: 40–41). Among the middle classes quite a number of women could speak French as well as Dutch, but Latin usually remained a male preserve (Frijhoff, 2017: 58). In the seventeenth century French gained ground as the language of social distinction, and in the latter half of the century it began to replace Latin as the international intellectual language.

Spanish played only a limited role. In the sixteenth century, and leaving aside the merchant communities in the urban centres, it was used only by the highest echelons of the Spanish Habsburg administration in Brussels and in the Army of Flanders. In the Republic it all but disappeared after 1600, even though Spanish novels and plays remained popular. In the early seventeenth-century Spanish Netherlands, half the army consisted of Spanish and Italian troops, and Spanish continued to be used in the top layers of the administration, together with French and Dutch for public-facing activities (Israel, 1997: 4–7). In the north, both Spanish and Portuguese could be heard in the small Jewish communities in the major cities, especially Amsterdam, which in the seventeenth century had its own synagogue. Portuguese mattered mostly overseas, in Brazil and also in Asia, where it served as a lingua franca at the time the VOC was establishing itself in India, Ceylon (now Sri Lanka) and on the islands of what is now Indonesia. I will return to this point.

Naturally, the reality on the ground was much richer than this simplified picture suggests. The Republic, for instance, counted a number of 'Walloon' churches preaching in French. In Amsterdam the Jewish synagogue used Hebrew alongside Portuguese, and the city had Lutheran churches catering in German for both German and Scandinavian immigrants. There were English communities, too: in the Republic as a result of English military assistance to the Revolt, and in the Spanish Netherlands because the area became a haven for exiled English Catholics. Italian played a part throughout the period due to trading communities in the cosmopolitan centres and Italy's cultural attractiveness as a Grand Tour destination. It was also the trading and diplomatic lingua franca in the eastern Mediterranean. When shortly after 1611 Cornelis Haga, the Republic's first ambassador to the Ottoman Empire, gave his inaugural address in Constantinople in the presence of the sultan, he spoke in Italian.

The main factor affecting the linguistic situation was migration, which came in two kinds: refugees and economic migrants. In the sixteenth century the rise of Protestantism, its repression by the Habsburg authorities and the ensuing Revolt led to at least 60,000 Protestants fleeing abroad, mostly to Germany and England (Janssen, 2018: 51). Around 1600 many of them returned, with foreign languages, and settled in the Republic. At this time up to half of the population in the major towns of Holland was foreign-born – although this terminology can be misleading, since 'foreign' might refer to people from another province as well as to those from another country, and thus 'foreigners' included the large numbers – estimated at 200,000 or more – of Protestant immigrants from the southern parts of the Low Countries, including the Francophone areas (Janssen, 2018: 50). At the end of the seventeenth century the revocation of the Edict of Nantes in 1685 led to tens of thousands of French Huguenots settling in the Republic. The French translators who ensured John Locke's European fame hailed from these circles, and their translations were printed in Amsterdam.

Economic migrants were attracted by the Dutch Republic's economic miracle. The rapid expansion in manufacture and trade laid bare the country's demographic shortfall and created a constant need to import labour, much of it unskilled. The Republic's army recruited half of its soldiers abroad, and almost half the crews on VOC ships were of foreign origin (Janssen, 2018: 53). By no means all economic migrants were unskilled. One-third of professors at Dutch higher education institutions – universities and 'illustrious schools' – were foreign (Frijhoff, 2010: 28). At the end of the seventeenth century Pierre Bayle lived in Rotterdam for twenty-five years without feeling the need to learn Dutch; he got by perfectly well with French and Latin (Frijhoff, 2010: 29). In the Dutch colony of New Amsterdam, which in 1674 was definitively taken over by the English and renamed New York, only half of the settlers were actually Dutch, and while Broadway, Wall Street and Staten Island are adaptations of originally Dutch names, the Bronx was named after a Danish farmer (Janssen, 2018: 60).

For the Dutch overseas, however, the most important language was Portuguese, widely used as lingua franca along the African coast, in

Brazil and throughout the Far East. The Portuguese preceded the Dutch in these parts by a hundred years. Both the first Dutch expedition that left for the Indies in 1595 under the De Houtman brothers and the voyage that Jacob van Neck undertook in 1600 were issued with letters of goodwill by Prince Maurice in Portuguese and Arabic – the latter version added because the East had been reported to be Muslim. The first treaty which the Dutch signed in the East, on 1 July 1596, between the ruler of Bantam and Cornelis de Houtman, was in Portuguese (Heeres, 1907: 3–4). The importance of Portuguese for the Dutch overseas continued well into the seventeenth century. In 1616, the Dutch in Bantam wrote in Portuguese to the English East India Company warning them not to meddle (Van Goor, 2015: 252, 261). In Ceylon a 1638 treaty between king Raja Sinha II and VOC admiral Adam Westerwolt sealing an anti-Portuguese alliance was drafted in Dutch but then translated into Portuguese for the official text authenticated by both parties – a treaty in Portuguese aimed at thwarting the Portuguese (Paulusz, 1980). The VOC embassy to Edo (now Tokyo) in 1627 arrived with letters translated from Dutch into Japanese via Portuguese (Clulow, 2014: 78, 91–93, 275; Matsutaka, 2018: 83–85). In 1641, after the Portuguese were expelled from Japan, the recently built Portuguese trading post on the little island of Deshima, in the bay of Nagasaki, was handed to the Dutch and became the only point of contact between Japan and the European world, but for the next thirty years or so Portuguese continued to be used as the intermediate language (Clements, 2015: 145–146; Joby, 2016: 221). In Brazil, the WIC sought to oust the Portuguese and gained a foothold in 1630, but with never more than about 3,000 Dutch settlers surrounded by some 20,000 Portuguese colonists the going was tough and 'Dutch Brazil' was lost in the 1650s (Emmer and Gommans, 2012: 213). Negotiations between the WIC and local rulers in the Congo basin, aimed at dislodging the Portuguese from Luanda, were also conducted in Portuguese (Meuwese, 2012: 210–211). In the Far East the VOC established its headquarters in Batavia (now Jakarta), founded in 1619 and a multi-ethnic and multilingual place from the start. Its first census, in 1632, recorded 8,000 inhabitants, half of them being enslaved people, mostly from South India; a quarter were Chinese and the rest predominantly Javanese. The most common languages were Portuguese and Malay (Blussé, 1986; Van Goor, 2015: 383).

Individuals

Societies are made up of individuals. Who were the polyglots in the Early Modern Low Countries? They came in various shapes and categories, but of those who acquired more than the standard French and/or Latin, most had international experience. Apart from merchants and diplomats who journeyed for professional reasons, there were refugees and economic migrants, aristocrats and patricians who travelled for leisure or education, interpreters and missionaries, and finally armchair polyglots who learned foreign languages without physically crossing borders.

Jan Ympyn (c. 1485–1540) is an example of an early international merchant. He hailed from Antwerp, was said to have lived in Spain and then Venice for twelve years and wrote a book (1543), in Dutch, based on Italian sources, on Italian-style double book-keeping, which was translated into French by his wife Anna Swinters (1543). An English version appeared in London shortly afterwards (1547).

Among the more famous diplomats of the sixteenth century was Ogier Ghiselin de Busbecq (1522–1592), ambassador to the Ottoman court in Constantinople for the emperor Ferdinand, brother of Charles V. Busbecq apparently spoke French, Dutch, German, Italian, Spanish and Croatian, but the 'Turkish Letters' that made his reputation were written in Latin. A rather more curious figure was Theodore Rodenburgh (1574–1644), who spent years living in France, Portugal, Spain, Italy, England and Denmark as a diplomat and merchant. As a playwright he translated and adapted works from French, Spanish, Italian and English into Dutch. In one play, *Melibea* (1618), a love intrigue set in The Hague, he has, for no apparent reason, characters speaking substantial passages – from half a page to four pages – in French, Spanish, English, Italian, Portuguese and Latin (Smits-Veldt and Abrahamse, 1993).

Among the many refugees who went into exile during the Revolt, we can name Vincentius Meusevoet (c. 1560–1624) and Johannes Lamotius (c. 1570–1627), both from Flemish Protestant families that had fled to England and on their return settled in the Republic. Both became prolific translators. In the first three decades of the seventeenth century they produced between them around seventy titles, mostly from English, occasionally from French or Latin, invariably Puritan works that helped shape the so-called Further Reformation, a conservative but highly influential religious movement that sought to push the Reformation further into people's daily lives. Their counterpart in the Spanish Netherlands, and equally prolific, was the Jesuit Franciscus de Smidt (1567–1659), who spent some time in Spain but produced all his translations in Antwerp – hence not a migrant. He worked from Latin, French and Spanish into Dutch and on one occasion from Dutch into French and matched the narrow ideological focus of his northern colleagues by translating almost exclusively other Jesuits, invariably devotional works strengthening the Catholic identity of the southern provinces. As for economic migrants, there was, for instance, the adventurous Jakob Rabe (?–1646), a German who entered the service of the WIC and went to Brazil. In 1642 he was tasked with liaising with the warlike Tarairiu, indigenous allies of the Dutch against the Portuguese. He appears to have gone native and was eventually murdered at the instigation of a Dutch WIC officer. Apart from German and Dutch he must have had at least some Portuguese as well as Tarairiu and probably also Tupi, since he was married to an indigenous woman who had Tupi as her first language (Meuwese, 2005). Later in the century the French Huguenot Barthélemy Piélat (1640?–after 1687?) settled in the Dutch Republic, although the reasons for his move remain unclear. In the 1670s and '80s he authored a number of books teaching French; on the title page of one of them he declares himself qualified to teach Hebrew, Greek, Latin, Italian, French, German Dutch and English (Piélat, 1681; Frijhoff, 2017: 63).

We know of quite a number of patricians and aristocrats with international travel or grand tour experience, so let me mention just two of the most proficient linguists. In the sixteenth century the botanist Carolus Clusius (1526–1609) moved in high places throughout Europe and kept up an extensive correspondence in six languages. He translated in multiple directions: from Dutch, French, Italian, Spanish and Portuguese into Latin; from Dutch and Latin into French; and from English into Latin and French. His work was highly relevant for the growth and dissemination of botanical and pharmaceutical knowledge. One of the best-known seventeenth-century literary virtuosos was Constantijn Huygens (1596–1687), personal secretary to the Prince of Orange. Writing poetry in his spare time he wove in and out of, and translated from and into, eight languages (Latin, Greek, Dutch, French, Italian, Spanish, German and English). Both his high social standing and his virtuosity helped to raise the status of Dutch as a literary vehicle among the classical and vernacular languages.

Little work has been done on the history of interpreting in Early Modern Europe, which seems especially surprising in the case of the Dutch Republic and its vast overseas trading and colonial enterprise. Some particular cases, however, are reasonably well documented. I already mentioned the Dutch embassy, from 1612 onwards, at the Ottoman court in Constantinople. The Dutch interpreters there were not themselves Dutch; most came from cosmopolitan Jewish, Greek or Armenian families and were conversant not just with Turkish and Arabic but also with Ottoman diplomatic protocol and written usage. The intermediate language tended to be Italian, and because the interpreters often worked for different embassies and had family ties among themselves, their reliability was a constant source of concern to their European employers. The Venetians and subsequently the French trained up their own youth from the age of about ten onwards (the boys were known as *enfants de langue*, language children), but the Dutch – and likewise the English – remained reluctant to follow suit, due to the risk associated with such a long-term investment.

Jaques Joosten (1613–?), who claimed to be of Polish descent, authored a *Kleyne wonderlijcke werelt* ('Little wondrous world') in 1649 and then a slightly enlarged *Grote wonderlijcke wereldt* ('Large wondrous world') ten years later, opening both books with short poems in ten different languages to demonstrate his linguistic prowess and presenting himself as a merchant and commercial interpreter. However, it is hard to know how seriously to take him; he may have been no more than a charlatan. Apart from a fair number of improbabilities which he claimed to have seen on his travels, such as mermaids in the Danube, entire passages in both his books were plagiarised from earlier travel writers like the Frenchman Nicolas de Nicolay.

The outstanding figure among Early Modern Dutch interpreters was Herbert de Jager (1636–1694), a language prodigy who spent his whole adult life in Asia. At university he studied mathematics, engineering and Eastern languages, including Arabic and Persian. The language of instruction, of course, was Latin, and he picked up French and German along the way. In 1662 he signed up for VOC service and left for Batavia, where he acquired Malay. From 1665 to 1670 he was stationed in Isfahan, perfecting his Persian. The next ten years were spent on the Coromandel Coast in South-East India, where he studied Sanskrit and became proficient in Tamil and Telugu. By 1680 he was back in Batavia and took up Javanese. Following another stint in Persia (1683–1687) he returned again to Batavia and set about learning Japanese. He died in Batavia in 1694. A year after his death a chest containing his papers arrived in Holland but subsequently went missing (Leupe, 1869).

Dutch missionaries overseas often found themselves in multilingual surroundings. Abraham Rogerius (c. 1609–1649), for example, spent nine years on India's Coromandel Coast, where he learnt some Tamil but preached mostly in Portuguese. Later, in Batavia, he translated the catechism from Dutch into Portuguese. He became famous for his *Open deure tot het verborgen heydendom* (1651; 'Open door to hidden paganism'), the first comprehensive and remarkably unbiased description of Hinduism in a European language. The book also contained translations from Sanskrit, again the first in a European tongue. Rogerius obtained his information from local Tamil-speaking brahmins with whom he talked mainly in Portuguese before writing up his book in Dutch (Noak, 2012: 355). The book's importance was soon recognised, and it was translated into German (1663) and French (1670).

And then there were the armchair polyglots, members of those social classes with the leisure to engage in serious language learning, often academics. Most were not entirely sedentary. In the sixteenth century, for example, Bonaventura Vulcanius (1538–1614), from Bruges, had Dutch, French, Latin and Greek, and also Spanish, having lived in Spain for eleven years (Van Ommen and Cazes, 2010: 62, 117). He took an interest in cryptography, hieroglyphics, etymology and ancient languages. One of his books, from 1597, featured Gothic texts, runic inscriptions and samples of Old High German, Welsh, Basque and Persian, part of the budding European interest in comparative and historical linguistics (Van Ommen and Cazes, 2010: 123–125).

Vulcanius became a professor at Leiden University, where he counted the Frenchman Josephus Justus Scaliger (1540–1609) among his colleagues. Scaliger had travelled in Italy and the British Isles but spent the last sixteen years of his life in Leiden. He was famous for the range of languages at his disposal: apart from French, Latin and Greek he studied Hebrew, Syriac, Aramaic, Ethiopic and Coptic. He had reasonably good Arabic (in 1600 he produced the Arabic version of the goodwill letter for Jacob van Neck's voyage mentioned above) and some Persian and Turkish – over ten languages in all.

Scaliger looked east, and so did Jacobus Golius (1596–1667), the most famous Arabist of his time. He spent a year and a half in Morocco (1622–1624) and then travelled for three years in the Middle East (1626–1629), and could manage Latin, Greek, Hebrew, Arabic, Persian, Turkish and Armenian. He compiled three dictionaries: Latin-Arabic (1653; 1,500 pages and unsurpassed until the nineteenth century), Latin-Persian (completed in 1643 and published posthumously in 1669), and Latin-Turkish (unpublished). One of his students was the German Georgius Gentius (1618–1687), who had Latin, French and Italian as well as the Arabic, Turkish and Persian he had studied under Golius. Gentius brought out a bilingual Persian and Latin edition of a major work by the medieval Persian writer Saadi (*Rosarium politicum*, Amsterdam 1651), which was translated into German by Adam Olearius (*Persianischer Rosenthal*, Schleswich 1654), which in turn was translated into Dutch by the Amsterdam bookseller Jan van Duisberg (*Perssiaansche roosengaard*, 1654). I will return to these chains of indirect translations below.

Not all the polyglots were academics. Some were some genuine amateurs, like Johan de Brune (1588–1658), a lawyer who served as pensionary in the province of Zeeland and said he learned ten languages, including Hebrew, as indeed his 1644 psalm translation showed (Van der Wal, 1990: 59). At his death in 1728 the rabbi David Nuñes Torres, who had lived in Amsterdam and then The Hague, left a library that, apart from the Hebrew works, comprised 522 books in French, 305 in Latin, 278 in Spanish, 270 in Dutch, 47 in Portuguese and a smattering in Greek, Italian and English (Den Boer, 1995: 109). The most remarkable among the amateurs was Anna Maria van Schurman (1607–1678), who became fluent in no fewer than fourteen languages including Aramaic and Syriac, and who wrote in Dutch, German, Latin, Greek, Hebrew, Italian, French, Arabic, Persian and Ethiopic.

All the examples so far have concerned individuals who acquired multiple languages. It may also be possible to think of multilingualism in a more distributed form, as something brought about collaboratively by several individuals pooling their linguistic resources for particular purposes or projects, one person's competence being complemented by another's and made available through translation. Multilingualism could thus become a jointly or collectively produced property otherwise beyond the reach of the individual participants, not unlike the recourse to an interpreter or to a lingua franca as a solution to a linguistic deficit.

A good illustration is the Dutch-Latin-Chinese glossary which the Dutch minister Justus Heurnius (1587–1652) produced in Batavia in 1628 with the help of a Chinese schoolteacher (his name has not been recorded) who had learned some Latin – and perhaps Portuguese – in Macau. Heurnius knew no Chinese; the Chinese schoolteacher did not speak Dutch. Their shared language was Latin. Occasionally the glossary shows the two collaborators getting their wires crossed in the transition: the Dutch entry *boeck* ('book') appears in Latin as *liber*, but *liber* can mean both 'book' and, as an adjective, 'free', and it is this latter meaning which is captured in the two corresponding Chinese phrases *zì zhŭ* ('act on one's own, decide for oneself') and *wú zhŭ rén guăn* ('not having a master who is in charge') (Kuiper, 2005: 117–118). Heurnius hoped his glossary would be of use in future trade between the VOC and China, but this never happened and his manuscript remained unpublished.

In the Republic the merchant and poet Jan Six van Chandelier (1620–1695), who did not have Hebrew, translated the psalms into Dutch in 1674 on the basis of existing Dutch, French and Latin versions, but he also consulted three Hebrew specialists, who all three published statements, signed with their names, affiliations and titles, confirming they had worked closely with the translator, had checked the translation and could vouch for its accuracy (Six van Chandelier, 1674: x–xvi).

Collaborations of this kind – little communities of practice – became common, even routine, for drama productions in Amsterdam around the middle of the seventeenth century. In 1637 the Amsterdam Theatre opened in a specially designed building and was run as a commercial enterprise. Spanish plays in particular proved popular, and to meet the demand plays were often first translated literally into prose by one person and then put to rhyme as a playtext by someone else, usually an experienced actor, with no knowledge of Spanish. The practice itself was not new, but it was now applied on a larger scale than ever before, a well-organised 'creative industry'. Almost half of the thirty-odd Spanish plays staged at the Amsterdam Theatre between 1641 and 1671 were based on intermediate prose versions. None of these have been preserved, presumably because they were seen as mere tools to arrive at a playtext in verse and discarded as soon as they had served their purpose. Jacobus Baroces (1617–1671), about whom little more is known than that he belonged to the Sephardic Jewish community in Amsterdam and probably had Spanish as his first language, supplied at least eight such intermediate prose versions which others then put to rhyme. Sometimes also an existing French version of an originally Spanish play was rendered into Dutch prose first and then rhymed for the stage by someone else – a translation chain of a very particular kind (Jautze *et al.*, 2016).

Texts

With their high levels of trade, urbanisation and literacy, the Early Modern Low Countries accommodated a major printing and publishing industry, the main centres being Antwerp in the sixteenth century and then Amsterdam in the seventeenth. The industry was multilingual from the start, not only because Latin and, later, French books made up a large part of the printed output but also because the Dutch language had only limited reach. Publishers could significantly increase their turnover by printing books in more languages than one, and they possessed the resources and expertise as well as the international contacts and distribution channels to do so. For most of the 1550s, for example, Antwerp printed more books in Spanish than any city in Spain. Soon after the conclusion of the Council of Trent the Antwerp publisher Christopher Plantin acquired a monopoly on Latin liturgical works for the Spanish crown; in the 1570s alone he shipped close to 50,000 breviaries, missals, hymnals and books of hours to Spain. In Amsterdam the volume of Spanish-language printing increased throughout the seventeenth century, but it now served a different audience, namely the Sephardic Jewish community in the city itself and similar communities elsewhere in Europe (Wilkinson, 2018: 282–284, 287, 293). In 1608–1610 Cornelis Claesz, the most successful publisher in Amsterdam at the time, issued separate catalogues advertising his stock of Latin, Dutch, French and German books (Pettegree and Der Weduwen, 2019: 40–41).

Multilingual publishing took essentially two forms: individual books in which several languages coexisted on the page and parallel editions of the same work in different languages.

The most obvious examples of multilingual books are the continually expanding phrasebooks of the sixteenth century. The most successful of these was the *Vocabulare* of the Antwerp schoolteacher Noël van Berlaimont which first appeared in 1527 and in the next fifty years went through around 150 impressions and adaptations. Originally bilingual Dutch and French, by the end of the century it featured eight languages printed in parallel columns across two pages, its dialogues reflecting the practical needs of travelling salesmen (Van der Sijs, 2000: 11–31). A seventeenth-century variant, didactically more advanced and intended for use in schools, was devised by the educational reformer Jan Amos Comenius, whose *Orbis sensualium pictus* (1658), for instance, depicted everything under the sun in a series of short lessons, each lesson consisting of a visual image and accompanying descriptions in Latin and a vernacular language. A system of numbers connected elements in the picture with key words in both languages. By triangulating the picture with the verbal descriptions, and by cross-checking the two matching descriptions, users could learn languages while visualising particular scenes and situations. The method, a form of translating by numbers, allowed for infinite extension and refinement.

Some multilingual books were a matter of elite publishing without commercial purpose and aimed at readers who were themselves multilingual. This was the case, for instance, with the collection of epitaphs in twelve languages on the death of King Henry II of France, which the Flemish patrician Carolus Utenhove and some of his friends published in Paris in 1560 (Utenhove, 1560). Of an altogether different order, in eight volumes and vastly more significant, was the polyglot Bible which Christopher Plantin printed in Antwerp in the years 1568–1572, the most impressive typographical monument of the age, with texts in Latin, Greek, Hebrew, Aramaic and Syriac. The team of scholars which Plantin gathered from all over Europe to prepare the edition stayed at his house during the project and used Latin as their lingua franca around the dinner table. Less exclusive but still not intended for the common reader were multilingual emblem books. Their illustrations made them expensive to produce and their refined wit appealed to an intellectual audience, so publishers were keen to reach educated readers in cosmopolitan cities. In 1607 the painter and humanist Otto Vaenius (c. 1566–1629) brought out his *Emblemata horatiana* in two versions, one in Latin only, the other in Latin, French and Dutch; the second edition, five years later, added Spanish and Italian. Vaenius's best-known emblem book, *Amorum emblemata* (1608), appeared simultaneously in four trilingual editions: Dutch-Latin-French, Latin-French-Italian, Latin-Spanish-Italian, and Latin-English-Italian (Porteman, 1975: 168–169). Later in the century, as especially religious and moralising emblem books gained popularity and were printed in smaller and more affordable formats, they also became less multilingual.

A different kind of multilingualism, on a smaller scale and for more specialist readerships, could be found in scientific and medical works, particularly in the later sixteenth and early seventeenth centuries, when a good deal of practical knowledge and applied science was being transferred from Latin to the vernacular. The *Florilegium* (1612) of Emanuel Sweerts featured four introductions, respectively in Latin, Dutch, French and German, and while the body of the book identified individual flowers by their Latin names only, three indices at the back gave the names in Dutch, French and German, taking care in each case to refer back to the illustrations.

Botanical works routinely incorporated several tongues, even though they mostly employed a single expository language. Plants were of interest primarily for their medicinal uses, and it was important for pharmacists and surgeons to be able to identify the correct plant, so lists of plant names in several languages were added. One of the more famous botanists of the sixteenth century, Rembert Dodoens, wrote his *Cruijdeboeck* (1554; 'Herb-book') in Dutch because he wanted to appeal to lay readers as well as professionals, but for each plant he still added the names in Latin, Greek, French, German, English and Czech. He later translated his book into Latin, while Carolus Clusius, whom we met earlier, provided a French version. Their colleague Matthias Lobelius translated the 1,500 pages of his Latin *Plantarum seu stirpium historia* (1576) into Dutch in 1581, adding lists of all the plant names mentioned in Dutch, Latin, French, German, Italian, Spanish, Portuguese and English; individual illustrations sometimes also featured Greek and Arabic (De Nave and Imhof, 1993).

The outstanding achievement in botanical publishing was the *Hortus malabaricus,* published in Amsterdam on the initiative of Hendrik van Rheede tot Drakenstein, who acted as VOC governor on the Malabar coast in South-West India from 1670 to 1677. Its twelve volumes, printed at Van Rheede's own expense between 1678 and 1693 and containing around 750 illustrations, were the work of a large editorial team comprising both Indian and European botanists and medics – a transcultural community of practice. Plant names were recorded in four languages and four scripts, identified as 'Latina', 'Malabarica', 'Arabica' and 'Lingua Bramanica antiqua', i.e. Sanskrit. They had been taken down first in Malayalam and Konkani, then rendered into Portuguese by the 'sworn translator' Manoel Carneiro, a VOC employee, and subsequently translated from Portuguese into Latin by Christiaan van Donep and Johannes Casearius, the collaborative chain overcoming the linguistic limitations of individual participants.

For works that addressed a broad readership it was more common to issue parallel editions in different languages than to print single multilingual books. Works celebrating grand public events that were deemed to have international resonance or that could enhance the status of a particular city, for instance, were often printed in Dutch and Latin and sometimes French versions as well. This was also true of political statements with an international dimension, including polemic and propaganda. To mention just a couple of the more famous documents: in 1581 William of Orange, the leader of the Revolt, who had been proscribed by the Spanish king Philip II, published a defence of his actions which appeared simultaneously in Dutch, French, Latin and English versions. In 1619, a coup by William's son Maurice led to his main opponent being sentenced to death; the verdict was published in Dutch, Latin and French (Pettegree and Der Weduwen, 2019: 64).

In some cases more complex webs emerged, as translations for propaganda purposes in different languages were coordinated and followed one another in quick succession. Two little books celebrating miracles attributed to intervention by the Virgin Mary in the Spanish Netherlands can serve as illustrations. While ostensibly religious in nature, both books carried an evident political load, since the belief in miracles and the cult of the Virgin Mary were eminently Catholic practices, strongly promoted by the authorities in Brussels as part of the Counter-Reformation campaign that preached loyalty to church and state. In 1604 the town secretary of Brussels, Philips Numan, gathered witness statements about recent miracles in Scherpenheuvel, a small town north-east of Brussels. Being bilingual, Numan published his account in both a Dutch and a French version. Around the same time the Leuven university professor Justus Lipsius brought out a similar treatise, in Latin, about miracles in Halle, just south of Brussels. Within a year Lipsius had translated Numan's book about Scherpenheuvel into Latin, and Spanish and English versions followed a year later, all printed in the Spanish Netherlands but obviously meant for dissemination abroad. Lipsius's own book about Halle was rendered into French in 1605, but then something unexpected happened: a Dutch translation appeared in Delft, in the Protestant Republic. The translation itself remained unobjectionable, but its abundant marginalia were vehemently anti-Catholic. Numan was asked to provide a Catholic counter-translation, and he obliged immediately. Thus, in the space of just two years, we have two little treatises leading to versions in five languages, a total of nine texts, six of them translations, including two rival renderings (Hermans, 2015).

More often than not, however, purely commercial considerations prevailed, notably in the case of illustrated books. Illustrations, especially the copper engravings that increasingly replaced the traditional wood carvings, were expensive to produce, and publishers could obtain a larger return on their investment by printing different language versions while recycling the same pictures. The translations were comparatively cheap, which may explain why in most cases we don't know the names of the translators.

As early as 1539 the artist and publisher Pieter Coecke van Aelst, who had been to Italy, translated some of Sebastiano Serlio's architectural work from Italian into Dutch for his own press in Brussels, re-using the illustrations for a German edition three years later and a French version another three years on. The French traveller Nicolas de Nicolay brought out an account of his journey to the Near East in Lyon in 1567; ten years later the Antwerp publisher Willem Silvius re-issued the French text together with versions in Dutch, German and Italian, all four versions featuring the same set of around sixty illustrations (Hamilton, 2001: 41). Sometimes the publisher leaned on the author to provide text in another language before commissioning the illustrations. This happened with a book of a hundred emblems in Dutch by the Jesuit Jan David: his publisher Jan Moretus was unwilling to go ahead with production unless the author supplied a Latin translation first. The author obliged, and the translation, *Veridicus christianus* (1603), appeared even before its Dutch original (Simoni, 1976: 68).

As the Dutch expansion overseas got underway from the 1590s onwards, accounts of these expeditions and works on navigation became extremely popular. In 1598 the Amsterdam publisher Cornelis Claesz launched simultaneous and lavishly illustrated versions in Dutch, French and Latin of two of the most eye-catching early expeditions, namely the (failed) attempt to find a north-east passage to China which resulted in the crew spending the winter of 1596–1597 on the island of Nova Zembla, and the (successful) first journey to the Far East via the Cape of Good Hope by the De Houtman brothers in 1595–1597. A few years later Claesz published versions in Dutch, French, German and Latin of the first Dutch voyage around the world. Perhaps the grandest publication in this genre followed the VOC mission to Beijing in 1655, the first Western embassy to reach the Qing court. The account, a folio sporting 150 illustrations, appeared in Amsterdam in 1665, simultaneously in Dutch and French, with a German translation a year later and a Latin version in 1668, all printed for the same publisher. Although the French edition clearly targeted the French market and was dedicated to Louis XIV's minister of finance, Jean-Baptiste Colbert, its illustrations featured captions in Dutch as well as French. In the German edition the captions remained, even more incongruously, in Dutch and French. In the Latin edition they appeared in Dutch and Latin, although the Dutch was now obviously redundant. It seems evident that the various editions were prepared with minimum additional expenditure on the illustrations.

For their navigation on the open seas the Dutch had initially relied on Spanish and English manuals. In 1584–1585 Lucas Jansz Waghenaer produced his own two-volume *Spieghel der zeevaert* ('Mirror of navigation') in Dutch, complete with maps, illustrations and mathematical tables. It was soon followed by editions in Latin, French, German and English, most of them printed by or for Cornelis Claesz. After Claesz's death in 1609 his role was taken up by Willem Jansz Blaeu, who published his own *Licht der zeevaert* ('Light of Navigation') first in Dutch in 1608 and subsequently in French (1612) and English (1619). The towering achievement in cartography came half a century later with the *Atlas maior* of Joan Blaeu, the son and successor of Willem Jansz Blaeu. In the years between 1662 and 1672 the *Atlas* appeared in parallel Latin, Dutch, French, German and Spanish editions, each version comprising ten or so large volumes containing around 600 illustrations and accompanying text. Fate ensured that the *Atlas maior* remained a unique venture: all the plates used for the illustrations were lost when Blaeu's workshop burned down in 1672 (Pettegree and Der Weduwen, 2019: 110–115).

We saw above that, in speaking of multilingual people, we could think of multilingualism as concentrated in one individual or, in an extended sense, as produced by several individuals collaborating. It is not hard to envisage a textual counterpart to this. Just as there are multilingual books and parallel multilingual versions of the same work, we can stretch the idea of multilingualism by thinking of it as distributed across several texts complementing one another across languages, in a process that necessarily involves translation. There would appear to be at least two variants of this kind of distributed multilingualism, and both are played out as part of a process of translation.

One involves translators working not just from the source text but additionally consulting existing translations in other languages. They may do this to help solve problems or for purposes of verification. In 1580, for instance, Marten Everaert translated Pedro de Medina's navigation manual from Spanish into Dutch, but the title page declared that the book had been translated from Spanish and French, and in his dedication (written in German, the dedicatee being the archduke Matthias of Austria) the translator explained he had worked from both the Spanish original of 1545 and Nicolas de Nicolay's French version of 1554 (Meskens, 2013: 145–146). In 1605 another translator, C. A. Boomgaert, translated Plutarch, not from Greek but from the French of Jacques Amyot, stating in his preface that he had also consulted Latin versions. Of course, in both these cases – and there are plenty of others – we are dealing with statements by translators. Their claims may be no more than a marketing ploy to lend the translation authority. In some cases, however, there is textual evidence to verify the claim, just as there are other cases where a translation is presented as being based on the original but the textual evidence shows or suggests the translator also used or consulted one or more existing versions in other languages.

The other variant consists of indirect translations, i.e. translations not based directly on the original but on an existing translation of it in another language. For most of the Early Modern period, the practice of indirect translation was considered unexceptional. All sixteenth-century translations of Greek texts into Dutch (bar a single possible exception) were done via intermediate versions in either Latin or French. Depending on the languages and the genres in question, the chain of intermediate versions could be long. Lodovico Varthema's Italian travel book of 1502 was rendered into Latin, the Latin then into German and the German into Dutch (in 1563). The anonymous Dutch Qur'an of 1641, purportedly printed in Hamburg but almost certainly in Amsterdam, derived from a German version that derived from an Italian version that derived from a medieval Latin version of the Arabic text. It may be arguable whether in cases like these we can still speak of a collaborative or distributed form of multilingualism. The series of translations is played out over a period of time and without personal interaction. Nevertheless, the practice enabled translators to extend their linguistic range by treating preceding versions as intermediaries giving access to a more distant original. In this sense the translation chain effectively generates multilingualism. The intermediaries were not always acknowledged, presumably because, by and large, direct translations were preferred if practicable. Around the middle of the seventeenth century, for instance, Ariosto's *Orlando Furioso* and Tasso's *Gerusalemme liberata* were rendered into

Dutch on the basis of French versions, but the title pages made no mention of this (Smit, 1975: 544, 559).

It seems fitting to end by highlighting some facets of the work of the seventeenth-century arch-translator Jan Hendrik Glazemaker, in whom several of the things mentioned in the preceding pages come together. Glazemaker's fame rests on his translations of the virtually complete œuvre of René Descartes and some key works of Baruch de Spinoza, but he translated all manner of genres. With around seventy translations to his name he was one of the most prolific translators in Early Modern Europe. He worked primarily from French and Latin, and to a lesser extent from German and Italian, into Dutch. For texts originally in Greek, Spanish, Portuguese, English or Arabic he made use of intermediate French or Latin versions, although he did not always acknowledge this. He learnt Latin when he was already in his twenties, and among his earliest translations was a version of John Barclay's Latin novel *Argenis* done from French, a fact he did not publicly acknowledge until almost forty years later when he translated the book again, now from the original Latin. On at least one occasion he produced, via the French, a literal translation of a Spanish play that was later put to rhyme for the Amsterdam Theatre by a professional actor. In the preface to his translation of Seneca he mentioned that, in addition to the original Latin, he had consulted French versions, and while revising his rendering of Descartes' *Discourse on Method* he consulted the Latin translation which had appeared in the meantime. In translating some of Descartes' more demanding work on mathematics and music theory he invoked the help of specialists in these fields – not multilinguals, perhaps, but individuals with complementary expertise nonetheless (Thijssen-Schoute, 1967: 226–261).

Conclusion

The most widely read sixteenth-century description of the Low Countries, Lodovico Guicciardini's *Descrittione di tutti i Paesi Bassi* of 1567, already remarked on the linguistic prowess of their inhabitants, especially those living in the metropolitan cities and trading hubs. A number of factors contributed to this multilingualism, although the picture remained uneven while also changing over time. We have traced some of its contours and manifestations at the level of communities, individuals and texts. The treatment has been selective, at times anecdotal, with the aim of providing concrete instances rather than general patterns. Nevertheless, it has shown, I hope, the social, political and commercial factors determining the prevalence of multilingualism, and the forms of translation to which multilingualism gave rise. Exploring these forms turned out to have some theoretical purchase of its own by pushing the conventional boundaries of multilingualism. If we can begin to see multilingualism in performative terms as a collaborative project involving the activation of complementary linguistic competences in the effort to surmount personal limitations, it becomes a richer and more dynamic concept with a wider range of applications, from individual translators pooling resources at a particular moment in time to chains of translations of translations, in principle unlimited and spread over any number of years.

References

Blussé, L. (1986). *Strange Company: Chinese Settlers, Mestizo Women and the Dutch in VOC Batavia.* Dordrecht: Foris.

Clements, R. (2015). *A Cultural History of Translation in Japan in the Early Modern Period.* Cambridge: Cambridge University Press.

Clulow, A. (2014). *The Company and the Shogun: The Dutch Encounter with Tokugawa Japan.* New York: Columbia University Press.

De Nave, F. and Imhof, D. (1993). *De botanica in de zuidelijke Nederlanden (einde 15de eeuw-ca. 1650).* Antwerp: Museum Plantin-Moretus.

Den Boer, H. (1995). *La literatura sefardí de Amsterdam.* Alcalá: Universidad de Alcalá.

Eckert, P. and McConnell-Ginet, S. (1992) Think practically and look locally: Language and gender as community-based practice. *Annual Review of Anthropology*, 21, pp. 461–490.

Emmer, P. and Gommans, J. (2012). *Rijk aan de rand van de wereld. De geschiedenis van Nederland overzee 1600–1800.* Amsterdam: Bert Bakker.

Frijhoff, W. (2010). *Meertaligheid in de Gouden Eeuw.* Amsterdam: KNAW Press.

Frijhoff, W. (2017). Frans onderwijs en Franse scholen. In: M. Koffeman, A. Montoya and M. Smeets, eds., *Literaire bruggenbouwers tussen Nederland en Frankrijk. Receptie, vertaling en cultuuroverdracht sinds de Middeleeuwen.* Amsterdam: Amsterdam University Press, pp. 49–82.

Grutman, R. (2009). Multilingualism. In: M. Baker and G. Saldanha, eds., *Routledge Encyclopedia of Translation Studies.* 2nd ed., London and New York: Routledge, pp. 182–185.

Hamilton, A. (2001). *Arab Culture and Ottoman Magnificence in Antwerp's Golden Age.* London and Oxford: Oxford University Press.

Heeres, J. E. (1907). Corpus diplomaticum Neerlando-Indicum. Eerste deel (1596–1650). *Bijdragen tot de taal-, land- en volkenkunde van Nederlandsch-Indië*, 57, pp. xv–xxxii, 1–514.

Helmers, H. (2018). Popular Participation in Public Debate. In: H. Helmers and G, Janssen, eds., *The Cambridge Companion to the Dutch Golden Age.* Cambridge: Cambridge University Press, pp. 124–146.

Hermans, T. (2015). Miracles in Translation. Justus Lipsius, Our Lady of Halle and Two Dutch Translations. *Renaissance Studies*, 29, pp. 125–142.

Israel, J. (1997). The Court of Albert and Isabella, 1598–1621. In: J. Israel, ed., *Conflicts of Empires: Spain, the Low Countries and the Struggle for World Supremacy 1585–1713.* London and Rio Grande: Hambledon, pp. 1–23.

Janssen, G. (2018). Migration. In: H. Helmers and G, Janssen, eds., *The Cambridge Companion to the Dutch Golden Age.* Cambridge: Cambridge University Press, pp. 49–66.

Jautze, K., Álvarez Francés, L. and Blom, F. (2016). Spaans theater in de Amsterdamse Schouwburg (1638–1672). Kwantitatieve en kwalitatieve analyse van de creatieve industrie van het vertalen. *De zeventiende eeuw*, 32, pp. 13–39.

Joby, C. (2016). Recording the History of Dutch in Japan. *Dutch Crossing*, 40, pp. 219–238.

Kuiper, Koos (2005). The Earliest Monument of Dutch Sinological Studies. Justus Heurnius's Manuscript Dutch-Chinese Dictionary and Chinese-Latin *Compendium Doctrinae Christianae* (Batavia 1628). *Quaerendo* 35, pp. 109–139.

Leupe, P. A. (1869). Herbert de Jager. *Bijdragen tot de taal-, land- en volkenkunde van Nederlandsch-Indië*, 16, pp. 67–97.

Matsutaka, F. (2018). Contacting Japan. East India Company Letters to the Shogun. In: A. Clulow and T. Mostert, eds., *The Dutch and English East India Companies: Diplomacy, Trade and Violence in East Modern Asia*. Amsterdam: Amsterdam University Press, pp. 79–98.

Meskens, A. (2013). *Practical Mathematics in a Commercial Metropolis. Mathematical Life in Late 16th Century Antwerp*. Dordrecht: Springer.

Meuwese, M. (2005). The Murder of Jacob Rabe. Contesting Dutch Colonial Authority in the Borderlands of Northeastern Brazil. In: J. Smolenski and T. Humphrey, eds., *New World Orders: Violence, Sanction and Authority in the Colonial Americas*. Philadelphia: University of Pennsylvania Press, pp. 133–156.

Meuwese, M. (2012). *Brothers in Arms, Partners in Trade: Dutch-Indigenous Alliances in the Atlantic World 1595–1674*. Leiden and Boston: Brill.

Noak, B. (2012). Kennistransfer en culturele differentie. Abraham Rogerius en zijn *Open deure tot het verborgen heydendom* (1651), *Tijdschrift voor Nederlandse taal- en letterkunde*, 128, pp. 350–364.

Paulusz, J. (1980). The 1638 Westerwolt Treaty in Ceylon: Charges of Dutch Deceit Disproved. *Bijdragen tot de taal-, land- en volkenkunde van Nederlandsch-Indië*, 136, pp. 321–352.

Pettegree, A. and Der Weduwen, A. (2019). *The Bookshop of the World. Making and Trading Books in the Dutch Golden Age*. New Haven and London: Yale University Press.

Piélat, B. (1681). *L'anti-grammaire. D'Oude spraek-konst verworpen*. Amsterdam: Wed. J. Janssonius van Waesberge en soonen.

Porteman, K. (1975). Miscellanea emblematica. *Tijdschrift voor Nederlandse taal- en letterkunde*, 17, pp. 161–193.

Prak, M. (2018). Urbanization. In: H. Helmers and G. Janssen, eds., *The Cambridge Companion to the Dutch Golden Age*. Cambridge: Cambridge University Press, pp. 15–31.

Pratt, M. L. (1987). Linguistic Utopias. In: N. Farb, D. Attridge, A. Durant and C. MacCabe, eds., *The Linguistics of Writing: Arguments between Language and Literature*. New York: Methuen, pp. 48–66.

Simoni, A. (1976). A Ghost No More: A Contribution to the Bibliography of Joannes David S.J. *De gulden passer*, 54, pp. 64–71.

Six van Chandelier, J. (1674). *Davids psalmen*. Amsterdam: Jakob Lescalje.

Smit, W. A. P. (1975). *Kalliope in de Nederlanden. Het renaissancistisch-klassicistische epos van 1550 tot 1850. Deel 1: Prolegomena. Opkomend tij (1550–1700)*. Assen: Van Gorcum.

Smits-Veldt, M. and Abrahamse, W. (1993). Een Nederlandse polyglot in het begin van de zeventiende eeuw: Theodore Rodenburgh (1574–1644), *De zeventiende eeuw*, 8, pp. 232–239.

Thijssen-Schoute, C. L. (1967). *Uit de republiek der letteren. Elf studies op het gebied der ideeëngeschiedenis van de Gouden Eeuw*. The Hague: Martinus Nijhoff.

Utenhove, C. (1560). *Epitaphium in mortem Herrici Gallorum regis christianissimi, eius nomini secundi, per Carolum Utenhovium Gandavensem, & alios, duodecim linguis [...] Epitaphe sur le trespas du roy treschrestien Henri Roy de France, II de ce nom, en douze langues*. Paris: Robert Estienne.

Van der Sijs, N. (2000). *Wie komt daar aan op die olifant? Een zestiende-eeuws taalgidsje voor Nederland en Indië, inclusief het verhaal van de avontuurlijke gevangenschap van Frederik de Houtman in Indië*. Amsterdam and Antwerp: L.J. Veen.

Van der Wal, M. J. (1990). Taalidealen, taalnormen en taalverandering: Johan de Brune in linguïstisch perspectief. In: P.J. Verkruijsse, ed., *Johan de Brune de Oude (1588–1658)*. Middelburg: Koninklijk Zeeuws Genootschap der Wetenschappen, pp. 54–58.

Van Goor, J. (2015). *Jan Pieterszoon Coen 1587–1629: Koopman-koning in Azië*. Amsterdam: Boom.

Van Ommen, K. and Cazes, H. (2010). *Facebook in the Sixteenth Century? The Humanist and Networker Bonaventura Vulcanius*. Leiden: Leiden University Library, Scaliger Institute.

Wilkinson, A. S. (2018). Printing Spanish Books in the Southern and Northern Netherlands, 1520–1700. *Quærendo*, 48, pp. 277–299.

Part II
The Defence of Latin

6 Should Latin Be Spoken?

The Controversy between Sanctius Brocensis, Henry Jason and the Irish Jesuits of Salamanca[1]

Eustaquio Sánchez Salor

Introduction

In the sixteenth century, Latin was spoken in two different ways. Most classical humanists would attempt to use the syntax, lexicon, twists, and idioms typical of classical Latin, while others, who spoke the language only to get by, did not care too much about the elegance of their style and calqued phrases from Hispanic, Italian, French or English onto the lingua franca. In other words, they used Latin terms, not always classical, to translate phrases from the vernacular language. In the case of Spain, this is what we are going to call *sermo hispanolatinus*. For example, the Latin phrase *agere gratiam* ("dar gracias" in contemporary Spanish) would be rendered as *dare gratias* in the *sermo hispanolatinus*. This is not the same thing as the so-called macaronic Latin, which originated in poetry and had its own technique.[2] The grammarian Cornelius Valerius (1512–1578), at the end of his *Syntax* described it thus:

> Those who do not observe the Latin feature in the joining of words or are not careful doing so, the only thing they do is to map foreign sentences into Latin. This is what normally happens to those who twist the Latin language in order to translate it into the vernacular language.
>
> (Valerius, 1575: 257)[3]

Similarly, Iacobus Lodovicus Strebaeus, in his *De electione et oratoria collocatione* (1540: 41), says that "there are those who do not seem to speak Latin, but destroy all Latin with barbaric constructions".[4]

Francisco Sánchez de las Brozas (1523–1600), also known as Sanctius and El Brocense, was an illustrious Spanish humanist, rhetorician and grammarian. As a rhetorician he was the author of a *De Arte dicendi* (1556) and an *Organum dialecticum et retoricum* (Lyon, 1579). As a grammarian he was, together with the Englishman Thomas Linacre (1465–1524), the most important representative of rational Grammar of the sixteenth century. His *Minerva* or *De causis linguae latinae* was

DOI: 10.4324/9781003092445-9

the first rational Grammar of Latin to be written in Europe (Sánchez de las Brozas, 1587) and served as a model for later schools such as Port Royal, Enlightened Grammar and indeed for Chomsky (2009), in our own day.[5]

Sanctius believed that it was necessary to study and read Latin in order to understand the rational basis of language and enjoy and learn from Latin texts, but that it should not be spoken. Indeed, he severely criticised those that spoke Hispanic Latin, on the grounds that this corrupted Latinity itself: "Those who quack Latin, corrupt Latin itself"[6] (Sánchez de las Brozas, 1587/1995: 266v/672). For him, the only thing these speakers did was "either to express thoughts with Latin words or meddle in the conversations of those who speak Latin"[7] (Sánchez de las Brozas, 1587/1995: 266v–267r/672). Expressing thoughts with Latin words was of course a reference to the *sermo hispanolatinus* since the person speaking was thinking in Spanish but using Latin terms.

Indeed, the most distinguished humanists held that the practice of translating sentences from the vernacular languages into Latin should be avoided since this would corrupt the genuine Latin which they themselves were trying to recover. In what follows, we will focus on Sanctius's pronouncements on the matter.

Speaking Latin destroys the elegance of the language

Sanctius's *Paradoxa*[8] entitled *Qui latine garriunt corrumpunt ipsam latinitatem* [Those who quack Latin corrupt Latin itself], later included in his masterpiece *Minerva*, begins by stating the principle that Latin must be studied and written but not spoken. Indeed, Sanctius harshly criticises the ignorance of those who insist on speaking Latin:

> Well, is there anyone, not only in Spain but also in Europe – except for four or six wisemen – who does not hold and command that the Latin language must be exercised through speaking in order to be able to promptly and easily express the bad ideas that come to our minds? Which schoolteacher – and wisemen may forgive me – does not shout at their children like this: "Good or bad, but speak to Mark"? So great is the ignorance, wickedness and stubbornness of the ignorant people.
>
> (Sánchez de las Brozas, 1587/1995: 266v/672)[9]

He believed that the Latin taught to children by schoolteachers of the time was an improper Latin, and that, if Latin was learnt wrongly from childhood, it would never be corrected later in life:

> No one in his right mind will approve this precept: that incompetent nursemaids teach something which later must be cast aside. Me, at

least, having had many disciples, I have never consented to something like this, because I have learnt from Quintilian that you cannot teach children expressions that they will later need to forget. And also, what is this good for, if the right thing is learnt with the same effort and perhaps easily?
(Sánchez de las Brozas, 1587/1995: 269r/676)[10]

Quintilian – the testimony is quoted by Sanctius himself – had already complained in the harshest terms (*Inst.* 1.1) about nursemaids who, unable to speak Latin correctly themselves, teach it to the children in their charge:

> Quintilian, Book 1, Chapter 1: "Given that it is the nursemaids whom children first hear, their vocabulary would be the first one that they will first attempt to imitate. And we, by nature, usually keep tenaciously what we learnt in the first two years; the new vessels and the dyes that have covered the primitive whiteness of wool are indelible. Furthermore, those worst impregnations are the most durable; thus, the flavour first absorbed has persistence. A virtue changes easily towards the evil but, when does vice turn into virtue? Therefore, do not allow children to become accustomed, particularly when they cannot speak yet, to some expressions which later they will subsequently have to unlearn".
> (Sánchez de las Brozas, 1587/1995: 269v/676)[11]

Sanctius's criticism is based not only on the testimony of Quintilian but also on Cicero.

> Cicero, Book 1 of *De Oratore*, speaking of exercising, says this: "But most of them, in their practice, try only to exercise their voice, and they do so without method; they exercise their lungs, develop the agility of their tongue, and are pleased with the flow of their words. What deceives them is that they have heard it said that speech is learned by talking. But it is no less true that it is also said that bad speaking is the surest way of learning to speak badly".
> (Sánchez de las Brozas, 1587/1995: 269r–269v/676)[12]

Sanctius describes those who insist on speaking Latin as ignorant and stubborn because they boldly use the language to express inappropriate ideas. They use Latin to express their ideas and thoughts without elaborating them further, inevitably using the enunciative schema of Spanish rather than those proper to Latin and therefore speaking a language that is halfway between Spanish and Latin. Indeed, there is nothing more reprehensible than a student expressing his thoughts in Latin:

> But me, who think that good reasons are stronger than the precepts of many, I declare that there cannot be a more repugnant thing for

a young lover of Latin language than expressing their thoughts in Latin or meddling in others' conversation.
(Sánchez de las Brozas, 1587/1995: 266v–267r/672)[13]

A young student should not speak Latin because he does not know how to speak it. Indeed, correct Latin cannot be learnt by speaking it. It is learned by reading the Latin Classics and, at the most, by writing it; since one who writes does not create sentences impulsively but can think and translate them into Latin formulae, that is, into pure Latin.

Indeed, those who have finally achieved a technical knowledge of Latin language – I refer to, for example, Petrus Bembus, Osorius, or our Priscianus – have done so, not by speaking but writing, thinking deeply and imitating.
(Sánchez de las Brozas, 1587/1995: 267r/672)[14]

Sanctius quotes from various other authorities too: Erasmus of Rotterdam (Desiderius Erasmus Roterodamus, 1466–1536) (1568: 636), who said that good Latin can be written but not spoken because, when writing, we act with serenity and knowledge while, when speaking, impulsively and thoughtlessly; Guillaume Budaeus (1467–1540) (1557), who said that he did not oblige his disciples to express everything they had to say in Latin, as often happened in schools; and Bartholomaeus Riccius (1490–1569), who, at the end of Book 3 of *De Imitatione*, (Riccius 1599: 65–66), coined the term *quotidianus sermo* to refer to what we have called *sermo hispanolatinus*, claiming "the term *sermo* in no way seems to characterise Latin phrases in terms of elegance".[15]

And Sanctius goes on, pointing out that Hebrew and Greek are not learned to be spoken but in order to enable the scholar to understand the texts written in those languages: Latin should be treated in the same way. If spoken Latin were required, it would have to be the Latin spoken at the time of Cicero, for fear of corrupting the Latin language.

One must diligently cultivate the style; in fact, as Marco Tullius says, the best teacher in the art of speaking; the style itself will teach us how those who do not have wisdom try to destroy – and how! – the Latin language in squares and even at gymnasiums.
(Sánchez de las Brozas, 1587/1995: 267r/672)[16]

Sanctius then lists a series of expressions commonly used by those who try to speak Latin, but which are not pure Latin expressions, but rather Castilian expressions translated into Latin. These are reproduced below, with the pure Latin phrases given by Sanctius on the left and the

Hispanolatinus phrases of those that speak the language wrongly on the right (Sánchez de las Brozas, 1587/1995: 267v–268r/674):

Locutiones latinae	Locutiones hispano-latinae
habere orationem [give a speech]	*facere orationem*
uerba facere [speak]	*agere uerba*
agere gratias [give thanks]	*facere gratias*
fer opem [provide support]	*da opem*
dare uerba [speak]	*tradere o praebere uerba*
speculantur de monte [watch from the mountain]	*vigilant milites in monte*
conatur aciem perrumpere [try to break lines]	*tentat frangere aciem*
dimisit copias seu exercitum [released the army]	*dimisit suos milites*
interclusit commeatum [intercept the supplies]	*impediuit commeatum*
re frumentaria carebat Caesar [Caesar was short of food]	*uictu carebat Caesar*
egit uineas [take war machines]	*duxit uineas*
consilii principes [first to decide]	*primi in consilio*
egerunt praedas [they took the spoils]	*reportarunt praedas*
milites hortatus est [appealed to the soldiers]	*milites monuit*
signum dedit [made a sign]	*signum fecit*
restituit seu redintegrauit proelium [renewed the fight]	*renouauit proelium*
aciem instruxi [arranged the army]	*aciem ordinauit*
receperunt se milites [soldiers came back]	*redierunt milites*
misit subsidio [sent to help]	*misit ad succurrendum*
impetum fecerunt [made an attack]	*fecerunt uim,*
magnis itineribus contendit [advanceat great speed]	*magnis uiis contendit*
amissit occasionem [missed the opportunity]	*perdidit opportunitatem*

Sentences like *Libris opus habeo, Adhibeo tibi fidem, Crimen laesae maiestatis, Ille tenetur hoc facere, Ego amo deum* [I need books, believe in you, crime of lèse-majesté, he is forced to do this, I love Lord] are grammatically correct but not correct Latin, as they would never have been produced in Roman times. Similarly, *perdidit opportunitatem* is not the same as *amissit occasionem* [s/he lost the chance]. The first expression is the Latin-vernacular one since it is formed according to the Spanish model ("perdió la oportunidad"), while the second expression, *amissit occasionem*, is the authentic Latin one. As Sanctius says, calquing Castilian sentences onto Latin is not the same as speaking Latin.

The problem of idioms

Idioms and idiomatic expressions also play an important role in this matter. These expressions are distinctive of a particular language and do not usually have any literal translation. A basic principle is that idiomatic expressions typical of one language cannot be expressed *verbum ex verbo* [word by word] in another.

In the sixteenth and seventeenth centuries, many Latin and Spanish scholars argued that Spanish idioms could not be translated into Latin without disfiguring the text. This is Sanctius' opinion. For example, in

Spanish, the phrase "ir de punta en blanco" is often used to describe someone that is dressed up to the nines. However, for Sanctius, it is quite unacceptable for a theologian to say *de cuspide in albo* [go from tip to blank], though the Latin expression must have been quite common in sixteenth- and seventeenth-century Spanish (it is used quite frequently in comic and burlesque texts to refer to the braggart soldier stock character – the *miles gloriosus* of Plautus). This particular idiom also attracted the attention of Bernardo de Aldrete at the beginning of the seventeenth century, who said that idioms are not essential elements of a language but accidental; if they were essential, they could be translated word by word from one language into the other and would be understandable in both languages (1606: 190–192). But the Latin expression *armatus de cuspide in albo* used to express the Castilian one "armado de punta en blanco" would not have been understood by a Roman Latin-speaker since it is formed according to an accidental characteristic, not to an essential one, of the Castilian language (Aldrete 1606: 193).[17]

Sanctius also refers to the Spanish phrase "válgame Dios", used to ask God for help, which was often translated into Latin as *Valeat me Deus*. For him, this is unacceptable, particularly coming from a great theologian, since in proper elegant Latin, the correct phrase would be *ita me deus adiuvet*. Another Spanish idiom is "bailar sin ton ni son" [literally, to dance without tone or sound] to refer to someone dancing without following the rhythm of the music. This Spanish idiom cannot be expressed in Latin as *saltare sine tono et sine sono*, as used by some Latin speakers of the sixteenth century. The Latin expression that meant the same as "bailar sin ton ni son" was *saltare extra chorum*. According to Sanctius, Latin was used so inaccurately in the sixteenth century that he had recently heard a loquacious preacher saying in Spanish "saltar fuera del coro" without even knowing what it meant (Sánchez de las Brozas 1587/1995: 153v/412–413).[18]

The quod *particle*

The continuous use of the *quod* ["that"] particle is considered as one of the misuses and abuses of the Latin language. The *quod* particle is obviously Latin, but its use was restricted in classical Latin (for example, it was not used to introduce a completive clause). However, in late or medieval Latin, it was overused and became a universal particle or connector, probably due to the influence of the Portuguese, Spanish and French "que" and the Italian "che".

Sanctius argues vociferously that such usage contaminated Latin and that the particle had been destroyed by the Scholastic use of Latin for the dialectics and philosophy of Aristotle and Plato. He even dares to criticise Erasmus of Rotterdam for the excessive use he makes of the *quod* particle in his translation of the New Testament, saying that Erasmus did not know or could not avoid "this plague that has destroyed the Latin language"[19] (Sánchez de las Brozas, 1587/1995: 153v/412). Indeed, Erasmus often repeats expressions such as *dico quod, dixit quod, credo quod, sciendum est quod* [I say that, I said that, I think that, It must be known that].[20]

Sanctius's dispute with Henry Jason

At the end of the sixteenth century, a strange but bitter dispute took place between Sanctius and an Irish master of the liberal arts settled in Salamanca. The controversy was about whether Latin should or not be spoken.

José María Maestre Maestre (2007: 181–231) has shown that Sanctius' document, first entitled *Latine loqui corrumpit ipsam Latinitatem* ("Speaking Latin corrupts Latin itself") (Sánchez de las Brozas, 1578), which would later turn into the famous *Paradoxa II* of the fourth book of *Minerva* titled *Qui latine garriunt corrumpunt ipsam latinitatem* ("Those who quack Latin corrupt Latin itself"), arose from a conflict between Sanctius and Henry Jason, an Irish Catholic exiled in Spain on account of the religious repression suffered under Elizabeth I (Maestre Maestre, 2007: 194–202). In the course of 1577–1578, Jason signed up for a class in Rhetoric for theologians given by Sanctius. However, as he could not speak Castilian, he asked that Latin be spoken, in accordance with the Statute of Salamanca University. When Sanctius refused, Jason raised some objections. Sanctius, whose pride was probably hurt by an attack from such a distinguished student, answered publicly in the cited document of 1578, to which Jason responded immediately by writing his extensive *Disquisitio Responsoria* (Jason, seventeenth cent.; Maestre Maestre, 2007: 202–204).[21] In it, he argued that although spoken Latin was not the most elegant Latin, it could be decent enough and did not have to be mere transformation of vernacular sentences into Latin.

The controversy between Jason and Sanctius offers important information about the matter of whether Latin should be spoken, and its details clearly show the direction in which these positions were heading. Those who argued that Latin could be spoken based their position on a new and less demanding concept of linguistic elegance and taught different ways of saying the same vernacular expression in Latin. They were, in short, those who taught *copia verborum*,[22] including Erasmus himself.

Sanctius, in his conflict with Jason, insisted that he would not harm the Latin language by speaking it,[23] to which the Irishman, in the second part of *Disquisitio responsorial* (seventeenth cent.), replied:

> You do not want to speak Latin so as not to harm it yet you make use of *copia verborum*, a typical procedure of those who speak Latin, in order to insult us; you have called us 'stupid crowd', 'grumpy',

'chatterboxes', 'foolish', 'lack of common sense', and you do this to defend the Latin language.

(quoted in Maestre Maestre, 2007: 195, note 63)[24]

That is to say, he accuses Sanctius of insulting them by means of procedures of *copia* so appreciated by those who, like Erasmus, wanted to be able to express a single vernacular expression in various ways in Latin. Not even Erasmus himself would have found so many Latin terms for foolish chatterboxes.

In another interesting passage, Jason distinguishes between scholarly and everyday speech. For normal communicative purposes, he argues, there is no need to speak a scholarly or elegant language; ordinary common speech is enough; otherwise, we would never speak at all (Maestre Maestre, 2007). He also points out that languages are learnt by speaking them. Sanctius had replied that, though this may be true for living languages, it was not appropriate for Latin. But Jason insisted that even Latin could be learnt by speaking it. Indeed, this was the basic principle of the various treatises known as *Ianua linguarum*, which offered an important third alternative in the debate about the speaking of Latin.

The *Ianua linguarum* [The gateway of languages]

Jason may have dared to stand up to the Salamanca master because he had behind him the many English and Irishman that studied in Salamanca. These will mostly have been Jesuits from the Society's College in Salamanca,[25] amongst whom were several good Latin grammarians, including the authors of one of the various treatises circulating at the time known as *Ianua linguarum* [The Gateway of Languages]. This work specifically teaches how to build Latin sentences from vernacular ones, using sentences that are not necessarily based on classical authors. As this work is diametrically opposed to Sanctius' position, it is worth looking at it in more detail.

The full title of the work is *Ianua linguarum sive Modus maxime accommodatus, quo patefit aditus ad omnes linguas intelligendas. Industria patrum hibernorum Societatis IESV, qui in Collegio eiusdem nationis Salmanticae degunt... Salmanticae Anno MDCXI* [The Gateway of Languages or very proper method, in which it is provided access to learn all languages. Work by the Irish Fathers of the Society of Jesus who live in their National School in Salamanca] and it is attributed to William Bathe, S.J. (1564–1614), assisted by John Bathe and Stephen White (1574–1646) (Mantuna, 1986). The title already hints at some of the characteristics of the treatise (Bathe, 1611): firstly, that it is a method of teaching languages; secondly, that the method, in this specific manual, is applied to Latin; and thirdly, that the method consists of teaching the most common and important uses and words of the language in question (in this case, Latin).

The manuals of Latin grammar produced by the Jesuits throughout the whole seventeenth century did exactly this: they taught the Latin forms of the most common terms and phrases in Castilian. In this *Ianua linguarum,* this principle is elevated to a doctrine and a practice. However, it seems that there was some reticence about publishing this new method of *Ianua,* perhaps on the part of the Superiors of the Order. Therefore, the manuscript was sent to different priests of their Order and to contemporary authorities on grammar asking for letters of recommendation. Those recommendation letters are all gathered together in the first pages of the *Ianua.* For example, there is a letter from the priest Hernando Vazquez de Guzman of the Society of Jesus addressed to an Irish priest in Salamanca (presumably William Bathe, who appears to be the author of the treatise):

> I received the abbreviated method of learning languages that you introduced to me; I have read all the sentences, and it seems to me the most ingenious and fruitful thing I have ever seen with this purpose, apart from being an abbreviated means of learning any language. The sentences are all about good manners, which I soon wish to see printed so that they can be read in our schools... Madrid, January 20, 1609
> (quoted in Bathe, 1611: 1)[26]

Recommendation letters were also requested from other Jesuits that were missionaries in America to show that the work would be effective even for learning the languages of the Indians, thereby facilitating the missionaries' evangelizing task. For example, the following recommendation was issued by the priest Luis de Valdivia, S.J. (1561–1642),[27] a missionary in Chile, during his stay in Spain between 1609 and 1610:

> *Pax Christi* etc.
>
> After I saw the treatise *Ianua Linguarum* I was very eager to have it printed before I went back to the Indies where I had been for 21 years. And I can assure your Reverences, as being the one who has learned with great labor many languages of Indians, that the one which has taken your Reverences must save this work for others in learning them... Madrid, December 12. 1609.
> (quoted in Bathe, 1611: 2)[28]

Another was provided by a professor in Law, Bartolomé Sánchez,[29] who, despite not being a grammarian himself, issued a recommendation about the *Ianua* addressed the Provincial of the Order:

> Letter from Doctor Bartolomè Sanchez, professor of Clementines at the University of Salamanca, to Father Cristobal de los Cobos, Provincial of the Society of Jesus in Castile.

Because His Majesty the King sent me to take charge of the instruction of an illustrious Irish gentleman, it was an occasion for me to have a special relationship with the Fathers of the Society of Jesus of the same nation, who communicated with me a method of learning the Latin language with ease. I, who at the time was Professor of Rhetoric and Grammar, and of Greek at the University of Salamanca, put it in use, and I sought the same experience in the Greek language. And although I was amused by the pretension of the professors in Law, which is my own profession, I could not attend with the truths that were required, I experienced that in three months I had better results by this way than by the ordinary one in three years, and thus I pledged them to publish it... Salamanca December 1, 1608.

(quoted in Bathe, 1611: 4)[30]

Yet another very favourable endorsement came from a distinguished professor of Prima at Salamanca University addressed the same Provincial of the Order, while the following is by none other than Juan Luis de la Cerda, S.J. (1558–1643), author of the Reform of Nebrija's Grammar known as *Regia Art*:

Approval of Father Juan Luis de la Cerda and Father Antonio Sanchez.

The method taught in these sentences for learning the Latin language seems to me to be good and purposeful, both for the brevity it contains and for the benefit it will continue to bring. Madrid, January 27, 1609.

(quoted in Bathe, 1611: 1)[31]

In addition to praising the work, many of these informers also express their desire to have it printed ("desseo verlas ya impressas" [I wish to see them soon printed]; "Por lo qual pido...que se imprima" [With this purpose... I am asking to be printed]; "assi les suplique la publicasen" [and so I pledged for publication]; "mueua con su autoridad à estos Padres à que las impriman" [use your authority to move these Fathers to print].

In the initial pages of the treatise (Bathe, 1611: 7–8), the Jesuits list the reasons why they think their work will be very useful. The *Ianua* will help missionaries learn indigenous languages *in infidelium regionibus* (in the lands of the infidels); it will assist confessors who travel around foreign lands to hear confession, older people that do not get admitted to the Order through lack of study, anyone that does not want to use the dictionary constantly and those who sweat when reading the Gospel and the prayers. It will also be useful for grammarians and rhetors (of course), and for preceptors and teachers, who will be able to teach all the main words of a language (in this case Latin) with no more than three student books; and finally, travellers to foreign countries, who will be able, with this method, to quickly learn the most essential things of the language of the country they are travelling to. In short, the work encourages the use of Latin as a *lingua franca*, spoken not as Cicero would have spoken it, but certainly in the most decent way possible.

Thus, a new method of teaching languages is proposed. In the first chapters, it is explained that there are three ways of learning a language, but that, until the *Ianua* appeared, only two ways were routinely used. The first of these, called the "regular" method, proceeds through the learning of grammar rules (*regularis, qualis est ad congruitates obseruandas Grammaticae*), while the second, called "irregular", involves using the language to communicate with the speakers of it *(et irregularis, est discentium vsus, per lectionem et loquelam in linguis vulgaribus)* (Bathe, 1611: 13). The first one is safer [*plus certitudinis*] but the second is easier [*plus facilitates*]. The first is the most appropriate way to learn a language that is no longer spoken (*Prior, vbi lingua communiter non usurpatur, praeferenda*), while the second is better for a living language (*Posterior, vbi lingua est vulgaris*).

There is, however, a third intermediate way which is both safe and easy,[32] and it is this that is taught in the *Ianua*. In order to demonstrate it, the work begins by listing the components of a language that must be taken into account when learning it. These are: the *Vocabula* (or words making up the Dictionary); the *Congruitas* or syntax (the heritage of Grammar); the *Sententiae* (illustrative sentences taken from the work of respected authors); and the *Elegantiae* (the heritage of Rhetors).[33]

The remaining chapters reveal a very modern attitude to the teaching of language on the part of the Jesuits. For example, in Chapter 3, they attempt to systematise the learning of Vocabulary by reducing the list to only the most essential words,[34] focusing on word-building[35] and ensuring that the words are contextualised into sentences in order to make them meaningful.[36] Similarly with Syntax or *Congruitas*, the author of the *Ianua* maintains that this is best taught not with abstract rules alone, but also with concrete examples in the form of sentences,[37] a resource that can be applied to the learning of any language (but is particularly useful in the case of the vernaculars, where there is less need to learn the Grammar scientifically).[38] As regards the *Elegantiae*, these can be learned by memorising short sentences taken from good authors,[39] though this aspect is left for subsequent editions.[40] Finally – and most significantly for the argument being presented here – the sentences are written both in Latin and Castilian: thus, students that know Castilian will be able to understand the Latin,[41] while the person who already knows the Latin language will better understand the vernacular.[42]

Thereafter follow the *Copia* of *sententiae* ordered into *Centurias* (blocks of a hundred) on themes such as temperance and intemperance, justice and injustice, fortitude and cowardice, presented as parallel texts with one page in Latin and the other in Castilian. Finally, there is an Appendix of ambiguous words (*De ambiguis*), illustrated through paired sentences contextualising each of the different meanings,[43] and an Index, or short dictionary [*Index sive dictionarivm breve, continens omnia vocabula familiaria fundamentalia linguae latinae ex Calepino et aliis excerpta*] containing the fundamental terms of Latin extracted from the Calepino.[44]

The *Ianua* achieved great popularity in the seventeenth century and was published many times in various languages (Mantuna, 1986). For instance, in 1615, William Welde presented an English translation of it in London, eliminating the Castilian. Then in 1617, also in London, Jean Barbier made a new edition, combining the previous two and adding a French translation. In 1623, in Portugal, Amaro de Roboredo added the Portuguese translation, and in 1629, Isaac Habrech published in Strasbourg (Argentinae) a new edition in French, German, English and Spanish (Habrecht, 1629). Indeed, the *Ianua* of the Irishmen of Salamanca was so successful that it easily found funders, as Comenius himself pointed out in 1631.

Conclusion

There were three different positions in the sixteenth century on the question of whether Latin could or should be spoken. The first group argued that, if Latin had to be spoken, it was necessary to imitate the elegant Latin of Cicero and the Classics; but as this was impossible for the vast majority of people, it was better not to speak it at all. This was Sanctius' position in *Paradoxa* (1578) and *Minerva* (1587). The second position was that of those who boldly dared to speak Latin by simply translating Romance structures into it, producing a severely distorted form of Latin that offended the taste of the purists. This is the group that Sanctius confronts in his *Minerva*, led by Jason in *Disquisitio responsoria* (seventeenth cent.). Finally, we have those who argue that Latin has to be spoken because it is the *lingua franca* of the moment, and for this, it has to be done in the best possible way, not as Cicero and the Classics did it, but decently enough. It was this impulse that led to the appearance of the treatises known as *Ianua linguarum*, firstly by the Irish Jesuits of Salamanca (1611), then by Comenius (1631) and later by others.

Notes

1. This chapter was prepared in the context of the projects "Grammars in Europe (seventeenth and eighteenth centuries). Studies and editions" (FFI2016-78496-P), financed by the Ministerio de Economía, Industria y

Competitividad – Agencia Estatal de Investigación and by the European Regional Development Fund.
2. Macaronic Latin has been defined by José Miguel Domínguez Leal (2007: 103) as "a type of composition that uses Latin quantitative metrics, fundamentally the hexameter, and it is written in an intentionally hybrid language, the result of the fusion of Latin with other languages, Romance or otherwise, in a supposedly homogeneous linguistic code that integrates Latin words with others from a vulgar language with a Latin ending or appearance" [*La poesía macarrónica o macarroea es un tipo de composición que emplea la métrica cuantitativa latina, fundamentalmente el hexámetro, y que está escrita en un lenguaje intencionadamente híbrido, fruto de la fusion del latín con otras lenguas, romances o no, en un código lingüístico pretendidamente homogéneo que integra palabras Latinas junto a otras de una lengua vulgar con terminación o apariencia latina*]. All translations were done by the author unless otherwise stated.
3. *Hanc proprietatem in uerborum coniunctione qui non obseruat, nec delectum habet ullum, is barbara locutione omnem peruerterit Latinitatem: quod iis fere solet accidere, qui linguam Latinam ad idioma uernaculum detorquent.*
4. *sunt qui non latine loqui mihi videntur quam barbarica phrasi omnem inuertere latinitatem.*
5. Chomsky (2009: 134) says: "Apart from its Cartesian origins, the Port Royal theory of language, with its distinction between deep and surface structure, can be traced to scholastic and renaissance grammar; in particular, to the theory of ellipsis and 'ideal types' that reached its fullest development in Sanctius's *Minerva* (1587)."
6. *qui latine garriunt corrumpunt ipsam latinitatem.*
7. *aut uerbis latinis effutire cogitata, aut loquentium profluentiae interesse.*
8. The Latin texts of the *Paradoxa* included in the *Minerva* have been reproduced from the critical edition by Eustaquio Sánchez Salor: Sánchez de las Brozas, Francisco (1587/1995). *Minerva o De causis linguae Latinae. Libri I, III, IV (introducción y edición E. Sánchez Salor). Liber II (edición C. Chaparro Gómez)*. Cáceres: Institución cultural El Brocense – Universidad de Extremadura. All Latin texts have been translated into English by the author.
9. *Quis enim est, non dico in Hispania, sed etiam in tota Europa – quatuor aut sex doctos excipio – qui non et sentiat et praecipiat uerbis latinis exercendam linguam, ut prompte et celeriter possis, quae male cogitaueris, expromere? Quis porro ludi magister grammaticus non subinde pueris crepat – honor sit auribus doctorum –* "*Vel male uel bene, loquere cum Marco*"? *Tanta est stultorum hominum ignorantia, peruersitas et pertinacia.*

(Sánchez de las Brozas, 1587/1995: 266v/672).

10. *Nemo sanae mentis tale consilium probabit, ut ineptae nutrices doceant, quae postea sint dedocenda. Ego certe, qui plurimos liberos sustuli, nunquam id sum passus, qui Quintiliano auctore didicerim, non assuescendum puerum sermoni, qui dediscendus sit. Quid quod optima eodem labore aut fortasse facilius edocentur.*

(Sánchez de las Brozas, 1587/1995: 269r/676).

11. Quintilianus, lib. 1 cap.1: "*Ante omnia ne sit uitiosus sermo nutricibus: has primum audiet puer, harum uerba fingere imitando conabitur; et natura tenacissimi sumus eorum quae rudibus annis percipimus, ut sapor, quo noua imbuimus, durat, neque lanarum colores, quibus ille simplex*

candor mutatus est, elui possunt. Et haec ipsa magis pertinaciter haerent, quae deteriora sunt, nam bona facile mutantur in peius: nunc quando in bonum uerteris uitia? Non assuescat ergo, ne dum infans quidem est, sermoni cui didiscendus sit".

(Sánchez de las Brozas, 1587/1995: 269v/676).

12. Cicero, lib. 1 De orat., de exercitatione agens, sic inquit: "Sed plerique in hoc uocem modo, neque eam scienter, et uires exercent suas, et linguae celeritatem incitant uerborumque frequentia delectantur. In quo fallit eos quod audierunt dicendo, homines ut dicant, efficere solere. Vere enim etiam illud dicitur: peruerse dicere homines peruerse dicendo facillime consequi".

(Sánchez de las Brozas, 1587/1995: 269r–269v/676).

13. At ego, apud quem pluris est rectae rationis pondus quam multorum praescriptum, assero nihil pestilentius posse iuueni linguae latinae cupido euenire quam aut uerbis latinis effutire cogitata, aut loquentium profluentiae interesse.

(Sánchez de las Brozas, 1587/1995: 266v–267r/672).

14. Quicumque enim aliquando peritiam linguae latinae est assequutus, Petrum Bembum dico, aut Osorium, aut nostrum Pincianum, non loquendo, sed scribendo, meditando et imitatione id sunt assecuti.

(Sánchez de las Brozas, 1587/1995: 267r/672).

15. *nihil admodum latinae orationi prodesse uidetur ad eam dignitatem.*

(Riccius, 1599: 117)

16. Stylus exercendus est diligenter; hic enim, ut Marcus Tullius ait, est egregius dicendi magister; hic uere nos docebit communi sensu illos carere, qui linguam latinam in plateis, aut etiam in gymnasiis, miris modis conantur dilacerare.

(Sánchez de las Brozas, 1587/1995: 267r/672).

17. "Si la esencia de la lengua consistiera en estos modos de decir, con qualesquiera vocablos y gramática que se dixeran, fueran de la lengua cuya era el modo de decir. Y assi aqueste, Armatus de cuspide in album, fuera romance, porque dize vn modo de hablar castellano, "armado de punta en blanco" ..., pero sin duda es latin, mas no propio, de manera que no lo entenderà el latino, porque no sigue la propiedad de su lengua, sino de otra, que en esto no se conforma con ella". ["If the essence of language consisted of these modes of speech, with whatever words and grammars were said, they would be of the language whose mode of speech was. And so if this Armatus de cuspide in album would be romance, because it corresponds to a way of speaking Castillian, "armado de punta en blanco" ..., but it is undoubtedly Latin, but not proper Latin, so that it will not be understood by Latin, because it does not follow the property of its language, but of another, which in this does not conform to it".]

(Aldrete 1606: 193).

18. An ferenda sunt illa quae summus theologus passim in scholis inculcabat, hoc argumentum tangit de cuspide in album, et o ualeat me deus? Quid si uelis hispane dicere "saltar fuera del coro", sicut latine dicitur extra chorum saltare, ut loquacem satis concionatorem dicentem nuper audiui?

(Sánchez de las Brozas, 1587/1995: 153v/412–413).

19. hanc pestem quae linguam latinam pessum dedit.

(Sánchez de las Brozas, 1587/1995: 412).

20. Quo magis irascor Erasmo Roterodamo qui, quum in latinam linguam nouum testamentum uertere tentauerit, hanc pestem quae linguam latinam pessum dedit nescierit aut non potuerit euitare.

(Sánchez de las Brozas, 1587/1995: 412).

21. This manuscript is preserved in the Library of the Real Academy of History of Madrid (codex 9/5792; see Jason seventeenth cent.), together with the only known copy of the first edition of the *Paradoxa* (Sánchez de las Brozas, 1578).
22. The manuals called *De copia verborum* [Of abundance of words] offer the student vernacular language phrases (Spanish, Italian, French, etc.) followed by several Latin phrases which can be used to translate that basic idea. The most important author of a treatise of this type is Erasmus of Rotterdam.
23. *Ego latinam linguam non damno.*
24. (…) nos omnes damnas et sane pluribus nominibus nos damnas propter linguam Latinam, dum nos 'stultorum turbam", 'obganientes', 'blaterones', 'onocrotalos' et 'communi sensu carentes' uocitas (…) tu nobis plures odiosissimas inussisti easque omnes propter linguam Latinam.

(quoted in Maestre Maestre, 2007: 195, n. 63).
25. Jesuit Colleges in various Hispanic cities welcomed young people fleeing the Protestant prosecution in Ireland, such as the College of the Conception of Our Lady and Santa Fe in Seville, and those in Santiago and Lisbon, as well as Salamanca.
26. Recibi el método breue de aprender lenguas que V. P. me embio; he leydo las sentencias todas, y me parece lo cosa mas ingeniosa y prouechosa que jamas he visto a este proposito, fuera de ser vn medio para aprender qualquier lengua muy breue. Las sentencias son todas a proposito de las buenas costumbres, que desseo verlas ya impressas para que se lean en nuestras escuelas... Madrid, Enero 20 de 1609.

(quoted in Bathe, 1611: 1)
27. Luis de Valdivia (1561–1642), born in Granada, joined the Order in 1581. In 1583, he went to Chile dedicating himself to evangelise the natives of the south. Scholar of the Mapuche, he published a Grammar of this language in 1606 (Lima). At the end of 1609 and during 1610, he was in Spain to declare before the Court-Martial of Indias in relation with the War of Arauco. His stay in Spain and his knowledge on teaching native languages would encourage the authors of *Ianua* to ask him for a letter of recommendation.
28. *Pax Christi* etc.

Despues que vi el trastado de *Ianua Linguarum* he quedado muy desseoso de que se imprima antes de que me buelva à las Indias, donde he estado veynte y vn años. Y puedo asseuerar à vuestras Reuerencias, como quien ha aprendido con grande trabajo muchas lenguas de Indios, que el que han tomado vuestras Reuerencias ha de ahorrar este trabajo à otros en aprendellas... Madrid y Diciembre 12. 1609.

(quoted in Bathe, 1611: 2)
29. Sánchez specialised in the Decretals of Pope Clement V, the collection known as the *Liber Clementarium*, which completed the *Corpus Iuris Canonici*.
30. *Carta de Doctor Bartolomè Sanchez, cathedratico de Clementinas en la Vniversidad de Salamanca, al padre Cristoual de los Cobos, Prouincial de la Compañía de Iesvs en Castilla.*

Por auerme mandado su Magestad el Rey nuestro Señor le siruiesse en encargarme de la institución de vn Cauallero illustre Irlandes, fue occasion de que tuuiesse trato particular con los Padres de la Compañía de Iesvs de la misma nación, los quales comunicaron conmigo vn método de aprender con facilidad la lengua latina. Yo que à la sazon era Cathedratico de Prima de Rhetorica, y Gramatica, y de Griego en la Vniversidad de

Salamanca, la puse en vso, y procure la misma experiencia en la lengua Griega. Y aunque por andar diuertido en la pretensión de las Cathedras de propiedad de Derechos, que es mi propia profession, no pude atender con las veras que se requería, experimente que en tres meses hazia mas fructo por esta via que por la ordinaria en tres años, y assi les suplique la publicasen ... Salamanca 1 de Diciembrre de 1608.

(quoted in Bathe, 1611: 4)

31. *Aprobacion de Padre Ivan luys de la Cerda y del Padre Antonio Sanchez.* El método que se enseña en estas sentencias para aprender la lengua Latina me parece à propósito y bueno, assi por la brevedad que contiene como por el prouecho que se seguirá saliendo à luz. Madrid 27 de Enero de 1609.

(quoted in Bathe, 1611: 1).

32. Sin autem via tertia media excogitari queat, quae certitudine regularem facilitate irregularem adaequet, multis profectò numeris vtramque superaret, qualem hic nos diuino fauente numine demonstrandam suscepimus).

(Bathe, 1611: 13)

33. *Vocabulis, congruitate, phrasibus, et elegantia. Vocabula dictionarium, congruitates Grammatica, phrases autores, elegantiam suis schematibus rhetores depingunt; phrases vocamus idiotismos, siue pecualiares cuiuslibet linguae loquendi modos.*

([Bathe], 1611: 13)

34. "There are a lot of strange and useless words in the Dictionary and consequently, it is not normally necessary to learn all of them" (*quia in vocabulario multa verba rara et ad propositum multorum inutilia iacent*). (Bathe, 1611).

35. If one understands how words are built, then from knowing only one word, the essential one, it is possible to know the meaning of many related ones (*tanta est inter nonnulla affinitas, vt cognito vno fundamentali, velut alliorum fonte, caetera inde facillimè colligantur*). This is the case, for example, with words that have the same root, such as *turbo, perturbo, conturbo, disturbo, turbatus, turbans, turbatio*; knowing one of them, it is possible to deduce the rest with no special effort (*et alia plurima quae ex unius significatione praehabita facilè innotescunt, ita vt specialem discentis conatum non mereantur*).

36. The sentences are as brief as possible to facilitate memorization, and repetitions are avoided so as not to overload the Copia (Ad subueniendum tertio, sententiae memoriae aptae, breuitate summa componuntur, quippè cum nullo verbo bis repetito charta oneretur).

(Bathe, 1611: 14–15)

37. Omnia enim quae in Grammaticae regulis praescribuntur, possunt etiam sententiis commode doceri, it vt facilius, citius, et certius animis inhaereant, quam nudis regulis grammaticalibus per se fieri queat.

(Bathe, 1611: 19)

38. Et hoc ad finem et proprium institutum addiscendi linguam sufficient, idque maximè in linguis vulgaribus, in quibus non est necesse scientifice percipere quae ad methodum Grammaticalem pertinent.

(Bathe, 1611: 19)

39. Vt vocabula sententiis, ita phrases et elegantiae continuato discursu summa breuitate commodissimè comprohendi possunt.

(Bathe, 1611)

40. sed quia executio huiusce multos operarios requirit, vt expeditè et perfectè fiat, necesse est hoc ad vlteriores editiones remittere.

(Bathe, 1611: 20)

41. vnus, vt qui linguam vulgarem iam callet, sententias sic Latinas intelligat.
(Bathe, 1611: 21)
42. alter, vt qui linguae Latinae iam est peritus, sit etiam et linguae vulgaris.
(Bathe, 1611: 21)
43. For example, *Offendo*, in the sentence *Neminem dum possis offendas*, means "offend"; but in the sentence *Et gemmam pacis offendes*, it means "find".
44. The Calepino was a Latin dictionary by Ambrogio Calepino (1440–1510), published in 1502 in Reggio di Calabria. Known as the Cornucopia ("horn of plenty"), it was reprinted multiple times during the sixteeenth century, with more and more languages constantly being added. In the Basel edition of 1590, there are eleven languages, as announced in its title: *Ambrosii Calepini dictionarium undecim linguarum; respondent autem latinis vocabulis hebraica, graeca, gallica, italica, germanica, belgica, hispanica, polonica, ungarica, anglica*.

References

Primary sources

Bathe, W. (1611). *Janua Linguarum sive modus maxime accomodatus, quo patefit aditus ad omnes linguas intelligendas*, Salmanticae: apud Franciscum de Cea Tesa.

Jason, H. (seventeenth cent.). *Disquisitio responsoria Henrici Iason, ingenuarum artium professoris, in magistri Francisci Sanctii editam assertionem de non loquendo Latine*. Manuscript. Madrid: Biblioteca de la Real Academia de la Historia, Signatura [Codex] 9/5792.

Sánchez de las Brozas, F. (1578). *Latine loqui corrumpit ipsam latinitatem*, Salmanticae: Pedro Lasso.

Sánchez de las Brozas, F. (1587). *Minerva seu de causis linguae Latinae*, Salmanticae: apud Ioannem, et Andream Renaut, Fratres.

Sánchez de las Brozas, F. (1995). *Minerva o De causis linguae Latinae. Libri I, III, IV (introducción y edición E. Sánchez Salor). Liber II (edición C. Chaparro Gómez)*, Cáceres: Institución cultural El Brocense – Universidad de Extremadura. (Original work published 1587).

Secondary sources

Aldrete, B. de (1606). *Del origen, y principio de la lengua castellana o romance que oi se usa en España*, Roma: Carlo Wllieto.

Budaeus, G. (1557). *Budaei operum tomus iiii, in quo commentarii linguae Graecae habentur ab authore accurate regcogniti*, Basileae: apud Nicolaum Episcopium Iuniorem.

Chomsky, N. (2009) *Cartesian Linguistics: A Chapter in the History of Rationalist Thought*. 3rd ed. Cambridge, New York: Cambridge University Press.

Comenius, J. A. (1631). *Ianua linguarum trilinguis reserata et aperta. Sive seminarium linguarum & scientiarum omnium, hoc est, compendiaria latinam, anglicam, gallicam (& quamvis aliam) linguam una cum artium & scientiarum fundamentis sesquianni spatio ad summum docendi & perdiscendi methodus, sub titulis centum, periodis mille comprehensa. Latine primum, nunc vero gratitudinis ergo in illustrissimi principis Caroli Britannicaeque Gallicae & Hybernicae*. Londini: Excudebat Georgius Millerus.

Domínguez Leal, J. M. (2007). La poesía macarrónica en España: definiciones y ejemplos. *Per Abbat: boletín filológico de actualización académica y didáctica*, 2, pp. 103–110.

Erasmus, D. (1568). *Apophthegmatum ex optimis utriusque linguae scriptoribus per Des. Erasmum Roterodamum collectorum libri octo*. Lugduni: apud Ioan. Tornaesium et Gul. Gazeium.

Habrecht, I. (1629). *Ianua linguarum silinguis, latina, germanica, gallica, italica, hispanica, anglica sive modus ad integritatem linguarum compendio cognoscendam maxime accommodatus*, Argentinae: Sumptibus Eberhardi Zetzneri.

Maestre Maestre, J. M. (2007). El Brocense contra el inglés Henry Jason: una nueva interpretación de la paradoja *Latine loqui corrumpit ipsam Latinitatem* y de sus posteriores cambios textuales. *Humanistica lovaniensia: Journal of Neo-Latin Studies*, 56, pp. 181–231.

Mantuna, S. P. Ó. (1986). *William Bathe, S. J., 1564–1614: A Pioneer in Linguistics*, Amsterdam and Philadelphia: John Benjamins.

Riccius, B. (1599) *Bartholomaei Riccii de imitatione libri tres ad Alfonsum Aestium principem*, Venetiis MDXXXXIX.

Strebaeus, L. (1540). *De electione et oratoria collocatione verborum libri duo*, Parisiis: apud Michaëlem Vascosanum.

Valerius, C. (1575). *Grammaticarum institutionum libri IIII*, Coloniae Agrippinae: Apud haeredes Arnoldi Birckmanni.

7 Pro lingua Latina

Girolamo Lagomarsini's Oration in Defence of Latin in Eighteenth-Century Italy[1]

Juan María Gómez Gómez

Introduction

During the first half of the eighteenth century, the Italian States (Tuscany, Genoa, Naples, and Venice), influenced by the enlightened currents coming from Western Europe (mainly France and England), began to feel the need to reorganise their education systems at both university and middle (pre-university or para-university) level. The reformist pedagogues believed that education should serve to form good citizens acting in the interests of the state rather than the Catholic Church or Pope. Thus, attempts were made to impose a utilitarian style of teaching to the detriment of the traditional Humanities curriculum, largely in order to wrest the monopoly of education from the religious orders, especially the Jesuits. For this purpose, attempts were made to attract teachers with more innovative ideas, enlightened intellectuals from different parts of Europe. The result was an opening-up of Italy to the Cartesian rationalism and Jansenism of Port Royal, which began to take root in Florence from the 1730s, with attempts to apply their methods for the teaching of more practical subjects (Balani and Roggero, 1976: 65; Venturi, 1998: Chapters 1 and 4).

In this context, the study of the vernacular languages took precedence to the detriment of Latin, especially in primary and middle education, as had already been happening in France from the second half of the seventeenth century (Garin, 1987: 245–251; Pieroni Francini, 2002; Espino Martín, 2010). Modern enlightened pedagogues brought with them the notion that Latin, the basic pillar of the Jesuit curriculum, was an obstacle to progress (Brizzi, 1995; Stiffoni, 1988). The vernaculars had, of course, undergone unprecedented development in the sixteenth and seventeenth centuries, and Spanish, French, English and Italian were now all languages of literary and cultural transmission in Europe (Garin, 1987: 245). French, for its part, had already begun to impose itself as the language of international diplomacy.

In Italy, as in other parts of Europe, Latin was the basic language used in grammar schools until the end of the seventeenth century (IJsewijn,

DOI: 10.4324/9781003092445-10

1990: 62; Sacré, 2014: 879–903). But in the Settecento, Italian was also introduced into schools, and texts written in that language became models for teaching alongside those in Latin. Thus, the privileged place that Latin had traditionally occupied as the basic language for teaching and culture started to be questioned in Italy too (Garin, 1987: 245 ss.; Marazzini, 2002: 355; Migliorini, 1978: 519–522).

In this way, a controversy was generated about the importance that Latin should have in relation to Romance in education and the transmission of culture. As in other parts of Europe, modern pedagogues considered that mastery of Latin was only necessary for a minority of young people destined to become members of the intellectual elites, while those destined to work in agriculture, crafts and trade were better served by the modern syllabus that would prepare them to contribute to the progress of the state (Marazzini, 2002: 358).

It was in this context that we encounter the figure of Spanish-Italian Jesuit teacher Girolamo Lagomarsini (1698–1773),[2] as a defender of Latin. Between 1734 and 1740, he gave a series of seven lectures in Florence, six defending the educational system used in the schools of the Society of Jesus, and one extolling the figure of François Étienne de Lorraine, Great Duke of Tuscany (1737–1765).[3] The *editio princeps* of these orations was printed in Augsburg (*Augusta Vindelicorum*) in 1740,[4] which means that it would not have included the third of his orations devoted to the defence of state schools, which was only delivered in that year (this appears in the 1753 edition printed in Rome). The titles of the lectures are sufficiently eloquent: I. *Multam dandam esse litteris, at non multis operam* ("One should dedicate much endeavour to the study of Humanities, but only to a few of its branches") (1734); II. *Pro Grammaticis Italiae scholis*, ("In defence of Italy's grammar schools") (1735); III. *Pro lingua Latina*, ("In defence of the Latin language") (1736); IV. *Pro scholis publicis prima* ("First oration in defence of state schools") (1737); V. *Pro scholis publicis secunda* ("Second oration in defence of state schools") (1738); VI. *In adventu Francisci tertii, Lotharingiae, Barri et magni Etruriae ducis ad Florentinos* ("Oration upon the arrival of Francis III, Duke of Lorraine and Bar and Grand Duke of Etruria, before the Florentines") (1739); VII. *Pro scholis publicis tertia* ("Third oration in defence of state schools") (1740).[5]

The oration that we will look at here, the *Pro lingua Latina* (Florence, 1736), constitutes a valuable testimony to the frequent conflicts between Jesuits and enlightened rationalist pedagogues, the former attempting to retain their monopoly on education and the latter bent on taking it away "for the sake of progress and benefit of the State". In this oration, Lagomarsini focuses on defending Latin in the socio-pedagogical context of Tuscany in the first half of the eighteenth century against the pedagogical tendencies of Port Royal, which, among other aspects, promoted the use of the vernacular languages in education, as we have said.

Through the progressive exposition and commentary of the most relevant passages of the oration, we will show how the Jesuit bases his defence not only on arguments related to the cultural dignity of the Latin language but also (crucially) on utilitarian principles, a basic criterion for the reformist proposals.

Arguments for the dignity and utility of Latin in the *Pro lingua Latina* oration

According to the title, this lecture was delivered in Florence on the *idus* of January 1736 (i.e. on the thirteenth of that month).[6]

The discussion about the need or not for Latin, and the suitability or otherwise of its study in schools, was a very topical matter in the first half of the eighteenth century. It is well known that the Jesuits attached great importance to the study of Latinity in their schools and this was one of the fundamental reasons why it was critiqued by enlightened reformers, who attempted, for pragmatic reasons, to impose the study of the vernacular languages, and other "useful" subjects, to the detriment of Latin. Lagomarsini will conclude that Latin must coexist together with vernaculars since they are equally worthy languages in terms of intrinsic dignity, but that Latin is ultimately more useful than Italian and its different dialects. Let's look closer at the progression of his argument.

From the beginning, linking the exordium with the *narratio*, Lagomarsini poses a general *quaestio*: whether the Italian language is preferable to Latin or Latin to Italian – a dilemma long debated by learned men.[7] Indeed, the assessment of how one's own language ranked in relation to others had been a constant in Europe throughout the Early Modern period, particularly with the rise of the nation states (Burke, 2004: 61–68). However, the Italian states – due to their special connection with Latin – had maintained a more conservative position towards the medieval lingua franca.

In fact, each state defended its language as the best. On some occasions, it was argued that a particular tongue had a privileged connection with a supposed first, natural and more perfect language, from which all the others had emerged (Eco, 1994). On other occasions, the supremacy of a particular language was defended in more rational terms on the grounds that it reflected the spirit of the people who spoke it, meaning that a people that was more developed, scientifically and rationally, would have a language that was more elaborate, complex and profound than those of the culturally less developed. This would produce a close link between language and culture.[8]

Throughout the eighteenth century, there was an abundance of treatises comparing languages, or examining the different manifestations of a particular language at various stages of its history, usually emphasising qualities such as harmoniousness, majesty, purity, clarity or lexical abundance. Prominent representatives of this kind of treatise included Benito Jerónimo Feijoo (1676–1764), Gregorio Mayans (1699–1781) and Antonio Capmany (1742–1813) in eighteenth-century Spain (Checa Beltrán, 1991; Lázaro, 1985), and Ludovico Antonio Muratori (1672–1750), Giovanni Vincenzo Gravina (1664–1718) and Melchiorre Cesarotti (1730–1808) in the Italian Settecento (Puppo, 1966). Lagomarsini would obviously have been aware of these controversies.

But Lagomarsini, from the beginning of his oration, does not involve himself with these disquisitions; indeed, he refuses to defend the superiority of one language over another in terms of innate linguistic dignity. According to him, the learned men who spent so much time on such disputes failed to consider a fundamental axiom: namely, that no language is intrinsically superior to another, but that it is the users of it who confer such attributes upon it.

> [...] Thus, first of all, the discourse of those who assume to affirm a language and elevate it above the others must be established and the following must be stated as an irrefutable principle: that one and the same is the communicative capacity and the nature of all languages, and that no one surpasses another for its intrinsic dignity, but for the opinion of men [...]
>
> (Lagomarsini, 1753: 52)[9]

Next, Lagomarsini admits that people from different regions believe their respective languages to have natural qualities, though no one, including language scholars, has been unable to agree as to which language possesses these qualities to the greatest degree (Lagomarsini 1753: 52–54). In the light of this disagreement, Lagomarsini raises the possibility that there might be one main language (*principem*), even while admitting that all languages are intrinsically equally worthy. Using one of the *exordium* formulas (*captatio benivolentia a rebus*, i.e. giving importance to the topic that will be covered), he affirms that this is a very important topic (*res praeclara*) that deserves to be discussed (*digna in quam conferamus*):

> [...] Can we agree Etruscans with Gauls, Gauls with Hispanics, but, above all, Latins both with the above mentioned peoples and with the others who compete over the primacy of their language, and make that, once deposed their rivalry, all choose a single language as the main one and equally all recognize that, even though theirs is not the main one, yet it is not inferior to any other in dignity? In my opinion, we can; and it is a really important matter and worthy of us contributing to it what we can [...]
>
> (Lagomarsini, 1753: 53)[10]

This concludes the *exordium* joined to the *narratio*.

Lagomarsini now moves on to the *argumentatio*. Assuming that languages are similar as regards their intrinsic value, Lagomarsini claims that external factors determine whether one language is to be considered more worthy than another,[11] the opinion a community has rather than the nature of people or things.[12] Lagomarsini then wonders what specific criteria might contribute to that favourable opinion. One determining factor, he suggests, is the number of excellent writers who wrote in that language.[13] In this sense, the community of speakers would consider languages more or less important depending on the greater or lesser number of excellent writers who had written in them and not on the expressive capacity nor on the nature of the language itself; by their nature, languages would be equally worthy.[14] But Lagomarsini is aware that a dilemma could arise, one which he exemplifies with the figures of Cicero and Petrarch. Do writers decide to write in a given language because the community considers it to be the most dignified, or is the language deemed to be more worthy due to the fact that the best writers write in it?[...] For example:

> What do you think? That Cicero has chosen and used the Latin language, Petrarch the Etruscan, and likewise that some good writers have chosen and used some languages and other good writers others – which we confess that they have excelled and made them distinguished, for so to speak, and valued by learned men – mainly because these languages were better than the others? Or do you think that these languages have become better than the others mainly because were chosen and used by men?" [...]
> (Lagomarsini, 1753: 62–63)[15]

Lagomarsini is clearly in favour of the second option: "I think the latter is the really true; the former is completely false" (Lagomarsini, 1753: 63),[16] he says. The best writers are those who give dignity[17] to their languages by using the style they work with best (Lagomarsini, 1753: 65); a "humble" *a priori* language can be elegant if it has authors who know how to exploit its resources (Lagomarsini, 1753: 66).

Thereafter, Lagomarsini continues to defend Latin by providing analogies with what happened with Greek in ancient Rome. This gradually leads to arguments about the utility of Latin. Lagomarsini says that even in the golden age of Latin literature when Roman letters enjoyed the highest consideration due to authors such as Cicero, Virgil and Horace, the study of Greek was not neglected in Rome; rather, it was eagerly studied from childhood (Friedlander, 1944; Marrou, 1985: 314–343; Blumenthal and Kahane, 1979; Joyal *et al.* 2009: 151 ss.).

> [...] But, if Latins were ever able to agree with their achievements, it was at the time that Tullius, Virgil, Horace and other excellent

writers flourished, whose teaching and elegance of discourse made us call their time the Golden Age. [...] Still, during that illustrious and productive golden age, although it seemed that nothing was lacking in Lazio as far as any of the liberal arts were concerned, nothing that had not been treated and perfected by the Latin writers themselves from these same disciplines, however, Latins not only did not neglect Greek studies, but practiced it uninterruptedly and with great diligence from childhood. [...]

(Lagomarsini, 1753: 74–75)[18]

What is more, the Romans endeavoured to translate the works of the Greeks, if only to prevent Greek literature from being lost. Cicero, for example, translated the *Phaenomena* of Arato, *Oeconomica* of Xenophont and Plato's *Timeus*, and came to recognise in *De oratore* (1,155) that the translation of Greek speeches by the best orators enabled him to refine his vocabulary and even to introduce neologisms into the Latin language.[19] Therefore, if the Romans acted this way with the Greek legacy, it will have been because the practice was useful or, at least, ennobling; hence, the Florentines, and contemporary Italians in general, should be inspired by the good practices of their illustrious ancestors to act in a similar manner.

Indeed, there have been distinguished Italian orators and poets that have proceeded in a similar way with Latin works, such as the illustrious "Christian Cicero", the Jesuit Paolo Segneri (1624–1694),[20] who polished his style by reading, explaining and translating Cicero's orations against Verres into Italian; and before him, the most excellent poet Torcuato Tasso (1544–1595), to whom an Italian translation of the *Aeneid* has been attributed (Lagomarsini 1753: 76). Thus, Lagomarsini fully recognises the usefulness of translating Latin works into Italian, both to develop the resources of the vernaculars and to make those Latin works accessible to those who do not know Latin. The Romans did the same with Greek works by translating them into Latin.[21]

These arguments for the study of Latin could be more easily accepted in Italy than in any other part of Europe since Italians had a greater awareness of the extent to which their vulgar tongue derived from Latin. Thus, it was appreciated that a good knowledge of classical Latin would naturally lead to a deeper mastery of the vernacular language (Garin, 1987: 91). And although the fifteenth and sixteenth centuries constituted the main period of neo-Latin literature, Latin continued to play a vital role in poetry, history and didactic prose in the seventeenth century and the first half of the eighteenth in Italy, as elsewhere in Europe (IJsewijn, 1990: 39–82; Sacré, 2014: 879–903).

On the other hand, regarding criticisms from modern pedagogues that teaching Latin was a waste of time, Lagomarsini is clear that his criterion is quite different from theirs (he refers to this rather contemptuously through his use of the demonstrative pronoun in the genitive and nominative masculine plural: *istorum... isti*). He believes that it would take much longer, and involve much greater effort, to teach the sciences and arts in the vernacular languages of the various nations – ancient and modern – rather than to simply teach them in Latin, since they would have to learn several languages instead of just one.[22] This, he says, can be achieved by anybody who is not stupid or lazy and who is prepared to invest some degree of effort.[23] However, those kind and compassionate men, who release us from the duty of learning Latin with their methods, force us, at the same time, to learn Latin alongside other languages.[24]

This is, once again, a pragmatic argument. Lagomarsini is advocating that Latin remain a *lingua franca* of education, in opposition to the modern enlightened pedagogy of the Jansenists (and other religious orders, such as Oratorians and Piarists) who advocated that young people be educated in the vernacular language (Nava, 1992: 86-88; Espino Martín, 2010).

Closely related to this, Lagomarsini argues at the end of his oration that when someone chooses to write in their vernacular language – either out of personal desire or through ignorance of Latin – they effectively condemn those works to obscurity.[25] It is therefore preferable that knowledge that is useful to all be written in a language that is known by everyone, such as Latin.[26]

Thus, Lagomarsini defends Latin as the vehicular language of scientific exchange, thereby wading into the ongoing controversy about which vehicular language should be used for science (Puppo, 1966: 17). He does so by using a pragmatic argument, which, *mutatis mutandis*, is not very far removed from those put forward later by the illustrious encyclopaedists Jean le Rond D'Alembert (a very forthright critic of the pedagogical methods used by the Jesuits) and Nicolas Beauzée. As Waquet points out (Waquet, 1998: 310–311), D'Alembert, in his *Discours préliminaire de l'Encyclopédie*, recognised that Latin could be useful for the transmission of philosophy, since such works require a high degree of clarity and precision, and proposes recovering Latin as a universal philosophical language (although he was skeptical about whether this could be achieved). D'Alembert approved the widespread practice of writing in the vulgar languages, but he also warned about the dangers of it: for if each philosopher (he was referring to any person of science) wrote in their vernacular tongue, then a philosopher interested in knowing about the advances of his colleagues would have to learn seven or eight different languages, and would spend most of his time doing this – time that would be taken away from his real task of apprehending and acquiring the knowledge transported by these works.

As for Beauzée, he also supported Latin as a lingua franca of science in his article "Langue" of the *Encyclopédie*. Thus, after presenting Latin as the "langue commune de tous les savants de l'Europe", he goes on to say that its use should be generalised in the domain of science in order to facilitate the international communication of the scientific achievements of each nation; otherwise, many scientific works would remain unknown due to a lack of understanding of the language in which they are written (Waquet, 1998: 385, n. 27).

All in all, it is clear that these philosophers of the *Encyclopédie* – and in general the enlightened thinkers who advocated Latin as a lingua franca of cultural and scientific exchange – were thinking only of extending it among the socio-cultural elites of the time, those who had access to the universities where Latin continued to be used (Waquet, 2015). For the rest of the population – those engaged in agriculture, crafts, or trade, that is, for the majority of people – it would not be necessary to learn Latin. Indeed, it was felt that its extensive use would actually delay the progress of the state, as mentioned above.

Thus, Lagomarsini, at the end of his speech, establishes that Italian, which has a rich (*copiosus*) and useful (*commodus*) lexicon, has been cultivated by the best authors and is therefore indispensable for both Italians and those who live among them, should coexist alongside Latin. However, Italian should not compete in terms of dignity with Latin, since Latin is not inferior to Italian in its expressive force and is superior as regards the importance attributed to it and its usefulness:

> [...] The Italian language will grow, I say, it will grow in Italy, and it will not be destroyed by any circumstances or contingency. And that it really grows, because it is abundant in terms, appropriate, refined, it is polished and perfected by the greatest geniuses and it is indispensable both for us Italians and for those who live among Italians. However, that it is very condescending with Latin and does not rival it in dignity, **because, as it has been shown, Latin by its expressive capacity and by its nature is not inferior to Italian at all, it is more, according to the opinion of all peoples and for its own usefulness, Latin is far superior.** I said. [...]
>
> (Lagomarsini, 1753: 84)[27]

Lagomarsini concludes in this way by returning to the initial idea, at least as far as Latin and Italian are concerned: that languages, according to strictly linguistic criteria, are equally worthy, and that what makes them superior are external factors such as opinions held about them. But, in addition to this, he also highlights utility as a fundamental criterion for maintaining the study of Latin.

Final remarks

As I said at the beginning, my main interest in this work has been to bring to light a sample of eighteenth-century deliberative rhetoric in which a Jesuit, Lagomarsini, makes a forceful plea in defence of the teaching of Latin against the Jansenist pedagogical methods and reforms spreading throughout Europe. At a time when enlightened pedagogues judged the importance of a discipline by its usefulness to the state, Lagomarsini bases his defence of Latin mainly on utilitarian arguments: the exercise of Latin translation enriches the resources of the vernacular language while contributing to the dissemination of culture and facilitating access to knowledge.

Of course, Lagomarsini, in this lecture, is also pursuing a pragmatic objective on behalf of the Society of Jesus. By defending one of the fundamental pillars of the Jesuit curriculum, namely the teaching of Latin, he no doubt hoped to contribute to the perpetuation of the secular socio-educational monopoly that the Society of Jesus had exercised over society in general and the nobility in particular since the sixteenth century (Brizzi, 1976). But it is also clear that Latin continued to be an important tool for humanistic and scientific learning, particularly in the universities. Thus, its usefulness remained evident in the eighteenth century, and to deny less privileged classes the opportunity of learning it would effectively remove a means by which they could access much of the culture and knowledge of the time, thereby depriving them of an important tool for reflection and progress.

Notes

1. This chapter was prepared in the context of the projects "Grammars in Europe (17th and 18th centuries). Studies and editions" (FFI2016-78496-P), financed by the Ministerio de Economía, Industria y Competitividad – Agencia Estatal de Investigación and by the European Regional Development Fund, and "Text and images from memory II: Arts of memory and rhetoric in the fifteenth and sixteenth centuries" (FFI2017-82101-P), financed by the Ministerio de Ciencia, Innovación y Universidades – Agencia Estatal de Investigación and by the European Regional Development Fund. I thank Professor Sánchez Salor for his corrections and suggestions for this chapter.
2. On the life and works of Lagomarsini, see Astorgano, n.d.: s.v. Lagomarsini, Girolamo; Zanfredini (2001): s.v. Lagomarsini, Girolamo; Arato (2014): s.v. Lagomarsini, Girolamo. These dictionary entries make use of ancient bibliographic sources about Lagomarsini.
3. This is Francis (1708–1765), Holy Roman Emperor and Grand Duke of Tuscany.
4. *Hieronymi Lagomarsini e Societate Jesu, Orationes publice dictae Florentiae ab ipso auctore, studiorum ibidem praefecto, et iam cum speciali per provinciam Germaniae superioris Soc. Iesu facultate,* Typis impressae Augustae Vindelicorum, A Joanne Michaële Labhart, Reverendiss. et Celsiss. Principis et Episcopi Augustani ac Civitatis Typographo, 1740.
5. I shall be using the edition *Hieronymi Lagomarsinii e Societate Jesu, Orationes septem: editio sexta retractior et auctior. Accedit epistola semel jam edita, qua quid in M. Tulli Ciceronis contra L. Pisonem oratione interciderit demonstratur.* Romae: typis Generosi Salomoni, 1753, for all examples of oration *Pro lingua Latina*. At present, we are working on a critic edition of these orations with their Spanish translation.

6. *Pro lingua Latina* habita Florentiae idibus Januarii MDCCXXXVI. Coram Francisco Maria Martellio Archiepiscopo.

(Lagomarsini, 1753: 51)

7. Diu multumque, quod non ignoratis, Florentini, ab eruditissimis viris quaesitum est italicane latinae, an italicae latina lingua praestaret

(Lagomarsini, 1753: 51)

8. See Sánchez (2019: 172–173); Puppo (1966: 21), commenting the main ideas of Muratori.

9. [...] *Illud igitur ante omnia ponendum est in oratione eius qui linguam aliquam commendandam prae reliquis atque efferandam suscipit, idque omni vera ratione confirmandum: unam esse omnium linguarum atque eamdem vim ac naturam; neque ullam ulli sua ipsius dignitate, sed hominum opinione praestare* [...] (Lagomarsini 1753: 52). The author of the chapter has modernised the punctuation of Latin texts and translated them into English to facilitate their understanding.

10. [...] Possumus Etruscos Gallis, Gallos Hispanis, praesertim vero Latinos et iis et reliquis qui de linguae principatu contendunt conciliare; et efficere ut, depositis simultatibus, unam omnes principem deligant, atque ita suam non esse principem fateantur, ut nulli tamen de dignitate concedat? Possumus, ut opinor; et profecto praeclara res est et digna, in quam, quidquid possumus, conferamus. [...].

(Lagomarsini, 1753: 53)

11. [...] Nam, ut omnes sermones vi sua sint atque ipsa natura pares, illud tamen reliquitur, ut alter alteri extrinsecus adiectis atque attributis dotibus praestare possit [...].

(Lagomarsini, 1753: 59)

12. [...] Sed neque linguarum praestantiam illam neque hominum hanc nobilitatem rerum ipsarum natura facit, sed, quemadmodum dictum est, opinio. Tolle opinionem; fient continuo omnia paria [...].

(Lagomarsini, 1753: 60)

13. [...] Qua in re tamen id esse eos potissimum sequutos possumus animadvertere, ut, quae linguae scriptoribus optimis abundarent, praeferrent eas ferme reliquis [...].

(Lagomarsini, 1753: 61)

14. [...] si consensu hominum eae linguae reliquis praelatae sunt, quibus excellentes scriptores esse usos viderunt, non vi sua atque natura linguas linguis, sed ipsorum hominum opinione ac voluntate praestare ac propterea, si per se ipsae spectentur, esse omnes inter se pares [...].

(Lagomarsini, 1753: 61–62)

15. [...] Nam quid putatis? Ciceronem, exempli causa, latinam linguam, Petrarcham etruscam, bonos item scriptores alios alias earum, quas ab iis illustratas, et tamquam nobiles factas, eruditisque hominibus commendatas fatemur, delegisse potissimum atque usurpasse, quod eae reliquis meliores essent; an ideo reliquis eas factas esse meliores, quod ab iis delectae potissimum atque usurpatae sint? [...].

(Lagomarsini, 1753: 62–63)

16. Equidem hoc alterum verissimum iudico: primum illum omnino falsum.

(Lagomarsini, 1753: 63)

17. Lagomarsini, in this point, agrees with one of the main opinions of Muratori in his teatrise *Della perfetta poesia italiana* (Módena, 1706) (Puppo, 1966: 21, 128–129).

18. [...] Quod si umquam latini contenti suis esse potuerunt, fuit id certe per ea tempora, quibus Tullius, Virgilius, Horatius aliique praestantissimi scrip-

tores floruerunt, quorum tum doctrina tum sermonis elegantia factum est, ut illorum illam aetatem Auream nominaremus. [...] Exacta autem aurea illa felicique aetate, cum nihil Latio deesse videretur, quod quidem ad liberales quasque disciplinas pertineret, quod non ab suis ipsorum scriptoribus et tractatum et perfectum esset, graeca tamen studia a latinis non modo non negligebantur, verum a prima usque pueritia diligentissime colebantur [...].

(Lagomarsini, 1753: 74–75)

19. [...] At certe, inquiunt, multa graecorum in latinum sermonem romani homines convertebant [...] Quaedam ex graeco sermone Cicero in latinum transtulit, Arati Phaenomena, Xenophontis Oeconomica, Platonis Timaeum [...].

(Lagomarsini, 1753: 75–76)

20. Paolo Segneri, the Elder (Nettuno, 1624 – Rome, 1694) was an Italian Jesuit, preacher, missionary and ascetical writer. He entered the Society of Jesu I 1637. After St Bernardine of Siena (1380–1444) and Girolamo Savonarola (1452–1498), Segneri was considered one of the greatest Italian orators.

21. [...] Italice scripturis utile est, quemadmodum olim latinis latine graeca convertere, sic iis horum latine scripta, italica interpretando facere; neque vero ipsis modo, verum iis etiam qui latine nesciunt, est id vehementer utile [...].

(Lagomarsini, 1753: 76–77)

22. [...] Ego enim sic statuo: multo esse ad diuturnitatem longius, multo ad laborem molestiamque gravius, si vernacula lingua, quam si latina, doctrinae artesque tradantur. Thus, if they are transmitted in Latin, it is sufficient with learning Latin well: Etenim, si hoc fiat, satis est latinam linguam ab litterarum studiosis perdisci, [...].

(Lagomarsini, 1753: 77)

23. id quod labore certe aliquo, at non admodum improbo, at non sane diuturno consequi non hebes neque indiligens quivis potest [...].

(Lagomarsini, 1753: 77)

24. [...] Isti autem misericordes homines atque humani, ut nos labore latinam linguam discendi levent, tum latinam ipsam nos discere, tum reliquas omnes praeterea cogunt [...].

(Lagomarsini, 1753: 78)

25. [...] Verum hoc tantum popularium linguarum studium, et haec nonnullorum patrio sermone scribendi sive voluntas, quod ita malunt, sive necessitas, quod latine non possunt, facit ut et illi nostris, et nos illorum litteris indigeamus.

(Lagomarsini, 1753: 83)

26. At certe utrique malle debemus ut quae cognita sunt omnibus profutura, ea ab omnibus non ignoto, ut cuique sunt fere peregrini, sed noto, qualis latinus est, sermone scribantur [...].

(Lagomarsini, 1753: 83)

27. [...] Vigebit, vigebit, inquam, italicus in Italia sermo, nec ullo umquam tempore, aut ulla peregrinitate delebitur. Et vigeat sane, nam et copiosus est, et commodus, et summis ingeniis excultus atque perfectus, et certe nobis, sive italis, sive inter italos agentibus, necessarius. Verumtamen latino plurimum tribuat, nec cum illo de dignitate contendat: **qui, quemadmodum ostensus est, sua vi atque natura nihilo inferior est, omnium vero gentium opinione, atque ipsa utilitate, multo superior. Dixi.**

(Lagomarsini, 1753: 84)

References

Primary sources

Lagomarsini, G. (1740). *Hieronymi Lagomarsini e Societate Jesu, Orationes publice dictae Florentiae ab ipso auctore, studiorum ibidem praefecto, et iam cum speciali per provinciam Germaniae superioris Soc. Iesu facultate.* Typis impressae Augustae Vindelicorum, A Joanne Michaële Labhart, Reverendiss. et Celsiss. Principis et Episcopi Augustani ac Civitatis Typographo. Available at: https://books.google.es/books?id=1kmUvAXrIGoC [Accessed on 17 Feb. 2021].

Lagomarsini, G. (1753). *Hieronymi Lagomarsinii e Societate Jesu, Orationes septem: editio sexta retractior et auctior. Accedit epistola semel jam edita, qua quid in M. Tulli Ciceronis contra L. Pisonem oratione interciderit demonstratur.* Romae: typis Generosi Salomoni. Available at: https://books.google.es/books?id=MaYBDwFCxawC. [Accessed on 17 Feb. 2021].

Secondary sources

Arato, F. (2014). Lagomarsini, Girolamo, In: *Dizionario Biografico degli Italiani*, Vol. 63. Available at: http://www.treccani.it/enciclopedia/girolamo-lagomarsini_(Dizionario-Biografico)/. [Accessed on 17 Feb. 2021].

Astorgano, A. (n. d.). Lagomarsini, Girolamo. In: *Diccionario Biográfico de la Real Academia de la Historia*. Available at: http://dbe.rah.es/biografias/47200/girolamo-lagomarsini. [Accessed on 17 Feb. 2021].

Balani, D. and Roggero, M. (1976). *La scuola in Italia della controriforma al secolo dei lumi*. Torino: Loescher Editore.

Blumenthal, H. and Kahane, R. (1979). Decline and survival of western prestige languages. *Language*, 55(1), pp. 183–198. Available at: https://www.jstor.org/stable/412522 [Accessed on 17 Feb. 2021].

Brizzi, G. P. (1976). *La formazione della classe dirigente nel Sei-Settecento. I seminaria nobilium nell' Italia centro-settentrionale*. Bologna: Il Mulino.

Brizzi, G. P. (1995). Les jésuites et l'école en Italie (XVI–XVIII siècles). In: Giard, L. ed., *Les jésuites à la Renaissance: Système éducatif et production du savoir*. Paris: Presses Universitaires de France, pp. 35–53.

Burke, P. (2004). *Languages and Communities in Early Modern Europe*. Cambridge: Cambridge University Press.

Checa Beltrán, J. (1991). Paralelos de lenguas en el siglo XVIII: de Feijoo a Vargas Ponce (1726–1793). *Revista de Literatura (RLit)*, 53(106), pp. 485–512. Available at: http://digital.csic.es/handle/10261/12437 [Accessed on 17 Feb. 2021].

Eco, U. (1994). *La búsqueda de la lengua perfecta en la cultura europea*. Translated by Pons, M. Barcelona: Crítica.

Espino Martín, J. (2010). Enseñanza del latín e historia de las ideas. La revolución de Port-Royal y su repercusión en Francia y España durante el siglo XVIII. *Minerva*, 23, pp. 261–284.

Friedlander, P. (1944). The Greek behind Latin. *The Classical Journal*, 39(5), pp. 270–277. Available at: http://www.jstor.org/stable/3292418 [Accessed on 17 Feb. 2021].

Garin, E. (1987). *La educación en Europa, 1400–1600. Problemas y programas*. Translated by Méndez, M. E. Barcelona: Crítica.
IJsewijn, J. (1990). *Companion to Neo-Latin Studies: Part. I. History and Diffusion of Neo-Latin Literature*. Second entirely rewritten edition. Louvain: Peeters.
Joyal, M., McDougall, I. and Yardley, J. C. (2009). *Greek and Roman Education: A Sourcebook*. London and New York: Routledge.
Lázaro, F. (1985). *Las ideas lingüísticas en España durante el siglo XVIII*. Barcelona: Crítica.
Marazzini, C. (2002). *La lingua italiana*, Bologna: Il Mulino.
Marrou, H. I. (1985). *Historia de la educación en la Antigüedad*. Translated by Vargas, Y. Madrid: Akal.
Migliorini, B. (1978). *Storia della lingua italiana*. Firenze: Sansoni Editore.
Nava, M. T. (1992). *La educación en la Europa moderna*, Madrid: Síntesis.
Pieroni Francini, M. (2002). Los Jansenistas y la Escuela. *Cuadernos de Historia Moderna. Anejos, I*, pp. 127–150.
Puppo, M., ed. (1966). *Discussioni linguistiche del Settecento*. Torino: Unione Tipografico – Editrice Torinese.
Sacré, D. (2014). Neo-Latin Prose in the Twilight Years (1700–Present). In: Ford, P., Bloemendal J. and Fantazzi C., eds., *Brill's Encyclopaedia of the Neo-Latin World. Macropaedia*. Leiden and Boston: Brill, pp. 879–903.
Sánchez, E. (2019). *Gramática del siglo XVIII, Gramática y Lógica, Gramática y Lingüística, Gramática Escolar*. Alcañiz: Instituto de Estudios Humanísticos and Lisboa: Centro de Estudos Clássicos.
Stiffoni, G. (1988). Ilustración y educación en Italia. In: Ministerio de Educación y Ciencia. *Simposium internacional sobre Educación e Ilustración: Dos siglos de Reformas en la Enseñanza. Ponencias*. Madrid: Centro de Publicaciones del Ministerio de Educación y Ciencia, pp. 67–92.
Venturi, F. (1998). *Settecento riformatore I. Da Muratori a Beccaria*. Torino: Einaudi.
Waquet, F. (1998). *Le Latin ou l'empire d'un signe, XVIe–XXe siecle*. Paris: Albin Michel.
Waquet, F. (2015). Latin et vernaculaires dans l'Université du XVIIIe siècle/ Latin and Vernacular Languages in the Eighteenth-Century University". In: Bloemendal, J. ed., *Latin and Vernacular Cultures: Examples of Bilingualism c. 1300–1800*, Leiden – Boston: Brill Studies in Intellectual History, Vol. 239, pp. 176–186.
Zanfredini, M. (2001). Lagomarsini, Girolamo. In: O'Neil, C. E. and Domínguez, J. M. (S.I.), eds., *Diccionario histórico de la S.I. Biográfico, temático*, Roma: Institutum Historicum S.I and Madrid: Universidad Pontificia Comillas, Vol 3.

8 Petropolis
The Place of Latin in Early Modern Russia[1]

Brian P. Bennett

Foreign visitors to Muscovy often remarked on the Russian ignorance of classical languages. According to Richard Chancellor, an Englishman who travelled there in 1553, "All studies and letters of humanity they utterly refuse; concerning the Latin, Greek, and Hebrew tongues, they are altogether ignorant in them" (Chancellor, 1968: 36). In 1582 Antonio Possevino, a Jesuit priest and papal legate, met with Ivan the Terrible and discussed the relationship between the Catholic and Orthodox Churches. In his subsequent report, he remarks that "the only language the Muscovites know is their own" and "The Muscovites possess only a handful of people who know Latin" (Possevino, 1977: 52–53). In his account of 1647, the German scholar and diplomat Adam Olearius states: "no Russian, whether ecclesiastic or layman, of high rank or low, understands a word of Greek or Latin" (1967: 238). Elsewhere he writes that Russians are completely ignorant of arts and sciences. And so, when "you observe the spirit, the mores, and the way of life of the Russians, you are bound to number them among the barbarians" (130). In *A Curious and New Account of Muscovy in the Year 1689*, Foy de la Neuville, the *nom de plume* of an unknown diplomat, claims that "Only four in that whole, vast country speak Latin" (1994: 24). Later in the text, he offers a sweeping judgement of Russian character: "To tell the truth, the Muscovites are barbarians. They are suspicious and mistrustful, cruel, sodomites, gluttons, misers, beggars and cowards ..." (1994: 57). These authors connect the absence of classical languages with supposed Russian backwardness (Poe, 2002: 149). The lack of Latin, in particular, led some to conclude that "the Muscovites were not Europeans and scarcely Christians" (Okenfuss, 1995: 4). Despite the self-serving nature of this Early-Modern version of ethnography – they are ignorant and crude; we are learned and cultured – it is true that Latin was for all intents and purposes *lingua non grata* in the Muscovite principality.

Now imagine a visitor a century after de la Neuville, around 1790. The Tsardom of Muscovy has become the Russian Empire. It is re-centred on St. Petersburg, Peter the Great's "window onto Europe," sometimes referred to in Graecised-Latinised form as Petropolis. With its canals

DOI: 10.4324/9781003092445-11

and maritime climate, the city was often likened to Amsterdam or Venice. Others proclaimed it a new Rome (Wes, 1992: 40). Strolling through the new capital, our imaginary sightseer could stop at the Imperial Academy of Sciences and attend a lecture being delivered in Latin or peruse volumes of the institute's flagship journal, *Commentarii Academiae Scientiarum Imperialis Petropolitanae* (Transactions of the Imperial Academy of Sciences of St. Petersburg). Having crossed from Vasilievsky Island to the main part of the city, wandering along the grand boulevards, this time-traveller might catch sight here and there of Latin inscriptions, perhaps accompanied by figures from antiquity like Mars, Neptune or Hercules. The best-known specimen of Latin in the city is the laconic inscription on the pedestal of the famous Bronze Horseman statue of Peter the Great:

PETRO PRIMO CATHARINA SECUNDA MDCCLXXXII
[To Peter the First from Catharine the Second, 1782]
(Budaragina, 2010: 75–76)

Continuing down to the end of Nevsky Prospect, the city's main thoroughfare, our visitor would reach the Slavonic-Greek-Latin Seminary, which was established in 1726 and later renamed the Alexander Nevsky Seminary. Latin occupied a central place in the curriculum. For example, a Latin-language homiletics manual, *Rhetoricae sacrae de inventione argumentorum et moendis affectibus libri duo. Conscripti in usum studiosorum Seminarii Petripolitani Alexandro-Nevensis,* [Two Books on Sacred Rhetoric: On the Arrangement of Arguments and Emotional Appeals. Written for Use by Students at the Alexander Nevsky Seminary in St. Petersburg] would be published in 1790. Ten years later a Russian prelate could declare: "Our clergymen are regarded by foreigners already as almost illiterate, unable to speak either French or German. Our honour is supported by the fact that we can speak and write Latin" (quoted in Kislova 2018: 216). We have come a long way from the contemptuous comments offered by Olearius, de la Neuville, and other Western European observers. This is the surprising story of Latin in Early Modern Russia. Why "surprising," exactly?

Latin, of course, was the learned lingua franca (or vehicular language) of Western Europe. According to Janson, "After antiquity Latin was the international language which made it possible for western Europe to preserve and establish bonds right across the Continent" (2004: 175–176). Latin, says Ostler, "is the story of western Europe – right up to the point when Europe made its profound impact on the world; Latin is the one common thread that runs right through it" (2007: 3). Russia, however, was made of different religious, cultural, and political fibres. Muscovite culture was Orthodox, not Catholic or Protestant. Christianity had come to Russia packaged in Church Slavonic, a language developed by the legendary missionaries Saints Cyril and Methodius with the purpose of *not* being Latin, of being directly accessible to neophyte Slavic Christians (Bennett, 2011: 118–120). Slavonic was chockfull of Byzantine theological terms – in a way, the language was like one gigantic calque of Greek. But Greek itself was not well known in Russia. By the Early Modern era, Slavonic had become the bookish idiom set over the rumbustious vernacular. As H. W. Ludolf, who lived in Muscovy for two years, famously said in his *Grammatica Russica* of 1696: "loquendum est Russice & scribendum est Slavonice" (one is to speak in Russian and to write in Slavonic) (Dunn, 1993). A variety called "chancery" Russian was used for governmental matters and occupied a kind of linguistic middle ground (Cracraft, 2004: 257; Kislova, 2018: 194–195).

Pace the disparaging remarks by Western travellers, Latin was not entirely unknown in Muscovy. A "professional" tongue, it was sometimes used by those in the ambassadorial and apothecary chanceries (Kislova, 2018; Vorob'ev, 1999: 14–23). Moreover, Moscow's Slavonic-Greek-Latin Academy, the first formally organised school in Russia, opened in 1685 (Chrissidis, 2016). As the name suggests, Latin was a basic part of the curriculum. That being said, Latin was a rare linguistic commodity in Muscovite society, largely restricted to doctors and diplomats. It was definitely perceived as foreign, as something out of place.

Not only was Latin absent from the cultural inventory, a longstanding anti-"Latins" discourse was entrenched in Muscovy. The language had become a symbol for Catholicism and all of its theological, liturgical, and institutional differences from Orthodoxy – and then, by extension, for Western Europe. "Latins" was a term of abuse. Syphilis was labelled the "Latin sickness" (Billington, 1970: 96, 86). *Latinstvo* (the Latin world or "Latindom") was pictured as a foul and foreign realm, the threatening "Other" to Holy Russia. This dualism helped define Muscovy's cultural, ideological, and political borders, providing a sense of Russian unity and superiority (Dunn, 2004: 13–14).

When the Rus' (the medieval forerunners of Russians, Ukrainians, and Belarusians) officially converted to Christianity in the tenth century, they received, along with other trappings of the Orthodox faith – devotional literature, icon painting, etc. – a storehouse of criticisms against the "Latins" (Popov, 1875; Rock, 2007: 62–65). A diatribe inserted into the *Primary Chronicle* (a monastic compilation of the tenth and eleventh centuries that mediates between imported Byzantine and indigenous Slavic viewpoints) warns, "Do not accept the teachings of the Latins, whose instruction is vicious. For when they enter the church, they do not kneel before the images…. Avoid their doctrine; for they absolve sins against money payments, which is the worst abuse of all. God guard you from this evil…." (quoted in Rock, 2007: 62–63). If we fast-forward to the latter part of the seventeenth century, we still find, on the eve of Peter the Great's cultural revolution, the strains of this *odium theologicum* (theological hatred). According to one cleric, Latin books "are filled with guile and deception, heresy and godlessness" (Strakhov, 1998: 36).

And yet Muscovy at that time was a "culture in flux" (Chrissidis, 2016: 195). The linguistic culture – "the set of behaviours, assumptions, cultural forms, prejudices, folk belief systems, attitudes, stereotypes, ways of thinking about language, and religio-historical circumstances associated with a particular language" (Schiffman, 1996: 5) – was shifting. Attitudes towards the occidental lingua franca were warming. "Latin was seen as the crucial element of the new, emergent culture" (Kislova, 2015: 76). Of course, not everyone welcomed this development. The fundamentalist priest Avvakum, for example, thought that the advent of Latin was a sign of the Antichrist (Wes, 1992: 25). But others, including churchmen, viewed Latin as a more or less neutral and necessary vehicle of knowledge (Chrissidis, 2016: 89, 194–195).

The disruption or transformation of Russia's linguistic culture is associated above all with Peter I (the Great). Without adjudicating the long-running debate about whether the towering figure (he was 6′8″) was more of an innovator or accelerator (Bushkovitch, 2015: 314; Franklin, 2019: 10–11), we can at least register some of the major changes that happened during his reign: the reorganisation of government chanceries into various 'colleges' in accordance with Scandinavian models, including subordinating the Church to secular control via the Holy Synod (hence this is sometimes termed the Synodal period in Russian Orthodox history); the restructuring of the army and the creation of a bona fide navy; support of new scientific and manufacturing ventures; the introduction of Western-style clothes, buildings, and even hairstyles (Offord et al., 2018: 92). Of course, we must add to this list the creation of an entirely new capital, St. Petersburg built in the swampy land along the Gulf of Finland, a most unlikely location. Dostoevsky called it "the most intentional city" (Munro, 2008).

Equally improbable was the importation of Latin. Peter realised that science, manufacturing, and a strong military – indeed, empire-building – required the knowledge of the major Western European languages. And so, following Peter's lead, Russians dramatically altered the linguistic culture of Muscovy. This is the period when "huge new vocabularies" entered from Dutch, French, German, Italian, and other languages (Cracraft, 2004: 257; Worth, 1963). Polyglot glossaries and phrase books started to appear. As for Latin, an ideological justification was articulated in a landmark text, whose title might be translated as *Trilingual Lexicon. A Treasury of Slavonic, Greek, and Latin Words, Collected from Ancient and Recent Books, and Arranged according to the Order of the Slavonic Alphabet*, published in 1704 by Fedor Polikarpov-Orlov, a prominent writer, printer, and alumnus of the Slavonic-Greek-Latin Academy (Polikarpov-Orlov 1704; Ramazanova 2009). Polikarpov-Orlov was an Orthodox traditionalist, but he may have seen the writing on the wall in terms of the shifting linguistic culture. In the forward to this thick tome, he states that Greek is the language of the original "holy books and church rituals" (that is, the source materials received from Byzantium), while Slavonic is the language of praise (*slava* said to be a cognate of Greek *doxa* and Latin *gloria*). As for Latin, it

> ... has been included as a third language because today this language is used around the world more than others in civil and educational matters. The same [is true] for all kinds of sciences and arts that are necessary for human society. A great many books have been translated [into Latin] from other languages, and many are still composed in this language. To sum up, there is no one who can do without it, who would not desire to have it available for his needs, whether an artist or a soldier skillful in military matters.
>
> (quoted in Zhivov, 2009: 62)

Though he possessed some Latin books (4.3% of his library), including *Urbis Romae Topographia* and *Romanae Historiae Scriptores* (Vorob'ev, 2015: 70), and though he sometimes signed his name as *Petrus* (Vorob'ev, 1999: 32, 35), Peter the Great probably did not know the language. He was, however, certainly aware of its symbolic potency. During his Grand Embassy of 1697–1698, he would have seen and heard Latin in the libraries, observatories, botanical gardens, and universities he visited in Western Europe. The vehicular quality of Latin seems to have fit well with "Peter's soaring political and scientific or technical ambitions" (Cracraft, 2004: 254).

Latin – or, to be precise, Neo-Latin, the scholarly name given to the variety used across Europe from about 1400 to 1800 – was not "reborn" in Russia the way it was in certain countries, like Italy, with their long vicissitudinous history of the language ("Dark Ages," medieval Scholasticism, Renaissance humanism, Reformation, etc.). Rather, we might say that, at the urging of a domineering father figure, Russians "adopted" it as a prestigious resource for various purposes and projects, the three most important of which were science, religion (specifically, the priesthood), and imperial propaganda. Predictably, the melding of Latin and Russian traditions was neither a smooth nor immediate process. Chew's comparative analysis (2009) suggests that lingua francas are typically linked to dominant social/cultural/political powers. Being associated with phenomena such as language shift and language death, their appearance will be met in some quarters with scepticism and calls to go "back to basics." As we will see, various negative attitudes towards Latin were voiced as the language settled into place in Early Modern Russia.

Recent years have seen the publication of a number of general books on the history and influence of Latin (e.g. Waquet, 2002; Janson, 2004;

Ostler, 2007; Leonhardt, 2013). Yet Russia largely remains *terra incognita* in these treatments. IJsewijn's essential handbook on Neo-Latin dedicates but a few pages to Russia, remarking (not unjustly) that Latin literature is a "late and peripheral phenomenon" there (1990: 254). The excellent survey of Korenjak (2016) does not add much. And for all their wealth of information, two major handbooks on Neo-Latin barely mention Russia (Ford *et al.*, 2014; Knight and Tilg, 2015). Actually, it was Peter Burke who, in his influential book, *Languages and Communities in Early Modern Europe* (2004), alighted on some of the key factors pertaining to Latin in Russia, including the status of Church Slavonic as well as the use of Latin in science and seminary education. This chapter cannot rectify this persistent lack of attention (an exception is Katzer, 2001). Its goal is much humbler: to provide an overview of Latin in Russia's "long" eighteenth century (ca. 1685–1825), charting where and how the language was used and, in the process, making available some of the results of Russian scholarship on the subject (especially Vorob'ev, 1999, 2015). Token texts are provided for each domain. The exposition simplifies a sprawling topic, rather like a subway map's cartoony schematic rendering of a multibranched underground transportation system. Important topics are bypassed, including the reception of classical authors like Vergil (Torlone, 2015) and the ways that Latin influenced the vocabulary and syntax of the emerging Russian national literary language (Zhivov, 2009.) Though progress has been made over the past years, research into the emplacement of Latin in Russian cultural history is just beginning.

Science

In 1735 the Imperial Academy of Sciences in St. Petersburg sent a package containing several learned tomes to the Royal Academy of History in Lisbon:

> Excellentissiimis, illustrissimis
> atque praestantissimis
> regiae academiae ulyssipponensis
> collegis
> s. d.
> Joannes Albertus Korff
> serenissimae Russorum Imperatricis camerarius
> regendae academiae petropolitanae
> praefectus.
> [To the most excellent, most illustrious
> and most eminent
> colleagues
> of the royal academy of Lisbon –

Joannes Albertus Korff.
chamberlain of the most serene Empress of the Russias
prefect of the sovereign Petersburg academy,
sends greetings.]
(Sukhomlinov 1890: 378; my translation)[2]

Six of the texts were in Latin and one was in French. They included the first volumes of the Academy's journal, as well as a treatise on plants (*Plantarum minus cognitarum centur. I, II, III, complect. Plantas circa Byzantium et in Oriente observatas per J.C. Buxbaum*), a work of history (*Historia Osrhoena et Edessena ex numis illustrata*), and a description of Chinese (*Museum sinicum, in quo sinicae linguae et litteraturae ratio explicatur*). (Sukhomlinov, 1890: 379). This gift aptly symbolises Russia's growing participation in the world of European learning. Though the Russian language would eventually be an influential medium for math and science, it was the vehicular nature of Latin that provided the framework and impetus for the national language's later ascent.

Latin and scientific inquiry were major innovations in Russia at this time. "It is a striking statistic that in the whole of the seventeenth century fewer than ten secular titles came off Muscovite presses, which were devoted mainly to the production of liturgical and devotional texts" (Hughes, 1998: 5). Given the fact that scholars have debated the causes and consequences of medieval Russia's supposed "intellectual silence" (e.g. Prestel, 2019), there may be some justification for saying that the creation of an Academy of Sciences was Peter's greatest accomplishment. Its establishment undermined the intellectual hegemony of the Church (Vucinich, 1963: 72; Gordin, 2000: 21).

Peter pushed to set up an academy that would be similar to those in the great capitals of Europe. He had visited the Royal Society in London in 1698, where may have met Isaac Newton. (The Academy's first formal communication – which was in Latin – was to Newton on October 11, 1726.) Later, Peter experienced the Académie Royale des Sciences in Paris in 1717. But the greatest influence seems to have been that of Gottfried Wilhelm Leibniz and the Berlin Academy of Sciences (Gordin, 2000: 4). The Russian equivalent would house Peter's growing collection of books, scientific instruments, and curiosities (Cracraft, 2004: 244). Its discoveries would bring glory to Russia – and its ruler. But creating the Academy was rather like putting the horse before the cart, since Russia did not yet have a school system that could support and feed such an institute of advanced learning (Gordin, 2000: 12). The academicians themselves had to be lured from Germany and Switzerland. It is revealing that the first Latin grammar in Russia, printed at the Academy in 1746, was a translation of a German handbook (*Compendium grammaticae latinae, oder Kurtzer Auszug aus der grösseren lateinischen Grammatica Marchica, zur Erlernung der lateinischen Sprache*).

At that time, Latin, of course, was considered the premier international medium of scholarship (Korenjak, 2016: 234–253). Not surprisingly, then, it was the expected vehicle for research conducted at the Academy of Sciences, the "sign of authentic scientificness (*znakom podlinnoi nauchnosti*)" (Vorob'ev, 1999: 110). The venerable language was supplemented here and there, depending on the situation, by German and French. Over time, Russian too earned a place at the table. According to the charter of 1747, which regulated practices that had not been explicitly codified at the establishment of the Academy (Gordin, 2000: 2), lectures were required to be given only in Latin and Russian. "The bilingual system," says Buck, "symbolically combined the identity of the Academy as an institution of the Russian state with its identity as a member of the international scholarly community" (1984: 192).

These scholars brought with them the full *instrumentarium* of Western European academic genres. Dissertations, formal debates, announcements, inaugural addresses, orations and lectures, orders and decrees, statutes, minutes, mottos, petitions, panegyrics, condolences, maps, and so forth – Latin was the natural linguistic resource for all such matters (Vorob'ev, 1999). The academicians were tasked with composing odes and inscriptions for various occasions, thereby extending the reach of Latin beyond the Academy's walls. Further afield, scholars in places like Vienna, Stockholm, London, Uppsala, Edinburgh, Padua, and Leipzig sometimes wrote to their counterparts in Petropolis. However, out of one collection of 1365 letters of the Petersburg Academy of Sciences, only 49 were in Latin (Vorob'ev, 1999: 159).

The Academy produced a number of noteworthy Latin publications. The most important were the *Commentarii Academiae Scientiarum Imperialis Petropolitanae* (Transactions of the Imperial Academy of Sciences of St. Petersburg), 14 volumes of which were published between 1727 and 1751. In Gordin's words, "The Latin publication was…for the face that pointed towards Paris, London, and Berlin" (2000: 13). The journal was then renamed *Novi Commentarii Academiae Scientiarum Imperialis Petropolitanae* (New Transactions of the Imperial Academy of Sciences of St. Petersburg), and continued for another 20 substantial volumes until 1775. It then became *Acta Academiae Scientiarum Imperialis Petropolitanae* (Acts of the Imperial Academy of Sciences of St. Petersburg) followed by *Nova Acta*.

One of the most outstanding scientists at the Academy was the Swiss-born Leonhard Euler. An astonishing talent who was versatile in several distinct research areas, he did two stints in St. Petersburg: 1727 to 1741 and then, after a prolific time in Berlin, 1766 to 1783 (Gautschi, 2008). Euler made some 150 contributions to the Petersburg journal (Korenjak, 2016: 239–240). His first period in Russia saw the publication of major works in physics and naval architecture. His two-volume *Mechanica, sive motus Scientia analytice exposita* (Mechanics, or a Science of Movement Explained Analytically) was most important, but he also penned *Tentamen novae theoriae musicae* (An Attempt at a New Theory of Music) (Gautschi, 2008: 11–12). Studies in algebra, statistics, agriculture and lunar theory issued forth in his second period in Petropolis. His voluminous correspondence with other scholars occurred in Latin, French, and German (Offord *et al.*, 2018: 322–323). Euler's grave in St. Petersburg is adorned with a Latin inscription that was originally erected in his honor in 1837 by the Academy of Sciences:

> LEONHARDO EULERO
> ACADEMIA PETROPOLITANA
> MDCCCXXXVII
> [To Leonhard Euler
> St. Petersburg Academy
> 1837]
>   (Budaragina, 2010: 124–125)

But Latin was not the exclusive intellectual property of the foreign-born. Mikhail Lomonosov was a graduate of the Slavonic-Greek-Latin Academy in Moscow. A polymath like Euler, he made notable contributions in science, history and philology. He was also an accomplished Latinist, said to be among the finest in all of Europe. A sampling of his scientific works may be judged from articles appearing in just the first volume of the Academy journal in 1750 (Vorob'ev, 1999: 70–75):

- *Meditationes de caloris et frigoris causa* (Reflections on the Cause of Warmth and Cold).
- *Tentamen theoriae de vi aeris elastica* (Attempt at a Theory Regarding the Elasticity of Air).
- *Dissertation de actione menstruorum chymicorum in genere* (Discourse regarding Chemical Dissolving Liquids in General).

The great Lomonosov Moscow State University, founded in 1755, is named after the figure sometimes called the Russian da Vinci.

The Academy was located on Vasilevsky Island across from the main part of St. Petersburg. The first resident scholars referred to the institution in their native German as "our island" (*unsere Insel*) in part because their Latin-based scientific work was such a rarity in Russia at that time (Okenfuss, 1995: 165). Yet, over the course of the eighteenth century, there was an incremental shift from the international idiom to the national languages of German, Russian, and French. In the early nineteenth century the Academy journal was given a French title, *Mémoires de l'Académie Impériale des Sciences de St. Pétersbourg*. There was a precipitous drop in Latin-language articles (Offord *et al.*, 2018: 319–320). Thus, in our imaginary tour *circa* 1790, Latin was actually *losing* ground at the Academy of Sciences after having played a distinguished role in the inauguration of Russia's world-famous traditions in math and science.

Religion

"When I began to read Greek books," wrote one seventeenth-century Muscovite cleric, "I came to know the Latin deceit and to understand the innovations and errors and depravities [contained] in their writings; and I spat upon all of them...." (quoted in Strakhov, 1998: 40). A century later, the main textbook used in Russian seminary education was the Latin *Commendium Orthodoxae Theologicae Doctrinae* (Compendium of Orthodox Theological Doctrine). The fact that a language once conspued as heretical had become ensconced in the church education system is the most unexpected plot twist in the story of Latin in Early Modern Russia. Strange to say, after centuries of anti-"Latins" discourse, "'Latin literacy' (*latinskaia obrazovannost'*) became the symbolic core of ecclesiastical education" (Kislova, 2015: 80). Indeed, Orthodox parish priests were the most "Latinized" of all social groups in Imperial Russia (Vorob'ev, 2015: 71), leading to another kind of insularity – as a sacerdotal caste (Okenfuss, 1995: 165). But we are getting ahead of the story.

As we have seen, Latin, as the recognised vehicle of knowledge and education across Europe, was integral to the start of scientific inquiry in Russia. The Russian Orthodox Church would similarly appropriate the language for its own discourses (catechisms, theological treatises, homiletic manuals, and so on), though never for the Divine Liturgy, the centrepiece of the faith. Unlike the scientific tradition, this strand of Latinity was not imported from German-speaking lands but came primarily through Ukraine.

As a result of the Protestant Reformation, the Roman Church had lost membership in northern Germany, Scandinavia, the Baltic area, England, and elsewhere. New ecclesiastical initiatives were required to win converts. Renowned for their organisation, mobility, educational prowess, and obedience to the Pope, the Society of Jesus was the spearhead of this Counter or Catholic Reformation. Most relevant for our story is the fact that they were effective proselytisers and agents of westernisation in the Polish-Lithuanian Commonwealth. By 1570 there were 23 Jesuit *collegia* in that vast multilingual, multiconfessional and multinational territory (Shore, 2019: 320–321; Thomson, 1993: 77). These prestigious schools, with their rigorous Latin-heavy *Ratio studiorum* (the plan of studies), motivated some Ukrainians and Belarusians to convert to Catholicism (Dunn, 2004: 9–10). Faced with this perceived existential threat, a group of Orthodox churchmen decided to fight fire with fire, "to reform and modernise their own Church in order to complete with the more learned Ukrainian and Latin Catholics" (Dunn, 2004: 10–11). They intended to fortify the Orthodox faith using the theological discourses that prevailed in Catholicism. Some Eastern clerics adopted a kind of Latinate armature to define and defend Orthodoxy and thus resist Catholic encroachment (Vucinich, 1963: 18). The Kyiv (Kiev) Academy, set up by Petro Mohila (Peter Mogila) in 1632, was the central locus for this project. Its Jesuit-like curriculum would be transplanted to Russia, where it served as the model and blueprint for seminary education into the nineteenth century (Kislova, 2015: 77).

Peter wanted an educated clergy. From his vantage point, there was a need for priests who could articulate the faith, defeat schismatics, extirpate superstition, and be respected members of society – good order depended on it (Freeze 1977: 79). Latin was viewed as a "synonym of the progress, Europeanization and enlightenment of the clerical community" (Kislova, 2018: 200). And so, Ukrainian churchmen were installed in important positions in the Russian ecclesiastical hierarchy and implemented the Latin-based curriculum (Okenfuss, 1995; Shore, 2019: 325). From Kyiv to Moscow, this pedagogical approach was extended to St. Petersburg, Kazan, Tver, Nizhny Novgorod, Ryazan, Kolomna, and other cities throughout the Empire (Kislova, 2015: 77). "By the 1780s the new [Latin] schools flourished in every diocese and exerted an ever-increasing influence over the careers and culture of the parish clergy. More broadly, the new schools were essential to the Church's task of modernizing or revitalizing the traditional religious culture" (Freeze, 1977: 78). Again, it must be remembered that Latin was the language of theological discourse; Church Slavonic remained the medium of prayer and devotional literature.

Though there were changes and adjustments over the course of the eighteenth century, the Russian Orthodox seminary curriculum was broadly similar to (indeed, ultimately modelled on) the Jesuit system found across Europe. The primary level involved grammar, first in Russian/Slavonic, then in Latin. The basic textbook was Emmanuel Alvarez's *Institutiones linguae Latinae* (Foundations of the Latin Language) – the same one used by Jesuit schools around the world since the sixteenth century. This was supplemented by various grammatical aids written by Russians (Kislova 2015: 84–85). The secondary level involved poetics and rhetoric. Students might study classical works by Ovid, Virgil, Horace, Cicero, as well as some Neo-Latin authors including Lomonosov (Kislova 2018: 207). The tertiary step was dedicated to philosophy and theology, which were studied and discussed in Latin, though very few students reached that level (Freeze, 1977: 91–92).

As noted earlier, one of the most widely used theology manuals was the *Compendium* of Hyacintus (Iakinf) Karpinski (1786), a monk at the prominent Kirillo-Belozersky Monastery (Vorob'ev, 2015: 89). Here is a partial look at the table of contents:

> Prolegomena
> Caput I. De Scriptura sacra
> Sectio I. De Scriptura in communi
> Sect. II. De Scriptura Vet. Testam.
> Sect. III. De Scriptura Novi Testam.
> Cap. II. De Deo
> Sectio I. De Deo absolute considerate
> Secti. II De Sancta Trinitate
> Cap. III. De operibus Dei
> Sectio I. De Creatione
> Sect. II. De Angelis
> Sect. III De operibus Dei primo die productis
> Sect. IV. De Creaturis relquorum quinque dierum
> Sect. V. De Homine ...
> [Prologue
> Chapter. I. On Sacred Scripture
> Section I. On Scripture in general
> Sect. II. On the Old Testament
> Sect. III. On the New Testament
> Chap. II. On God
> Section I. On the Godhead
> Sect. II. On the Sacred Trinity
> Chap. III. On the Works of God
> Section I. On Creation
> Sect. II. On Angels
> Sect. III. On the Works of the First Day of Creation
> Sect. IV. On Creatures from the Five Remaining Days
> Sect. V. On Man...]
> (Karpinski, 1786; my translation)

Each section of the handbook contains a dogmatic part (*pars dogmatica*) in which different propositions relating to the topic are enumerated, explained, and supported by scriptural quotations (from the Latin Vulgate, the traditional Bible of Catholicism), followed by a polemical part (*pars polemica*) in which various questions are raised (*objicitur*: "it is objected"). Responses, typically with scriptural backing, then refute the objections. Though all of this is stock-in-trade Baroque Scholasticism, it does look quite strange compared to the traditional Orthodox genres of spiritual writing. It is perhaps understandable why the twentieth-century churchman Georges Florovsky applied the term *pseudomorphosis* to this period of Russian Orthodox history (Thomson, 1993).

Whether at a religious institution like the Alexander Nevsky Seminary or a secular one like Moscow University, Russian students had to learn to speak the Latin code. According to an internal church report from 1766:

> This language is already studied in our seminaries and, moreover, a great number of useful books are in Latin, which can be regarded as a language of learned people, insofar as all learned people in Europe can converse and communicate in it.
>
> (quoted in Freeze 1977: 80–81)

To that end, the multilingual conversation books that were then commonplace in western Europe were adapted to the Russian milieu. They contained useful phrases like:

"*Salve, mi amice! Zdravstvui, drug moi!* [Hi, my friend!]."
"*Quid loqueris, inepte? Chto ty govorish, durak?* [What are you saying, fool?]"

A popular booklet called Colloquia Scholastica - Shkol'nye Razgovory - Schul-Gespräche (School Conversations) consisted of parallel columns of French, German, Russian and Latin dedicated to topics such as the following:

On morning affairs
On washing
On school affairs
On books
On wisdom
On the creation of the world
On theft and lying
On birds
On dogs
On sickness

(Vorob'ev, 1999: 155–156; my translation)

Though Russian hierarchs preached the value of Latin for overcoming ignorance and attaining honor in the eyes of Western Europeans, "most youths found the Latin studies an exasperating experience; coming from culturally deprived backgrounds, they found the material totally alien and incomprehensible" (Freeze, 1977: 92). The main duty of the parish priest was to perform the Divine Liturgy, which was (and still is) in Church Slavonic. Students griped. Some tried to escape; others had to be beaten into obedience (Freeze, 1977: 86). Though somewhat outside our temporal framework, the memoir of I.S. Beliustin (published in 1858) expressed a sentiment that was no doubt widely shared:

The main subject, which receives the overwhelming share of attention, is Latin....It is a strange, incomprehensible phenomenon, possible only in the education of Russian clergy: the heart of education for a future village priest is a dead language, which will be about as useful in real life as Sanskrit! To be a good pastor, now one must first be a good Latinist.... For a whole six years the boy wastes his abilities on the study of a language that he will forget in his first two years of priesthood, for in all his life he will not encounter a single letter of that language!

(Beliustin, 1985: 78)

Parishioners also complained. Latin had become the cant of the priestly caste, further alienating them from their flock. In 1835, Count Nikolai Protasov issued a blistering critique:

You are our teachers in faith. But we cannot understand you ... you have invented a sort of a language for yourselves like physicians, mathematicians and sailors. It is impossible to apprehend you without interpreting. It is no good at all. Speak to us a language which we know, teach us the law of God in a manner that every peasant can understand you at once!

(quoted in Kislova, 2018: 215)

By the middle of the nineteenth century, Latin was still taught as a subject matter but had ceased being used as a language of instruction (Vorob'ev, 1999: 66). All told, its place in the seminary lasted longer than in the laboratory.

Imperium

Latin was a valuable resource not only for the church but the state. According to Ostler, "...in politics too Latin was highly influential for the Early Modern world. With its aura of antiquity – an aura that grew as the language appeared less and less in day-to-day business – the use of Latin gave majesty and authority to any field" (2007: 283). The ancient language meant not only *stadium* and *sacerdotium* but *imperium*.

The connection between Latin and political power was articulated in Polikarpov-Orlov's Slavonic-Greek-Latin dictionary of 1704, discussed earlier, which echoes a longstanding Christian theme. According to the Gospel of John 19:20, three languages were used in the inscription on Christ's cross: Hebrew, Greek, and Latin. Augustine's exegesis would be influential in the premodern era. According to this interpretation, each language had its own providential meaning: Hebrew was for God's law, Greek represented human wisdom, and Latin was about ruling might – here pointing to the belief that the *Pax Romana* was instrumental in the spread of the Gospel (Resnick, 1990: 64). In the forward to the

Trilingual Lexicon we read: "Nam Hebraea lingua, est lingua sacra, Graeca lingua, est lingua sapientiae, latina lingua, est lingua imperii (For the Hebrew language is a sacred language, the Greek language is a language of sagacity, the Latin language is a language of empire)" (Polikarpov-Orlov, 1704: 4).

Peter pressed Latin into the service of imperial ceremony and propaganda (Zhivov, 2009: 59). He adopted titles like *Imperator, Pater Patriae*, and *Maximus* (Hughes, 1998: 27). The imperial ethos was reflected in the very layout of his new capital:

> For two centuries Saint Petersburg was the capital of a vast and complex empire, a symbol of the implacable will that forged Russian into a modern European state. The city rose from a collision of two cultures, Muscovite and European, and the ensuing tensions formed one of the most persistent themes of a remarkable succession of writers, enthralled not only by the spirit of the city but by its very appearance. And with reason, for the architecture of Saint Petersburg – grandiose, overpowering at times, obsessed with a rational design – remains the clearest statement of purpose that Imperial Russia ever made: to measure, to build, to impose order at whatever cost.
>
> (Brumfield, 2008: 1)

We might say that Petropolis was the urban equivalent of Latin (rational, artificial, international, imperial), whereas "picturesque and disorderly" Moscow (Hughes, 1998: 209), chockablock with churches and curving lanes, corresponded to the ornate letterforms of Slavonic.

A perambulation through Petropolis *circa* 1790 would reveal bits of Latin writing scattered across the cityscape. Strolling by the Sheremetev Palace on the Fontanka Embankment, for example, our imaginary traveller would catch sight of an elaborate herald on the northern wing containing the Latin motto *Deus conservat omnia* (God conserves all things) (Budaragina, 2010: 22–23). Entering into the mansions and palaces of the northern capital, a visitor could encounter Latin lettering on a wide range of material objects and surfaces: coats of arms, gold and silverwork, guns, snuffboxes, and clocks (Vorob'ev, 1999: 184–185). It is possible that some Latin books might be found on the bookshelf, though most likely just for display purposes. For the Russian upper classes were never much interested in Latin; they were enamoured of German and especially French (as anyone who has read Tolstoy's *War and Peace* can attest). The classic account of this topic is Okenfuss's *The Rise and Fall of Latin Humanism in Early-Modern Russia: Pagan Authors, Ukrainians, and the Resiliency of Muscovy* (1995), which argues that, despite the inroads Latin made in the domains of science and theology, the Russian nobility consistently said "no" to a classical education. "The history of a defeat" is the subtitle of a more recent investigation into the issue

(Rjéoutski, 2018). Latin was derided as a "doctor" jargon – one not fit for high society. "The Latin book," concludes Okenfuss, "did not find a niche in Russian cultural life" (1995: 157). Nonetheless, our time-traveller might well find an emblem book in one of these stately manors or palaces (Gordin, 2000: 17).

Peter had become interested in the genre during his tour of Western Europe in 1697–1698. *Simvoly i emblemata* (*Symbols and Emblems*) was originally printed in 1705 by Peter's order and then reprinted in 1719. The Russian translation was based without attribution on a French original *Devises et emblémes*. The volume contains more than 800 numbered images of plants, animals, various and sundry objects, and mythological themes. Each image is accompanied by a motto in Dutch, Russian, Latin, French, Italian, Spanish, English, and German. The text became a beloved possession of Peter the Great (Sashalmi, 2013: 460–461). In the eighteenth century, emblematics spilled over from the page and appeared on household items (silver beakers, trays, etc.), ships, gates, firework displays, and elsewhere (Maggs, 1976: 31).

The frontispiece of *Simvoly i emblemata* comprises a Westernised portrait of Peter in battle armour, looking something like an idealised Roman emperor, surrounded by eight medallions with mottos in Russian and Latin. Images include an olive branch, a two-headed eagle, a sword, sun with rays, a lion attacking a wolf, and a figure of (most likely) Hercules. Sashalmi decodes this montage to mean something like: "In the service [of] his burdensome office (as the Russian Hercules) Peter leads Russia towards glory and the golden age (the Sun at its zenith) via war" (2013: 472). Underneath the ensemble of images is a long Russian inscription. A Latin translation sans imagery appears on the next page:

SYMBOLA
ET
EMBLEMATA
Jussu atque auspiciis
SACERRIMAE SUAE MAJESTATIS
AUGUSTISSIMI AC SERENISSIMI
IMPERATORIS MOSCHOVIAE
MAGNI DOMINI CZARIS, ET
MAGNI DUCIS
PETRI ALEXEIDIS
totius Magnae, Parvae & Albae Rossiae, nec non aliarum
multarum Potestatum atque Dominiorum
Orientalium, Occidentalium, Aquilonariumque
SUPREMI MONARCHAE,
Excusa
[SYMBOLS
AND

> EMBLEMS
> Printed by decree and under the auspices
> OF HIS MOST SACRED MAJESTY
> THE MOST AUGUST AND SERENE
> EMPEROR OF MUSCOVY
> THE GREAT LORD TSAR,
> AND GREAT LEADER
> PETER ALEXEIVICH
> of all of Great, Little, and White Russia,
> as well as of many other
> Oriental, Occidental, and Northerly
> Powers and Dominions
> THE SUPREME MONARCH]
> (quoted in Sashalmi, 2013: 462; my translation)

It is noteworthy that Peter is here called emperor (IMPERATORIS) some fifteen years before he officially assumed this title.

Peter altered not only the linguistic culture of Russia but its visual landscape or "graphosphere" (Franklin, 2019: 128). Latin was used on banners, pedestals, triumphal gates, obelisks, and medals, and in spectacles that glorified the state and its ruler (Vorob'ev, 1999: 169–176). "Temples" were constructed honoring the divinities of Virtue, Peace, Wisdom, and Glory and were adorned with Latin inscriptions. Ordinary Russians had to be instructed about the meaning of this strange "pantheon" by means of leaflets and brochures. One explained to the unlettered that "Jupiter was accepted by the ancient pagans as the first and foremost almighty power" (quoted in Hughes, 1998: 208). Another sought to reassure spectators that the triumphal arches erected in the wake of military victory "are not a temple or church in honour of a deity, but political, that is, civilian, praise to those working for the wholeness of their fatherland" (quoted in Maggs 1976: 37). Firework displays might involve "transparents" (placards) containing emblems and mottoes illuminated from behind. Latin was integral to this imperial spectacle. But as Maggs notes, "How much more mystifying and incomprehensible this strange symbolic language, often accompanied by inscriptions in Latin, a foreign language written in a foreign alphabet, must have been to the Russian spectator" (1976: 39). Indeed, there are contemporaneous reports of bystanders hurling profanities at the structures of this new cultus (Franklin, 2019: 151).

Latin was also used to project Russia's newfound imperial might beyond its borders – another form of linguistic vehicularity. Commemorative medals intended for propaganda abroad featured Mars, Mercury, Hercules, Minerva, and Victoria, with inscriptions in Latin. Lomonosov's Latin panegyric of Empress Elizabeth (daughter of Peter the Great) circulated in the West. A telling example is an inscription commissioned by Peter in

1718 for the town of Spa in Belgium. Even though it commemorates the occasion when the emperor spent five weeks "taking the waters" for stomach and other maladies, the tone is grandiose:

> Petrus Primus, D. G. Russorum
> imperator,
> Pius, Felix, Invictus,
> Apud suos militaris disciplinae restitutor,
> Scientiarum omnium, artiumque protosator,
> Valadissima bellicarum navium
> Proprio marte constructa classe,
> Auctis ultra finem exercitibus suis,
> Ditionibus tam avitis quam bello partis,
> Inter ipsas Bellonae flammas in tuto positis,
> ad exteros se convertit...
> [Peter the First, by the grace of God of all the Russias
> Emperor
> Pious, fortunate, unconquered,
> The restorer of military discipline
> And the promoter of all the sciences and arts,
> Having by his genius
> Established a formidable Navy,
> Considerably increased his Armies,
> And placed in security amidst the flames of war
> His hereditary and his conquered States,
> Undertook a journey to foreign lands...]
> (Cutler, 1871: 46–47)

Much of this novel cultus – the streamers, pedestals, wooden triumphal gates – was ephemeral and has been lost to time, preserved only indirectly in brochures or engravings from the era (Maggs 1976: 28). But one innovation has endured: the so-called civil script.

This chapter of the story has been told before (e.g. Shitsgal, 1959; Franklin 2019: 105–107). Peter was greatly concerned with changing the appearance of things – beards, clothes, houses...cities – which he often did quite forcefully (Gordin, 2000: 17). His cultural revolution had a semiotic thrust to it (Zhivov, 2009: 50). Peter apparently favoured the Latin typefaces he encountered while travelling in Western Europe. So, working with Dutch printers, he intervened to modify the historic Slavonic Cyrillic alphabet, doing away with diacritics (of which there are many), eliminating some letters, and simplifying the shapes of the letterforms. The end result was the *grazhdanskii shrift* or civil script. Peter's role is clear:

> The great reformer gave the orders which originated the project and commissioned workers to carry it out. He kept a careful eye on the

development amidst all his other great responsibilities. He corrected specimen sheets in his own hand and approved the final outcome. Thus, it is not inappropriate to call *grazhdanskii shrift* Tsar Peter I's type.

(Kaldor, 1970: 136)

Peter's graphic intervention was likely motivated by his quest for a "simple" – and secular –Russian language that could be readily understood by merchants, sailors, artisans, and others responsible for building the new mighty Russian empire, unlike the hieratic Slavonic script (Cracraft, 2004: 221). But the political symbolism should not be ignored. As Hughes says, "Roman historical imagery infiltrated many areas of the secular state, from the imperial titles adopted in 1721 (Imperator, Pater Patriae, Maximus) to the Latinate letters in the reformed civil script" (1998: 207). This penchant for empire-building ultimately led to a momentous bifurcation in Russian cultural history. Though it did not happen overnight and though there were gradations and exceptions, the Church Slavonic alphabet was henceforth conserved for devotional texts and contexts, while the Latinate civil script was designated for secular materials. There would be two scripts now, just as there were two capitals: westernised St. Petersburg and byzantine Moscow. The Bolsheviks also modified the Cyrillic alphabet, further distancing it from the "look and feel" of old Slavonic (Bennett, 2012).

Conclusion

The conspicuous absence of Latin in Muscovy contributed to foreign perceptions of Russians as a rude and barbarous people. Not only was Latin not studied in the premodern principality, but it was also portrayed in Russian folklore and church apologetics as downright dangerous and heretical. And yet, *mirabile dictu*, the lingua franca became "the mark of the new, Petrine Imperial culture" (Kislova 2015: 77; cf. Franklin 2019: 124). Though the history of Russian Latinity did not start with Peter the Great, his initiatives catalysed the phenomenon and helped transform the country's linguistic and graphic culture. But the acclimatisation of Latin in Russia was an uneven and contested process across the domains of science, religion, and imperial power.

As the European medium of scholarship, Latin found a natural home in the fledgling Imperial Academy of Sciences in the newly built city of St. Petersburg. It served as a kind of Early-Modern internet, linking Petropolis to Lisbon, Berlin, London, and other centres of learning. Important research was published in the Academy's *Commentarii* and subsequent journals, including works by prodigiously talented scholars like Euler and Lomonosov. Yet by the end of the eighteenth century, Latin was being overtaken by French and Russian in the scientific domain.

More enduring – and surprising – was the influence of Latin in the religious, especially sacerdotal, sphere. Despite a history of polemics against *Latinstvo* ("Latindom"), a Jesuit-inspired curriculum transformed (or, according to some Orthodox religionists, deformed) the Russian Church in the Early Modern era. One final statistic may drive home this point: an inventory of the Smolensk seminary in 1802 listed 1,240 books in Latin, 467 in Russian/Slavonic, 167 in Greek, 40 in German, 39 in French, 33 in Hebrew and 3 in Swedish (Vorob'ev, 2015: 73). There is no doubt, though, that some, perhaps most, of the seminarians would have agreed with Beliustin's *cri de coeur* that Latin was "something utterly useless for a rural priest" (1985: 79).

Finally, Latin had long been an icon of imperial power. Peter and subsequent rulers capitalised on this symbolic meaning in a newfangled civic cultus:

> Eighteenth-century panegyrists elevated Peter to the status of a god: he was Titan, Neptune and Mars rolled into one. They compared 'Petropolis' to ancient Rome. It was a link that Peter also made by adopting the title of 'Imperator' and by casting his own image on the new rouble coin, with laurel wreath and armour, in emulation of Caesar.
>
> (Figes, 2002: 5)

These semiotic novelties were met in some quarters with bafflement and reproach. As one clerk lamented, "They have changed the words and names of our Slavonic language and our clothing, shaved heads and beards and abusively dishonored their persons; we no longer look different or have moral distinction from people of other faiths" (quoted in Zhivov, 2009: 52). Though Latin inscriptions can still be found here and there in St. Petersburg, on homes, schools, and institutions, it is the Petrine civil script – the ordinary Cyrillic alphabet used in Russia to this day – that is the true legacy of the Latin interregnum, hiding in plain sight.

Notes

1. A shorter journalistic version of this article was published as "How the Jesuits helped to bring Latin to Russia" in *America: The Jesuit Review* (https://www.americamagazine.org/faith/2020/03/20/how-jesuits-helped-bring-latin-russia).
2. I would like to thank Daniel Gallagher (Cornell University) for assistance with some of the translations.

References

Beliustin, I. S. (1985). *Description of the Clergy in Rural Russia. The Memoir of a Nineteenth-century Parish Priest*. Gregory L. Freeze, ed. Ithaca: Cornell University Press.

Bennett, B. (2011). *Religion and Language in Post-Soviet Russia*. London and New York: Routledge.

Bennett, B. (2012). Orthography and Orthodoxy in Post-Soviet Russia. In: A. Jaffe, J. Androutsopoulis, M. Sebba, and S. Johnson, eds., *Orthography as Social Action*. Berlin, Boston: De Gruyter Mouton.

Billington, J. (1970). *The Icon and the Axe: An Interpretative History of Russian Culture*. New York: Vintage.

Brumfield, W. (2008.) St. Petersburg and the Art of Survival. In: H. Goscilo and S. M. Norris, eds., *Preserving Petersburg: History, Memory, Nostalgia*, pp. 1–38.

Buck, C. (1984). The Russian Language Question in the Imperial Academy of Sciences, 1724–1770. In: R. Picchio and H. Goldblatt, eds., *Aspects of the Slavic Language Question*, Volume II, *East Slavic*. New Haven: Yale Concilium on International and Area Studies, pp. 187–233.

Budaragina, O. (2010). *Latinskie nadpisi v Peterburge/Latin Inscriptions in Saint Petersburg*. Kolo: Saint Petersburg.

Burke, P. (2004). *Languages and Communities in Early Modern Europe*. Cambridge: Cambridge University Press.

Bushkovitch, P. (2015). Change and Culture in Early Modern Russia. *Kritika: Explorations in Russian and Eurasian History*, 16(2), pp. 291–316.

Chancellor, R. (1968). The First Voyage to Russia. In L. E. Berry and R. O. Crummey, eds., *Rude & Barbarous Kingdom: Russia in the Accounts of Sixteenth-Century English Voyagers*. Madison, Milwaukee, and London: The University of Wisconsin Press, pp. 9–41.

Chew, P. (2009). *Emergent Lingua Francas and World Orders. The Politics and Place of English as a World Language*. New York: Routledge.

Chrissidis, N. (2016). *An Academy at the Court of the Tsars: Greek Scholars and Jesuit Education in Early Modern Russia*. DeKalb, Illinois: Northern Illinois University Press.

Cracraft, J. (2004). *The Petrine Revolution in Russian Culture*. Cambridge, Massachusetts and London, England: The Belknap Press of Harvard University Press.

Cutler, T. (1871). *Notes on Spa, and Its Chalybeate Springs, etc.* London: J. & A. Churchill.

de la Neuville, F. (1994). *A Curious and New Account of Muscovy in the Year 1689*. Edited and introduced by L. Hughes. Translated from French by J. A. Cutshall. London: School of Slavonic and East European Studies, University of London.

Dunn, J. (1993). What Was Ludolf Writing About? *The Slavonic and East European Review*, 71(2), pp. 201–216.

Dunn, D. (2004). *The Catholic Church and Russia: Popes, Patriarchs, Tsars and Commissars*. Burlington, Vermont: Ashgate.

Figes, O. (2002). *Natasha's Dance: A Cultural History of Russia*. London: Penguin Books.

Ford, P., Bloemendal, J., and Fantazzi, C., eds. (2014). *Brill's Encyclopaedia of the Neo-Latin World*. Leiden and Boston: Brill.

Franklin, S. (2019). *The Russian Graphosphere, 1450-1850*. Cambridge; New York, NY: Cambridge University Press.

Freeze, G. (1977). *The Russian Levites: Parish Clergy in the Eighteenth Century*, Cambridge, Massachusetts and London, England: Harvard University Press.
Gautschi, W. (2008). Leonhard Euler: His Life, the Man, and His Works. *SIAM Review*, 50(1), pp. 3–33.
Gordin, M. (2000). The Importation of Being Earnest: The Early St. Petersburg Academy of Sciences. *Isis*, 91(1), pp. 1–31.
Kaldor, I. (1970) The Genesis of the Russian *Grazdhanskii Shrift* or Civil Type. Part II. *The Journal of Typographic Research*, 4(2), pp. 111–138.
Hughes, L. (1998). *Russia in the Age of Peter the Great*. New Haven and London: Yale University Press.
IJsewijn, J. (1990). *Companion to Neo-Latin Studies. Part I. History and Diffusion of Neo-Latin Literature*. Second entirely rewritten edition. Leuven: Leuven University Press; Louvain: Peeters Press.
Janson, T. (2004). *A Natural History of Latin*. Translated by M. D. Sørensen and N. Vincent. Oxford and New York: Oxford University Press.
Karpinski, H. (Iakinf). (1786). *Compendium Orthodoxae Theologicae Doctrinae*. Lipsiae: Breitkopf. https://digital.staatsbibliothek-berlin.de/werkansicht?PPN=PPN654677034&PHYSID=PHYS_0011&DMDID [Accessed 24 June 2019].
Katzer, N. (2001). Latinitas Russiae. Römisches Erbe und lateinische Philologie in Rußland. *Beiträge zur deutschen und europäischen Geschichte*. Bd. 28: M. Hundt, ed., *Geschichte als Verpflichtung. Hamburg, Reformation und Historiographie: Festschrift für Rainer Postei zum 60. Geburtstag*. Hamburg, pp. 229–260.
Kisolova, E. (2015). 'Latin' and 'Slavonic' Education in the Primary Classes of Russian Seminaries in the 18th Century. *Slovene: International Journal of Slavic Studies*, 4(2), pp. 72–91.
Kislova, E. (2018). Latin as the language of the Orthodox clergy in eighteenth-century Russia. In: V. Rjéoutski and W. Fijhoff, eds., *Language Choice in Enlightenment Europe: Education, Sociability, and Governance*. Amsterdam: Amsterdam University Press, pp. 191–224.
Knight, S. and Tilg, S., eds. (2015). *The Oxford Handbook of Neo-Latin*. Oxford and New York: Oxford University Press.
Korenjak, M. (2016). *Geschichte der neulateinischen Literatur: Vom Humanismus bis zur Gegenwart*. Munich: C.H. Beck.
Leonhardt, J. (2013). *Latin: Story of a World Language*. Translated by K. Kronenberg. Cambridge, Massachusetts and London, England: The Belknap Press of Harvard University Press.
Maggs, B. (1976). Firework Art and Literature: Eighteenth-Century Pyrotechnical Tradition in Russia and Western Europe. *The Slavonic and East European Review*, 54(1), pp. 24–40.
Munro, G. (2008). *The Most Intentional City: St. Petersburg in the Reign of Catherine the Great*. Madison, [New Jersey]: Fairleigh Dickinson University.
Okenfuss, M. (1995). *The Rise and Fall of Latin Humanism in Early-Modern Russia. Pagan Authors, Ukrainians, and the Resiliency of Muscovy*. Leiden: Brill.
Olearius, A. (1967). *The Travels of Olearius in Seventeenth-Century Russia*. Translated by Samuel H. Baron, ed. Stanford, California: Stanford University Press.

Offord, D., Rjéoutski, V., and Argent, G. (2018). *The French Language in Russia: A Social, Political, Cultural, and Literary History*. Amsterdam: Amsterdam University Press.

Ostler, N. (2007). *Ad Infinitum: A Biography of Latin*. New York, New York: Walker & Company.

Poe, M. (2002). *"A People Born to Slavery." Russia in Early Modern European Ethnography, 1476–1748*. Ithaca, New York: Cornell University Press.

Polikarpov-Orlov, F. P. (1704). *Leksikon treiazychnyi, sirech' rechenii slavianskikh, ellino-grecheskikh i latinskikh sokrovishch iz razlichnykh drevnikh i novykh knig sobrannoe i po slavianskomu alfavitu v chin raspolozhennoe*. Moskva: typografiia tsarskaia. https://www.prlib.ru/item/342071 [Accessed 13 Aug. 2020].

Popov, A. (1875). *Istoriko-literaturnyi obzor drevne-russkikh polemicheskikh sochinenii protiv latinian, (XI-XV v.)*. Moscow: Tipographiia T. Ris.

Possevino, A. (1977). *The Moscovia of Antonio Possevino, S.J.* Translated with a Critical Introduction and Notes by H. F. Graham. Pittsburgh, Pennsylvania: University of Pittsburgh Press.

Prestel, D. (2019). Kievan Rus' Theology: Yes, No, and It Depends. *Russian History*, 46(2–3), pp. 177–192.

Ramazanova, D. N. (2009). "Leksikon treiazychnyi" Fedora Polikarpova v sobranii museia knigi Rossiiskoi gosudarstvennoi biblioteki. In: A. Iu. Samarin, ed., *Bibliofika: Istoriia knigi i izuchenie knikhnikh pamiatnikov*, Vol. 1. Moscow: Pashkov dom, pp. 156–176.

Resnick, I. (1990). Lingua Dei, Lingua Hominis: Sacred Language and Medieval Texts. *Viator*, 21, pp. 51–74.

Rjéoutski, V. (2018). Latin in the Education of Nobility in Russia: The History of a Defeat. In: V. Rjéoutski and W. Fijhoff, eds., *Language Choice in Enlightenment Europe: Education, Sociability, and Governance*. Amsterdam: Amsterdam University Press, pp. 169–189.

Rock, S. (2007). *Popular Religion in Russia: "Double Belief" and the Making of an Academic Myth*. London and New York: Routledge.

Sashalmi, E. (2013). The Frontispiece of Peter the Great's *Simvoly i Emblemata* (1705): An Iconographical Analysis. *Canadian-American Slavic Studies*, 47, pp. 459–472.

Schiffman, H. (1996). *Linguistic Culture and Language Policy*. London and New York: Routledge.

Shitsgal, A. (1959). *Russkii grazhdanskii shrift 1708–1958*. Moskva: Isskustvo.

Shore, P. (2019). The Jesuits in the Orthodox World. In: I. G. Županov, ed., *The Oxford Handbook of the Jesuits*. Oxford, England and New York, New York: Oxford University Press, pp. 318–348.

Strakhov, O. (1998). *The Byzantine Culture in Muscovite Rus': The Case of Evfimii Chudovskii (1620–1705)*. Cologne: Böhlau Verlag.

Sukhomlinov, M. I. (1890). *Materialy dlia istorii Imperatorskoi akademii nauk*. Vol. 6. Istoriia Akademii nauk G.-F. Millera s prodolzheniiami I.-G. Shrittera, 1725–1743. https://books.google.pt/books?id=7ltDAQAAMAAJ&printsec=frontcover&hl=pt-PT&source=gbs_ge_summary_r&cad=0#v=onepage&q&f=false [Accessed 30 June 2019].

Thomson, F. (1993). Peter Mogila's Ecclesiastical Reforms and the Ukrainian Contribution to Russian Culture. A Critique of Georges Florovsky's Theory of *The Pseudomorphosis of Orthodoxy*. *Slavica Gandensia*, 20, pp. 67–119.

Torlone, Z. (2015). *Vergil in Russia: National Identity and Classical Reception*. Oxford: Oxford University Press.

Vorob'ev, Iu. K. (1999). *Latinskii iazyk v russkoi kul'ture XVII – XVIII vekov*. Saransk: Izdatel'stvo Mordovskogo Universiteta.

Vorob'ev, Iu. K. (2015). *Latinskii iazyk v rossii XVI – pervoi treti XIX veka (kul'turologicheskii aspect)*. Saransk: Izdatel'stvo Mordovskogo Universiteta.

Vucinich, A. (1963). *Science in Russian Culture: A History to 1860*. Stanford, California: Stanford University Press.

Waquet, F. (2002). *Latin, or, The empire of a Sign: From the Sixteenth to the Twentieth Centuries*. Translated by J. Howe. London, England and New York, New York: Verso.

Wes, M. (1992). *Classics in Russia 1700-1855: Between Two Bronze Horsemen*. Leiden: Brill.

Worth, G. H. (1963). *Foreign Words in Russia: A Historical Sketch, 1550–1800*. Berkeley and Los Angeles: University of California Press.

Zhivov, V. (2009). *Language and Culture in Eighteenth-Century Russia*. Boston, Massachusetts: Academic Studies Press.

Part III
Pidgins, Jargons, Lingua Francas

9 On the Existence of a Mediterranean Lingua Franca and the Persistence of Language Myths

Joshua Brown

Introduction

This paper deals with the very existence of the so-called Mediterranean lingua franca (MLF) – an extinct trade language, with a Romance lexical base, used around the Mediterranean basin, from anywhere between the late medieval to early modern periods. Therefore, part of the analysis which follows traces how researchers have aimed to discern the presence of MLF in historical documents. The reality of Lingua Franca "is not easily tangible, as has been remarked throughout the history of its study, analysis and description". Indeed, for over a century, "the notion of Lingua Franca has been constantly constructed and deconstructed" (Selbach, 2017: 253). I suggest that what is missing from current analyses of MLF is not a disregard of the tools from historical linguistics, but that they have been applied incorrectly or inconsistently. This approach has led to some instances of circular reasoning and what is known as a "sorites paradox" (sometimes known as the "paradox of the heap"). A simple definition of this situation is provided below:

> The paradox consists of two main premises. Base premise: Clearly, 1 grain of sand does not qualify as a heap. Inductive premise: Adding a single grain of sand is never sufficient to turn a collection of sand grains that is not a heap into one that is a heap. If we accept both of these premises, then it follows that no matter how many grains of sand are added to the first grain, the result will never be a heap. Yet eventually, if we add enough sand, there will come a point at which there is a heap, and we have arrived at a paradox.
> (Barker, 2009: 1037)

This paper argues that a sorites paradox arises in almost all discussions of MLF. Selbach (2017: 253) notes how certain researchers:

> seemingly over-endorse the notion [of lingua franca] and have a tendency to provide a larger and highly inflated corpus (e.g. Rossetti, 2002); others

DOI: 10.4324/9781003092445-13

deconstruct the notion of Lingua Franca at large, questioning the very idea of a specific language entity (e.g. Aslanov, 2002).

(Selbach, 2017: 253)

It is (presumably) a similar language, if not the very same, to which Burke (2004: 127) refers when he describes "the original lingua franca" as being "a mix of Venetian, Portuguese and Arabic that was known in the Mediterranean world in the Middle Ages". Even a study looking specifically at MLF in the Mediterranean in a historical framework, where we may hope to find traces of its presence, warns us not to confuse the term "lingua franca" with *Lingua Franca proper*" (Cremona, 1997: 53, his emphasis). Here we are told that, during the seventeenth century, MLF was "much in evidence during this period in spoken exchanges between Moslems and Christians" (Cremona, 1997: 53).[1] Nolan has recently investigated the "fact and fiction" of Lingua Franca studies, noting that "the potential unreliability of some witness' accounts combines with the native language(s) bias of the writers and idiolectal variation, rendering their examples of Lingua Franca less credible" (2020: 83). In yet another case, Wansbrough's study conflates, in a purposeful way, both transfer mechanisms and the object of his analysis, which spans a period from 1500 BCE to 1500 CE. His focus is on the standard procedures of contact, noting that "*Lingua franca* refers to the several natural languages that served as vehicle in the transfer, but also to the format itself" (1996: vii).

Problems of identification, selection, and interpretation of MLF, are symptomatic of the broader issues throughout the literature. Scholars have generally considered MLF "a pidgin with a Romance base" (Cifoletti, 1989: 5).[2] In a recent investigation, Mallette (2014: 334) concluded that the "plasticity of the language and the ephemeral nature of the written record can be accounted for by the simple fact that the *lingua franca* never creolized". In a chapter entitled *Lingua Franca: Historical Problems*, Whinnom (1977: 298) asks much of his reader. He identifies some major difficulties in the study of MLF, such as the paucity and unreliability of documents, the ambiguous, indirect historical evidence and other red herrings, noting that "these are fundamental issues". One question that remains unresolved is whether MLF may be considered a distinct linguistic variety – a question often dismissed in earlier research. For example, Whinnom (1977: 298) calls for a degree of creative hypothesising: "if we can assume that Lingua Franca is something other than Italian [learnt as a second language] (however we choose to define "pidgin"), that it had a long and continuous history, and that it was Italian-based, we can move on to other and perhaps more subtle points".

Today the term "lingua franca" is habitually used to refer to any language that is used for communication between speakers of different mother tongues. However, the name has its origins in a trading language

Existence of a Mediterranean Lingua Franca 171

used around the Mediterranean basin. In his review of Dakhlia (2008), Aslanov (2010: 105) writes:

> It seems that this abusive extension of the notion of *lingua franca* to the east of the Mediterranean has resulted from a misunderstanding deriving from the polysemy of the term *lisān al-faranj* which can denominate any spoken language by the (Western) Franks perceived from a levantine point of view.[3]

Ever since, this term has become ever more polysemous, encompassing many communicative instances where two interlocutors may communicate in a code that is not native to either one.

Part of this paper provides an analysis of one of the most well-known documents which purportedly records MLF phenomena – the *Dictionnaire de la langue franque ou petit mauresque* of 1830. The *Dictionnaire*, composed by an anonymous author, and published in Marseille, has been termed "the only comprehensive source" [*die einzige umfassende Quelle*] by Schuchardt (quoted in Coates, 1971: 25). I argue that the "myth" of MLF has been perpetuated by at least two (semi-related) notions: (a) the act of naming the MLF itself and its associated "glottonym" and (b) the historical context surrounding the writing of the *Dictionnaire*. When these factors are taken into consideration – that is, when the text is placed within its proper sociolinguistic and historical context – the unremarkable linguistic phenomena recorded in the *Dictionnaire* are brought to light. Indeed, recent work by scholars has already begun to trace the "standard" language origins of MLF (Cifoletti, 2002; Operstein, 2017, 2018). The final part of the paper offers an alternative typology for classifying the MLF data recorded in the *Dictionnaire*, and suggests that the majority of forms recorded are the same (or very similar) to standard Italian, thus presenting evidence against the hypothesis that MLF can be considered a separate language variety. Overall, this chapter stresses the way in which the creation of the *Dictionnaire* coincided with a broader trend to include language as part of a nationalist discourse more generally, thus helping to perpetuate its myth. Very little literature, so far, has questioned the existence of the MLF variety itself. This chapter acts a corrective to this record. It has implications for the way researchers consider mixed-language phenomena in the past and emphasises the need to continually evaluate the social element in historical linguistic research more generally.

The act of language naming and "glottonyms"

One question that is rarely addressed in a direct way is the meaning attached to MLF itself. The act of language naming, and their resultant names ("glottonyms"), has meant that MLF is often highly polysemous and applied to a broad range of contact phenomena where speakers do not share a common code. Regardless of the historical period, geographical area, or nature of the data that researchers work with, a traditional approach has seen scholars take their data *a priori* to be a MLF variety. In some cases, this may be because the most copious material for our knowledge of MLF comes from the *Dictionnaire* itself, whose title contains the words *langue franque*, (thus presenting – seemingly – a description of an as-yet unrecorded language variety). Upon closer inspection, its material appears suspiciously to conform to any mixed-language phenomena of one or more contact varieties, as we will see in section 5 below. This has been the case particularly since Schuchardt's seminal study of 1909, entitled *Die Lingua Franca*, which Selbach (2017: 253) has said "called to life" this language in the field of Pidgin and Creole studies. This description suggests a variety that was somehow mythically resurrected.[4] Indeed, Selbach concludes that "there is no primary evidence in support of the traditional definition of Lingua Franca" (2017: 269).

Other researchers have attempted to seek the origins of MLF, without providing an assessment of exactly which varieties contributed to it, or how it was formed in the first place. In a magisterial chapter, Mallette (2014: 334) writes that "if the grammatical structure and the lexicon [of MLF] are difficult to pin down, the origin of the language is altogether lost in the mists of time". Acknowledgement of MLF sources is deemed to vary "widely". Nevertheless, there is still a tendency to accept certain textual samples as representative of "some valid version of Lingua Franca". If one cannot do so, "the only other course of action is to ignore the subject completely" (Collier, 1977: 281). Despite these efforts, "not much general agreement has been reached concerning its origin" and "many questions remain unanswered" (Sedlaczek, 2017: 16–17).[5] The name *lingua franca* itself is enticing for any researcher looking for evidence of a "common language" between peoples of distant geographical regions in the past. But the act of naming any variety (whether it exists or not is irrelevant), as the anonymous author of the *Dictionnnaire* did in 1830, is crucial for our understanding of exactly which variety is being described. The porous definition and lack of data in MLF research have meant that most researchers rely on the *Dictionnaire*, or have gone seeking evidence of MLF in historical texts to fit a pre-established category.[6] If we pose that the variety did exist, then we should remind ourselves that: (1) all named languages are contact languages; they have always borrowed from, and mixed with other languages and language varieties and (2) the naming of languages is a political and ideological act and has been closely connected with the creation of the nation-state (Barbour, 2000; Wright, 2000).

In this sense, the key dates in the historiography of MLF are crucial. The first of these is 1830, the year of publication of the *Dictionnaire*.

This appears to be the first attempt to codify the variety and which contains an explicit reference to the term *lingua franca* in its title. In none of the previous works identified in Selbach's (2017) corpus – which is itself simplified from Arends (1998) – does the term MLF appear. Table 9.1 reports all 49 items listed in Arends' corpus. This corpus spans a period from 1204 to 1887. It includes texts from a wide variety of authors, places, and genres. The items included from one century to the next have been shaded in order to demonstrate how successive centuries contain more and more texts, which (presumably) corresponds to the growing nature and diffusion of MLF around the Mediterranean.

Even a cursory glance at this table is enough to show the small corpus of texts included for the eighteenth century – the period immediately preceding the publication of the *Dictionnaire*. Out of the 13 items included in the period from 1735 to 1798–1800, seven are derived from the writings of just one author. All have a literary nature. Arends himself noted the relative paucity of the data. Indeed, for items 5, 10, 20, and 32, he writes that these texts contain "only one LF sentence". In the last of these, for example, we are told that the *Account of an Algerine Corsair* of 1760 contains just one simple phrase: "*Inglaterra! Inglaterra! Bona Inglaterra!*". It is on evidence of this order that such documents have been included in descriptions of MLF and its analysis. Further, it is not entirely clear which criteria were used to include or exclude documents from the corpus. The consequence has been for scholars to search for historical instances of MLF in texts which bear little resemblance to Schuchardt's original study (1909). In short, scholars have gone looking for evidence of MLF which are either ill-defined, or identified in an anachronistic way.

The question of naming the language variety described in the *Dictionnaire* is crucial for the way in which researchers have subsequently categorised the data they have worked with – be it from the *Dictionnaire*, or any other source. The problem is particularly acute when the goal has been to ascribe MLF phenomena to *other* linguistic varieties. These varieties have usually been national standards of Romance vernaculars (excluding some obvious influences of Arabic and Turkish), thereby disregarding the potential dialectal variation around the Mediterranean basin and which may have contributed to the formation of MLF. In this regard, the glottonym *lingua franca* is no different to any other linguistic descriptor. As Pountain (2016: 638) has said, "use of a language name does not imply the existence of a readily identifiable *Abstand* language".[7] Similarly, the adoption of the term *lingua franca* by the anonymous author of the *Dictionnaire* does not imply a corresponding reality in either a diachronic or synchronic sense.

The glottonym *lingua franca* is related to the broader historical context and linguistic historiography of late nineteenth-century philology in which Schuchardt was himself immersed. This, too, has had implications

174   J. Brown

Table 9.1 A reproduction of Arends' (1998) corpus of primary documents containing evidence of the Mediterranean Lingua Franca (MLF)

#	Year	Title	Author	Place	Genre
1	1204?	Credo in latinike glotta	anonymous	n/a	religious
2	1300	Contrasto della Zerbitana	anonymous	n/a	poem
3	1353	Zerbitana Retica	anonymous	Djerba	poem
4	c.1410	Das Lied von der Kreuzfahrt	Oswald von Wolkenstein	Eastern Mediterranean	poem
5	1484	dialogue fragment	Fabri	Alexandria	travel report
6	1520	Villancico	Encina	Holy Land	song
7	1528	dialogue fragment in letter to pope	Giovio	Djerba to Rome	letter
8	1545	Zingana	Giancarli	Rovigo	play
9	1581	Matona mia cara	Orlando di Lasso	Eastern Mediterranean	poem
10	1600	The diary of Master Thomas Dallam	Dallam	Rhodos	gentleman travel report
11	1612	Topographia de Argel	Haedo (ed.)	Algiers	slave travel report
12	1637	Histoire de la Barbarie et de ses corsaires	Pierre Dan	Barbary	redemptionist missionary travel report
13	1644	Jesuit dialogue fragment	P. Jose Tamayo	Algiers	prose fragment
14	1662	Relation de la captivite et liberte du sieur Emanuel de Aranda, mene esclave a Alger en l'an 1640 et mis en liberte l'an 1642	Emanuel de Aranda	Brussels	report
15	1664	Voyage de la France Equinoxiale en l'isle Cayenne, entrepris par les Francois en l'annee MDCLII	Antoine de Biet	Barbuda	travel report
16	1667	Le sicilien	Jean-Baptiste Poquelin de Moliere	Eastern Mediterranean	n/a
17	1670	Dicionario des escritores trinitarios de Espana y Portugal, vol. IX	Antonio de la Asuncion (1899)	Algiers	Word list
18	c.1670	Libro en que se da razon del viaje que hicimos a la ciudad de Argel el ano de 1670	Bartolome Serrano	Algiers	Word list
19	c.1675	Histoire chronologique du Royaume de Tripoly	anonymous		History
20	c.1683	No title	Otto Friedrich von der Groeben	Liberia	travel report
21	1697	L'Europe galante	M. de la Mothe	Eastern Mediterranean	n/a
22	1735	Memoires du chevalier d'Arvieux	Laurent d'Arvieux	Tunis	memoirs
23	1735	La birba	Goldoni, Carlo	Eastern Mediterranean	literary
24	1737	Lugrezia Romana in Constantinopoli	Goldoni, Carlo	Eastern Mediterranean	literary
25	1749	La famiglia dell'antiquario	Goldoni, Carlo	Eastern Mediterranean	literary
26	1751	I pettegolezzi delle donne	Goldoni, Carlo	Eastern Mediterranean	literary
27	1755	Le donne de casa soa	Goldoni, Carlo	Eastern Mediterranean	literary
28	1760	L'impresario delle Smirne	Goldoni, Carlo	Eastern Mediterranean	literary
29	1760	La fiera di sinigaglia	Goldoni, Carlo	Eastern Mediterranean	literary
30	1741	El mercante Armeno	Malamani, V	Eastern Mediterranean	literary
31	c.1740	Un Turco inamora'	Malamani, V	Eastern Mediterranean	literary
32	1760	Account of an Algerine Corsair, on the Coast of Cornwall	anonymous	Algiers	report
33	1789	Reise in die Barbarey oder Briefe aus Alt-Numidien	Jean L. M. Poiret	Barbary	travel report
34	1798-1800	Nachrichten und Bemerkungen uber den algierschen Staat	Anonymous	Algiers	travel report
35	1805	Ragguaglio del viaggio compendioso di un dilettante antiquario sorpreso da corsari, condotto in Barberia e felicemente ripatriato	Felice Caronni	Tunis	travel report
36	1817	Avventure ed osservazioni sopra le coste di Barberia	Filippo Pananti	Algiers	travel report
37	1822-1825	MS in the Archivio del Consolato sardo, Tripoli	Yusuf Qaramanli	Tripoli	n/a
38	1830	Dictionnaire de la Langue Franque ou Petit Mauresque	Anonymous	Algiers	dictionary
39	1830	Gemalde von Algier	M. Renaudot	Algiers	n/a
40	1834	Notice sur Tunez et biographie du Bach Mamelouk Hassine. Revue de l'Histoire des Colonies Francaises	Louis Calligaris	Tunis	report
41	1850	Tunis: Description de cette Regence. L'univers Pictoresque	Louis Frank	Tunis	travel report
42	1852	La langue Sabir	Anonymous	Algiers	report
43	1863	Drei Jahre im Nordwesten von Afrika	Heinrich Freiherr von Maltzan	Barbary coast	travel report
44	1870	Schicksale und Wanderungen eines deutschen Renegaten in Nordafrika	Heinrich Freiherr von Maltzan	Barbary coast	travel report
45	1882	Letter to Hugo Schuchardt	Emil Jellinek	Barbary coast	letter
46	1884	L'alliance francaise pour la propagation de la langue francaise dans les colonies et les pays etrangers	L. Faidherbe	Algiers	general
47	1884	Review of Faidherbe	Victor Waille	Algiers	review article
48	1887	L'Algerie qui s'en va	Bernard	Algiers	travel report
49	1887	Voyage dans le sud de la Tunisie	Valerie Mayet	Tunisia	travel report

Source: © Joshua Brown

for perpetuating the MLF myth.[8] Let us briefly consider this context before moving to the previous taxonomies that have been proposed for MLF data.

The historical context of the *Dictionnaire*

Discussions surrounding MLF often take place without sufficient consideration of the socio-historical context within which such texts were written. This also goes for the creation of the *Dictionnaire*. There are at least two characteristics of late eighteenth-century and early nineteenth-century Europe which should be taken into consideration whenever dealing with MLF. The first is the context of dictionary writing which proliferated in Europe more generally. The second concerns the relationship between language and nationalism in the same period.

The nineteenth century has been called the "century of dictionaries" (Marazzini, 1994: 385). This period is characterised by an impressive number of dictionaries and dictionary writing, some of which have a comparative or "encyclopedic" nature. Several make explicit references to concepts such as *universale*, *totius*, or historical periods referred to as *epoche*.

In fact, the appearance of the *Dictionnaire* occurs precisely at the midpoint of an extraordinary activity of dictionary production. Between 1765 and 1840, nearly a dozen dictionaries were produced in Romance languages (Spanish, French and Italian) as well as in Latin, including the *Traité de la formation mécanique des langues* (1765), *Catálogo de las lenguas de las naciones conocidas* (1800), Villanova's *Dizionario universale critico enciclopedico della lingua italiana*, and Foscolo's *Epoche della lingua italiana* (1823). Many of the dictionaries record a variety which was to become a national standard, in the effort and interest of "building the nation". This century has also been described as a period of "re-awakening" of interest in the variety of local speech communities, whose production included, especially in France and Spain, "a vast series of glossaries, dictionaries and elementary descriptions of dialects and *patois*" (Simone, 1998: 189). It is no coincidence, therefore, that the year 1830 also marks the conquest of Algeria by France and an attempt by the anonymous author of the *Dictionnaire* to enshrine this military "victory" also in linguistic terms. The social value of its creation and the enthusiasm with which its author composed it has also been commented upon. Aslanov (2014: 128), for example, notes: "*Eager as they were* to give an account of the contact vernacular used in the Regency of Algiers, the author or the authors of the Dictionnaire probably condensed into one book two varieties of the Lingua Franca" [my emphasis]. In other words, the *Dictionnaire* is written in the broader context of a general desire to codify as yet unrecorded language varieties. Throughout Europe, and particularly France, "there was interest in and curiosity about the languages and cultures of ancient India, and documents and evidence of that world were collected" (Simone, 1998: 212). At the same time as linguists were aiming to study language and make mixed-language phenomena "fit" a standard language, nationalism was using language to help fulfil its goals of "making the nation". This enthusiasm may have contributed somewhat to producing a dictionary of MLF for both a nationalist and militaristic narrative.

Secondly, nationalism and nationalist discourses may also help to shed light on Schuchardt's original analysis (1909). The concept of the nation is a particularly European idea, and develops clearly from the eighteenth century onwards (Barbour, 2000: 14). The idea that a nation closely identifies with one particular language is even more restricted, and little more than two centuries old. For individual nations, "the potential for a shared first language can facilitate greater economic and political cooperation between citizens" (Barbour, 2000: 15). Multilingual states were seen by emerging national elites as barriers to progress. Indeed, the concept of "one nation, one language" throughout Europe was heavily influenced by the French case, "where the common language was promoted by the revolutionary state as a means of achieving democracy and equality". Nationalism's attitude towards language was "one of minimizing internal linguistic difference in the community in question, formalizing language in a way that would empower intellectual classes, and emphasizing external linguistic difference" (Ruzza, 2000: 173). How do these elements, then, influence the way we should read the *Dictionnaire*? These movements provide the broader context within which we must see its creation and the variety it contains. In short, there is little attempt to consider the possibility that "lingua franca" may simply be a hybrid, mixed variety. The aim of its creator was to provide a one-to-one translation of certain lexemes into "standard French". The aim for Schuchardt was to consider the mixed phenomenon of MLF, but through a lens of discerning the languages of nation-states, rather than as a potential written reflection of mixed, local varieties.

In order to see how these two characteristics (dictionary writing and nationalist narratives) of early modern Europe have coloured earlier analyses of MLF, it will be useful to look at some examples of previous taxonomies and how they have been designed in favour of classifying MLF phenomena within a framework of standard languages. In turn, this will allow a new taxonomy to emerge in Lexical entries in the Dictionnaire.

Previous taxonomies of MLF phenomena

One question that remains unresolved is the lexical base of MLF, despite a general consensus that the variety has a mixed Romance origin. It has been estimated that the Italian lexical component comprises "approximately half of the approximately 2,000 MLF lexical items listed in the *Dictionnaire*" (Operstein, 2017: 107). One difficulty which researchers face is precisely the impossibility of separating out Italianisms from other Romance varieties, as has been previously pointed out (Minervini, 2014: 73). Minervini, as well as Operstein (2017: 111, n.6), highlight "specific correspondences between selected LF items derivable from Spanish (or Italian) and their cognates in Genoese and/or Portuguese (e.g. *agoua* 'water', *amigo* 'friend', *nome* 'name')". Operstein concludes this note by saying that "a more thorough study of the lexical contribution of these languages to LF would be highly desirable".[9] Minervini looked at "Italianisms" in a range of MLF writing, noting how many Jews of Italian origin had undergone a process of "Sephardization" (2014: 67). But since standard Italian is in fact none other than the continuation of Tuscan, this is unhelpful. Indeed, Baglioni (2016: 139) stresses the non-Tuscan nature of MLF: "it was likely a form of Italian that was distant from the literary language, in which non-Tuscan elements and items from other languages must have been more frequent".[10]

A second obstacle must be overcome. It is not a simple matter, for example, to define exactly *which* vernaculars contributed to the lexical stock of MLF. Italian dialects are not "dialects of Italian", but rather daughter languages of Latin, and vary widely at all levels of linguistic abstraction, including lexis. This variation continues today, although convergence processes have reduced the most conspicuous examples.[11] Previous researchers have sometimes substituted Italian to mean "Tuscan", thus precluding non-Tuscan dialects as a potential lexical source.[12] The hypothesis that MLF has a Tuscan base is further complicated by the ambiguity surrounding exactly what is meant by "origins".[13] If, as Minervini (2010: 802) believes, it is documented only from the late 1500s along the coasts of the Mediterranean, then it seems plausible that the matrix language may be composed not only of Tuscan, given the prominence of seafaring companies from that region around the Mediterranean, but also from the powerful companies working further north, as in Genoa, or along the Adriatic coast, such as Venice.[14]

Varieties other than Italo-Romance identified by previous researchers as contributor varieties to MLF lexis cover an extraordinary range, as shown in Table 9.2 on the next page. They include the following (listed in alphabetical order of variety). Note that, for the most part, the variety identified corresponds to a modern, standard glottonym.

Italo-Romance vernaculars that contributed to the lexical base of MLF have also been identified. In some cases, the descriptors are used to cover wide geographical areas. These are included in Table 9.3.

Whether these varieties contributed to MLF or not remains to be proven. Baglioni (2016: 138) is one of the few researchers to reject the inherent geographical variation of MLF: "Sporadic, but very interesting evidence, document the circulation in the Mediterranean not of varieties that are diatopically characterised, but rather of Italian".[17] In short, the exact mechanisms through which these varieties contribute to the

Table 9.2 Varieties other than Italo-Romance previously identified in MLF

Variety	Example(s)	Cited by
Arabic[15]	*tarjuman* "translator"	Aslanov (2014: 126)
		Burke (2004: 127)
		Minervini (2010: 802)
Catalan	*baschiar* "to descend"	Cifoletti (1989: 65)
Latinisms	*brakio* "malt"	Cifoletti (1989: 65)
Luso-Arabic	no example given	Aslanov (2014: 131)
French	*biéra* "beer"	Schuchardt (1909: 41)
Greek	*aspra*[16] "money"	Cifoletti (2004: 42, n.1)
Occitan	*gorba* "basket"	Aslanov (2014: 129)
Portuguese	*ficar* "to remain"	Aslanov (2014: 125; 131)
		Minervini (2014: 73)
Provençal	*boulégar* "to move"	Cifoletti (1989: 65)
	cadiéra "chair"	
Spanish	*bentana* "window"	Operstein (2017: 107)
Turkish	*pasa* "Pasha"	Aslanov (2014: 126)
		Minervini (2010: 802)

Source: © Joshua Brown

formation of MLF are unclear. In some cases, such as the word *mi*, we are dealing with pan-Romance lexemes, and items that can be traced to a wide variety of texts, places, and times. In other cases, such as *giaba* "to scam (something)", little evidence has so far suggested itself as to exactly when or where such lexemes entered MLF.

On the existence of the Mediterranean lingua franca: A sorites paradox?

The method of classifying MLF phenomena according to these previous criteria has led to a situation known as a "sorites paradox" – a paradox that arises from vague predicates (Barker, 2009: 1037). While this notion is not generally adopted in studies of language contact, or at least with much frequency, it *has* been referenced recently by Börjars *et al.* (2015: 364)

Table 9.3 Varieties of Italo-Romance previously identified in MLF

Variety	Example	Cited by
Venetian	*mi* 'I'	Cifoletti (1989: 64–65)
		Cifoletti (1991: 35)
		Burke (2004: 127)
Genoese	*giaba* "to scam [sthg.]"	Cifoletti (1989: 65)
		Minervini (2014: 73)
		Whinnom (1977: 298)
Southern Italo-Romance	*aca* "here"	Cifoletti (1989: 64–65)
Sicilian	*mischinu* "unfortunate"	Aslanov (2014: 127)

Source: © Joshua Brown

in their review of Traugott and Trousdale's 2013 study of constructionalisation and constructional changes. Although the definition of "change" provided in the study by Traugott and Trousdale appears intuitive, the reviewers note that it is toothless when considering "change as innovation" alongside the undefined concept of "population". The reviewers wonder whether a hundred speakers are enough (perhaps two hundred?), before one is able to adequately measure "change" in a "population". It is in this context, they note, that a sorites paradox arises. The concept is equally useful when considering so-called contact varieties, such as MLF, and the question of precisely when one can establish that a contact variety can be said to have formed historically.

Tracing the provenance of linguistic phenomena – whether it be at a phonological, morphological, lexical level, whatever – proves highly problematic when we are dealing with a "language" that supposedly covers such a broad chronological period, and so few documents. The problem stems from the notion that MLF is itself susceptible to impotency without a proper understanding of the nature of language contact, and without a corpus that will allow scholars to investigate whether a new variety emerged at all. In the absence of reliable tools, we cannot reject the hypothesis that MLF data may represent surface phenomena that are characteristic of most typologically similar varieties whenever they come into contact. This is where the paradox occurs. Since the forms generally reckoned to be MLF are traceable, if not identical, to forms in other Romance languages, is it still possible to talk about a distinct variety if we subtract x number of words from the *Dictionnaire*? What about if we dismiss a certain number of items from Arends' corpus, some of which, as he explains in the bibliography, only include "one line in LF"?

Previous researchers concede that attempts at seeking dialectal boundaries between MLF and Romance are flawed. Aslanov, for example, notes that the isogloss "between Lingua Franca and Provençal (at least as far as the use of the demonstrative is concerned) is too general to be ascribed to a direct contact" (2014: 133). On the same page, he speaks only of a "partial isogloss" (but according to which feature?). Not only is a matrix language dismissed, but the question of defining its importance in the first place is equally disregarded:

> whatever the importance of the Portuguese-based nucleus of Lingua Franca may be, it is obvious that the main bulk of the linguistic material represented by this contact vernacular has to do with the two major Romance languages of Western Mediterranean: Spanish on the one hand and Italian on the other.
>
> (Aslanov, 2014: 133)[18]

Similar comments can be said to characterise an earlier study (Aslanov, 2000), which "concerns a strange coexistence of French and

Italian within the same sentence" – in other words, just one. In a later work (2014: 132), precisely on myth and MLF, Aslanov expresses doubt regarding the existence of MLF and the nature of its contact: "Lingua Franca crystallized as a result of the convergence between two or three Romance languages on the basis of a primordial nucleus that *may have been a real contact vernacular*" (my emphasis).

A clearer picture of the "donor" varieties to MLF lexis may emerge by considering the lexical entries of the *Dictionnaire*, and the extent to which they show similarity, if not a precise correspondence, to forms of standard Italian.

Lexical entries in the Dictionnaire

The *Dictionnaire* contains 2,120 entries. As noted above, the work does not provide definitions. Rather, it lists the French entry in the left-hand column while providing the corresponding MLF term in the right-hand column in a one-to-one mapping. Images of the title page of the *Dictionnaire*, and the first page of recorded forms for the letter "A", are provided below in Figures 9.1 and 9.2, respectively.

Many of the MLF terms appear numerous times for different French terms. For example, the MLF entry *adesso* is given as the corresponding element for both the French *maintenant* and *présent*. Similarly, MLF *cascar* is provided as the only entry for French *s'écrouler, glisser, tomber, couler, écouler*. This may be evidence for a lack of lexical diversification in MLF. Other studies of contact languages have shown that, after initial mixing takes place, we are likely to see wide polymorphy before levelling occurs (Britain, 2012: 224).[19] It is only in a subsequent period that multiple features may become levelled, but different semantic terms are likely to remain. In this sense, the entries recorded in the *Dictionnaire* do not appear to be representative of a separate variety, whether it has creolised or not.[20]

If one eliminates the duplicates in the MLF column from the 2,120 total number of entries in the *Dictionnaire*, 1,887 unique lexemes remain. Even a cursory glance at these entries, however, suggests a lack of complexity and diversity. As such, it is difficult to understand how they could be presented as evidence for a distinct variety of Romance. Of these 1,887 unique items, 697 are written the same as standard Italian.[21] Of these 697, a further 583 items may be subtracted whose orthography is clearly designed to mirror Italian pronunciation, but whose phonology is ultimately unknown. These include items such as *taska, soupa, pépé*, etc. Combining both categories (same lexeme and orthography), one arrives at a figure of 1,280 unique MLF items; in other words, a sizeable 68% of the total corpus can be said to be the same as standard Tuscan forms. This figure can be further increased, by considering items whose stem is exactly the same as standard Italian, but whose

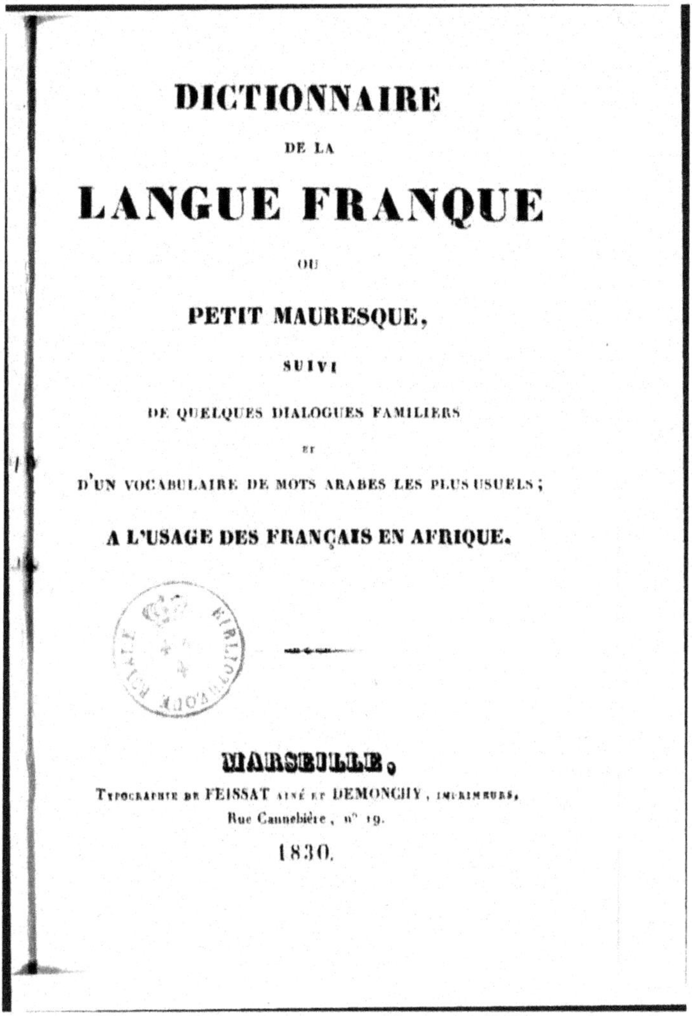

DICTIONNAIRE

DE LA

LANGUE FRANQUE

OU

PETIT MAURESQUE,

SUIVI

DE QUELQUES DIALOGUES FAMILIERS

ET

D'UN VOCABULAIRE DE MOTS ARABES LES PLUS USUELS;

A L'USAGE DES FRANÇAIS EN AFRIQUE.

MARSEILLE,

TYPOGRAPHIE DE FEISSAT AÎNÉ ET DEMONCHY, IMPRIMEURS,

Rue Cannebière, n° 19.

1830.

Figure 9.1 Title page of the *Dictionnaire de la langue franque ou petit mauresque* printed in Marseille in 1830

Source: https://gallica.bnf.fr/ark:/12148/bpt6k6290361w.texteImage/Bibliothèque nationale de France

desinence shows a non-Italian element (e.g. *dios, attention, pensiéré*). These items bring the total count to 1,366, or 72% of the total corpus. Of the remaining elements, one finds a different lexical root (as in *boriqua* "donkey") or some feature indicative of phonetic change (*poder* "to be able"). Nevertheless, these categories combined are relatively small when compared to the overall corpus, representing only 26% of all MLF entries. The total constitution of all items in the *Dictionnaire* according to these categories is best visualised in Figure 9.3.

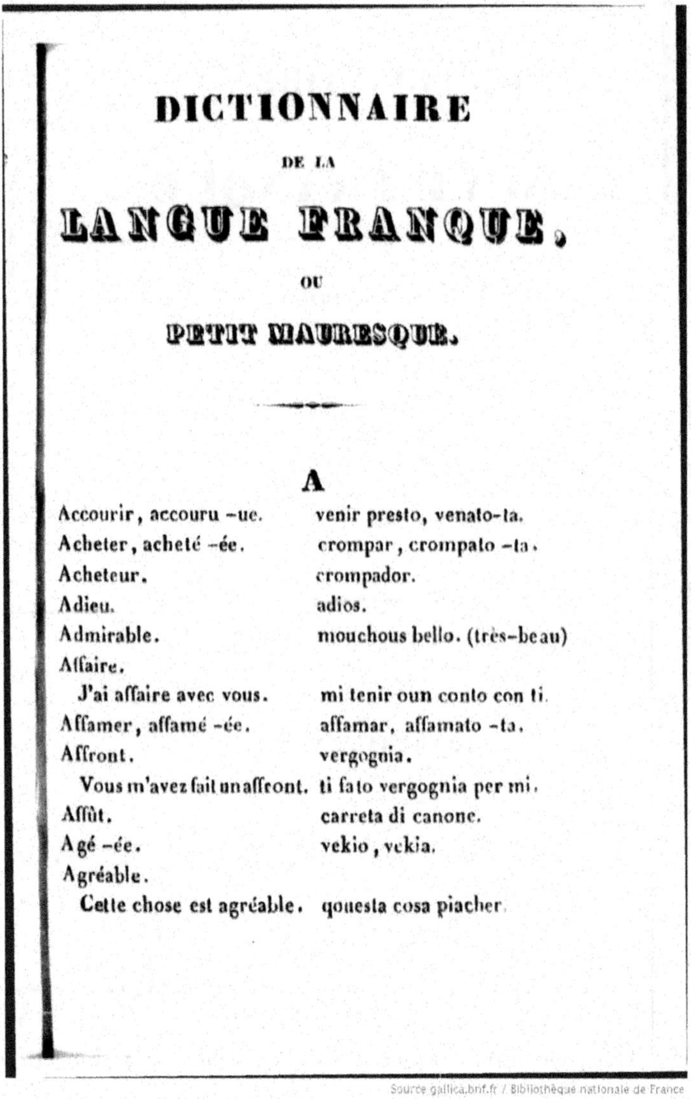

DICTIONNAIRE

DE LA

LANGUE FRANQUE,

OU

PETIT MAURESQUE.

A

Accourir, accouru -ue.	venir presto, venato-ta.
Acheter, acheté -ée.	crompar, crompato -ta.
Acheteur.	crompador.
Adieu.	adios.
Admirable.	mouchous bello. (très-beau)
Affaire.	
J'ai affaire avec vous.	mi tenir oun conto con ti.
Affamer, affamé -ée.	affamar, affamato -ta.
Affront.	vergognia.
Vous m'avez fait un affront.	ti fato vergognia per mi.
Affût.	carreta di canone.
Agé -ée.	vekio, vekia.
Agréable.	
Cette chose est agréable.	qouesta cosa piacher.

Figure 9.2 The first page of the *Dictionnaire de la langue franque ou petit mauresque* (1830) showing correspondences between French (left column) and the Mediterranean Lingua Franca (right column).

Source: https://gallica.bnf.fr/ark:/12148/bpt6k6290361w.texteImage/Bibliothèque nationale de France

In short, these statistics point to strong evidence for a sorites paradox. At what point can we say this variety ever existed, particularly when the recorded forms show such a high degree of similarity, if not exactitude, with standard Italian, let alone other Romance varieties? This is not to deny that the author of the *Dictionnaire* recorded forms that historically

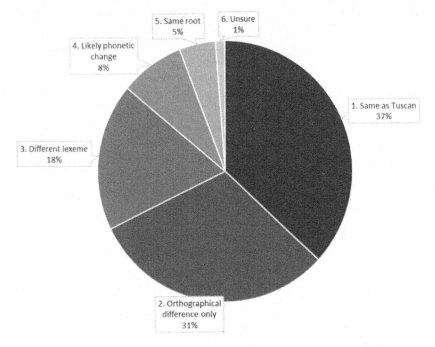

Figure 9.3 Taxonomy of Mediterranean Lingua Franca items listed in the *Dictionnaire de la langue franque ou petit mauresque* (1830).

Source: © Joshua Brown

existed, or that what has been passed down is a faithful attempt to record these items by the author. But they are not unexpected in an environment of language contact, and show no evidence of having creolised or having undergone any subsequent development as a contact variety.[22] It may be typologically convenient to refer to the mixed phenomenon as a separate "pidgin", "lingua franca", etc., but the phenomena described are the expected results whenever any two (or more) varieties come into contact, especially when such varieties are in such a state of flux over a long period of time and are typologically related.

Conclusion

This chapter has considered a specific variety of lingua franca, called the "Mediterranean Lingua Franca". First described in these terms by Schuchardt (1909), the vicissitudes of its study have seen it supported along nationalistic arguments at times, and along a desire to see in it some form of mythical cross-cultural communication at others. This chapter, and the linguistic data contained within it, are situated within a framework known as a sorites paradox. On the one hand, this decision has been based on the repeated (sometimes successful) attempts by scholars to find correspondences in MLF data with standard languages. On the other hand, a sorites paradox allows us to interrogate a large dataset ("heap"), such as the forms recorded in the *Dictionnaire*, in order to show how the variety's existence can be defined in terms of only a small amount of mixed-language forms. Whether these forms themselves can be said to constitute a linguistic reality seems to have little support in the literature, or little evidence historically. It has now been over fifty years since Coates (1971: 25) first reported that one is obliged "to rely on historical records for our knowledge of [MLF], and those records are unfortunately few, brief, and rather unreliable". In a recent investigation, Baglioni has noted that "labels such as 'mixed language' or 'langue métisse' (as in the title of Dakhlia, 2008) appear inappropriate and even misleading when referred to the LF" (2018: 203). Despite often being touted as a trade language between different peoples of the Mediterranean, Selbach also concluded that one is left "with a literary study of an oral language. And a myth on shaky grounds" (2017: 269).

What, then, is one to make of the forms recorded in the *Dictionnaire*? In all likelihood, the linguistic phenomena that are generally taken to be MLF never represented a divergent, separate language variety. Nor would they have been considered so by the people who used them, assuming someone did. This evaluation has recently been observed by Schulte (2018: 623) in terms of Romance in contact with Romance more generally: "the closer the contact languages are in structural terms, the more likely it becomes for speakers not to have completely separate cognitive representations of the different languages involved". The author(s) of the *Dictionnaire* may have considered some form of Italian as a lingua franca, with transfers from several languages around the Mediterranean Sea basin, including Catalan, Arabic, Portuguese, etc. In short, MLF did not exist as such on the basis of the extant documents; rather, it was a sort of nineteenth-century myth.

Mallette (2014: 332) has written, specifically of MLF, that "scholars today agree that almost all of these records represent other linguistic phenomena generated by the collision of Latin-Romance, Greek and Arabic language systems and that, while they are interesting in themselves, they have little to do with the *lingua franca* as such". While the term *lingua franca* continues to be highly polysemous, one must be cautious in applying it to varieties for which the historical record is particularly fragmentary, and to linguistic phenomena which can be best explained when the appropriate sociolinguistic context is taken into consideration.

Notes

1. This appears to be the same sense in which Migliorini (1960: 559) adopts the term as well: "Along the coasts of the Mediterranean, especially in the east, Italian is still very well known in spoken usage in the simplified

form of "lingua franca", and in written usage as a diplomatic language" [Sulle coste del Mediterraneo, specialmente orientale, l'italiano è ancora molto noto nell'uso parlato sotto la forma semplificata di "lingua franca", e nell'uso scritto come lingua diplomatica]. The non-singularity which *lingua franca* encompasses has been noted by Tommasino (2017: 35), who writes that it must include "markedly different linguistic varieties". For a study of the use of Italian as a lingua franca as a "common" language in Italy during the nineteenth century, see Colombo and Kinder (2012).
2. Cf. Diaz (2016: 224) describes MLF as a "paralanguage". She adopts a broad view, deciding that MLF was "born out of the mix between one or several Romance languages and any eastern or Levantine language".
3. "Il semble que cette extension abusive de la notion de *langue franque* à l'Orient de la Méditerranée résulte d'une équivoque résultant de la polysémie du terme *lisān al-faranj* qui peut nommer n'importe quelle langue parlée par des Francs (Occidentaux) perçus d'un point de vue levantin". All translations are my own unless otherwise stated.
4. Schuchardt's essay is available online at: http://schuchardt.uni-graz.at/. Venier (2012) has provided a translation of this work into Italian, as well as commentary and analysis of some aspects. On the beginnings of pidgin and creole studies, and Schuchardt's contribution, see Meijer and Muysken (1977).
5. A recent exception to this general pattern is the comments provided by Biosca and Castellanos (2017: 40), who note the following, while not questioning either the existence of MLF or that a pidgin was formed: "it is reasonable *to assume* that, as [Mediterranean Lingua Franca] took shape, it was influenced by the remnants of Vulgar Latin (...) contact with speakers of non-Latin languages accelerated the pidginization (morpho-syntactic simplification and hybridization) that gave rise to this language" [my emphasis]. Cf. also Mallette (2014: 332) "We do not possess substantial positive evidence of the lingua franca until the opening decades of the seventeenth century".
6. Other similar comments are found in Selbach (2017: 253): "Scholarship has thus been chipping away at larger and smaller parts of the Lingua Franca myth for over a century, yet with little consensus, and little impact on general knowledge".
7. Following Kloss (1967), Pountain defines *Abstand* as "what we might regard as distinguishable naturally occurring spoken languages" (2016: 634). Pountain points to the list of languages in which Wikipedia pages are available, noting how "Emilian-Romagnol" is in reality "a group of Romance varieties defined only by their geographical location in the Emilia-Romagna region created by the Italian constitution in 1948".
8. Here it is worth noting that Schuchardt makes reference to the French orientalist Jacques Auguste Cherbonneau's *Observations sur l'origine et la formation du langage arabe africain* of 1855. Cherbonneau described the *langage arabe africain* as "a curious amalgamation of Spanish words, Italian terms, and French expressions" [un amalgame curieux de mots espagnols, de termes italiens et de tournures françaises]. In a footnote to her translation of Schuchardt's work, Venier (2012: 15, n.1) comments on this description, noting that "this alternation of nouns leads one to suppose a relationship *that, in reality, does not exist*" [questo alternarsi di sostantivi lascia supporre una relazione *che nella realtà non sussiste*] (my emphasis).
9. Operstein (2017: 107), citing Cornelissen (1992: 220), estimates that 39% of lexical items from the Haedo (1612) can be traced back to more than one Romance language. For the *Dictionnaire*, 27% of words exist in more

than one Romance language. Aslanov (2014: 128–130) deals with some of these issues in his section "Hispanized Italian or italianized Spanish?", concluding that these forms represent a "hybrid linguistic object" (2014: 128), and rejecting a separate MLF variety.

10. verosimilmente si trattava di un italiano distante dalla lingua letteraria, in cui elementi non toscani e inserti di altre lingue dovevano essere assai frequenti.
11. Vincent (1988: 310) reports one empirical study by Swiss linguist Robert Rüegg in the early 1950s: "only one of the 242 concepts investigated, 'strong black coffee served in a bar', had a common designation for the 124 informants from 54 provinces, namely *espresso*!".
12. Symptomatic in this regard is Cifoletti (1989: 63): "If we look now at the origin of words used in lingua franca, one notices immediately that they are, for the most part, derived from Italian" [Se si guarda ora all'origine delle parole usate nella lingua franca, ci si accorge subito che esse sono in massima parte derivate dall'italiano].
13. While I do not enter into a discussion here of the chronological limits of MLF, it will suffice to mention that previous researchers have estimated its origin anywhere from the tenth century, the fifteenth century (Castellanos, 2007: 2) to the late sixteenth century (Minervini, 2010: 802). Castellanos (2007: 2) sees the creation of MLF as a result of the commercial expansion of the Franks, who came into contact with North African Arabs and Berbers. It was only in subsequent centuries that this contact then became Italianized.
14. On the question of whether MLF can be considered a Mediterranean trade pidgin at all, see Selbach (2017), who rejects this hypothesis.
15. Cf. Aslanov (2014: 124): "As for the genuinely Arabic words that occasionally appear in Lingua Franca, they are hardly more abundant than the Arabic component in Sicilian, Castilian and Portuguese".
16. Cf. Cifoletti (2004: 42, n.1): "Reported by several other sources (Serrano, Tamayo, etc.), this is one of the few Greekisms in lingua franca" [Riportato da diverse altre fonti (Serrano, Tamayo ecc.) questo è uno dei pochi grecismi della lingua franca]. The transcription provided by Cifoletti on pages 57–75 provides no other cases of *grecismi*.
17. Testimonianze sporadiche ma interessantissime documentano poi la circolazione in ambito mediterraneo non di varietà diatopicamente caratterizzate, bensì dell'italiano.
18. Cf. his statement on p. 128: "Lingua Franca is in fact the result of a synthesis between some Romance languages". What this 'synthesis' consists of is not further defined.
19. Britain (2012: 224) describes levelling as "the eradication of marked linguistic features, marked in the sense of being in a minority in the ambient linguistic environment after the contact 'event', marked in the sense of being overtly stereotyped, or marked in the sense of being found rarely in the languages of the world and/or acquired late in first language acquisition".
20. Derivational morphology also helps to explain other forms recorded in the *Dictionnaire*. But these endings similarly reflect patterns of already attested word-formation in other Romance varieties. In most cases, infinitives, always placed into the *-ar* category, are simply derivations from the form given for singular, masculine nouns (e.g. *dopio* > *dopiar*; *pranzo* > *prantzar*), with each item listed as a separate entry.
21. In this count, I have included infinitives whose final vowel is subject to apocope (also considered a feature of standard Italian in certain phonetic

environments, e.g. *parlar*). I have also included items showing diacritics, whose value is unknown in the *Dictionnaire*, as well as items whose orthography appears designed to mirror standard Italian (Tuscan), e.g. *médiko, melio, bagniar, picolo*.

22. See also Operstein (1998: 379): "The answer to the question whether LF was ever creolized, seems to be negative". The term "creole" is "used in sociolinguistics to refer to a pidgin language which has become the mother-tongue of a speech community, as is the case in Jamaica, Haiti, Dominica, and several other ex-colonial parts of the world. The process of creolization expands the structural and stylistic range of the pidginized language, so that the creolized language becomes comparable in formal and functional complexity to other languages" (Crystal, 2008: 122).

References

Arends, J. (1998). A bibliography of Lingua Franca. *The Carrier Pidgin*, 26(4–5), pp. 33–35.
Aslanov, C. (2000). Interpreting the language-mixing in terms of codeswitching: The case of the Franco-Italian interface in the Middle Ages. *Journal of Pragmatics*, 32(9), pp. 1273–1281.
Aslanov, C. (2002). Quand les langues romanes se confondent…La Romania va ailleurs. *Langage et société*, 99(1), pp. 9–52.
Aslanov, C. (2010). Débat sur l'ouvrage de Jocelyne Dakhlia, Lingua franca: histoire d'une langue métisse en Méditerranée. *Langage et société*, 4(134), pp. 103–113.
Aslanov, C. (2014). Lingua Franca in the Western Mediterranean: Between myth and reality. In: J. Besters-Dilger, C. Dermarkar, S. Pfänder and A. Rabus, eds., *Congruence in Contact-induced Language Change: Language Families, Typological Resemblance, and Perceived Similarity*, pp. 122–136. Berlin and Boston: De Gruyter.
Baglioni, D. (2016). L'italiano fuori d'Italia: dal Medioevo all'Unità. In: S. Lubello, ed., *Manuale di linguistica italiana*, pp. 125–145. Berlin: De Gruyter.
Baglioni, D. (2018). The vocabulary of the Algerian Lingua Franca. *Lexicographica*, 33(1), pp. 185-205.
Barbour, S. (2000). Nationalism, language, Europe. In: S. Barbour and C. Carmichael, eds., *Language and Nationalism in Europe*, pp. 1–17. Oxford: Oxford University Press.
Barker, C. (2009). Vagueness. In: K. Allan, ed., *Concise Encyclopedia of Semantics*, pp. 1037–1040. Amsterdam: Elsevier.
Biosca, C. and Castellanos, C. (2017). Maltese, Mediterranean Lingua Franca and the Occitan-Catalan linguistic group. In: B. Saade and M. Tosco, eds., *Advances in Maltese Linguistics*, pp. 39–66. Berlin: De Gruyter Mouton.
Börjars, K., Vincent, N. and Walkden, G. (2015). On constructing a theory of grammatical change. *Transactions of the Philological Society*, 113(3), pp. 363–382.
Britain, D. (2012). Koineization and cake baking: Reflections on methods in dialect contact research. In: B. Wälchli, A. Leemann and A. Ender, eds., *Methods in Contemporary Linguistics*, pp. 219–238. Berlin: De Gruyter Mouton.
Burke, P. (2004). *Languages and Communities in Early Modern Europe*. Cambridge: Cambridge University Press.

Castellanos, C. (2007). La lingua franca, una revolució lingüística mediterrània amb empremta catalana. *XII International Colloquium of the North American Catalan Society. Halifax, Nova Scotia, Canada. 11–13 May 2007.* Available at http://www.uab.cat/Document/439/403/castellanos_linguafranca2007.pdf.

Cifoletti, G. (1989). *La lingua franca mediterranea.* Padua: Unipress.

Cifoletti, G. (1991). L'influsso arabo sulla Lingua Franca. In: A. Loprieno (ed.), *Atti della quinta giornata comparatistica,* pp. 34–39. Perugia: Dipartimento di Linguistica e Filologia Romanza.

Cifoletti, G. (2002). Coincidenze lessicali tra la lingua franca e l'arabo tunisino. *Incontri linguistici,* 25, pp. 125–150.

Cifoletti, G. (2004). *La lingua franca barbaresca.* Rome: Il Calamo.

Coates, W. A. (1971). The lingua franca. In: F. Ingemann, ed., *Proceedings of the Fifth Annual Kansas Linguistics Conference,* pp. 25–34. Lawrence: University of Kansas.

Collier, B. (1977). On the origins of lingua franca. *Journal of Creole Studies,* 1, pp. 281–298.

Colombo, M. and Kinder, J. J. (2012). Italian as a language of communication in nineteenth century Italy and abroad. *Italica,* 89(1), pp. 109–121.

Cornelissen, R. (1992). Zur Lingua Franca des Mittelmeers. In: G. Birken-Silverman and G. Rössler, eds., *Beiträge zur sprachlichen, literarischen und kulturellen Vielfalt in der Philologien,* pp. 217–228. Stuttgart: Franz Steiner.

Cremona, J. (1997). Acciocché ognuno le possa intendere: The use of Italian as a lingua franca on the Barbary Coast of the seventeenth century. Evidence from the English. *Journal of Anglo-Italian Studies,* 5, pp. 52–69.

Crystal, D. (2008). Creole. *A Dictionary of Linguistics and Phonetics.* Oxford: Blackwell, pp. 122. https://www.wiley.com/en-us/A+Dictionary+of+Linguistics+and+Phonetics,+6th+Edition-p-9781405152969

Dakhlia, J. (2008). *Lingua franca. Histoire d'une langue métisse en Méditerranée.* Arles: Actes Sud.

Diaz, E. M. (2016). An approach to the lingua franca of the Mediterranean. *Quaderns de la Mediterrània,* 9, pp. 223–227.

Kloss, H. (1967). "Abstand" languages and "Ausbau languages". *Anthropological Linguistics,* 9, pp. 29–41.

Mallette, K. (2014). Lingua Franca. In: P. Horden and S. Kinoshita, eds., *A Companion to Mediterranean History,* pp. 330–344. West Sussex: John Wiley.

Marazzini, C. (1994). *La lingua italiana: profilo storico.* Bologna: Il Mulino.

Meijer, G. and Muysken, P. (1977). On the Beginnings of Pidgin and Creole Studies: Schuchardt and Hesseling. In: A. Valdman, ed., *Pidgin and Creole Linguistics,* pp. 21–48. Bloomington: Indiana University Press.

Migliorini, B. (1960). *Storia della lingua italiana.* Florence: Sansoni.

Minervini, L. (2010). lingua franca, Italiano come. *Enciclopedia dell'italiano,* pp. 802–804. Available online at: http://www.treccani.it/enciclopedia/lingua-franca-italiano-come_%28Enciclopedia-dell%27Italiano%29/ [Accessed 2 Jul. 2021]

Minervini, L. (2014). El léxico de origen italiano en el judeoespañol de Oriente. In: W. Busse, ed., *La lengua de los sefardíes: Tre contribuciones a su historia,* pp. 65–104. Tübingen: Stauffenburg Verlag.

Nolan, J. (2020). *The Elusive Case of Lingua Franca. Fact and Fiction.* London: Palgrave Macmillan.

Operstein, N. (1998). Was lingua franca ever creolized? *Journal of Pidgin and Creole Languages*, 13(2), pp. 377–380.

Operstein, N. (2017). The Spanish component in lingua franca. *Language Ecology*, 1(2), pp. 105–136.

Operstein, N. (2018). Inflection in lingua franca: From Haedo's *Topographia* to the *Dictionnaire de la langue franque*. *Morphology*, 28(2), pp. 145–185.

Pountain, C. J. (2016). Standardization. In: A. Ledgeway and M. Maiden, eds., *The Oxford Guide to the Romance Languages*, pp. 634–643. Oxford: Oxford University Press.

Rossetti, R. (2002). La Lingua Franca: una langue méditerranéenne à travers les siècles. *Université de Nantes, 22/23 Avril 2002, Chaire Du Bellay de l'Académie de la Méditerranée*, pp. 1–15.

Ruzza, C. (2000). Language and nationalism in Italy: Language as a weak marker of identity. In: S. Barbour and C. Carmichael, eds., *Language and Nationalism in Europe*, pp. 168–182. Oxford: Oxford University Press.

Schuchardt, H. (1909). Die lingua franca. *Zeitschrift für romanische Philologie*, 33, pp. 441–461.

Schulte, K. (2018). Romance in contact with romance. In: W. Ayres-Bennett and J. Carruthers, eds., *Manual of Romance Sociolinguistics*, pp. 595–626. Berlin: De Gruyter.

Sedlaczek, M. (2017). On the importance of history and historicity in the (Socio-)linguistic reconstruction of pidgins and creoles: The case of the original lingua franca. *Colloquium: New Philologies*, 2(2), pp. 15–27.

Selbach, R. (2017). On a famous lacuna: Lingua franca the Mediterranean trade pidgin? In: E. M. Wagner, B. Beinhoff and B. Outhwaite, eds., *Merchants of Innovation. The Languages of Traders*, pp. 252–271. Berlin: De Gruyter Mouton.

Simone, R. (1998). The early modern period. In: G. Lepschy, ed., *History of Linguistics. III. Renaissance and Early Modern Linguistics*, pp. 149–236. London and New York: Longman.

Tommasino, P. M. (2017). Travelling east, writing in Italian. *Philological Encounters*, 2(2), pp. 28–51.

Traugott, E. C. and Trousdale, G. (2013). *Constructionalization and Constructional Changes*. Oxford: Oxford University Press.

Venier, F. (2012). *La corrente di Humboldt. Una lettura di "La lingua franca" di Hugo Schuchardt*. Rome: Carocci.

Vincent, N. (1988). Italian. In: M. Harris and N. Vincent, eds., *The Romance Languages*, pp. 279–313. London: Croom Helm.

Whinnom, K. (1977). Lingua franca: Historical problems. In: A. Valdman, ed., *Pidgin and Creole Linguistics*, pp. 295–310. Bloomington: Indiana University Press.

Wansbrough, J. E. (1996). *Lingua Franca in the Mediterranean*. London and New York: Routledge.

Wright, S. (2000). *Community and Communication: The Role of Language in Nation State Building and European Integration*. Clevedon: Multilingual Matters.

10 Immortal Passados
Early Modern England's Italianate Fencing Jargon on Page and Stage

Laetitia Sansonetti

"Tempestuous termes"

Fencing increasingly became part of a gentleman's education in early modern England, at the same time as swords and techniques were imported from the Continent, together with the specialised lexicon to describe the new moves. The 1590s are a particularly interesting period for tracing the linguistic evolution of the fencing lexicon in England, as they saw the publication of several major works, all of which drew on foreign, and more specifically Italian, sources, but in different ways. William Segar's *Booke of honor and armes* and John Smythe's *Certain discourses* were both issued in 1590 by the same publisher. The mid-1590s saw the publication one year apart of two books directly influenced by the Italian language, an anonymous translation of Giacomo di Grassi's *Ragione di adoprar sicuramente l'arme si da offesa, come da difesa* (Grassi, 1594) and Vincentio Saviolo's *Practise* (Saviolo, 1595). While the anonymous translator of Grassi's manual provided English equivalents for the technical terms, Saviolo, a native of Padua who had settled in London and by 1591 operated a thriving fencing school, adhered to his native terminology.[1] George Silver's *Paradoxes of Defence*, published in 1599, was intended as a polemical response to the increasing popularity of techniques promoted by Italian masters settled in London and described in detail in manuals derived from Italian practice, such as Saviolo's.

Silver's indictment of the foreign origin of Italianate fighting is reinforced by his mockery of the lexicon associated with it: "can they vnlace his Helmet, vnbuckle his Armour, hew asunder their Pikes with a *Stocata*, a *reuersa*, a *Dritta*, a *Stramason*, or other such like tempestuous termes?", he asks jeeringly. The answer is obviously a negative one, for "these toys are fit for children, not for men, for stragling boyes of the Campe, to murder poultrie" (Silver, 1599: A5v). Voicing suspicion towards foreign behaviours through a criticism of linguistic borrowing was not new, of course, and Thomas Wilson's indictment of English travellers coming back from

DOI: 10.4324/9781003092445-14

Continental journeys with a store of foreign words and structures is well known:

> Some farre iorneid gentlemen at their returne home, like as thei loue to go in forrein apparell, so thei wil pouder their talke with ouersea language. He that cometh lately out of France, wil talke Frenche English, & neuer blushe at the matter. Another choppes in with Angleso Italiano.
>
> (Wilson, 1553: 86)[2]

But forty years later, borrowings are no longer ascribable solely to English travellers abroad; now they are imported together with foreign books and foreign fashions – brought to England by "aliens" (such was the term predominantly in use).[3]

While Segar and Smythe got their information from French, or Italian, or Spanish soldiers, or from reading Continental sources (such as Froissart's *Chronicles* for Smythe [1590: 13v, 31, 36–37]), and could control its reception by establishing a linguistic hierarchy in which classical Latin remained at the top, the translation of Grassi's manual and Saviolo's own contribution worked differently. The anonymous translator of *True arte* provides English equivalents for all the technical terms specific to the language of fencing without deriving them from the Italian original terms. In the preface to his translation, he explains why he chose to translate the generic word *spada* by a more specific term in English, a word associated with Continental techniques and derived from the French, but already nativised: "sometimes finding this word Sword generally used, I take it to have been the better translated, if instead thereof the Rapier had been inserted" (Grassi, 1594: "An Advertisement to the courteous reader", ¶¶).[4] The transmission of Italian fencing terms and their incorporation into the English lexicon appears here to be a multilingual process involving other Continental languages.

Comparing Grassi's English *True arte* and its Italian original enables us to identify two translating strategies. Some terms are rendered with the help of paraphrase: *imbrocata* (spelt with one –c– by Grassi) is "the thrust above hande" and *stoccata* "the thrust underhand" in a symmetrical phrasing that makes it easy to visualise the moves (Grassi, 1570: 29, 32; 1594: E2v, E4v).[5] When Italian words have close equivalents in English because of a common etymology, these are chosen: *riverso* is "reversed thrust" or "reversed blowes" (Grassi, 1570: 32, 54; 1594: E4v, H4v). One year after it had been proved that the English language could describe the new fencing moves imported from the Continent without having to import Continental words as well, Vincentio Saviolo published a treatise written in English which featured a deliberately Italian lexicon. From this choice, one understands that Saviolo is not just teaching fencing: he is selling Englishmen a whole way of life, complete with the adequate jargon, and the attractiveness of this "package" is exactly what Silver resents, as appears from his envious description of the fencing school set up by another Italian in London, Rocco Bonetti.[6]

Now the main elements of Silver's indictment of Italianate fencing – mocking the imported terminology, criticising the impractical nature of the weapon and techniques used, envying the social status and wealth gained by rivals in the trade – are to be found in a few plays written in the mid- to late 1590s featuring references to specifically Italian words and moves.[7] Shakespeare's *Love's Labour's Lost* (composed between 1594 and 1595, and published in 1598), *Romeo and Juliet* (ca. 1595, published in 1597 and 1599), and *Merry Wives of Windsor* (1597–1598, published in 1602) were composed before Silver published his treatise. Others, such as Ben Jonson's *Every Man In His Humour* (published in 1601), or *Patient Grissil* (written by Thomas Dekker, Henry Chettle, and William Haughton, published in 1603), were composed at the turn of the century. I would argue that these plays do not only reflect the growing popularity of Italianate fencing and technical vocabulary in London, but they also contribute to creating a form of lingua franca for English fencers.[8]

Denizening alien words[9]

If the fencing words were originally Italian, they were imported into English under Spaniardised forms, maybe via Frenchified versions, as is apparent in the transformation of *stoccata* into *stoccado*, *passata* into *passado*, or *imbroccata* into *imbrocado*,[10] the –d– for –t– substitution occurring in French adaptations (*estoccade* and *imbronccade* in Henry de Sainct-Didier's *Traicté contenant les secrets du premier livre sur l'espee seule* [Sainct-Didier, 1573: Biij[11]]) and the -ado/a ending being the Spanish ending for past participles (as -ato/a is in Italian). That fencing had become a trade and not a means of defence or an art is obvious in Silver's reaction to Bonetti's fees and Saviolo's fame: the new lexicon was not only useful to describe new moves, but it also served to signal one's awareness of new fashions and one's belonging to a community of people sharing a jargon. The words themselves became more than a means to communicate within a trade; together with knowledge of the art they were the very goods traded by the fencing teachers.

Some of these words had been known for years, long before the translation of Grassi's *True arte* (Grassi, 1594) and the publication of Saviolo's *Practise* (Saviolo, 1595). Thomas Wilson, whose distrust of Italian words and fashions had already been voiced in his 1553 *Arte of rhetorique*, uses the word *stoccado* metaphorically in his 1572 collection of "discourses" to refer to a blow in money matters, a situation in which a borrower loses both the money borrowed and the goods against which the money has been lent: "this is called a double stoccado, that is to saye, the stycking blowe, or the double stabbe" (Wilson, 1572: Diiij).

The metaphorical use, together with the font (blackletter like the rest of the text) and spelling (no capital initial), seem to indicate that the author expects his readers to be familiar with the word, even though it is translated twice. A more English spelling seems to have gained ground in John Hester's translation of Leonardo Fioravanti's *Compendium of the rationall secretes* ten years later: "[He] tooke hym by the coller and gaue him fiue stockadoes in the breast to haue slaine hym" (Fioravanti, 1582: II, Ch. xli, 123).

Vincentio Saviolo, an Italian fencing master writing in faultless English and doubtless aware of the fact that his readers may already be familiar with the technical terms for the moves he describes, nevertheless provides a full Italian lexicon, pairing Italian words with English equivalents until the readers have assimilated them and no longer need a translation. In the case of "stoccata", the word is first glossed ("the stoccata or thrust"), then taken up without translation ("the saide stoccata") before being paired again with its translation, this time appearing first as if to test the readers' memory by inviting them to recollect the Italian word as they read the English one ("a thrust or stoccata") (Saviolo, 1595: E, Gv). Likewise, for the "passata or remove" (H3r–v, mentioned three times), first glossed and then used without a translation (many times between I3v and K3).

When he mocks the Italianate vocabulary of the new-fangled fencing lexicon made popular by Saviolo among others, Silver spells these two words, *passata* and *stoccata*, *all'italiana*, or nearly so. *Paradoxes of Defence* features several mentions of "*Passata*" (Silver, 1599: B4v, H4r, I2v [there spelt "*Passatos*" in the plural form]) and "*Stocata*" (for instance B4v, H4r, Iv, K4v, often associated with "Vincentio" [Saviolo] and the Italian masters, and sometimes not italicised). Despite the missing –c– in *stoccata* and the one substitution of an –o for an –a in *passata*, Silver's spelling is consistent with Saviolo's Italian forms. Although they do it for opposite reasons, both Saviolo and Silver re-Italianise (as it were) words that had already started to be assimilated into the English fencing vocabulary.

Aiming to criticise his foreign rivals and their idiom, Silver tends to replicate the spelling he finds in Saviolo's manual. With his 1598 bilingual dictionary, *A World of Words*, John Florio's aim is quite different (and much closer to Saviolo's), since his ambition is to teach Italian to English native speakers. Florio, who was himself of Italian origin, was trying to counter negative stereotypes such as could be found in Wilson's works. The dictionary features a few fencing words: the Italian technical term *stoccata*, for instance, is translated and defined thus: "a foyne, a thrust, a stoccado given in fence" (Florio, 1598: 399). In a less elaborate way, *passata* is Englished as "passado a word in fencing" (261). We have seen that altered pronunciations of Italian words had been in use in English since the 1570s at least. Rather than translations of Italian words, *passado* and *stoccado* can be read as attempts to transcribe foreign pronunciation (at least as it might have sounded to English ears).

In 1591, Florio had published a bilingual language manual, *Second Fruits*, in which he mentioned Saviolo, praising his fencing techniques. While the English version claims that "[Saviolo] will hit any man, be it with a thrust or stoccada, with an imbroccada or a charging blowe, with a right or reverse blowe", the Italian side has proper Italian spelling: "o di punta, o di stoccata, o di stramazzone, o d'imbroccata, o di mandritto, o di riverso" (Florio, 1591: Q2v–Q4),[12] confirming that the –d– for –t– substitution is a spelling device designed to adapt Italian sounds to English speakers. One process of phonetic assimilation reflected in spelling is particularly apparent here, the weakening of the unstressed final vowel, written –o regardless of matters of grammatical gender – which were irrelevant to English speakers.[13] A similar process was registered in Sainct-Didier's French manual mentioned above, with -a endings changed to final silent -e, assimilating the words more clearly and signalling a now French pronunciation.

While Saviolo and the early Florio are trying to sell an aurally authentic experience to their customers, pronunciation indicates that a fencing jargon is being developed by mixing features of Continental (Italian and French, but also Spanish) origin. This process can be seen at work in plays of the 1590s featuring references to Italianate fencing, if we look at the spelling of technical terms in the published versions.[14]

Southward, ho

In Shakespeare's *Romeo and Juliet* (first printed in 1597), a play set in the *Italian* city of Verona, Mercutio lists the names of newly imported moves insisting on their non-Englishness in order to mock Tybalt's fashionable fencing: "The immortal Passado, the Punto reuerso, the Hay", which elicits Benvolio's puzzled exclamation – "The what?" (Shakespeare, 1597: Ev). The Englished spelling of *stoccata* seems to have been in less frequent use than the now-denizened "passado", for the 1597 edition has Mercutio's later challenge to Tybalt spelt "*Allastockado* caries it away" (F), while the 1599 edition reads "*Alla stucatho* carries it away" (Shakespeare, 1599: F3v).[15] *Love's Labour's Lost* (first published in 1598) features one occurrence of *passado*, paired with a reference to duelling in another approximately spelt Italian word which confirms the easy confusion between final -o and -a: "the *Passado* he respects not, the *Duella* he regards not" (Armado speaking; Shakespeare, 1598: B4). The word can be found once too in *The Merry Wives of Windsor* when Shallow refers to "yong/Tall fellowes with their stroke & their passado" (Shakespeare, 1602: C2). There is no mention of *stoccata* in the 1602 Quarto of *The Merry Wives of Windsor*, but the word "stock" is used as an English equivalent in a multilingual list of fencing moves which seems to have left the copyist puzzled: "to see thee passe the punto. The stock, the reuerse, the distance: the montnce [montant] is a dead my francoyes?" (the Host speaking) (Shakespeare, 1602: Dv). In a short passage that is not in the Quarto version, Shallow criticises fashionable techniques which he thinks compare unfavourably with more traditional moves, an argument reminiscent of Mercutio's jibes at Tybalt and the "new tuners of accents", "these fashionmongers" (Shakespeare, 1597: Ev): "In these times you stand on distance: your Passes, Stoccado's, and I know not what" (*Merry Wives*, Act 2, Scene 1; Shakespeare, 1623: 45).

As the playhouses were located in the liberties (privately administered areas that were not under the sovereign's jurisdiction), where fencing schools were also to be found, Shakespeare's audience could have been familiar with the moves and the sounds of the words to describe them.[16] In the case of Shakespeare's company, the Lord Chamberlain's Men, James Burbage bought rooms in the Blackfriars precinct including those where Rocco Bonetti had held his "college" (Smith, 1964: Document 19, 469–470). Fencing masters and their pupils, actors and their audiences, thus shared a "free" zone and the possibilities of a common language. When the plays were published first as quartos (versions usually considered closer to performance[17]), the readers (the more educated fringe of the audience) could try and pronounce the terms out loud, as they would do with the many language manuals which provided phonetic spelling.[18]

Now the example of Mercutio's *stockado/stucatho*, as well as the half-Italian-, half-Spanish-looking *passado*, show that these words seem to serve as pointers to the "Southern" origin of the fencing techniques that had become fashionable in late sixteenth-century England.[19] The digraph –th– is also used, for instance, to write the name of *Love's Labour's Lost*'s famous bragging Spaniard, Don Adriano de Armado, in the signature of Armado's second letter (Shakespeare, 1598: D3). The same spelling is found in mentions of the Spaniard by Costard at the beginning of Act 4 (D4; spelt "Armathor" in Shakespeare, 1623: 131), Jaquenetta later in the same act (Shakespeare, 1598: Ev), and Nathaniel in Act 5 (F2v), and in Ferdinand's reference to Moth as "Armathoes page" (H2). Outside the Shakespearean canon, there is contemporary evidence that Spanish intervocalic –d–, like Italian intervocalic –t–, could be written –th– in English while a final –a in both languages could become an English –o: *stucatho* for *stoccata*, *armatho* for *armada*.[20] This blending of Italian and Spanish identity is confirmed when Boyet calls Armado a "Monarcho" (D3v), referring to an *Italian* who lived at the court of Elizabeth in the 1570s and who was given this nickname, derived from a common masculine noun ending in -a in Italian (*monarca*), because he thought he was the king of the world. Conversely, in *Romeo and Juliet*, a (pseudo-) Spanish word is introduced to trigger a Spanish reference in an Italian context, with the word "ambuscado" in Mercutio's Queen Mab speech (Shakespeare, 1597: C2).[21]

Italian fencing masters seem to have been both specific targets and synecdochical representatives of Continental Catholic Europe, which also included Spain (the country which had sent a supposedly "invincible" *Armada* against England in 1588) and France (whose king had converted to Catholicism in 1593). In *Romeo and Juliet*, when Mercutio jeers at Italianate fencers, he includes their use of French phrases in his criticism, calling them "these pardonmees" by metonymy (Shakespeare, 1597: Ev). Likewise, in the Host's multilingual list of moves from *The Merry Wives of Windsor*, words of Italian origin are associated with French identity ("my francoyes" quoted above).[22]

The issues raised by spelling in early versions of Shakespeare plays are thus not only relevant to our assessment of the popularity of the new Italianate fencing jargon: they enable us to see instances of misunderstanding due to language differences in a European context, thus highlighting the complex dialectic of inclusion and exclusion that shapes communities.

Words, swords and status

A few patterns have emerged from this study of Italianate fencing in Shakespeare's plays composed between the publication of Saviolo's manual in 1595 and that of Silver's treatise in 1599: the topographical proximity between fencers and actors, which probably made for direct transmission of moves and technical terms; an interest in written texts as aids for oral expression (the play-text itself, as well as language manuals); the use of non-English words to satirise affectation; the multilingual context in which the foreignness of Italian jargon is negotiated. This combination is not specific to Shakespeare, although he was early (and particularly skilful) among playwrights in using it to achieve dramatic effectiveness. The anonymous authors of the Cambridge "Parnassus Plays", composed at the turn of the century, may have seen a performance of *Romeo and Juliet* in their students' days (Shakespeare, 2012: Introduction, 55–56) and remembered it a few months later when composing the scene of *The First Part of The Return from Parnassus* in which Ingenioso and Gullio discuss Spanish rapiers and social pretensions. Gullio claims to have bought his rapier, "a pure tolledo", in Padua, and to have killed with it "a Pollonian, a Germaine, & a Duche man, because the[y] would not pledge the health of Englande"; he boasts of being up to any opponent who has learnt the new Italian techniques: "Give mee a new knight of them all, in fencschoole, att a Nimbrocado or at a Stocado" (Act 3, Scene 1, lines 836–839, 866–867 in Leishman, 1949: 174, 177). The metanalysis turning "imbrocado" into "nimbrocado" translates visually Gullio's weak grasp of foreign words and swords (and may trigger aural associations with "ninny").

The satirical intent is also obvious in Ben Jonson's *Every Man In His Humour* (1601), whose character of Bobadilla[23] is the same bragging type as Gullio. In a scene of reverse translation, Bobadilla tells Matheo that a well experienced man "would passe vpon [him] at pleasure". He then explains for a puzzled Matheo what he means: "make a thrust at me; come in vpon my time; controll your point, and make a full carriere at the bodie: the best practis'd gentlemen of the time terme it the *passado*, a most desperate thrust, beleeue me". When Matheo, eager to learn, asks Bobadilla for just "one veny", the other comments on the inapt terminology: "Fie ueney, most grosse denomination as euer I heard: oh the *stockado* while you liue Signior, note that". He then offers to take Matheo to "some tauerne or so, & [...] send for one of these fencers" to teach him (Jonson, 1601: Act 1, Scene 3, C4r–v). But Matheo has no money... The role played by Italianate fencing and the mastery of the appropriate lexicon in establishing social hierarchies is one of the recurring elements in this play too.

The list of moves is completed later in the play, as Bobadilla plans to "teach [19 gentlemen of good spirit] the special tricks, as your *Punto*, your *Reuerso*, your *Stoccato*, your *Imbroccato*, your *Passado*, your *Montaunto*" (Act 4, Scene 1, I2). The approximate spelling reflects both an attempt to master a more authentically Italian pronunciation (with intervocalic –t– instead of the "Englished" –d– except for the now-nativised *passado*) and an assimilating tendency, with the neutralising of the gender factor in the choice of final vowel (the customary –o when some of the Italian words are feminine[24]). Bobadilla's inflationist Italianate jargon seems to be indefinitely expansible, for he adds such terms as the slightly more recondite "retricato", and even the mixed "assaulto", a combination of English "assault" (a word derived from Old French) and Italian "assalto" (Act 4, Scene 1, Kv). But Matheo "*runnes away*" when challenged by Giuliano, while Bobadilla himself remains safely out of the fray, prompting Lorenzo Junior to make derogatory comments on "your passados, & your Mountauntos" (Act 4, Scene 1, I3).

As appears from several dialogues, rapier fighting is presented as the prerogative of gentlemen, and so is the use of imported words, even when it comes to defining less dignified forms of fighting, such as cudgelling:

> *Matheo.* [Giuliano] brags he will give mee the bastinado, as I heare.
> *Bobadilla.* How, the bastinado? how came he by that word trow?
> *Matheo.* Nay indeed he said cudgill me; I termed it so for the more grace.
> *Bobadilla.* That may bee, for I was sure it was none of his word[.]
>
> (Act 1, Scene 3, C3v)

The association between Italianate fencing and Spanish vocabulary is present in the phrase "to lie in ambuscado" (Act 2, Scene 1, D4), which the trickster Musco uses to explain his impersonation of a soldier, and which the audience may remember from *Romeo and Juliet*. When the same Musco tries to sell a rapier to two gulls, he claims that "it's a most pure Toledo", to which one of the gulls replies: "I had rather it were a Spaniard" (Act 2, Scene 1, D4v). As unaware of the actual location of Toledo as they are of the trick that is being played on them, they eventually buy it, but when Bobadilla examines it, he declares it "not a Toledo": it is "a Fleming", "a prouant Rapier, no better" (Act 2, Scene 3, E4v).

We find the same combination of rapier fighting (real or planned, or prevented), Italianate vocabulary, and foolish affectation in *Patient Grissil* by Dekker *et al.* (1603), with Emulo's narrative of the imaginary duel he claims to have fought with Sir Owen. What matters more than the fight itself is Emulo's own refined apparel, which ultimately causes his defeat; the fantasised duel is narrated using strongly Latinate (or Italianate) vocabulary and fencing technical jargon: "My spangled garters in that imprision fell about my feet, and he, fetching a most valorous and ingenious career, invaded my rapier hand, entered this gilded fort, and in that passado vulnerated my hand thus deep" (Dekker *et al.*, [1603] 1841: Act 3, Scene 2, 41).[25] Several geographical areas are evoked – Italy, the location for the plot, as well as Wales, represented by two Welsh characters (Sir Owen Ap Meredith, a knight, and Gwenthyan, a widow) and their strong accent (and a few lines in Welsh). And the very story of Grissel's marriage to the Marquess of Saluzzo, found in Boccaccio's *Decameron* and Englished by Chaucer, hinges on inequality in social status, as Grissel is the daughter of a basket-maker.

Set in an Italian location and intended as a satire of the papacy, Barnabe Barnes's *Devil's Charter*, published in 1607, features a character of expert fencer, Frescobaldi, who is shown practising on stage. In his technical explanations, he uses words belonging to the Englished vocabulary of fencing with their typical –ado ending, interspersed with phrases in correct Italian:

he fenceth.

He makes a thrust, I with a swift passado,
Make quick auoydance, and with this stoccado
(Although he fence with all his finest force)
Bar'd of his body thrust him in the throate.
Guardatemi bene, signori honoreuoli.
Suppose this conduict or my duellist,
Should falsifie the foine vpon me thus.
Here will I take him, turning downe this hand.
      Enter Henrico Baglioni *looking earnestly vpon* Frescobaldi.
            Il punto verso indrizzato, thus.
Admit he force me with his ambroccado
Here I deceiue then, with this passado
And come vppon him in the speeding place.

> [...]
> *Henrico Baglioni* (by this sword)
> I am to morrow to performe a duell,
> And practising in this nights melancholie,
> How to dispatch it with a braue stoccadoe.
>   (Barnes, 1607: Act 3, Scene 5, Fv–F2, F3)

The original audience, which according to the title page included King James himself, was thus given a fencing lesson together with a reminder of the key terms in the appropriate lexicon. Despite the Italian context, the fencing lexicon is made of the mixed forms to which late Elizabethan (and now early Jacobean) audiences had grown accustomed.

Thomas Middleton and William Rowley's *Fair Quarrel* (1617) has no Italian setting, but the audience (here too including King James) is still taught a double lesson in Italian fencing and technical vocabulary. A mistaken analysis of the moves is provided, immediately corrected by a more expert observer. As two unnamed characters watch a duel between Captain Ager and the Colonel of his troop, they comment on the moves they see:

> 1. Stay, by this hand he offers; fights yfaith.
> Fights: by this light he fights sir.
> 2. So me thinkes sir.
> 1. An absolute Punto: hey.[26]
> 2. 'Twas a Passado sir.
> 1. Why let it passe, and 'twas, I'me sure, 'twas somwhat,
> Whats that now.
> 2. Thats a Punto.
> 1. O goe to then,
> I knew 'twas not farre off.
>   (Middleton and Rowley, 1617: Act 3, Scene 1, Fr–v)

When put in the right by his interlocutor regarding the exact move, the character numbered 1. plays on the two meanings of the verb "pass" in English, the one used in conversation to change the subject and the one used in the fencing jargon, which translates Italian *passare* whence *passata* (and therefore *passado*) is drawn. The humour comes from the fact that character 1. seems to know the name of only one move, which he ventures for the first pass he sees, but which turns out to be adequate for the second pass. The difference in rank between the Captain and the Colonel also points to another element recurrently associated with Italianate fencing and its jargon, namely social hierarchies and the assertion of a gentlemanly identity through the joint mastery of techniques and of the corresponding words.

As the last example illustrates, the Italianate fencing jargon acts as a sort of theatrical lingua franca, a language shared by playwrights and audiences, which they also have in common with the fencers themselves, allowing for communication – sometimes at the expense of the characters who use words and swords inexpertly. It is both a cypher testing (and enlarging) the audience's knowledge of current fashions and a code pointing to affectation, an index of irony.

An English blend

More examples could be adduced down to the mid-seventeenth century, even though French masters and techniques had started to supplant Italianate fencing after the great masters of the late sixteenth century had died. Forty-five years after the translation of Grassi's manual, the author of *Pallas Armata* (1639) included a glossary in his own fencing treatise for his readers to understand the international technical jargon. He included verbs and gave them English endings, going much further in the Englishing of some Italian words than his predecessors: "*Stringering* is the touching of thine adversaries point with thy point, which thou art to doe upon any occasion, that thou mayst secure thy selfe on eyther side from a thrust, which commonly is termed binding" (G. A., 1639: 5). *Stringering* is indeed an English derivation from the Italian verb *stringere*, which does mean "to bind", as is explained at the end of the entry.[27] The verb "*stringere*" is then used as if it were a native English word although it remains in italics, with the frequent imperative form, "then *stringere* him". Earlier borrowings were rather limited to substantives, but this late example incorporates infinitives as well. It shares in the other characteristics evidenced in earlier texts, namely the tendency to blend words of Italian, Spanish and French origins, as well as the function of this jargon in exchanges within a certain community that could be said to trade in words and not just goods or services. Further than the practical aspect manifest in the deformations to which the original Italian words were submitted while being adopted by English fencers and playwrights, the question of linguistic authority surfaces in any attempt to assess the importance of this technical lexicon and its status.

The history of the English language is one of successive borrowings, and most of the words from *Patient Grissil* cited above which have a directly French origin derive from Latin (only "garter" may be ultimately of Celtic origin, according to the *OED*).[28] Does it mean that when a Romance-sounding word is used, it wields the same authoritative force, the same prestige, as a Latin word? Or is there a subtle difference between Emulo's "valorous", a borrowing from the French, and his "invade", a verb created by direct derivation from a Latin root? The same questions arise with Italian, a Romance language even closer to Latin than French. Earlier generations were familiar with the Latin etymon of the Italian verb *stringere*, which they could have found in Thomas Elyot's Latin dictionary, *s.v. stringo*: "*Stringo, xi, gere*, to strayne or wrynge. Also to stryke, to make thynne in curtynge, to gather, to shaue, to wounde. *Stringere ensem*, to drawe a sworde" (Elyot, 1538: Aaiiiij). Could this have been the reason why G. A. chose to keep it in his lexicon?[29] An elite readership may have needed a technical explanation of the move, but they would not have needed a translation of the word. That G. A. himself knew Latin, which had served as the humanists' lingua franca earlier in the period and was still widely used in learned publications, is attested by the two prefatory addresses (to his friends and to the reader) written in this language (G. A., 1639: *2r–6v). *Stringere* would indeed have *looked* much more familiar than *strammazzone* – and it must have felt easier to pronounce (and to spell) correctly.[30]

The example of Italian fencing terms helps document the history of swordfight in England at a time when foreign influences were felt strongly – sometimes embraced, sometimes resented. It also tells us how technical knowledge was shared and transmitted, orally and textually, and how teaching by example (with lessons) and teaching by rule (with treatises and manuals) could interact. The physical presence of foreign words on the page, marked by typographical indicators such as italics and spelling, or their conspicuous absence, testify to strategies of self-promotion in which social, national, and linguistic identities are intertwined. Italian words thus act as pointers, but they seem to point in different directions depending on who is using them and how – and on who is capable of understanding them, thus delineating multilingual communities. If at first sight (and hearing) they can appear alien to the English language, the Italian words used in fencing treatises and bandied over on stages also reveal the essentially "multilingual" nature of English itself, a language made of successive borrowings.[31]

Notes

1. Two editions came out the same year, by the same printer (Thomas Scarlet), with two different publishers; the page numbers are identical: here, the first one listed in the STC will be used (STC number 21788).
2. See Warneke (1995).
3. See Scouloudi (1938), Dillon (1998, 162–186 in particular on foreign vernaculars in English plays in the context of legislation on aliens), Archer (2005), Kermode (2009: 1–22), Mayer (2008: 28–33 on French aliens in early modern London), Oldenburg (2014: 3–19, 138–170 more specifically on Shakespeare).
4. The first mention of 'rapier' recorded in the *Oxford English Dictionary* dates back to 1503–1504; it is found in the accounts of the Lord High Treasurer of Scotland: one Robert Selkyrk received payment "For gilt hilt and plomet to the rappyer and ane new scheith to it" (See Paul, 1900: 224).
5. The illustrations of the Italian edition are reproduced in the English translation, although in slightly coarser versions.
6. See Silver (1599: I4v–K), in particular the luxurious "greene carpet, done round with a very brode rich fringe of gold, always standing vpon it a very faire Standish couered with Crimson Veluet, with inke, pens, pin-

dust, and sealing waxe, and quiers of verie excellent fine paper gilded". On Bonetti and his Blackfriars school, see Smith (1964: 157–158, and Document 18, 468).

7. The case is different in *Hamlet*, which was also composed in the late 1590s, for the fencing match is associated with French rapiers, not Italian ones (see Act 5, Scene 2, lines 108–113 for the detail of the wager including "six French rapiers and poniards"), and the words shouted are all English ("hit" [206, 223, 228, 238], "touch" [229], "pass" [242], "have at you" [245], in Shakespeare [1997]). Similarly, Ben Jonson's *Everyman Out of His Humor* (1600) is much concerned with sword fight, but Italianate vocabulary is not used.

8. I am using this term in its figurative meaning, "any language that is used by speakers of different languages as a common medium of communication; a common language" (see *OED, s.v. lingua franca*). On lingua franca, see Ostler (2011) and Bennett (2020).

9. See Mulcaster (1582: 154–155): "This benefit of the foren tung, which we vse in making their termes to becom ours, with som alteration in form, according to the frame of our speche, tho with the continewing in substance of those words, which ar so vsed, that it maie appear both whence theie com, and to whom theie com, I call enfranchisment, by which verie name the words that ar so enfranchised, becom bond to the rules of our writing, which I haue named before, as the stanger denisons be to the lawes of our cuntrie".

10. Spelt *embrocado*, which makes it sound even more Spanish, in Dekker (1606: B): "hee [the devil] was the first that kept a Fence-schoole, when Cayn was aliue, and taught him the Embrocado, by which he kild his brother".

11. Sainct-Didier argues that *estoccade* and *imbronccade* are one and the same move.

12. In Florio's dictionary (Florio, 1598: 167), *imbroccata* is not translated/adapted (it is explained as "a thruste in fence, or a venie given over the dagger") – the word also exists in the masculine form, *imbroccato*; likewise for *stramazzone*, glossed as "a downe right blow", but also (and first) "a blow, a cap, a bang, a rap, a cuffe, a boxe, or whirret on the cheeke" (401). On Italian language learning in Elizabethan England, see Lawrence (2005) and Gallagher (2019).

13. Playwrights were not unaware of the Italian spelling of these words, as appears from a list in another of Dekker's works, in a passage describing a typical braggart: "Hées the best Fencer in the world: *Vincentio Sauiolo* is no body to him: He has his Mandrittaes, Imbrocataes, Stramazones, and Stoccataes at his fingers ends" (Dekker, 1603: D4).

14. On this issue, see Montgomery (2012: 1–20).

15. On the 1597 Quarto of *Romeo and Juliet*, see the introduction in Erne (2007). Cain (1942) discusses the possibility that *"allo steccato"* (defined in Florio [1598: 396] as "a place to combat in, [...] also a combat"), rather than *"alla stoccata"*, might be meant here. On duelling in *Romeo*, see Rossi (1993) and Niayesh (2014).

16. Competitions organised by fencing masters to promote their skills and attract pupils/customers often took place in the same venues as dramatic performances so as to accommodate the large crowds they would draw. See McElroy and Cartwright (1986: 193): "these bouts or 'prizes' [...] were played upon platforms or stages in the courtyards of inns and taverns, in open fields, or at the playhouses that lay north and south of the city". Also, see Anglin (1984: 402): "The 'Curtain' and the 'Theatre', in Holywell, were especially popular, as were two inns, the Bell Savage without Ludgate and the Bull within Bishopsgate, which also served as playhouses".

17. The Quarto texts of *The Merry Wives of Windsor* and *Romeo and Juliet* are often considered to have been abridged versions designed for touring the provinces, and sometimes based on memorial reconstruction by one or several actors (see René Weis's introduction to Shakespeare [2012: 56] and Giorgio Melchiori's introduction to Shakespeare [2000: 36]), but Lukas Erne has questioned this assertion, without denying that these texts are close to performance experience (Erne, 2007: 15, 21–22). For an assessment of the "memorial reconstruction" hypothesis, see Maguire (1996).
18. See Bellot (1586) for French.
19. For the argument that Mercutio criticises Tybalt's typically *Spanish* way of fighting (relying on arithmetic), see Soens (1969).
20. See, for instance, Henry Chettle's *Englands mourning garment*, which features the "Armatho" spelling twice (Chettle, 1603: B2v, C3v).
21. "And then dreames he of cutting forraine throats, / Of breaches ambuscados, countermines". See René Weis, Introduction, in Shakespeare (2012: 42–43), on the possible reference to Essex's Cadiz expedition. The version quoted by Weis is Shakespeare (1599), which reads "breaches, ambuscados, spanish blades" (C2). For *ambuscado*, the OED provides the following etymology: "An affected refashioning of ambuscade n. after Spanish. Here Englishmen may have confused the Spanish past participle *emboscado* ambushed, in *estar emboscado* to lie in ambush, with the feminine n. *emboscada* ambuscade; but compare the series of words in -ado suffix for French -ade, Spanish -ada".
22. As Richard Helgerson states, *The Merry Wives of Windsor* "works at its Englishness, insists on it, makes it fundamental to the definition of a domestic space that court and country can share" (Helgerson, 2000: 64). Also see Hoenselaars and Buning (1999: xiii–xvi) and Santos (2014).
23. In the 1616 edition of the *Works*, the names of the characters have been Englished, and the title page indicates that the play was "acted in the yeere 1598. by the then Lord Chamberlain his Servants" (Jonson, 1616: 4, 1).
24. Emended in Jonson (1616: Act 4, Scene 7, 54) to *Stoccata, Imbroccata, Passada*.
25. The digitised copy of Dekker *et al.* (1603) accessible via Early English Books Online misses the page on which this quotation appears, hence my use of a later edition. "Garters", "imprison", "valorous", "ingenious", "career", "rapier", "enter" and "fort" are borrowings from French; "invade" and "vulnerate" are derived from Latin. The dynamic alliteration in f– rests on words of Germanic origin.
26. I.e. *hai* [you have it], the Italian exclamation used in fencing already satirised by Mercutio in *Romeo and Juliet* quoted above.
27. See Florio (1598: 403).
28. See, for instance, Newstok (2015) and Durkin (2014).
29. The other "foreigne termes" G. A. adopts and adapts are similarly transparent, in their Latinate forms if not in their specific meanings: *Cavere, Tempo, Parere, Finda* [sic]*, Passere, Contratempo, Battere, Voltere. Passado* has been nativised (*Passade*) (G. A., 1639: B4r–B5r).
30. *Stringere* also has the advantage of looking like English "string", which has a Germanic origin (see OED, *s.v. string*, v. and n.).
31. "Hence, the alien will always be there in the midst; English will apparently never be fully itself but will always be multilingual" (Magnusson, 2008: 64); also see her rhetorical question about the multiple origins of English: "How could the language have a unitary identity if so many of its words were indistinguishable from French words, Latin words, Dutch words, or Spanish words?" (62). Magnusson borrows the idea of Shakespeare's English as "multilingual" from Parker (2003).

References

Anglin, J. P. (1984). The Schools of Defense in Elizabethan London. *Renaissance Quarterly*, 37(3), pp. 393–410.

Archer, J. M. (2005). *Citizen Shakespeare. Freemen and Aliens in the Language of the Plays*. Basingstoke: Palgrave Macmillan.

Barnes, B. (1607). *The Diuils charter a tragaedie conteining the life and death of Pope Alexander the sixt. As it was plaide before the Kings Maiestie, vpon Candlemasse night last: by his Maiesties Seruants*. London: John Wright.

Bellot, J. (1586). *Familiar dialogues for the instruction of the[m], that be desirous to learne to speake English, and perfectlye to pronou[n]ce the same*. London: Thomas Vautrollier.

Bennett, K. (2020). Lingua franca, translation. In: M. Baker and G. Saldanha, eds., *The Routledge Encyclopedia of Translation Studies*, third edition. London and New York: Routledge, pp. 290–294.

Cain, H. E. (1942). An Emendation in "Romeo and Juliet". *The Shakespeare Association Bulletin*, 17(1), pp. 57–60.

Chettle, H. (1603). *Englands mourning garment*. London: Thomas Millington.

Dekker, T. (1603). *The wonderfull yeare. 1603 Wherein is shewed the picture of London, lying sicke of the plague*. London: [N. Ling, J. Smethwick, and J. Browne].

Dekker, T. (1606). *Newes from hell brought by the Diuells carrier*. London: W. Ferebrand.

Dekker, T., Chettle, H. and Haughton, W. [1603] (1841). *Patient Grissil: A Comedy*. Ed. John Payne Collier, London: The Shakespeare Society.

Dillon, J. (1998). *Language and Stage in Medieval and Renaissance England*. Cambridge: Cambridge University Press.

Durkin, P. (2014). *Borrowed Words: A History of Loanwords in English*. Oxford: Oxford University Press.

Elyot, T. (1538). *The dictionary of syr Thomas Eliot knight*. London: Thomas Berthelet.

Erne, L., ed. (2007). *The First Quarto of Romeo and Juliet*. Cambridge: Cambridge University Press.

Fioravanti, L. (1582). *A compendium of the rationall secretes, of the worthie knight and moste excellent doctour of phisicke and chirurgerie Leonardo Phiorauante*. Trans. J. Hester. London: George Pen and J[ohn] H[ester].

Florio, J. (1591). *Florios second frutes to be gathered of twelue trees, of diuers but delightsome tastes to the tongues of Italians and Englishmen*. London: Thomas Woodcock.

Florio, J. (1598). *A worlde of wordes, or Most copious, and exact dictionarie in Italian and English*. London: Edward Blount.

G. A. (1639). *Pallas armata. The gentlemans armorie*. London: John Williams.

Gallagher, J. (2019). *Learning Languages in Early Modern England*. Oxford: Oxford University Press.

Grassi, G. di. (1570). *Ragione di adoprar sicuramente l'arme si da offesa, come da difesa*. Venice: Giordano Ziletti.

Grassi, G. di. (1594). *Giacomo di Grassi his True arte of defence [...] Englished by I.G. gentleman*. London: Isaac Jaggard.

Helgerson, R. (2000). *Adulterous Alliances: Home, State and History in Early Modern European Drama and Painting*. Chicago: University of Chicago Press.

Hoenselaars, A. J., and Buning, M., eds. (1999). *English Literature and the Other Languages*. Amsterdam: Rodopi.
Jonson, B. (1601). *Euery man in his humor As it hath beene sundry times publickly acted by the right Honorable the Lord Chamberlaine his seruants.* London: Walter Burre.
Jonson, B. (1616). *The workes of Beniamin Ionson.* London: Will Stansby.
Kermode, L. E. (2009). *Aliens and Englishness in Elizabethan Drama*. Cambridge: Cambridge University Press.
Lawrence, J. (2005). "Who the Devil Taught Thee So Much Italian?" *Italian Language Learning and Literary Imitation in Early Modern England*. Manchester: Manchester University Press.
Leishman, J. B., ed. (1949). *The Three Parnassus Plays*. London: Nicholson & Watson.
Magnusson, L. (2008). "To Gase So Much at the Fine Stranger": Armado and the Politics of English in *Love's Labour's Lost*. In: P. Yachnin and P. Badir, eds., *Shakespeare and the Cultures of Performance*. Aldershot: Ashgate, pp. 53–68.
Maguire, L. (1996). *Shakespearean Suspect Texts: The 'Bad' Quartos and Their Contexts*. Cambridge: Cambridge University Press.
Mayer, J.-C., ed. (2008). *Representing France and the French in Early Modern English Drama*. Newark: University of Delaware Press.
McElroy, M. and Cartwright, K. (1986). Public Fencing Contests on the Elizabethan Stage. *Journal of Sport History*, 13, pp. 193–211.
Middleton, T. and Rowley, W. (1617). *A faire quarrell with new additions of Mr. Chaughs and Trimtrams roaring, and the Bauds song, neuer before printed: as it was acted before the King, by the Prince His Highnesse seruants.* London: I.T.
Montgomery, M. (2012). *Europe's Languages on England's Stages, 1590-1620*. Farnham and Burlington: Ashgate.
Mulcaster, R. (1582). *The first part of the elementarie vvhich entreateth chefelie of the right writing of our English tung*. London: Thomas Vautrollier.
Newstok, S. (2015). Loving and Cherishing "True" English: Shakespeare's Twinomials. In: M. Saenger, ed., *Interlinguicity, Internationality, and Shakespeare*. Toronto: McGill-Queen's University Press.
Niayesh, L. (2014). "Make It a Word and a Blow": The Duel and Its Rhetoric in William Shakespeare's *Romeo and Juliet*. In: J.-M. Hostiou and S. Vasset, eds., *Quarrel Scenes,* Special Issue of *ARRÊT SUR SCÈNE/SCENE FOCUS*, 3, pp. 79–85.
Oldenburg, S. (2014). *Alien Albion: Literature and Immigration in Early Modern England*. Toronto: University of Toronto Press.
Ostler, N. (2011). *The Last Lingua Franca: The rise and fall of world languages*. London and New York: Penguin.
Parker, P. (2003). (Peter) Quince: Love Potions, Carpenter's Coigns and Athenian Weddings. *Shakespeare Survey*, 56, pp. 39–54.
Paul, J. B., ed. (1900). *Accounts of the (Lord High) Treasurer of Scotland*. Vol 2. Edinburgh: Her Majesty's Stationery Office.
Rossi, S. (1993). Duelling in the Italian Manner: The Case of *Romeo and Juliet*. In: M. Marrapodi *et al.*, eds., *Shakespeare's Italy: Functions of Italian Locations in Renaissance Drama*. Manchester: Manchester University Press, pp. 112–124.
Sainct-Didier, H. de. (1573). *Traicté contenant les secrets du premier livre sur l'espee seule, mere de toutes armes*. Paris: Jean Mettayer & Mathurin Challenge.

Santos, K. V. (2014). Hosting Language: Immigration and Translation in *The Merry Wives of Windsor*. In: R. Espinosa and D. Ruiter, eds., *Shakespeare and Immigration*. Farnham and Burlington: Ashgate.

Saviolo, V. (1595). *Vincentio Sauiolo his practise In two bookes. The first intreating of the vse of the rapier and dagger. The second, of honor and honorable quarrels*. London: John Wolfe.

Scouloudi, I. (1938). Alien immigration and alien communities in London, 1558–1640. *Proceedings of the Huguenot Society*, 16, pp. 27–49.

Segar, W. (1590). *The booke of honor and armes*. London: Richard Jones.

Shakespeare, W. (1597). *An excellent conceited tragedie of Romeo and Iuliet As it hath been often (with great applause) plaid publiquely, by the right Honourable the L. of Hunsdon his Seruants*. London: John Danter [and Edward Allde?].

Shakespeare, W. (1598). *A pleasant conceited comedie called, Loues labors lost As it vvas presented before her Highnes this last Christmas. Newly corrected and augmented by W. Shakespere*. London: Cuthbert Burby.

Shakespeare, W. (1599). *The most excellent and lamentable tragedie, of Romeo and Iuliet. Newly corrected, augmented, and amended: as it hath bene sundry times publiquely acted, by the right Honourable the Lord Chamberlaine his Seruants*. London: Cuthbert Burby.

Shakespeare, W. (1602). *A most pleasaunt and excellent conceited comedie, of Syr Iohn Falstaffe, and the merrie wiues of Windsor [...] As it hath bene diuers times acted by the right Honorable my Lord Camberlaines seruants. Both before her Maiestie, and else-where*. London: Arthur Johnson.

Shakespeare, W. (1623). *Mr. William Shakespeares comedies, histories, & tragedies Published according to the true originall copies*. London: Isaac Iaggard and Edward Blount.

Shakespeare, W. (1997). *The Norton Shakespeare*. Eds. S. Greenblatt, W. Cohen, J. E. Howard, and K. Eisaman Maus. New York: Norton.

Shakespeare, W. (2000). *The Merry Wives of Windsor*. Ed. G. Melchiori. London: Arden Shakespeare.

Shakespeare, W. (2012). *Romeo and Juliet*. Ed. R. Weis. London: Arden Shakespeare.

Silver, G. (1599). *Paradoxes of defence wherein is proued the true grounds of fight to be in the short aunctient weapons, and that the short sword hath aduantage of the long sword or long rapier*. London: Edward Blount.

Smith, I. (1964). *Shakespeare's Blackfriars Playhouse: Its History and Design*. New York: New York University Press.

Smythe, J. (1590). *Certain discourses, vvritten by Sir Iohn Smythe, Knight: concerning the formes and effects of diuers sorts of weapons, and other verie important matters militarie*. London: Richard Jones.

Soens, A. L. (1969). Tybalt's Spanish Fencing in *Romeo and Juliet*. *Shakespeare Quarterly*, 20(2), pp. 121–127.

Warneke, S. (1995). *Images of the Educational Traveller in Early Modern England*. Leyden: Brill.

Wilson, T. (1553). *The arte of rhetorique*. London: Richard Grafton.

Wilson, T. (1572). *A discourse vppon vsurye by vvaye of dialogue and oracions*. London: Richard Tottel.

11 Linguistic Expression of Power and Subalternity in Peixoto's *Obra Nova de Língua Geral de Mina* (1741)

Christina Märzhäuser and Enrique Rodrigues-Moura

Introduction

Antonio da Costa Peixoto's 1741 manuscript *Obra Nova de Língua Geral de Mina* ("New work on the general language of Mina") documents a variety of Gbe (sub-group of Kwa languages) spoken by slaves in the Brazilian city of Vila Rica (today Ouro Preto) in the eighteenth century, which Peixoto called *Língua Geral de Mina* (abbreviated here to LGM). This language, brought from overseas by enslaved West Africans, is one of the many vernaculars thought to have already disappeared in colonial Brazil. However, this eighteenth-century document, and today's reality, prove otherwise. In fact, the transatlantic linguistic link between the lexical material documented in Peixoto's manuscript and modern Fon (and also Ewe) is still present. Yeda Pessoa de Castro explains that, out of the 920 lexical entries in the manuscript, 755 have been recognised by the speakers of Fongbe (the majority ethnic language of the country of Benin), while 76 others have been identified as Mahi or Gun and 11 more as Ewe (Castro, 2022 forthcoming).[1] Vestiges of the *Língua geral de Mina*, can also be found in the vocabulary used by Afro-Brazilian religious communities identifying themselves as Mina-Jêje (Cobbinah *et al.*, 2022 forthcoming), an ethnic label that combines and blurs distinct West African origins from areas of modern Ghana, Benin and Nigeria (Castro 2002; Märzhäuser and Samla, 2022 forthcoming).

Peixoto's *Obra Nova* is essentially a glossary of terms supplemented by short dialogues in LGM with translations to Portuguese. It is interesting not only from the linguistic point of view but also socioculturally, since the scenes represented in the dialogues reflect the contradictory interests of different social agents, and the complexity of their interactions. Several dialogues in the glossary testify to a degree of agency on the part of the Africans that undermines conventional representations of colonial relations.[2] In the complex socio-economic setting of eighteenth-century Minas Gerais, a considerable number of slaves managed to buy their freedom and engaged in small trades, as many dialogues about economic interactions illustrate. There were *escravos de ganho* (slaves who were

DOI: 10.4324/9781003092445-15

able to make some money for themselves)[3] and quite a few *forros* (liberated or free-born slaves) who achieved economic independence, social status and power. Among these were many women, especially so-called *negras de tabuleiro* (literally "negresses of the trays", who sold food and drink on the street), and *negras das vendas* (who owned or worked at small shops), and whose social position gave them a certain bargaining power in the mining society (Almeida, 2010; Gonçalves, 2011).

This chapter is organised as follows. Key information about the manuscript and its author is given in sections 2 and 3. Section 4 provides the sociohistoric context for our analysis of the power relations in the complex multi-ethnic, multilingual slaveholding society of Minas Gerais during the gold rush era, power relations that were constantly being renegotiated within the sphere of individual biographies. Section 5 looks at key terms for the ethnically structured social hierarchy, social status and spaces, and dialogues describing acts of state control, incidents of violence and intimate gender relations, which capture, to some extent, an otherwise invisible discourse. Section 6 discusses how structural superiority (Portuguese, male) and subalternity (African or of African descent, and especially women) were renegotiated in the micro-situations described and ends with some broader reflections about *Obra Nova de Língua Geral de Mina*. Apart from the power dynamics reconstructed from the glossary's content, the re-negotiation of power and subalternity are also reflected in the facts that (i) Peixoto clearly acquired – and recommends that his fellow Europeans acquire – the African language in order to keep social peace in Minas Gerais and (ii) his (possibly female) African informants were not necessarily poorer than he was, a Portugal-born countryside clerk (Araujo, 2013, 2022 forthcoming).

Both findings go against "prototypical" colonial imagery. The fact that Peixoto learned and recommended learning the Gbe-variety *Língua Geral de Mina* can be interpreted as an attempt to draw closer to the other. This linguistic approximation by a white man towards a demographically dominant and socially heterogeneous African population group, like many of the contents of the *Obra Nova de Língua Geral de Mina*, reflects Spivak's observation that "the networks of power/desire/interest are so heterogeneous that their reduction to a coherent narrative is counterproductive" (Spivak, 1994: 66).

Manuscripts

Two original handwritten manuscripts of Antonio da Costa Peixoto's have been preserved. There is a shorter version, dating from 1731, entitled *Alguns apontamentos da Língua Mina com as palavras Portuguesas correspondentes* ("Some notes on the Mina language with the corresponding Portuguese words"), kept in Portugal's National Library in Lisbon, and an extended version from 1741, *Obra Nova de Língua*

Geral de Mina, stored in the Évora Public Library.[4] The 1741 version was intended for publication in print and sale, but it was never published during Peixoto's lifetime.[5]

The 42-page-long, 11.5 × 11 cm booklet of the 1741 manuscript contains 899 lexical entries, complex expressions and dialogues from different semantic domains relating to the gold trade and everyday life (body parts, food and agriculture, human interaction, and so forth) in LGM with their Portuguese translations,[6] preceded by a dedication, a prologue to the reader, and an "Advertencia" ("Warning") at the end of the glossary, which informs the reader about variations in the pronunciation of <ch>.[7] The paratexts also allow us to suppose that Peixoto sent his manuscript to Lisbon to be printed, as there was a ban on printing press in Portuguese America at the time.[8]

In the paratexts of *Obra Nova de Língua Geral de Mina*, Peixoto twice calls his glossary a "nova tradução" ("new translation", 1741: 3, 5), which could imply either "something recently done anew" ("cousa feita de pouco tempo a esta parte", Bluteau, 1716: 760), or a "new work that so far no one has tried" ("obra nova …que até agora ninguém tentou", Bluteau, 1716: 760).[9] Peixoto thus seems to be suggesting that he is offering something hitherto unknown, although some of his countrymen probably knew about Peixoto's familiarity with LGM and his 1731 attempt to compile a glossary. Moreover, his quite unusual commitment to spreading knowledge about LGM in written form was unlikely to have remained unknown in a society where very few could read and write. We thus interpret his use of the adjective "novo" as part of Peixoto's attempt to advertise a volume he hoped to sell in print soon.[10] But the manuscript never came back from Portugal in printed form[11] and did not bring its author the additional income he had hoped for.

Biographic information on the author Antonio da Costa Peixoto

On the title page, Peixoto is described as a "national of the Kingdom of Portugal, of the Province of Entre-Douro-e-Minho, of the county of Felgueiras".[12] This has allowed Araujo (2013, 2022 forthcoming) to reconstruct many aspects of Peixoto's biography by combining archival data and documents from both Portugal and Brazil with an attentive historical-cultural contextualisation.

Thus, we know that Antonio da Costa Peixoto was born in 1703 in Lamas, according to his certificate of baptism from the Church of S. Pedro de Torrados dating from 23 March 1703. He migrated to Brazil presumably as a 12 or 13 year old in 1716, heading for the gold-mining region of Minas Gerais. He lived in different settlements around the region's main town, Vila Rica, and worked as a writing clerk (*escrivão*) and municipal judge (*juíz de vintena*) from 1736 until his death.[13]

He died on 19 September 1763 in Casa Branca, leaving a will, which shows that he had four (illegitimate) children by different mothers, but no possessions (Araujo, 2013: 4, 2022 forthcoming).

An especially interesting aspect of his biography is the fact that his career in colonial administration was interrupted, when he worked in the municipality of S. Bartolomeu, because he was publicly scolded for socialising with the African population of Minas Gerais. A letter sent to Vila Rica's city council by the village's inhabitants dated 18 February 1741 led to his dismissal on the grounds that "he is not capable of serving the office, because he is a man who drinks and gets drunk on *cachaça,* and frequents the taverns with black women and men".[14] Despite this scandal (or attempt at blackmail), Peixoto managed to regain his administrative position, and from 16 February 1743 to 19 September 1763 was assigned to three municipalities: S. Bartolomeu, S. Antonio da Casa Branca, N. Sra. de Nazaré da Cachoeira do Campo. As reconstructed by Araujo, he was in good relations with Vila Rica's city council and important members of the local (European) community and was even a member of local Catholic fraternities (*irmandades religiosas*). He also maintained relations with local Africans and Afro-descendants, especially women. As already mentioned, historical documents prove that at least two of his four children had black mothers (a typical pattern in colonial Brazil, especially in Minas Gerais), who were both freed slaves (*forras*). His reference to female informants in his glossary offers evidence of his close contacts with African women; indeed, his intimate relations clearly played a role in the production of the more sexually explicit parts of his *Obra Nova*.

Given the multifaceted structure of this mining society, where the Africans were in the majority (though political and economic power clearly resided with the Portuguese), to speak LGM would have been an advantage for a white person in local administration, as well as in the local and regional trade networks (and probably even in the transatlantic gold, tobacco and slave trade).

To understand how and why a Portugal-born clerk engaged with the local Gbe-speaking community to such degree that he could transcribe all this linguistic information – and even (partly) acquire the language,[15] we need to know more about the sociohistoric context. Within this context, it also becomes clearer how his ideas about social control and crime prevention, and inter-ethnic relations, made him invest so much time and effort in producing this manuscript.

Sociohistoric context

From the time of Prince Henry the Navigator and the Portuguese explorations along the African coast in the first half of the fifteenth century, slavery was officially authorised by the Portuguese Crown. It was justified by the "just war theory" (*Bellum iustum* or *jus ad bellum*), which sanctioned war against the "unfaithful", permitting the taking of prisoners to be converted into Christians. Already in medieval times, it had been considered legitimate to wage war against and enslave Muslims, especially when captured in battle. However, from the fifteenth century onwards, under the influence of Prince Henry, Portugal officially turned into a slave-trading kingdom.

By the first two decades of the eighteenth century, there were about 30,000 slaves in Minas Gerais, but numbers exploded in subsequent decades, with most slaves being born on African soil.[16] By the middle of the eighteenth century, the population of this *capitania* was over 70% African and mestizo; more precisely, in 1786 out of ~350,000 inhabitants, nearly 300,000 were black (Castro, 2002: 49–50). Though this was a socially coercive system, it was also susceptible to acquisitions, resistance, accommodation, negotiations, and social pacts. It is known, for example, that slaves were able to set up families, including marrying in church, and that they could acquire significant material assets, including access to land for cultivation and a house that was differentiated from the collective slave quarters known as "*senzalas*".[17]

Peixoto considers that LGM is "important knowledge" ("emportante sabedoria", 1741: 5), and describes its usefulness explicitly in his introduction: if slaveholders, and even those colonialist that didn't own them, knew LGM, it would be possible to avoid many of the "insults, wrongs, robberies, deaths [...] and atrocities"[18] that happened in the colony. Peixoto opines that LGM would facilitate communication between masters and slaves and thereby help control subordinates and avoid frequent tumults and violent incidents.

Institutions of colonial power and their representatives followed the logic of "social disciplining" (*Sozialdisziplinierung*, Oestreich, 1969) in order to ensure greater control of all members of society and the effectiveness of policies in the interest of the Portuguese Crown. Propertied classes (both local Brazilian and those acting between the kingdom and the colony), gold seekers and local traders operated along economic logic. Subaltern groups of Africans and Afro-descendants strived for (more) freedom and for socio-economic advancement. As a village clerk, Peixoto surely knew about the necessity of mediating between these different groups.

In the dedication at the beginning of his manuscript, Peixoto highlights its usefulness by mentioning the various friends and interested parties that had asked him to write it.[19] He particularly singles out a certain Sergeant-Major Antonio de Souza Coimbra, to whom he explicitly dedicates the work. Although he acknowledges the limits of his knowledge – typical false modesty in a text part serving as *captatio benevolentiae* – Peixoto seems proud and convinced about the great utility of his glossary in Minas Gerais.

Peixoto's intellectual contribution, from which he also hoped to achieve direct economic profits, can be understood in this context as a tool for better control of the black population, and therefore, for more efficient management of human and economic resources.[20] Since every disturbance or revolt, however brief, would obviously damage the local economy and, consequently, the collection of taxes by the officials of the Kingdom of Portugal, Peixoto seems to have believed that his manuscript would be welcomed by both local authorities and the Lisbon Court.

However, the text was never printed, and colonial language policies soon changed. Just one decade after Peixoto tried to print his *Obra Nova*, the all-powerful Marquis de Pombal, chief minister of King Joseph I (1750–1777), imposed a Portuguese-only policy, corresponding to the idea of Brazil as a rationally organised, unified state to which multilingualism was considered an obstacle.[21] This policy was originally directed at indigenous Brazilians and the Jesuits' *Língua Geral* and did not immediately affect the slaves, whose African languages were not explicitly mentioned in the plan.[22] But the drive to learn other languages – something that had been diligently pursued before by religious orders like the Jesuits – now disappeared. Thus, Peixoto's manuscript arrived at the Lisbon court at a bad time.

Furthermore, a look at the content of this work shows that the logic of social control and self-defence against transgression by slaves and runaways with which Peixoto advertised his *Obra Nova* is only one position represented. In a number of the dialogues, power and subalternity seem to be negotiated between the various factions, as we shall see in the next section.

Power and subalternity in *Obra Nova de Língua Geral de Mina*

In this section, we discuss some of the terms mentioned in Peixoto's *Obra* and their sociocultural significance. They are divided into: (a) Entries relating to ethnicity, legal status, official functions and social spaces representing the colonial social structure; (b) Dialogues about the slave trade, state control and raids against whites showing different structural and situational aspects of violence and (c) Entries relating to the exercise and negotiation of power within a framework of inter-gender relations.

Ethnic terms, legal status, official functions and social spaces

In colonial Brazil, a person's legal status was closely linked to their ethnicity, skin colour and possessions. The ethnic categories employed in colonial Portuguese historiographic texts were first catalogued in the early nineteenth century work, *Discripção da Capitania de Minas Gerais* (ca. 1807) by António de Araújo e Azevedo, first Conde de Barca:

The non-European inhabitants of the *Capitania* and their descendants: blacks brought over from Africa; mulattos or *pardos* descending from a European father and an African mother; *cabras*, who are the children of a mulatto father and an African mother, or vice versa; blacks born in the country called creoles: and mestizos of a European father and an American mother or vice versa.[23]

In Peixoto (1741), ethnic/racial terms include *hihàbouno* and *gauheno*, both translated as *branco* ("white person"), *hihàbouce = molher br.*[ca] *ou Snar.* ("white woman or lady") and *hihàboubi = menino br.*[co] ("white child")[24]; *Bōbi = mulato, ou mulata* ("mulatto") (1741: 11) and *vigidòdé = crioulo, ou crioula* ("creole") (1741: 11–12) for people of mixed race; *melamdutô = carijó* (1741: 12) referring to enslaved indigenous people,[25] and, for Africans, the African ethnic terms *guno = gente mina* ("Mina people"), *aglono = g.*[te] *Angolla* ("Angolan people") and *gamlimno = gente cóbû* (1741: 12).[26]

The social structure is also reflected in spatial terms, including terms that include a reference to ethnicity. Official institutions include are *Avódumchuhê = Igreja* ("church"), *achósuchuhê = palacio* ("palace") and *gamchòme = cadeya* ("prison") (Peixoto, 1741: 13). As for the ethnic divide, we find the central terms *hihabouno chòme = caza de branco* ("house of white man") and *acruchòme = senzalas* ("slaves' quarters"). These reflect the typical division of a slaveholding household in colonial Brazil.[27]

As for the signs of African agency in local trade, especially by females working as *negras de tabuleiro* or *negras das vendas* (mentioned above), these activities produced considerable wealth for some members of the black community. LGM was used in trade interactions, as the numerous dialogues about trade in the glossary confirm.

Quite surprisingly, in the glossary we also find the phrase *hiháboutó mématimagu am = terra de branco não· tem guerra* ("white mans' land does not have war"), which may be understood as an indirect reference to the unstable situation in West Africa, where numerous groups and states were engaged in violent conflicts over power and territory – financed and armed, to a considerable degree, by the transatlantic slave trade.

The legal status of Africans and Afro-descendants included terms referring to slaves, to those that had been freed (*forro, afforado*), and to the free-born, but who were not "full" members of the Portuguese kingdom. In the manuscript, besides *mese sim = canhanbollas* ("escaped slaves") and *mebubû = g.*[te] *fugida, ou perdida* ("people who fled or are lost") (Peixoto, 1741: 16), we find a series of expressions providing answers to the question "Who is your master?" (*men cru hauhê = q.*[m] *hé teu senhor*): *methómereu ame = eu sou forro*[28] ("I am freed"), *snor. fuão· cruàme = eu sou do s.*[r] *fuão* ("I belong to Mr. So and so") and *hihàbouce dè cruàme = eu sou escravo de hua molher* ("I'm a woman's slave")[29] (Peixoto, 1741: 17).

In order for a free or freed black person to prove their legal status and be allowed to circulate independently, they would have to present a written document called a *escripto*, as shown in this dialogue:

guisi = tu andas fugido ("Are you a runaway?")
humsi = ando fugido ("I am runaway")
masihâ = não· anda [...] fugido não· ("I'm not a runaway")
sóhá huhema mápom = mostra o escripto p.ª ver ("Show me your document so I can see")
huhema matim = não· tenho escripto ("I don't have the document"), and neither the explanation *huhema hébú = perdi o escripto* ("I lost the document") nor
huhema hejáhi = cahiieme o escripto ("The document fell down") are convincing enough to avoid the legal consequences:
guácheguima tim huhema, ná blauhê = se não· tens escripto hei de amarrarte ("If you don't have the document, I will have to arrest you" (Peixoto, 1741: 16–17).

The scene ends with detention. The enforcement of state control needed local agents, and the *Obra Nova* also mentions some of the official positions in the colonial regime: *Achósû = governador* ("local governor"), *achólupê = soldados* ("soldiers") and *megulitô = capp.ᵐ do mato ou meirinhos* (the first Portuguese term, *capp.ᵐ do mato*, refers to a low-ranking military officer charged with hunting down slaves and, often violently, taking and enforcing legal decisions on the spot, while *meirinho* refers to a more prestigious administrative position in the judicial system) (all three terms in Peixoto, 1741: 12).[30] We also find *máhigamchóme = vou p.ª a cadeya* ("I'm being put into prison", 1741: 20). The behaviour of those responsible for enforcing the law, as well as slaveholders, was often cruel and violent, and the physical violence of whites against slaves black is very explicit, as reflected in the entry *hi hà bouno, hé nachuhé acrú susû = os br.ᶜᵒˢ castigão m.ᵗᵒ os escravos* ("whites punish slaves a lot", 1741: 29).

Dialogues on the slave trade and violence

Reference to different forms of violence is made in the *Obra Nova*. First, there is mention of state power against runaway slaves/criminals, reflected in the expressions *máhigulimesesim = vou amarrar canhanholas* ("I will arrest runaways", Peixoto, 1741: 22). Second, explicit mention of slave trade, as an inherently violent practice, is made in the lists of parallel expressions about selling and buying goods: *máhisáacru'hihō = vou vender negros novos* (1741: 23) and *máhichóacru'hihõ = vou comprar negros novos* ("I will sell/buy new black people") and *máhichóhinhono = vou comprar hũa negra* ("I will buy a black woman" (1741: 23). Besides slaveholding Europeans, free(d) blacks could also possess slaves, and female slave owners (as mentioned above) included *forras*, i.e. free African or Afro-descendant women.[31]

Besides these attestations of inherent structural violence, general reference to violence is made with *Aguam = guerra* ("war", 1741: 23) and *megutõ = matador de gente* ("killer of people", 1741: 19), the latter term following the short dialogue *mé nabi huguhi = q.^{tas} pessoas matastes* ("How many people did you kill?") answer: *magu méreha = não· matey nimguem* ("I didn't kill anyone") or alternatively *humgu meru pou = matey hua pessoa* ("I killed one person", 1741: 19).

Dialogues involving violence in which the relations of power and subalternity crystallise or shift include those relating to violence and crime against whites: *mesesim efim aquachepou = os canhanbolas furturamme o meu ouro todo* ("The runaway slaves stole all my gold", 1741: 27). The danger for white people becomes visible in a dialogue (1741: 33–35), which begins:

Maguhi hi habouno = matemos este Branco//("Let's kill this white man") [...]
Preg.^{to}, anihutũ nágume = e porque rezão· me quereis matar ("Why do you want to kill me?")
miná hinum poupouthòhẽ = queremos lhe tomar tudo ("We want to take everything you have")
hinum poupou [...] mágumehã = tomay tudo e não· me mateis ("Take everything but don't kill me")
héguhéthóhéhi-nhõ = tem m.^{ta} rezão· ("You are very right").

So in the dialogue, the white victim begs for his life successfully and tries to build trust saying *nhimáhinháram nácruhã = eu não· sou ruim p.^{a} os escravos* ("I don't treat slaves badly") – though this doesn't seem very convincing to his attackers, who reply *guidómórufidim = você diz histo aqui agora* ("You only say this now and here"). Although he insists (*humdómó tou pou pou me = eu digo o mesmo em q.^{al} q.^{r} p.^{te}*, i.e. "I say the same thing everywhere"), the dialogue ends with a negation of inter-ethnic solidarity: *mipoupou màhichomto = nos não· somos todos am.^{os}, ou camaradas* ("We are not all friends and comrades", and finally *Responde, mesesim matim hi há bouno hã = os canhanbollas não· tem am.^{os} Brancos* ("Answers, Runaway slaves don't have white friends"). The use of solidarity terms like *avódum chomto = comp.^{e}, ou comadre* ("male or female compadre") or *chomto = amigo, ou camarada* ("friend or comrade", 1741: 12) in inter-ethnic relations and friendships has to be further researched.

African women, sexual violence and intimate relations

As negras minas ricas, rich African ladies running slave-based trades and services, represented only one end of the social hierarchy for African women or those of African descent. Forced prostitution, sexual and physical attacks and abuse in slavery were characteristic of the slave women's lot in this male-dominated mining community. As Spivak states, "The question of 'woman' seems most problematic in this [i.e. colonial] context. Clearly, if you are poor, black and female you get in the three ways" (1994: 90).

The *Obra Nova* contains a number of disrespectful LGM expressions for women,[32] including *coisa* ("thing"), as in (1741: 35) *Anunhatõ cri cri* ("You('re a) bad, vulgar thing"); *anunhatõ veo* ("You'(re a) disgraced thing, you disgraced"), *anóhihófou* ("You thing, get undressed"), *anunhatõ angalito plou plou* ("You thing, get undressed"). Peixoto also includes *huhádumi* ("Come and eat me, fuck me") to solicit sexual intercourse, and also *huhádumi chuchũ* ("Come and eat me, you leprous dog"), where "leprous dog" is obviously directed at a male, indicating that the agency expressed by the other participant of the conversation is equally disrespectful. All expressions were very likely used in the context of prostitution.

Due to gender demographics, sexual intercourse and intimate relations between African women and European men were frequent,[33] a topic about which Peixoto is surprisingly explicit, as we can see in the following dialogue:

> *Nóhé name ayó parê* = mai dame hũ bocado de cono//("Give me a little bit of your cunt")
> *fihá náhiná nauhê* = aónde/hó hey de hir dar//("Where should I give it to you")
> *huhà mi hi zume* = vamos p.ª o mato//("Let's go to the woods")
> *zumehé mihom* = o mato está humido//("The woods are wet")
> *huhà mi hi zamgi* = vamos p.ª a cama//("Let's go to the bed")
> *hu hà mi hi* = vamos//("Let's go") (Peixoto, 1741: 40).

The decision to have sex seems to be consensual in this dialogue. Especially when the women were *forras*, inter-ethnic heterosexual relations were less imbalanced in terms of power and might also yield long(er)-term and more stable relationships which also provided financial benefits.

Regarding the financial transactions involved in prostitution, the glossary includes advice on how to trick a woman into bed without paying. Peixoto introduces the following dialogue with *Cá milhor praxe de que eu uzo, alguas vezes, hé esta* ("This is the best strategy, which I sometimes use"):

> *Nhi matim aquhédimhã* = eu naõ· tenho agora ouro ("At this moment, I don't have gold").

mématim aquhé má hóhayò hâ = q.ᵐ naõ· tem ouro, naõ· fode ("Those who don't have gold won't fuck").
name ayo dim, beré sû ná nauhé aquhé = dame agora o cono, eq.ᵃˡ q.ʳ dia te darey o ouro ("Give me your cunt now, I'll give you the gold another day") (Peixoto, 1741: 41).

But the lady reinforces her business policies: *nhimá ná ayóche achó hâ = eu naõ· dou o meu cono fiado* ("I won't give my cunt on credit"). If we consider this negotiation from a gender perspective, it is the woman who is in control of the situation.

For *minas forras* (free African women of Mina origin), prostitution was an (additional) source of income, in addition to selling agricultural products and *cachaça* (brandy) in their (heavily taxed) *vendas* (shops) Because these female businesses to some extent followed West African patterns of women-controlled finance (see Farias 2019), a number of African women were able to accumulate considerable wealth. Besides these dialogues about sex, Peixoto includes a wide number of entries on family issues (pregnancy, childbearing, baptism). His interest in these issues is understandable given that he had daughters in Cachoeira and S. Bartolomeu by *negras forras* (free(d) African women), and two other children also probably of African mothers.

What these dialogues show is that, although being black and female was usually associated with double subaltern status, producing atrocious situations of sexual and physical exploitation and violence, and with de-structured family relations, some African women managed to move up the socio-economic hierarchy and renegotiate their subaltern status.

Final reflections: Renegotiating the subaltern in socio-economic relations, violence and sex

Looking at the micro-level of inter-ethnic interactions represented in the dialogues from the *Obra Nova da Língua Geral de Mina*, it is clear that power positions were negotiated and frequently shifted. Despite its declaredly "control-oriented" intention, the manuscript provides multiple examples of African agency, challenging racially based socio-economic patterns and power relations, where being "black" was associated with being enslaved and poor.

Alongside the micro-incidents between "blacks" and "whites" represented in Peixoto's *Obra Nova*, the work also sheds light on the socio-economic logic of solidarity and competition between people from different social groups (as regards gender, ethnicity, legal status, fortune and religion) in Minas Gerais' colonial social structure. Questions such as how and with whom different people would fraternise and under what circumstances have been investigated by Araujo (2022 forthcoming), using documents by or mentioning Antonio da Costa Peixoto.

In this context of complex alliances, animosities, and threats, Peixoto chose to employ LGM apparently as a means of inter-ethnic and inter-gender communication. To interact in LGM with members of African communities as a European-born member of Minas Gerais society was helpful considering his administrative position and probably boosted his professional ascent.

From this perspective, then, we can interpret Peixoto's efforts to acquire and describe LGM as a strategy on the part of a "white" member of society to secure his own position through the successful control of (but also winning the trust of and cultivating good relations with) members of the local black community. However, it is also clear from his work that these communicative and intimate "borders" were by no means stable. Race relations were clearly very fluid in the context of this mining society, and race was only one relative factor contributing to socio-economic position and social ascension. This becomes especially visible in the intimate relations between European men and African women.

Notes

1. See Rodrigues (2003), Petter and Fiorin (2008).
2. As put forward in Gayatri Spivak's seminal article 'Can the subaltern speak?' (1994).
3. This occurred when they were allowed to keep, for their personal benefit and maintenance, any surplus gold mined over and above the daily quota required of them.
4. Original: "OBra nova de Lingoa g.^{al} de mina, traduzida, aó nosso Igdioma por Antonio da Costa Peixoto, naciognal do Rn.º de Portugal, da Provincia de Entre Douro e Minho, do comcelho de Filgr.^{as}".
5. In 2022, a critical edition of Antonio da Costa Peixoto's two manuscripts (1731, 1741) by Rodrigues-Moura will be published at *Bamberger Editionen* (University of Bamberg Press), which will take into consideration the observations made by Silveira (1944, 1945), Souza (2001), Castro (2002) and Fernandes (2012). This book, published together by Märzhäuser and Rodrigues-Moura, includes contributions in English by Fernando Araujo, Annegret Bollée, Yeda Pessoa de Castro, Alexander Cobbinah, Sandra Furtado, Marcela Farias Bernardo and Cléa Nunes, Christina Märzhäuser and Dzidula Samla, and Enrique Rodrigues-Moura (Märzhäuser and Rodrigues-Moura, 2017, 2019).
6. All examples are given in the original spelling of the Peixoto manuscript (1741) with page number according to the original. The English translations are our own.
7. Peixoto recommends "tomar parecer com algũ negro, ou negra mina, porq.to tem diferente pernumcia" (1741: 42), i.e. 'to consult with a black Mina man or woman about pronunciation', which shows that he tries to assure the practical utility of his transcriptions for the reader.
8. Portuguese printer Antonio Isidoro da Fonseca opened a press in Rio de Janeiro in 1747 but was forced to close it the same year. In 1750, he officially requested permission to print books in Brazil, but the ban was reaffirmed (Bragança, 2010; Hallewell, 1985: 1–23).

9. This dual interpretation of "novo" as 'recent, anew' or 'ex novo' is described by Carolina Michäelis de Vasconcelos in her foreword to Ribeiro and Falcão (1923) and also included in the *Dicionário de Regionalismos e Arcaísmos* (Vasconcelos, 1997–2017). The use of the adjective "novo" to qualify a scientific text already had a long tradition, being present in over a hundred scientific books published from the late sixteenth until at least the middle seventeenth century, as Rossi (1997: 60) recalls.
10. "me comprem outros velumes, que com ansia e fervor, fico dando ao prello, e brevem.te sahirão" ('buy other volumes from me, which with eagerness and fervour, I'm handing in to be printed, and which soon will appear' Peixoto, 1741: 41–41).
11. The 1741 manuscript was eventually published in 1944 by Luís Silveira through the Agência Geral das Colónias, Lisbon. One year later, in 1945, a second edition was required because some of its contents were deemed indecent by the censor (Castro, 2002; Fernandes, 2012; Araujo, 2013). The 1945 edition includes a philological comment by Edmundo Correia Lopes, who already identifies LGM as "Ogunu, Gunu, Gu or alada [...] a variety of the Fon or Daomé, one of the dialects that constitute the Evɔe language" (our translation), adding the conclusion that the dialect in question was, in eighteenth-century Brazil, the general language of the Mina people (Lopes, 1945: 45).
12. "naciognal do Rn.º de Portugal, da Provincia de Entre Douro e Minho, do comcelho de Filgr.as [Felgueiras]" (Peixoto, 1741: 1).
13. A *juíz de vintena* was elected by the parish council (in this case: Câmara Municipal de Vila Rica); he was responsible for 20 *vizinhos* (= heads of households together with all persons depending on them), and worked as judge for questions of small value (100–400 Réis). To fulfil these roles, Peixoto had to count as trustworthy (*homem bom* = 'a good man') for local administration because he "incarnated the image of justice for questions of daily life in these territories" (Camarinhas, 2015; Vainfas, 1986). As a general rule, a *homem bom* did not have a mechanical trade or Jewish ancestry, although exceptions to the latter rule are documented.
14. "como não seja capaz de servir o tal oficio, por ser homem que toma bebidas e se embebeda de cachaça e anda metido pelas tabernas com as negras e negros" (quoted in Araujo, 2013: 3).
15. Legal documents from Vila Rica mention that Peixoto was able to recognise and talk the African language.
16. In the first half of the eighteenth century, between 82.2% and 94.9% of slaves came directly from Africa. See Rezende (2006: 3) for a detailed demographic description of the enslaved population groups in Vila Rica.
17. In fact, there were several types of "senzalas" in accordance with the composition of its inhabitants. Other names were "choça", "palhoça", "mocambo", "casa dos negros" (Schwarcz and Gomes, 2018).
18. "tantos imsultos, ruhinas, estragos, roubos, mortes e [...] cazos atrozes" (Peixoto, 1741: 5).
19. "rogos de am.os e particulares peditorios de p.cas a q.m não devia faltar, e como vm.ce tambem comigo neste p.ar se empinhou, justo parece que a vm.ce lhe tribute a lemitada oferta de meu trabalho, e oscuro entendim.to" (1741: 3).
20. Peixoto criticises the "preguisa" ('laziness') and lack of "curuzid.e" ('curiosity') of Minas Gerais' white residents (1741: 6).
21. Though economic reasons prevailed in Pombal's political project, the idea that an empire had to have a single language had Iberian (Antonio de Nebrija, 1492) and Italian roots (Lorenzo Valla, 1449/1952) (Asensio, 1974; Rodrigues-Moura, 2021). The importance of teaching the Portuguese

language gained fundamental importance with Luís António Verney's *Verdadeiro método de estudar* (1746).
22. See the *Directório, que se deve observer nas povoações dos índios do Pará e Maranhão* (1755), (extended to the whole of Brazil in 1758), which declared indigenous people as free and vassals of the king, and in doing so suppressed their languages, rites, customs and beliefs as incompatible with an enlightened society.
23. "Os habitantes da Capitania não Europeos, e os seus descendentes: negros, que se transportarão de Africa; e mulatos ou pardos, que provêm de Europêo, e de Africana: Cabras, que são os filhos de mulato e negra, ou vice versa: aos negros nascidos no Paiz chamão crioulos: e mistiços em fim, aos que nascem de pai Europeo, e mãe[s] Americana, ou pello contrario" (Azevedo, n.d.: 59).
24. Enslaved African wet-nurses (*amas de leite*) commonly fed the offspring of Europeans (Freyre 1933/ 1998; Schwarcz and Gomes, 2018).
25. See Venâncio (1997) for further discussion of this aspect.
26. All terms appear on pages 11–12. See Castro (2002: 47 ff.) for further discussion.
27. In urban Vila Rica, the underground gold mine, *senzala* and *casa grande* (Freyre 1933/1998) often formed a spatial unit, as can still be observed in Ouro Preto today.
28. According to Bluteau (1713: v. 4, 182): "Escravo forro. Aquele a quem o seu proprio senhor tem dado liberdade" (trasl.: 'Liberated slave. The one to whom his own master has given freedom'). The act of manumission was considered a concession of the slave owner. Even so, the slaves of Minas Gerais could buy their liberty, against the will of their master, if they found a diamond above 20 carats. At the same time, a slave who denounced the embezzlement of diamonds by his master also gained freedom. Over time, because mining production declined, slaveholders granted manumission more frequently to cut the costs of keeping slaves. See also Schwartz (1974), Mattoso (1982) and Souza (1982).
29. The word "fuão" is the reduced form of "fulano", "so and so" ('man').
30. Castro classifies 25 terms in Peixoto's glossary as related to 'confusion, slavery, war and agents' ("confusão, escravidão, guerra e mandatários") (2002: 182–183). For more on the colonial administration, see Salgado (1985).
31. Legal documents analysed in Araujo (2013) refer to the *forras* Thereza Ferreira Souto, the wealthy owner of a *venda* in Casa Branca, and to Rita Dias, owner of a *venda* in S. Bartolomeu, mother of one of Peixoto's daughters. See Paiva (2009) and Lima (2014) on social behaviour and economic strategies of liberated African women in Minas Gerais.
32. These range among the expressions for which Peixoto doesn't provide translation: "Não· declaro em portuguez, por serem palavras menos desentes a nossa pulicia" ('I don't declare this in Portuguese, because these words are not appropriate for our good behaviour') (Peixoto, 1741: 35). We therefore base our translations on those presented in Castro: *Anunhatõ cri cri = sua coisa ruim, ordinária; anunható veo = sua coisa desgraçada, seu desgraçado; anóhihófou = seu coisa, vá te arreganhar; anunható angalito plou plou = sua coisa debochada, prostituta, filho/filha da puta; huhádumi = venham me comer, foder; huhádumi chuchū = venha me comer, seu cão leproso* (2002: 184).
33. Alongside, marriage between Africans was legal and frequent in Brazil throughout the eighteenth and nineteenth century, as documents show; sadly, African procreation was also exploited by slaveholders to increase their 'stock' of slaves, especially regarding mine workers.

References

Primary sources

Peixoto, A. da Costa. (1731). *Alguns apontamentos da Língua Mina com as palavras Portuguesas correspondentes*. Manuscript preserved at the Biblioteca Nacional de Portugal (Códice 3052, F. 2355).

Peixoto, A. da Costa. (1741). *Obra Nova de Língua Geral de Mina*. Manuscript preserved at the Biblioteca Pública de Évora (Códice CXVI/1-14).

Peixoto, A. da Costa. (1944). *Obra Nova de Língua Geral de Mina*. Ed. by L. Silveira. Lisboa: Agência Geral das Colónias.

Peixoto, A. da Costa. (1945). *Obra Nova de Língua Geral de Mina*. Ed. by Luís Silveira and commented by E. Correia Lopes. Lisboa: Agência Geral das Colónias.

Peixoto, A. da Costa. (2022 forthcoming). *Obra Nova de Língua Geral de Mina*. Ed. By C. Märzhäuser and E. Rodrigues-Moura Bamberg: University of Bamberg Press (Bamberger Editionen).

Secondary sources

Almeida, C. M. Carvalho de. (2010). *Ricos e pobres em Minas Gerais: Produção e hierarquização social no mundo colonial, 1750–1822*. Belo Horizonte: Argvmentum.

Araujo, F. (2013). *Fome do ouro e fama da obra. Antonio da Costa Peixoto e a "Obra Nova de Lingoa Geral de Mina" – alianças, proximidades e distâncias de um escritor português no Brasil colonial do século XVIII*.

Araujo, F. (2022 forthcoming). Antonio da Costa Peixoto and his *Obra Nova de Lingua Geral de Mina*. Transitions of a writer and his manuscripts between Northern Portugal and the pathways of colonial Minas Gerais. In: A. da Costa Peixoto, C. Märzhäuser and E. Rodrigues-Moura, eds. *Obra Nova de Língua Geral de Mina*. Bamberg: University of Bamberg Press (= Bamberger Editionen).

Asensio, E. (1974). La lengua compañera del imperio. Historia de una idea de Nebrija en España y Portugal. In: E. Asensio, ed. *Estudios portugueses*. Paris: Fundação Calouste Gulbenkian, 1–16.

Azevedo, A. de Araujo. (n.d.) [ca. 1807]. *Breve descrição geográfica, física e política da capitania de Minas Gerais*. Arquivo Distrital de Braga [PT_UM-ADB-FAM-FAA-AAA-L-004532].

Bluteau, R. (1712-1728). *Vocabulário português e latino*. Oito volumes. Coimbra: Colégio das Artes da Companhia de Jesus.

Bollée, A. (2022 forthcoming). The *língua geral de Mina* and the genesis of creole languages. In: A. da Costa Peixoto. C. Märzhäuser & E. Rodrigues-Moura, eds. *Obra Nova de Língua Geral de Mina*. Bamberg: University of Bamberg Press (= Bamberger Editionen).

Bragança, A. (2010). António Isidoro da Fonseca e Frei José Mariano da Conceição Veloso: precursores. In: A. Bragança and M. Abreu, eds. *Impresso no Brasil: Dois séculos de livros brasileiros*. São Paulo: Unesp, 25–39.

Camarinhas, N. (2015). Juiz de Vintena. In: J. V. Serrão, M. Motta and S. M. Miranda, eds. *e-Dicionário da Terra e do Território no Império Português*. Lisbon: CEHC-IUL. Available at: https://edittip.net/2015/02/15/juiz-de-vintena/ [Accessed 7 June 2019].

Castro, Y. Pessoa de. (2002). *A língua mina-jeje no Brasil: Um falar africano em Ouro Preto do século XVIII*. Belo Horizonte: Fundação João Pinheiro; Secretaria de Estado da Cultura.

Castro, Y. Pessoa de. (2022 forthcoming). Língua mina-jeje. Territories of resistance and African identity in Brazil. In: A. da Costa Peixoto, C. Märzhäuser and E. Rodrigues-Moura, eds. *Obra Nova de Língua Geral de Mina*. Bamberg: University of Bamberg Press (= Bamberger Editionen).

Cobbinah. A. Y., Furtado, S., Bernardo, M. Farias and Nunes, C. (2022 forthcoming). Living memory – The linguistic legacy of Fon in the Tambor de Mina. In: A. da Costa Peixoto, C. Märzhäuser and E. Rodrigues-Moura, eds. *Obra Nova de Língua Geral de Mina*. Bamberg: University of Bamberg Press (= Bamberger Editionen).

Farias, J. Barreto. (2019). Entre pretas minas e signares: discutindo gênero, escravidão e liberdade no mundo atlântico. Paper at *Simpósio Internacional A diáspora dos povos Mina: dinâmicas identitárias, linguísticas e culturais*, 10–12 June 2019, Rio de Janeiro.

Fernandes, G. (2012). A Língua geral de Mina (1731/1741) de António da Costa Peixoto. *Confluência, Revista do Instituto de Língua Portuguesa*, 43(2), pp. 28-46.

Freyre, G. (1998). *Casa-Grande & Senzala*. Rio de Janeiro: Record. (Original work published 1933.)

Gonçalves, A. L. (2011). *As margens da liberdade: Estudo sobre a prática de alforrias em Minas colonial e provincial*. Belo Horizonte: Traço.

Hallewell, L. (1985). *O Livro no Brasil*. São Paulo: Edusp.

Lima, D. (2014) *A polissemia das alforrias: significados e dinâmicas de escravos nas Minas Gerais setencistas*. Master thesis. Belo Horizonte: Universidade Federal de Minas Gerais.

Lopes, E. Correia. (1945). Os trabalhos de Costa Peixoto e a Língua Evɔe no Brasil. In: A. da Costa Peixoto and L. Silveira, eds. *Obra Nova de Língua Geral de Mina*. Lisbon: Agência Geral das Colónias, pp. 41-66.

Märzhäuser, C. and Rodrigues-Moura, E. (2017). *Antonio da Costa Peixoto's Obra nova de língua geral de Mina (1731/1741) – A print- and online-edition of an unique historical document on the Ewe-Fon-legacy in Brazil*. Conference Poster at IV.° Congresso Internacional de Linguística Histórica, University of Lisbon (17–21 July 2017).

Märzhäuser, C. and Rodrigues-Moura, E. (2019). *A Obra nova de Língua Geral de Mina (1731/1741) de Antonio da Costa Peixoto. Edição de um testemunho de língua(s) Gbe em Minas Gerais & Breve estudo do campo semântico «alimentos»*. Conference Poster at Lusitanistentag, University of Augsburg.

Märzhäuser C. and Samla, D. (2022 forthcoming). Search for the origins of Língua Geral de Mina. Slave trade and external language history on the African continent. In: C. Märzhäuser and E. Rodrigues-Moura, eds. *A. da Costa Peixoto. Obra Nova de Língua Geral de Mina*. Bamberg: University of Bamberg Press (= Bamberger Editionen).

Mattoso, K. de Queirós. (1982). *Ser escravo no Brasil*. São Paulo: Brasiliense.

Nebrija, Antonio. (1492). *Gramática castellana*. Salamanca: Juan de Porras.

Oestreich, G. (1969). Strukturprobleme des europäischen Absolutismus. In: G. Oestreich, ed. *Geist und Gestalt des frühmodernen Staates*. Berlin: Duncker & Humblot, pp. 179-197.

Paiva, E. França. (2009). *Escravos e libertos nas Minas Gerais do século XVIII: estratégias de resistências através dos testamentos*. 3rd edition. São Paulo: Annablume.
Petter, M. and Fiorin, J. L., eds. (2008). *África no Brasil: a formação da língua portuguesa*. São Paulo: Editora Contexto.
Rezende, R. Castro. (2006) Africanos, Crioulos e Mestiços: a população de cor em algumas localidades mineiras do século XVIII e a construção de suas identidades. *Anais do XV Encontro Nacional de Estudos Populacionais*, Sec. 11(6), pp. 11–21.
Ribeiro, B. and Falcão, C. (1923). *Obras. Nova edição conforme a edição de Ferrara, preparada e revista por Anselmo Braamcamp Freire e prefaciada por D. Carolina Michaëlis de Vasconcellos*. Coimbra: Imprensa da Universidade.
Rodrigues, A. Dall'Igna. (2003). Obra Nova da Língua Geral de Mina: A língua Ewe nas Minas Gerais. *Papia. Revista Brasileira de Estudos Crioulos e Similares*, 13, pp. 92–96.
Rodrigues-Moura, E. (2021). Prolegômenos. Letras na América Portuguesa. In: E. Rodrigues-Moura, ed. *Letras na América Portuguesa. Autores – Textos – Leitores*. Bamberg: University of Bamberg Press, pp. 6–41.
Rossi, P. (1997). *La nascita della scienza moderna in Europa*. Roma and Bari: Laterza.
Salgado, G., ed. (1985). *Fiscais e meirinhos. A administração no Brasil colonial*. Rio de Janeiro: Nova Fronteira, Pró Memória and Instituto Nacional do Livro.
Schwarcz, L. M. and Gomes, F., eds. (2018). *Dicionário da Escravidão e Liberdade. 50 textos críticos*. São Paulo: Companhia das Letras.
Schwartz, S. B. (1974). A manumissão dos escravos no Brasil colonial, 1684–1745. *Anais de História*, 6, pp. 71–114.
Spivak, G. C. (1994). Can the Subaltern Speak? In: P. Williams and L. Chrisman, eds. *Colonial Discourse and Post-Colonial Theory. A Reader*. New York: Columbia UP, pp. 66–111.
Souza, L. de Mello e (1982). *Desclassificados do Ouro. A pobreza mineira no século XVIII*. Rio de Janeiro: Edições Graal.
Souza, S. M. Cunha. (2001). *A predicação na "língua geral de mina": uma proposta de descrição*. Master thesis. São Paulo: Universidade de São Paulo.
Vainfas, R. (1986). *Ideologia e escravidão: os letrados e a sociedade escravista no Brasil colonial*. Petrópolis: Vozes.
Valla, L. (1952). Elegantiarum linguae Latinae libri sex. In: E. Garin, ed. *Prosatori latini del Quattrocento*. Milano and Napoli: Riccardo Ricciardi Editore. (Original work published 1449.)
Vasconcelos, J. Leite. (1997-2017). *Dicionário de Regionalismos e Arcaísmos (DRA)*. Edição de I. Castro and J. P. Silvestre, eds. Lisboa: Centro de Linguística da Universidade de Lisboa and Grupo de Filologia. Available at: http://teitok.clul.ul.pt/dra/index.php?action=home [Accessed 7 June 2019].
Venâncio, R. Pinto. (1997). Os últimos Carijós: Escravidão Indígena em Minas Gerais: 1711-1725. *Revista Brasileira de História*, 17(34), 165–181.
Verney, L. A. (1746). *Verdadeiro método de estudar: para ser util à Republica, e à Igreja: proporcionado ao estilo, e necesidade de Portugal*. 2 vol. Valença: na oficina de Antonio Balle.

12 "Long Time No See"
The Use of Chinese Pidgin English as a Cultural Identity Symbol by the Canton Anglophone Trading Community

Rogério Miguel Puga

Introduction

The earliest narratives sent to Europe from China were by European Catholic missionaries and dated from the sixteenth century, a time when China was still relatively unknown in Great Britain. These were gradually complemented and replaced by accounts by traders, colonial agents, and explorers. In this chapter, I am going to examine some of the descriptions of Chinese Pidgin English (CPE) in eighteenth-century English and North-American travel writing, looking first at the way it was represented in general terms, before focusing on the way it sounded to the Western ear. CPE was an element of the soundscape of several China Trade contact zones and a symbol of the identity of the eighteenth-century British and North-American commercial community, the Anglophone "golden ghetto" (Downs, 1997) or "gated community" (Lampe, 2014: 117–174) in Canton and Macau. Back in Great Britain or the United States of America, traders, their relatives and writers who were members of the financial and cultural elites continued to use and spread CPE words and expressions such as "savvy",[1] "no can do" and "long time no see", which are still used nowadays all over the world by English speakers.

For Chinese speakers, CPE was a foreign language, while for English native speakers it was "broken English" as spoken by Chinese. In Anglophone countries, it was used for comic effect in Orientalist works to ridicule and diminish the Chinese – works that Hayot *et al.* (2008: vii–xxi) classify as "sinographies", or writings that use the figure of Chineseness to organise thought itself and Englishness. All these texts implied the inferior status of this makeshift language as a corrupted "sinified" version of the English language. Curiously, though, once the western traders and their families had returned home, CPE words and expressions became exoticized public markers of their cosmopolitan experience, cultural agency, power and wealth, far away from the Chinese servants and merchants from whom they learnt them. They also became part of the soundscapes of cities like London, New York, Boston and Philadelphia.

DOI: 10.4324/9781003092445-16

Macao was established by the Portuguese around 1557 and was the only Western gateway into China (Canton) until the founding of Hong Kong in 1841–1842. From the seventeenth century onwards, this Sino-Portuguese enclave was the first home in China for western traders, such as the officials of the East India Company (EIC), who established direct trade with China in 1700, and American traders, who arrived in 1784. The Chinese authorities decided to use Macau, a walled city co-administered by the Portuguese, as the centre of Chinese and Portuguese control over all other Westerners who were prohibited from entering China (Puga, 2013: 79–82). Until the First Opium War, the China Trade took place in Canton, the main destination for British and American traders, who lived in Macau between the trading seasons (March–September) as the Chinese authorities forbade them to live all year round in Canton.

In Canton and Macau, Chinese servants, shopkeepers and traders and western merchants did not speak each other's language and communicated in Portuguese[2] through local (often mistrusted) translators. They would also use the existing Macau Pidgin Portuguese (MPP), a functionally restricted pidgin used mainly by Chinese traders in the Pearl River Delta from which CPE may have derived (Li, 2016a, 2016b; Li and Matthews, 2016: 141–183).[3] With time, the continuous contact between British and Chinese in the Canton factories (autumn-winter months) and in Macau (spring-summer months), the MPP, spoken mainly by Chinese traders, servants and shopkeepers, influenced the formation and development of the CPE, also referred to as Canton English, or China Coast Pidgin (Tryon *et al.*, 1996; Li and Matthews, 2012, 2016; Li, 2016b).[4] In the middle of the eighteenth century, traders in the Pearl River Delta therefore spoke Portuguese (Macau) and English (Canton, Whampoa) pidgins simultaneously (Williams, 1836: 429–432).

In 1731, Thomas Naish's report to London advises every vessel *en route* to Amoy to stop off in Macau for protection against typhoons and to take in supplies (East India Company Factory Records. *India Office Records* (*IOR*), G/12/32, 1731, fl. 15), testifying to the strategic value of Macau both for travellers and for British interests in the Far East. These business journeys and the continued EIC presence in the Macau-Canton circuit gave way to a degree of cultural exchange and financial power of which CPE was a symbol. By 1717, British trade in Canton had already surpassed Portuguese commercial power, and the EIC's investments and presence became essential for Macau's economy. As, from 1729 onward, trade relations between foreigners and the Chinese took place mostly in Canton, and given the commercial contact between Chinese traders and the "red-haired barbarians" (as the Chinese called the British) – each side being barred from learning the other's language[5] –, there soon arose in the Pearl River Delta a new pidgin aimed at meeting new trading Sino-British needs.

As the British spent more time in their ships in Whampoa (Osbeck, 1771, vol. 1: 183) and in the Canton factories, the MPP's influence on

CPE decreased (Baker and Mühlhäusler, 1990: 106). Among the British community and their Chinese trading partners, there is evidence of the gradual replacement of certain Portuguese lexical items by English ones, though with a strong influence from substrate Cantonese grammar (Li *et al.*, 2005; Ansaldo *et al.*, 2010; Ansaldo *et al.*, 2011). These two important contact varieties emerged and developed as a result of the Sino-western trade, conducted continuously (by the Portuguese, English, Americans, Chinese and others) since the sixteenth century in the enclaves of Macau and Canton. From there, CPE also migrated to other Chinese and Asian ports, while, as we will see, some terms and expressions, such as "savvy", "long time no see", and "no can do", migrated with the China Trade community to the United States of America and Great Britain, and are still used nowadays by English speakers all over the world.[6] These Anglophone commercial and cultural agents connected East and West and can be regarded as precursors of the modern networks (Czennia, 2021: 1), facilitating cultural transfer and the movement of commodities.

Hall (1944: 95) outlines four main periods in CPE's history: (1) Origin in Canton and Macau (1715–1748); (2) Classical period, use at Canton (1748–1842); (3) Period of expansion and greatest use in Hong Kong and the Treaty Ports, and Yangtze valley (1842–c. 1890) and (4) Decline, as a consequence of political and social disfavour, and preference for standard English (1890–1940s). The development of the key features of CPE is traced back to 1732, when Campbell (1732/1996) visited China, while major grammatical and lexical changes in the early nineteenth century coincide with the increase of Anglophone foreigners in the Pearl River delta. Morse (1926: 67) suggests that, in around 1715, both Chinese and English merchants spoke CPE, which thereafter became the "lingua franca of the China trade", and that by the beginning of the 1730s, CPE had replaced Macao Pidgin Portuguese (MPP), which was probably becoming confined to Macau (Li, 2016a: 299). Chinese and Anglophone traders used terms such as "joss" (meaning "god", from Portuguese "Deus") (Osbeck, 1771, vol. 1: 238), "joss house" (church)[7] and "good/bad joss" (good/bad luck"); "number one" (main), "long time no see" and "no can do" (literal translations from Cantonese); "savvy" (from the Portuguese "sabe"), *pickenini* (*pequenino*, small), and "amah" (Portuguese *ama*, nanny), as well as Portuguese commercial terms used among English traders, such as *conta* "bill") and *comprador* ("buyer").[8] Terms like *mandarim* and *sobrecarga* also entered the English language (as "mandarin" and "supercargo", respectively).

Today, we can only access the commercial language through written sources. There are hundreds of CPE words, expressions and dialogues recorded in Chinese phrasebooks[9] and Anglophone sources related to the China Trade. In what follows, we examine some textual representations of CPE made in the eighteenth century by Anglophones in the enclosed spaces of the Canton factories and Macau homes, drawing on travel narratives,[10] diaries and letters; memoirs by colonial officials and their families, newspapers, and even contemporary novelists (such as Goldsmith, Defoe), as well as official records and chronicles.

Representations of CPE in eighteenth-century anglophone accounts

The earliest Anglophone writers reporting from Canton and Macau represented Chinese cultural artifacts and an unknown way of life to a new audience back home. These transcriptions of verbal narratives were made during contact situations in which Chinese servants and merchants spoke CPE to try to force Westerners to respect "China fashion" or the Chinese "old custom" while they were in Canton. Many travellers, especially in the eighteenth century, reported interactions in CPE as if they had taken place in English and transferred knowledge by translating CPE words and dialogues and even introducing Chinese concepts into the English language. One such concept was "loss of face", which is still used nowadays: in 1784, after a conflict between Westerners and Chinese, the American consul Samuel Shaw reported how he heard the latter say: "all Fanquois [Europeans] have much lose his face in this business" (Shaw, 1847: 195).

Epistolary and diaristic texts, sent from China in the eighteenth and nineteenth centuries, were read in places like Salem, New York and Boston by the authors' relatives and friends, often out loud in groups before an extended audience (Kagle, 1986: 5). These public-private journals are examples of what we might call early North-American amateur Sinology.

The earliest attestation of CPE that we know of was provided in 1732 by Colin Campbell (1686–1757), the first supercargo of the Swedish East India Company ship *Fredericus Rex Sueciae*. Campbell was an English trader of Scottish descent who left London in 1723 to work for the Austrian-Belgian Ostend Company. He spent four months in Canton (September 1732–1733), and the diary he wrote for the Swedish EIC while he was there contains a detailed description of events in that city. He quotes the Chinese trader Hunqua saying "*Masquie*, or no matter", and gives voice to Chinqua (a local trader with whom the Swedish East India Company would need to trade in the future), also in CPE, refusing silk to a European supercargo (Morford) "by saying he had no silks, and then told us he no quiere[11] *trust so fashion man for he no have Good*" (Campbell, 1732/1996: 147, 148, my italics). Campbell uses the quasi-direct speech of Chinqua to accuse Morford of being untrustworthy (Benson, 2005: 74). CPE as a symbol of the Chinese merchant's voice was therefore used as a rhetorical device to reinforce Campbell's negative opinion about his colleague, much as Anderson would do years later when he quoted a Chinese merchant criticizing English slavery.

In 1748, British trader George Anson (1748: 404) observed that trade in Canton was carried out in a "ridiculous jargon of broken English, which some few of the Chinese learned, or by suspected interpretation of the linguists of other nations". He, like Benyowsky (1790: 72), described how Chinese pilots spoke "in broken Portuguese" (Anson, 1748: 351) on board English ships, and how he heard a Chinese translator describe the Chinese people, "in his broken jargon, *Chinese man very great rogue truly, but have fashion, no can help*" (Anson 1748: 397: author's translation: "The Chinese are scoundrels but that's the way they are, there's nothing one can do").

George Noble, describing a visit to Canton in 1747–1748, also stated that the Chinese spoke a "broken and mixed dialect of English and Portuguese", "a mixture of European languages, but mostly, ... of English and Portuguese, together with some words of their own" to enable trade (Noble, 1762: 210, 245, 262). At one point, he reports a Chinese man asking two English sailors if they wanted a big or small woman ("whore") using almost entirely Portuguese words: "Carei grandi hola, pickenini hola?", while another reputedly said: "I moiki grand chin-chin for he" ("I made my compliments to him") (Noble, 1762: 240, 263).

Toreen, a chaplain of the Swedish EIC, in his *Voyage to Suratte, China*, mentioned that in 1751 the Chinese used Portuguese terms when speaking CPE:

> They(?) say instead of *doctor* and *padri* [priest in Portuguese], *locta* and *pali*... They generally converse with the Swedes in broken English; and sometimes in broken Portuguese, French, and Dutch... A Chinese merchant being asked whether he had any stockings? Answered, no *habb*.... When he is to say greet or small, he says *grande* or *galande*, and *pequenini*.
>
> (Toreen, 1771: 237–238)

Another chaplain to the Swedish EIC, Osbeck, suggested that other languages sometimes entered the mix:

> They [traders] can avail themselves of the *French, Portuguese,* or *English* languages, which the *Chinese* servants employed in trade have learned; though they have a particular dialect [CPE], and think that he does not speak well who does not intermingle *English, Portuguese,* and *Dutch*.
>
> (Osbeck, 1771, vol. 1: 274–275)

In 1769, William Hickey (1795: 208) visited Canton and described how CPE was used during interethnic and transnational social events hosted by Chinese merchants attended by British, such as the dinner and theatre play hosted by the hong merchant Pankeequa. The play included a funny Chinese impersonation of an Englishmen:

> In one of the scenes an English naval officer, in full uniform and fierce cocked hat, was introduced, who strutted across the stage, saying "Maskee can do! God damn!" whereon a loud and universal laugh ensued, the Chinese quite in an ecstasy, crying out "Truly have muchee like Englishman.
>
> (Hickey, 1795: 223–224)

This Sino-British play reminds us that travel writers such as Hickey are cultural translators; for having (ear)witnessed such CPE cross-cultural dialogues, they were involved in the action they were "translating". They became performers, and translation from CPE became a "cross-identity performance" (St. André, 2018).

CPE was often presented in these texts as a Chinese practice, while standard English is associated with the Anglophone residents, although, as the texts I am dealing with show, many of the latter also learned and used CPE even in their Macau homes, where they spent the autumn and winter months. In 1784 Shaw described the Chinese speaking to him in CPE and distinguishing Americans from British traders:

> "You are not Englishman?" said he. "No". "But you speak English word, and when you first come, I no can tell difference; but now I understand very well… Truly, Massa Typan [chief supercargo], I see very well you no hapt [have] Englishman. All China-man very much love your country'".
>
> (Shaw, 1847: 199)

Descriptions of translated interaction(s) between Chinese shopkeepers and servants and British traders or visitors in Canton illustrate how widely and fluently CPE was already spoken, particularly in shops:

> "Hy you truly have much ee handsome… Truly you go with me, I cumshaw all things" [the Chinese said], pointing to various articles of China ware… The man coolly replied, "Maske Maskee you come along with me, can break you please."… "All those have too much ee grand Ladrones [big thieves in Portuguese], give me too much trouble, make handsome face, no pay, no take, so must ee hang up".
>
> (Hickey, 1795: 227)

In 1793, during the first British embassy to China, the English and Chinese communicated in Canton shops using CPE, and Anderson transcribed one such conversation with a local merchant who criticised the British slave trade in his "broken English":

> Aye, aye, black man, in English country, have got one "first chop, good mandarin Willforce, that have done much good for allau blackie man, much long time: allau man makie chin, chin, hee, because he have got more first chop tink, than much English merchant-men; because he merchant-man tinkee for catch money, no tinkee for poor blackie man: Josh, no like so fashion.
> (Anderson, 1795: 272–273)

Assuming that his implicit British readers probably did not understand CPE, Anderson takes the trouble to translate this exchange into standard English:

> The meaning of these expressions is as follows: "Aye, in England, the black men have got an advocate and friend, (Mr. Wilberforce) who has, for a considerable time, been doing them service; and all good people, as well as the blacks, adore the character of a gentleman, whose thoughts have been directed to meliorate the condition of those men; and not like our West India planters, or merchants, who, for the love of gain, would prolong the misery of so large a portion of his fellow-creatures as the African slaves. But God cannot approve of such a practice".
> (Anderson, 1795: 273)

Like Goldsmith who, in his *The Citizen of the World* (1762), uses the figure of the Oriental visitor-spectator to comment on Western society, Anderson here uses the Chinese merchant to criticise slavery, presenting an informed and sober[12] voice that was strategically exoticized to attack, in CPE, the traffic that was already being challenged in London by abolitionists.

Lord George Macartney's embassy (1792–1793), which constituted Britain's first, albeit diplomatically fruitless, attempt to improve trade between the two countries, led to the systematisation of knowledge about China and intensified Britain's interest in the country and the need to train British translators. Publications like Winterbotham's *View of the Chinese Empire* (1795: 369), which included Anson's interaction with a Chinese merchant in "broken English", gradually associated the pidgin with Sino-British contact in the British popular imagination.[13] Descriptions of the British embassy, like Staunton's *An Authentic Account of an Embassy* (1798) and Barrow's *Travels in China* (1804), also mentioned the Canton "broken English" and illustrated British imperial ambitions in China, namely through the importance of supercargoes speaking Cantonese:

Satisfied in transacting the Company's concerns through the medium of a jargon of broken English, which all the Hong merchants, and even the inferior tradesmen and mechanics, find it worth their while to acquire, they have totally neglected the [Chinese] language...
... Accomplishing this desirable object [speaking Cantonese is] extremely simple. If the directors of the East India Company were to make it a rule that no writer should be appointed to China until he had [learned...] five hundred or a thousand characters.

(Barrow, 1804: 417–418)

Barrow added that foreigners in Canton "communicated only with the natives in a jargon of their own language" (418) and warned the British government and the EIC of the danger of neglecting the study of Cantonese as in Canton "every petty officer of the government knows he can practice impositions on our trade with impunity, because we have not the means of bringing his villainy to the knowledge of his superiors" (1804: 418–419), and reflected on the importance of having skilled translators in Canton, rather than only using CPE, which, though useful in the factories, is less so in more official contexts.

After Lord Macartney's failed embassy,[14] a more negative image of (a backward, corrupt and proud) China began to appear.[15] Throughout the eighteenth century, CPE, seen as "broken English" spoken by Chinese servants and traders, helped to stress the already existing British and European ambiguity towards "industrious inhabitants" (Osbeck, 1771, vol. 2: 40; Eckeberg, 1771: 272) and the "great Monarchy" of China (Shelvocke, 1726: 460), also considered to be a "not very friendly country" (Downing, 1838: 113). Towards the end of the century, and especially after 1834–1842, cities like Hong Kong, Macau and Shanghai began to be viewed increasingly as (semi-)colonial spaces.

In the early eighteenth century, China had become associated with new modes of consumption that tested the stability of existing and emergent forms of English identity and taste. The growing range of "things Chinese" now available on the wider market conveyed signs of cosmopolitan prestige traditionally possessed by the aristocracy. As Jenkins (2013: 3) puts it, "Chinoiserie is identified in writing of the period with a kind of consumption that mimics diplomatic tribute and replaces inheritance as the foundation of identity". This process helps to explain the dissemination of CPE words in the late eighteenth century and first half of the nineteenth century. Whole Anglophone families went to live in Macau and Canton and wrote about the Pearl River Delta using CPE words which were part of their daily life in China. Once they were back home, the members of the American and British financial and cultural elites continued to use those expressions as identity traits and nostalgic symbols of their residence in China, negotiating their cosmopolitan self-awareness with nationalism. CPE – described in the sources that I used as a "broken" version of the language of the writing Anglophone Self used by the Chinese Other – puts the Anglophone Self in a mutually defining relationship with Chinese practices, providing opportunities for the display of wealth by those British and American users of CPE.

There was also an important gender dimension to CPE. As Chinese women were described as "continually confined, and in shops or working places are only men" (Osbeck, 1771, vol. 1: 219), and the few foreign women who travelled to Macau – the female space of the China Trade – were not allowed into China, the pidgin was predominantly a male language during the eighteenth century. However, as relatives of Anglophone traders started residing in Macau, this male commercial trade language in Canton gradually became a domestic contact language, also used by women and children. It was this that enabled it to become a family heritage and shared memory, as well as part of the identity of affluent communities back in Great Britain and the United States. The itinerant CPE expressions considered amusing by these English speakers were then also adopted by American social climbers who socialised with China Trade families and imitated their behaviour, further disseminating them.

Thus, while most eighteenth-century authors chose not to represent themselves as CPE speakers in China, using the pidgin exclusively to exoticize the Chinese, this attitude changed with time as more and more Westerners spoke it at home and on the streets.

How Chinese soundscapes and CPE sounded to the western ear

Eighteenth-century Chinese soundscapes can only be accessed through amateur transcriptions of dialogues and words in written sources, therefore in order to get an idea of what CPE sounded like to the Western ear, we must endeavour to undertake an acoustically attuned exploration of these written archives, searching for traces of "aurality" across Western textual and ideological sites of inscription (Ochoa Gaultier, 2014: 3).

Chinese sounds and noises amazed the Western newcomers and, like CPE, functioned as a culture shock and acoustic frontier. For instance, in 1793, during the first British embassy to China, George Barrow entered Beijing and described the city's strange cultural and ethnographic soundscape, which he compared to that of London:

> The buzz and confused noises of this mixed multitude, proceeding from the loud bawling of those who were crying their wares, the wrangling of others, with every now and then a strange twanging noise like the jarring of a cracked Jew's harp, the barber's signal

made by his tweezers, the mirth and the laughter that prevailed in every group, could scarcely be exceeded by the brokers in the Bank rotunda, or by the Jews and old women in Rosemary Lane.

(Barrow, 1804: 96)

Similar sounds were heard in Canton along with the more familiar CPE after the initial shock upon arrival at the "Pandemonium", as reported by the nineteenth-century traveller Downing:

A time comparatively quiet is broken the minute after by these sounds, and the clash and clamour gongs and other delicate music... The first journey up to Canton has made such an impression on me, that I think it never could be erased if I were to live for a thousand long years to come... A person would be excused, if upon his first progress up to Canton he should really believe that he was at the entrance of Pandemonium.

(Downing, 1838: 114)

Another account, by an anonymous correspondent in Jacob Abbott's miscellaneous *China and the English,* is suggestive of the soundscape in a small square opposite the Canton factories and the boats in the river, using adjectives and action verbs to describe all nationalities mingling in the small space where CPE was heard (except, significantly, the neutrally superior Westerners):

A cluster of stupid, thick headed Chinamen, looking with affected scorn and contempt; the staid and sedate Parsees or Persians; the supercargoes and other officers of the English and American ships... Jack Tar ... reeling about in a state of inebriety. The Lascars, or Malays, ... growling and quarrelling with everyone.

(Abbott, 1835: 80)

The Chinese soundscapes were also emphasised by the sensation of the spectacular when Westerners admired the narrow-crowded Canton streets, watched Chinese pantomimes or entered shops. Western traders and their wives, who spoke CPE, listened to Chinese with their "imperial ears" (Irvine, 2020: 6), just as they observed China with "imperial eyes" (Pratt, 1992), demarcating acoustic frontiers and accentuating the cultural difference in the commercial borderlands.

Thus, the China Trade experience was not only cultural and ethnographic but also sonic, as residents and travellers observed the performing Chinese and listened to them speaking CPE. The pidgin was also a matter of non-standard English pronunciation (for instance, the absence of the/r/phoneme), while for the Chinese the unfamiliar and hard to pronounce Western sounds must also have seemed amusing.

Nevertheless, using CPE as a means of communication helped the Chinese prevent foreigners from learning Cantonese and thus gaining direct access to the higher ranks of the Mandarinate. Anglophone merchants were vulnerable in Canton, enclosed in the factories and victims of Chinese violence if they tried to enter the city (Osbeck, 1771, vol.1: 215–216, vol. 2: 17–19) where they had no power. Chinese servants were in charge of their factories and homes and, like local merchants, did not care much about the norms of standard English spoken by their foreign employers and trading partners. If CPE suited Westerners, as it allowed them to trade and understand their servants, it also allowed the Chinese, from servants to the Mandarins, to defend their interests and power. The contact language was therefore used as a political and control tool.

As these texts reveal, for Anglophone speakers and earwitnesses, individualised Chinese servants and merchants were often reduced to CPE voices, perfunctorily sketched, like so many other aspects of Chinese culture. The textualisation of CPE turns it into a Chinese cultural symbol and literary strategy, an identity trait that was imported to the USA and GB as a form of literary and linguistic chinoiserie, along with China Trade export paintings, silk and ivory fans, export furniture and Chinese clothes, tea, chinaware, lacquerware and other artefacts and commodities. CPE would gradually become a recurrent symbol of the Chinese in Anglophone representations, to the extent that novels such as Defoe's *Colonel Jack* (1722), as well as many more recent works, have used the pidgin to add proto-ethnographic realism to dialogues in Chinese spaces (Puga, 2004).

These travel and fictional texts that give voice to CPE speakers can be read as what Aravamudan has called Enlightenment Orientalism, which was not a corporate institution for dealing with the Orient but rather

> ...a fictional mode for dreaming with the Orient – dreaming with it by constructing and translating fictions about it, pluralizing views over it, inventing it, by reimagining it, unsettling its meaning, brooding over it. In short, Enlightenment Orientalism was a Western style for translating, anatomizing, and desiring the Orient.
> (Aravamudan, 2011: 8)

Caricaturing the performing Other through the use of CPE in the shape of comic spectacle was a way to claim the cultural and linguistic superiority of the enclosed Self in Canton and Macau. From the eighteenth century onwards, these travelling authors, many of whom had had contact only with the enclosed spaces of Macau and the Canton factories, formally outside China, characterised themselves as cosmopolitan and refined. Their judgments about the Chinese merchants and servants, and the way they spoke CPE, were based on their sense of their own status and power – a linguistic manifestation of social and colonial hierarchies.

Conclusion

Recent scholarship on cultural relations between Britain and China has stressed that the literature of the long eighteenth century generated a model of English selfhood that was dependent on figures of China,[16] making Orientalism one of the most lasting effects of the literary incorporation of China into the English self-definition (Jenkins, 2013: 1–2; Min, 2018). For David Porter (2010b), the eighteenth century was the century of chinoiserie,[17] while Jenkins (2013) proposes that Chineseness, of which CPE was a fundamental part, was an English literary effect that helped to define Englishness.

This chapter has illustrated how CPE was effectively constructed by eighteenth-century travel narratives as a form of linguistic chinoiserie. In the texts analysed, the Chinese are always represented as performers communicating and interacting with foreigners (in "broken" English) in a commercial or master–servant relationship, within the semi-colonial spaces of the Canton factories and Macau. CPE is one of the themes and strategies used to increasingly exoticize the Chinese Other. With such speech (and listening) acts, these individuals are represented as performing an identity and revealing their sense of belonging and social and ethnic solidarity or difference (Page and Tabouret-Keller, 1985).

The pidgin was, from the very beginning, a comic performance for both Chinese and Westerners, a symbol of trade and interethnic communication in semi-isolated spaces like the Canton factories, Whampoa or Macau. Descriptions of CPE dialogues with and between Chinese servants and shopkeepers allow us to access the master-servant interactions taking place in shops, factories, ships and Macau homes, with CPE expressions such as "China fashion"[18] and toponyms like "Lob Lob Creek"[19] evoking the world of the Chinese servants, washerwomen, hawkers and shopkeepers, and the Tanka women who drove sampans and were prostituted in the periphery of a male commercial environment. These pidgin-speaking voices were voices "from below", giving glimpses of a very different world from the dinner parties hosted by Chinese merchants and attended by western traders (the China trade ruling class).

As more and more American and British private merchants and their families arrived in Canton from the end of the eighteenth century onwards, the Anglophone "golden ghetto" grew, increasing the numbers of western speakers of CPE. Upon returning home, those American and British traders took chinaware, Chinese furniture, and other commodities back as souvenirs and signs of their cosmopolitan social status. They also imported CPE expressions that were used in Canton mainly by the Chinese working class and traders – terms like "savvy", "no can do", or "long time no see" – domesticating and disseminating them with the help of other cultural agents. In America and Great Britain, these amusing linguistic symbols were used "from above" by the cultural and financial elite to construct, maintain and display their Canton Trade identity and wealth.

All along, CPE was the language of the foreign trading Other and, in the end, was no one's "broken" language. However, its importance for the Chinese and Western collective cultural memory was such that it needs to be placed in a much broader global commercial, colonial and cultural context, far beyond the boundaries of the geographical space(s) where it first arose.

Notes

1. Terms like "savvy" or "piccaninny" are used in several contacts languages and their origin is undetermined (Baker and Huber, 2001: 193, 202).
2. The importance of the Portuguese is testified by the fact that, in the seventeenth and eighteenth centuries, the EIC tried to hire supercargoes who could speak it (Campbell, 1732/1996: 138–139, 156-7). As early as 1703, Alexander Hamilton traded in Macau and Canton with the help of Portuguese interpreters, "linguists" from the French factory, and his own purser, "who spake good Portuguese" (Hamilton, 1727: 224–233).
3. See Baker (1987: 201, n. 15): "CPE may be, in part at least, a relexification of an earlier Portuguese-based Pidgin"; Baker and Mühlhäusler (1990: 105, 107); Holm (2004: 9); Tryon et al. (1996: 486–490). The extensive lexical and grammatical similarities between MPP and Macau Creole Portuguese (MCP) have led Li (2016b) to suggest that MPP was based on MCP (pidginisation of a creole) and that these varieties can be represented as a continuum, with varying degrees of (dis)continuity. The author concludes that the varieties of Portuguese spoken in Macau present a complicated linguistic scenario, with Portuguese as the administrative language, MCP as the local language for the Macanese and Christian Chinese; and MPP as the variety used by the Chinese.
4. According to Matthews and Li (2012), two of the grammatical properties of CPE (the use of "have" as locative copula, and the use of "for" as complementizer) may be explained by the influence of pidgin Portuguese.
5. Just as the Portuguese had concluded in the sixteenth century, the EIC realised that it was essential to have a good command of Cantonese, and in 1746 employed an interpreter, the young James Flint, who had lived in Southern China since 1736 in order to learn Cantonese (East India Company Factory Records, *IOR*. G/12/49, fl. 7; G/12/110, fl. 52), just as Thomas Bevan and Barton did in 1753. Their Chinese teacher was pressured by the Chinese authorities into desisting from teaching them. In 1793, faced with this linguistic blockade, three young men, B. Travers, T. C. Pattle, and J. Roberts secretly learnt Cantonese in Macau. As the Company's translator, Flint became a threat to the position of the Cantonese traders and of some officials; foreign supercargoes would be able to communicate directly with the *hopu* (Chinese Customs) and the viceroy, as well as negotiate more freely. Flint was arrested by the Chinese

and expelled in 1762 (East India Company Factory Records G/12/11, fls. 100–112), but the emperor ordered an inquiry into events in Canton and the *hopu* was punished (Puga, 2013: 94).
6. Indeed, CPE itself survived until at least 1971 (Baker, 1987: 164; Hall, 1944).
7. In 1784 and in 1882, the American diplomat Shaw (1847: 195–198) and the American trader Hunter (1882: 24, 29, 84, 93), respectively, used the same expressions and words ("chin chinning Joss", "Joss-house") several times in their texts, and the latter informed his readers about CPE and speculated on its origins suggesting theories that, as we have seen, are nowadays being proven by linguists (relexification of the PMP).
8. The foreigners' daily life depended on the action of the comprador(e) (Campbell, 1732/1996: 96), the "bicultural middleman" between Chinese and Westerners (Hao, 1970: 1–77, 154–223).
9. Compared with Macau Pidgin Portuguese (MPP), Chinese Pidgin English (CPE) is relatively well-documented. On Anglophone sources (travel books, articles, letters, diaries) and Chinese sources (MPP and CPE nineteenth-century phrasebooks, published mostly after the Nanking Treaty) see Bolton, 2003; Li, 2011: 270–271; Li, 2016a; Li *et al.*, 2005; Matthews and Li, 2013; Shi, 1993; Williams, 1838; Wu, 2001.
10. Please see the "Primary sources" section of our bibliography, *infra*.
11. Portuguese verb *querer* (to want), also used in Noble's (1762: 240) attestation of CPE ("carei").
12. Hayot (2009) and Kitson (2013: 9) recall that Chinese people frequently functioned in western discourse as philosophical and literary examples.
13. On the construct of China by English and European authors using the information provided by missionaries and travellers, see Hsia (1998), who calls this cumulative process "Sinism", and Min (2018).
14. Though the British mission did not bear diplomatic fruit, it had direct cultural repercussions in Europe and in China, for the young George Staunton (1781–1859), who took part in that expedition, exemplified the British desire to set up in trade in China, later becoming a sinologist, supercargo and EIC administrator.
15. According to Markley (2006: 1–4), an economic fascination with the riches of China underwrites English literary production in the seventeenth and eighteenth centuries (Defoe's *A New Voyage Around the World*, 1724; Swift's *Gulliver's Travels*, 1726). Markley sees China as the world's leading economy between 1500 and 1800 and a political, economic, and intellectual example to the West, "a fantasy space for mercantile capitalism", where trade was carried out with the help of CPE, also a symbol of wealth for Anglophone traders. Until 1800, if any economy had a "central" position and role in the world economy and its possible hierarchy of "centres", it was China (Frank, 1998: 5). The Western idea of China's inferiority gradually developed in the late eighteenth century (Porter, 2010a) but was already visible in Defoe's demonisation of China (inferiority of the Chinese to British Protestantism) in his *Farther Adventures of Robinson Crusoe* (1719).
16. Early eighteenth-century British literature even writes China into its self-representation (Markley, 2006; Porter, 2010b). Jenkins (2013: 5, 14) concludes that "the Oriental" that is so "vehemently resisted by the nineteenth-century English subject is, in fact, an eighteenth-century Englishness", while Yang (2011: 25–27, 31) states that an orientalist vision of China is a structure of ambivalence in British literature "resulting from

the desire for East Indies markets and the encounter with their superior moral *and* economic example, [revealing] fundamental contradictions of British consumer society by testing the changing boundaries between virtue and vice... [China was a] paradoxical temporality..., an instructive set of paradoxes. ... The paradox of its being an ancient yet modern, and far from defunct empire".
17. Porter (2010b: 20) concludes that the Chinoiserie style seems consistent "to have troubled this boundary between cultivated and vulgar taste, fine art and the fripperies of fashion. On the one hand, period satirists regularly denounced Chinese and Chinese-inspired goods as the best foolish trifles worthy of no more serious regard than this season's favourite hat or velvet glove, or at worst as emblems of aesthetic monstrosity or perversion trending only to vitiate the taste of their admirers".
18. This CPE term refers to the traditional Chinese customs and rules, as communicated to westerners by their servants (Low, 2002: 196).
19. Lob Lob (Love Love) Creek was an inlet on the Pearl River estuary between Whampoa and Canton where Western traders paid for sex with Chinese women, as described by William Hickey (1795: 208).

References

Primary sources

Abbott, J. (1835). *China and the English*. New York: Leavitt, Lord.
Anderson, A. (1795). *A Narrative of the British Embassy to China*. Dublin: P. Wogan.
Anson, G. (1748). *A Voyage Round the World, in the Years MDCCXL, I, II, III, IV*. London: John and Paul Knapton.
Barrow, J. (1804). *Travels in China*. Philadelphia: W. F. M'Laughlin.
Benyowsky, M. (1790). *Memoirs and Travels*. London: G.G.J. Robinson, Pater- Bister- Row.
East India Company Factory Records (1731-1762). G/12/11; G/12/32; G/12/49; G/12/110London. *India Office Records (IOR)*. British Library.
Campbell, C. (1996). A Passage to China: Colin Campbell' s Diary of the First Swedish East India Company Expedition to Canton, 1732–1733. In: P. Hallberg and C. Koninckx, eds., *Acta Regiae Societatis Scientiarum et Litterarum Gothoburgensis, Humanoria 37*. Gothenburg: Royal Society of Arts and Sciences (1732).
Downing, C. T. (1838). *The Stranger in China*. Vol 1. Philadelphia: Lea & Blanchard.
Eckeberg, C. G. (1771). A Short Account of the Chinese Husbandry. In: P. Osbeck, ed. *A Voyage to China and the East Indies*. Vol. 2. London: Benjamin White, pp. 267–317.
Hamilton, A. (1727). *A New Account of the East Indies*. Vol 2. Edinburgh: John Mossman.
Hickey, W. (1795). *Memoirs of William Hickey. Vol 1. (1749–1775)*. London: Hurst & Blacket.
Hunter, W. C. (1882). *The Fan Kwae at Canton before Treaty Days, 1825-1844*. London: K. Paul, Trench.
Low, H. (2002). *Life and Shadows of a Macao Life. The Journal of Harriet Low*. Winthrop: Bear Creek Books.

Noble, C. F. (1762). *A Voyage to the East Indies in 1747 and 1748*. London: T. Becket.
Osbeck, P. (1771). *A Voyage to the China and the East Indies*. 2 vols. London: Benjamin White.
Shaw, S. (1847). *The Journals of Major Samuel Shaw, the First American Consul at Canton*. Boston: Wm. Crosby and H. P. Nichols.
Shelvocke, G. (1726). *A Voyage round the World*. London: J. Senex.
Staunton, G. (1798). *An Authentic Account of an Embassy from the King of Great Britain to the Emperor of China*. Dublin: P. Wogan.
Toreen, O. (1771). A Voyage to Suratte, China, &c. From the 1st of April, 1750, to the 26th of June, 1752. In: P. Osbeck, ed., *Voyage to China and the East Indies*. Vol 2. London: Benjamin White, pp. 153–266.
Williams, S. W. (1836). Art. VII. Jargon Spoken in Canton: How it Originated and Has Grown into Use; Mode in which the Chinese Learn English; Examples of the Language in Common Use between Foreigners and Chinese. *The Chinese Repository*, 4(9), pp. 428–435.
Williams, S. W. (1838). Hungmaou Mae Mae Tung Yung Kwei Hwa, or those Words of the Devilish Language of the Red-Bristled People Commonly Used in Buying and Welling. *Chinese Repository*, 6(6), pp. 276–279.

Secondary sources

Ansaldo, U., Matthews, S. and Smith, G. (2010). China Coast Pidgin: Texts and Contexts. *Journal of Pidgin and Creole Languages*, 25(1), pp. 63–94.
Ansaldo, U., Matthews, S. and Smith, G. (2011). The Cantonese Substrate in China Coast Pidgin. In: C. Lefebvre, ed., *Creoles, their Substrates, and Language Typology*. Amsterdam: John Benjamins, pp. 289–302.
Aravamudan, S. (2011). *Enlightenment Orientalism: Resisting the Rise of the Novel*. Chicago: University of Chicago Press.
Baker, P. (1987). Historical Development in Chinese Pidgin English and the Nature of the Relationships between the Various Pidgin Englishes of the Pacific Region. *Journal of Pidgin and Creole Languages*, 2(2), pp. 163–207.
Baker, P. and Huber, M. (2001). Atlantic, Pacific, and World-wide Features in English-lexicon Contact Languages. *English World-Wide*, 22(2), pp. 157–208.
Baker, P. and Mühlhäusler, P. (1990). From Business to Pidgin. *Journal of Asian Pacific Communication*, 1, pp. 87–116.
Benson, P. (2005). The Origins of Chinese Pidgin English: Evidence from Colin Campell's Diary. *Hong Kong Journal of Applied Linguistics*, 10(1), pp. 59–77.
Bolton, K. (2003). *Chinese Englishes*. Cambridge: Cambridge University Press.
Czennia, B. (2021). Introduction: Oriental Networks in the Long Eighteenth Century. In: Czennia, B. and Clingham, G., eds. *Oriental Networks: Culture, Commerce, and Communication in the Long Eighteenth Century*. Lewisburg: Bucknell university Press, pp. 1–33.
Downs, Jacques M. (1997). *The Golden Ghetto: The American Commercial Community at Canton and the Shaping of American China Policy, 1784–1844*. Cranbury: Lehigh University Press.
Frank, A. G. (1998). *ReOrient: Global Economy in the Asian Age*. Berkeley: University of California Press.
Hall, R. A. (1944). Chinese Pidgin English Grammar and Texts. *Journal of the American Oriental Society*, 64(3), pp. 95–113.

Hao, Y.-P. (1970). *The Compradore in Nineteenth Century China*. Cambridge: Harvard University Press.
Hayot, E. (2009). *The Hypothetical Mandarin: Sympathy, Modernity, and Chinese Pain*. Oxford: Oxford University Press.
Hayot, E., Saussy, H. and Yao, S. G. (2008). *Sinographies: Writing China*. Minneapolis: University of Minnesota Press.
Holm, J. (2004). *An Introduction to Pidgins and Creoles*. Cambridge: Cambridge University Press.
Hsia, A. (1998). *Chinesia: The European Construction of China in the Literature of the 17th and 18th Centuries*. Tubingen: Niemeyer.
Irvine, T. (2020). *Listening to China: Sound and Sino-Western Encounter, 1770-1839*. Chicago: The University of Chicago Press.
Jenkins, E. Z. (2013). *A Taste for China: English Subjectivity and the Prehistory of Orientalism*. Oxford: Oxford University Press.
Kagle, S. E. (1986). *Early Nineteenth-Century American Diary Literature*. Boston: Twayne.
Kitson, P. J. (2013). *Forging Romantic China: Sino-British Cultural Exchange, 1760-1840*. Cambridge: Cambridge University Press.
Lampe, E. (2014). *Work, Class, and Power in the Borderlands of the Early American Pacific: The Labors of Empire*. Lanham: Lexington Books.
Li, M. (2011). Origins of a Preposition: Chinese Pidgin English Long and Its Implications for Pidgin Grammar. *Journal of Language Contact*, 4, pp. 269–294.
Li, M. (2016a). Trade Pidgins in China: Historical and Grammatical Relationships. *Transactions of the Philological Society*, 114(3), pp. 298–314.
Li, M. (2016b). Macau Pidgin Portuguese and Creole Portuguese: A Continuum?. In: A. Schwegler, J. H. McWhorter and L. Ströbel, eds., *Iberian Challenge: Creole Languages beyond the Plantation Setting*. Madrid: Iberoamericana Editorial Vervuert, pp. 113–134.
Li, M. and Matthews, S. (2016). An Outline of Macau Pidgin Portuguese. *Journal of Pidgin and Creole Languages*, 31(1), pp. 141–183.
Li, M., Matthews, S. and Smith, G. P. (2005) Pidgin English Texts from *The Chinese and English Instructor*. *Hong Kong Journal of Applied Linguistics*, 10(1), pp. 79–167.
Markley, R. (2006). *The Far East and the English Imagination, 1600-1730*. Cambridge: Cambridge University Press.
Matthews, S. and Li, M. (2012). Portuguese Pidgin and Chinese Pidgin English in the Canton Trade. In: H. C. Cardoso, A. Baxter and M. P. Nunes, eds., *Iberian-Asian Creoles*. Amsterdam: John Benjamins, pp. 263–288.
Matthews, S. and Li, M. (2013). Chinese Pidgin English. In: S. Michaelis, P. Mauer, M. Haspelmath and M. Huber, eds., *The Survey of Pidgin and Creole Languages*. Oxford: Oxford University Press, pp. 206–213.
Min, E. K. (2018). *China and the Writing of English Literary Modernity, 1690-1770*. Cambridge: Cambridge University Press.
Morse, H. B. (1926). *The Chronicles of the East India Company Trading to China, 1635-1834*. Vol 1. Oxford: Clarendon Press.
Ochoa Gaultier, A. M. (2014). *Aurality: Listening and Knowledge in Nineteenth-Century Colombia*. Durham: Duke University Press.
Page, R. B. and Tabouret-Keller, A. (1985). *Acts of Identity: Creole-Based Approaches to Language and Ethnicity*. Cambridge, Cambridge University Press.

Porter, D. (2010a). *Ideographia: The Chinese Cypher in Early Modern Europe*. Stanford: Stanford University Press.
Porter, D. (2010b). *The Chinese Taste in Eighteenth-Century England*. Cambridge: Cambridge University Press.
Pratt, M. L. (1992). *Imperial Eyes: Travel Writing and Transculturation*. London: Routledge.
Puga, R. M. (2004). Chinese Pidgin English as a Narrative Strategy and the Polyphonic Dimension of Austin Coates' *City of Broken Promises* (1967) and Timothy Mo's *An Insular Possession* (1986). *BELL 2004: Belgium Journal of English Language and Literatures*, 3, pp. 103–104.
Puga, R. M. (2013). *The British Presence in Macau: 1635-1793*. London: Royal Asiatic Society, Hong Kong: Hong Kong University Press.
Shi, D. (1993). Learning Pidgin English through Chinese Characters. In F. Byrne and J. Holm, eds., *Atlantic Meets Pacific*. Amsterdam: John Benjamins, pp. 459–465.
St. André, J. (2018). *Translating China as Cross-Identity Performance*. Honolulu: University of Hawai'i Press.
Tryon, D. T., Mühlhäusler, P. and Baker, P. (1996). English-derived Contact Languages in the Pacific in the 19th Century (Excluding Australia). In S. A. Wurm, P. Mühlhäusler, and D. T. Tryon, eds., *Atlas of Languages of Intercultural Communication in the Pacific, Asia, and the Americas 2(1)*. Berlin: Mouton de Gruyter, pp. 471–495.
Winterbotham, W. (1795). *An Historical, Geographical and Philosophical View of the Chinese Empire*. London: J. Ridgway.
Wu, Y. (2001). Pidgin English and Sino-Western Intercourse before the Mid-nineteenth Century. *Modern Chinese History Studies*, 123(3), pp. 172–202.
Yang, C.-M. (2011). *Performing China, Virtue, Commerce and Orientalism in Eighteenth-century England 1660-1760*. Baltimore: Johns Hopkins University Press.

Epilogue
Developing Historical Linguistic Awareness in a Multilingual World

Angelo Cattaneo

Looking at any phenomena from the point of view of a non-specialist is always a great opportunity. As a cultural historian I would like to reflect on the language dynamics of the past brought forward by the authors of this volume by reflecting on three main focal points which relate to the language dynamics of today and, more specifically, to the current state of the cultural-linguistic policies promoted by the European Union.

First, I would like to attempt a concise, critical assessment of the European Union's current political and cultural project on linguistic diversity and multilingualism, in order to highlight the nature of multilingualism implicitly underlined in the statements of the Council of Europe. Second, I wish to bring to this debate a comparative view, by taking into account the practices, sensibilities and complex geographic linguistics of the Early Modern Age as analysed by the studies contained in this volume, but also referring to debates on "global English" and the reasons which might encourage the mastering of a third language (besides one's native tongue, and the same "global English"). The fundamental question which underlies the observations that follow concerns the manner in which the linguistic dynamics of the past, preceding the affirmation of mono-linguistic principles of national states, and the cross-linguistic practices of today, can offer critical instruments which can better orientate and consolidate current policies intended to sustain and promote multilingualism: linguistic diversity, with the right to give value to the mother tongue of each interlocutor. Finally, with regard to this, I would mention the lack, in school and university textbooks of history, of any reference to the linguistic dynamics of the past as an essential basis for the study of cultures. A broad view of these dynamics would contribute to reviving and promoting a deeper knowledge of history connected by languages, in opposition to the emphasis which in the vast majority of states is placed on the prevalent national languages.

Starting with the current linguistic politics of the European Union, in May 2014 the Council of the European Union formulated and adopted

DOI: 10.4324/9781003092445-17

the following executive conclusions on multilingualism, language diversity and the mutual process of language learning:

> Languages unite people, render other countries and their cultures accessible, and strengthen intercultural understanding. Foreign language skills play a vital role in enhancing employability and mobility. Multilingualism also improves the competitiveness of the EU economy.
> (European Union, 2014)

Mutual language learning, multilingualism and linguistic diversity across Europe represent the cornerstones of the very political project that sustains the European Union, as encapsulated in the motto "united in diversity". These declarations of principles follow other formal points of view that aim to place in evidence the cultural importance of linguistic differences and pluralism: in particular the institution of an *International Mother Language Day*, first announced by UNESCO on 17 November 1999,[1] as part of a broader initiative "to promote the preservation and protection of all languages used by peoples of the world" as adopted by the UN General Assembly on 16 May 2007 in UN resolution 61/266.

What forms of multilingualism do the decisions of the Council of Europe refer to? And how could research on the linguistic dynamics of the past that precede the affirmation of national languages contribute, in an essential way, to this political and cultural project? The goal of the EU is that every citizen of the Union acquires linguistic competence in at least two languages beyond that of their mother tongue. This aim is being promoted in agreement with the State members through the teaching of at least two languages in schools. These abilities would reinforce individual mobility, thus favouring policies regarding employment, hiring, and the formulation of contracts, as well as facilitating a working life beyond the confines of the national state of each individual. One of the primary policies which, at the university level, have established a base for linguistic integration of the citizens of the European Union – also being adopted more recently on a global scale – has been, and without a doubt will continue to be, the Erasmus Programme (European Community Action Scheme for the Mobility of University Students): the student, teacher and administration exchange-programme established in 1987, to promote and reinforce ties and cultural exchange between institutions of a high level,[2] which is in fact one of its most significant instruments, and among the most pervasive practices for the learning of languages in contexts such as university courses – which imply and call for the most diverse cultural exchanges.

This exacting framework has been conceived within a context of linguistic practices that presents paradoxes and challenges which are by no means negligible. For some time now, linguists and historians of culture have had to come to terms with the spread of a near-global lingua franca defined as "Global English" (in a very broad and ever-expanding historiography, see for example, Jenkins 2007, 2014), a phenomenon, complicated by opposing forces of linguistic particularisms (forms of linguistic "jihad", see Bennett's "Introduction" in this volume), which is however surprisingly neglected, if not down-right ignored, in its multifarious complexity, by the *Conclusions* on linguistic matters of the European Council (Council of the European Union, 2014). By taking into consideration and sharing that which has already been underlined in the introduction to the book regarding conceptual affinities between Global English and late medieval and early modern Latin, Karen Bennett writes – referring to the research of Wright (2004) – that it is fragmented "into mutually incomprehensible tongues, combined with a drive to elevate a culturally pared-down version into a universal language of scholarship or administration" ("Introduction" p. 5). In terms which are certainly simplistic and anecdotal, it is very probable that if we were to take 24 groups of citizens of the European Union of school age, representing the 24 official languages of the Union, and were to ask them to converse all together in the language which united the greatest number of interlocutors with the abilities of *independent users*,[3] the majority would very probably agree to speak in one of the many linguistic variants of the current near-global lingua franca rooted in English. There are certainly diverse levels of linguistic competence, which depend on the quality of the language teaching received and the respective scholastic systems, but it is unlikely that other, even widespread languages, such as French, German, Spanish or Italian can show a degree of diffusion and pervasiveness comparable with that of Global English, even within Europe. This fact has arguably relevant consequences on the application and concrete feasibility of the European cultural project for the valorisation of multiple tongues.

Recently, the issue of "motivations for learning languages other than English in an English-dominant world" has received much scholarly attention but remains for the most part unresolved. In Europe, in particular, the learning of languages other than English (LOTEs) – whether by non-Anglophones choosing additional or alternative languages or Anglophones choosing to learn a different idiom – is contrasted by two converging and mutually reinforcing phenomena, which characterise the educational systems: the emphasis on the priority given to the understanding and teaching of national languages, and the teaching of English as a second language (see the ten articles collected in Dörnyei and Ushioda, 2017). In this sense, as a way of counteracting this linguistic and cultural simplification the learning of LOTEs could acquire a profound existential significance – for some individuals even a revaluing of their community of origin (whether real or imaginary). Reasoning in terms of motivation and educational methods, a substantial change in the evaluation of methods of teaching and understanding LOTEs has been urged, including not only linguistic considerations but also "intercultural capabilities" (Scarino, 2010). The well-known and recent political events involving Brexit have made this situation even more paradoxical with regard to the departure of the United Kingdom from the UE: English remains a *target language* for translation and the principal *second language*[4] in all the nations which constitute the European Union, although it is no longer the national language of any member state (Kużelewska, 2020).

As this volume amply documents, linguistic issues in past societies have received and are still receiving significant scholarly attention, so the question is how this rich academic research can be linked to relevant and ongoing contemporary debates. More precisely and with reference to current linguistic dynamics – which one might synthesize as an attribution of political-cultural value to multilingualism within a context which also witnesses the affirmation of a "fragmented lingua franca" such as Global English – what can the reflections, studies and discoveries of linguistic historians offer, beyond the horizon of academic erudition and debates? How can linguists and language historians interact and contribute to the current cultural policies on the issues of multilingualism and linguistic diversity?

Within the broad horizon of the humanities, historians of linguistics, languages and translation have an important role to play: by unveiling and creating living memories of the past of language dynamics and struggles, they can provide a historical context for the formation of the values of multilingualism, understood by the Council of Europe and the European Union as one of the pillars for the fostering of tolerance and mutual understanding. At the same time, a more active presence of scholars of historical linguistics, language history and translation in the (European) public sphere could strengthen such values in connection with the freedom of conscience and individual rights in EU countries.

The majority of contributions gathered in this volume were presented in the international conference "*A Host of Tongues...*" that took place in Lisbon in December 2018, organized by two centres of NOVA FCSH, the CETAPS (Centre for English, Translation, and Anglo-Portuguese Studies) and CHAM (Centre for the Humanities) as well as CEL (Centre for the Studies in Letters) of the University of Trás-os-Montes and Alto Douro (UTAD). Considering now in retrospect the significance of this collaborative effort and the publications which have resulted, one of the evident and felicitous consequences has to do with the emphasis given to the necessity of providing an historical dimension to linguistic education with the goal of building a common European cultural space. Even more importantly, this collective work has highlighted the importance of a correct knowledge of linguistic history in order to understand the long-term development of one of the cultural pillars of contemporary Europe:

multilingualism and linguistic diversity. We believe that a better understanding of the past proves to be not only a useful but indeed also an invaluable tool to understand the current challenges related to European citizenship and identity, an identity that promotes as its indispensable common goal the unity and convergence of heterogeneous groups, desiring to respect, protect and promote civil rights and diversity as a specific manifestation of pluralism.

It is my contention that by focusing on the role of schools and textbooks in shaping a more widespread knowledge of language history and historical linguistics, an operation which could be facilitated by the creation of a dedicated research infrastructure promoted by the European Research Council, one could contribute to the reframing of education as a process of transfer of knowledge – and possibly even exchange – from academia to a larger audience, promoting linguistic diversity as pillars for a cooperative and peaceful co-existence. Political statements such as "The harmonious co-existence of European languages is a powerful example of unity through diversity – a cornerstone of the European project" need and call for a more grounded historical foundation (European Commission, 2021).

The proposal of focusing on the inclusion of language histories in textbooks is linked to the consolidated attention that the European Union and other European institutions (Council of Europe, OSCE) have given to the role played by school textbooks in handing down correct information about our shared European past (Verga, 2017). On several occasions, the Council of Europe highlighted the role of school education as the foundation of the awareness of European citizenship, especially through the teaching of history at all levels of schooling and higher education.[5] School textbooks are among the most accessible and widely disseminated media, and – at least where primary and secondary education is compulsory – can be counted among the few books really read and shared by vast communities of readers: particularly with regard to those fields of knowledge which, like history or historical linguistics, are subsequently relegated to niche disciplines (Meloni and Oliva, 2019). Updating school and university history textbooks with fresh knowledge on the history of languages, of their pluralism and complex linguistic dynamics from an historical perspective, together with the training of school teachers on these topics from a transcultural view, could be a most effective way of achieving the goals set out in the recommendations, resolutions and treaties produced by European institutions on the promotion of transcultural communication and the acquisition of the largest possible number of secondary languages to foster a plurality of voices. In order to achieve a deeper awareness of scientific research on the historical dimensions of languages, and by incorporating the current practice of considering national languages as "containers of differences" rather than as monolithic and immutable blocks of knowledge, customs and practices (Della Valle and Patota, 2016), it would be essential for history textbooks to abandon exclusive national linguistic perspectives.

With methods and purposes similar to those that have recently led to the creation of the Research Infrastructure for Religious Studies (ReIReS) – a pioneering community of twelve European institutions funded under the EU's Horizon 2020 scheme committed to building a highly qualified infrastructure on religious studies with the scope of sustaining religious pluralism in Europe[6] – language historians, translation studies scholars and linguists might consider the creation of a research infrastructure with similar aims, to communicate their knowledge beyond the academic borders of their own disciplines and reach the widest possible civic audience.

The study of modern history highlights how the convergence and synergy between religious pluralism and linguistic pluralism are undoubtedly at the basis of the (difficult and sometimes contrasting) affirmation of civil rights, and the recognition of plural forms of citizenship that respect differences and identities. If at the centre of ReIReS' mission there is an awareness that "peaceful living together in a multi-religious society is increasingly coming under pressure and [...] knowledge of religious traditions helps us to reduce fear and anger brought about through prejudices and unfamiliarity with 'the other'", the communities of historical linguists could work together towards the creation of an infrastructure to collect scientific knowledge and training expertise that could be shared with the multifaceted European societies, with the goal of modelling their cultural dynamics through three main mass educational tools: school history textbooks, museums, and the creation of comprehensive research infrastructures to aggregate sources and linguistic historical expertise. All together, they could provide better insight into the ways in which linguistic history is crucial for an understanding of the narrative of the past while at the same time intersecting the social, political and cultural processes of today.

A renowned UNESCO resolution of 2003 included language as one of the vehicles of intangible cultural heritage, together with oral traditions and expressions, performing arts, social practices, rituals and festive events, knowledge and practices concerning nature and the universe, and traditional craftsmanship.[7] The safeguarding of languages has been addressed by UNESCO, through the creation of a *Register of Good Practices in Language Preservation*, the *Atlas of the World's Languages in Danger*, the *International Year of Languages* (2008) and, more recently, the *International Year of Indigenous Languages* (2019). Altogether, these initiatives of institutional recognition have reinforced public awareness that languages are an essential part of the intangible cultural heritage that deserves and needs preservation. The focus of these UNESCO initiatives is mainly on languages that are still spoken. But there is unquestionably little attention given to the linguistic dynamics of the past as phenomena that could be displayed and presented to the general audience as relevant collective memories and an intangible cultural heritage.[8] The most relevant example is the recently founded House of European History located in Brussels, whose primary mission is "to enhance understanding of European history in all its complexity, to encourage the exchange of ideas and to question assumptions" (Savelli, 2019). The House of European History, established by the European Parliament, aims to become the leading museum on European trans-national phenomena, by sharing experiences and their diverse interpretations intended "to initiate learning on trans-national perspectives across Europe".[9] However, the analysis of the six sections – "Shaping Europe", "A Global Power", "Europe in Ruins", "Rebuilding a Divided Continent", "Shattering Certainties" and "Europe Now" – that give shape to the permanent exhibition of the House, reveals that languages and the history of languages of Europe are not given any attention.[10] It is important to highlight how at present there is still no comprehensive museum of the history of European and Mediterranean languages. As highlighted in a recent path-breaking volume on the history and current development of language museums from a global perspective, "the planning of museums dedicated to languages with a much wider speech community" has been problematic (Cannata et al., 2020: 19). A remarkable exception seems to be a recent pioneering museum project under development at the Sapienza University of Rome, curated by Cannata, entitled "Eurotales: A museum of the voices of Europe", that aims to fill this cultural gap (Cannata et al., 2020: 206–218).

At the end of this brief reflection, in the light of recent EU cultural policies that have defined and promoted multilingualism and the safeguarding of linguistic diversity as pillars of the very basis of the European project, the need to explore the history of the continent's multilingual past is more cogent than ever. If the pioneering work of Peter Burke (2004) has opened a field of reflection that has called into question not only language and translation historians, and specialists of the numerous European languages, but also cultural historians (e.g. Braarvig and Geller, 2018), our hope is that these communities of scholars consider other tools and places for disseminating the knowledge of the linguistic past. Due to their extensive diffusion, history textbooks for primary and secondary schools, along with those of universities, represent an extraordinary vehicle for the formation of a historical sensitivity that would offer a context for current policies on linguistic issues beyond specific national horizons. History museums, moreover, would offer an opportunity for dissemination: Steven Conn reminds us that "we live in a museum age (…) more people are going to more museums than at any time in the past" (Conn, 2010: 1–19). The absence, even in recently founded history museums, of specific discourses on languages and their past dynamics, as in the case of the House of European History, encourages proactive intervention by communities of specialists in the history of linguistic disciplines and the past of languages.

Finally, by taking as a possible model the *Research Infrastructure for Religious Studies* (ReIReS), created and funded in the framework of *Horizon 2020*, it would be desirable to promote and create a similar research infrastructure which, by uniting academic communities and the main publishing houses dealing with historical linguistics, could aggregate knowledge of the European multilingual past with the goal of contextualizing and strengthening a European citizenship, based on multilingualism, language diversity, but also, if not mostly, on historical interactions among languages, n the forms of translations, mutual contaminations, and loanwords. This infrastructure could also collect documents, recommendations and resolutions taken by the European Union on these subjects, paying attention in particular to the Council of Europe and to the cultural agencies that focus on languages, with the goal of establishing an open dialogue between the academic communities and the public sphere.

The essays contained in this volume, their articulated linguistic geography, together with the rich scientific contexts and debates that have emerged, are a testimony that now, more than ever, is the moment in which language and translation specialists as well as cultural historians, amplify these topics beyond the confines of academic specialisms, and reach, through more widespread tools and institutions, large transnational communities of citizens, beyond national borders.

Notes

1. The International Mother Language Day (21 February each year) marks the anniversary of the day when the people of Bangladesh (then East Pakistan) fought for recognition for the Bangla language. Several people were killed and many others injured while protesting at the University of Dhaka in 1952 in favour of the use of the Bangla language. The idea of celebrating an International Mother Language Day was initiated by Bangladesh. It was approved at the 1999 UNESCO General Conference and has been observed throughout the world since 2000. https://en.unesco.org/commemorations/motherlanguageday [Accessed 8 June 2021].
2. Council decision, OJ L 166, 25 June 1987.
3. "The term *independent user* corresponds at least to level B1, as defined in the Common European Framework of Reference for language competences (CEFR)" (Council of the European Union, 2014: 5). B1 (Independent User) is defined as follows by the CEFR: "Can understand the main points of clear standard input in familiar matters regularly encountered in work, school, leisure, etc. Can deal with most situations likely to arise while travelling in an area where the language is spoken. Can produce simple connected text on topics which are familiar or of personal interest. Can describe experiences and events, dreams, hopes and ambitions and briefly give reasons and explanations for opinions and plans".
4. "The main language(s) of instruction is/are considered as the *first* language(s), while among additional languages, the one which is most widely

taught is considered as the *second* language studied. Each Member State shall determine the languages which are to be considered as *first* and *second* languages in its case" (Council of the European Union, 2014: 5).
5. The portal of the Council of Europe stores and makes accessible thousands of documents about the teaching of history. Consult and search https://www.coe.int/web/portal/home using as research string "history teaching" [Accessed 8 June 2021].
6. The ReIReS project started in February 2018 and continued for three-and-a-half years. The twelve funding partners include: Brepols Publishers NV, Belgium; the Consiglio Nazionale Delle Ricerche – National Research Council, Italy; the École Pratique des Hautes Études, France; the Fondazione per le scienze religiose Giovanni XXIII, Italy; the Johannes Gutenberg-Universität Mainz, Germany; KU Leuven, Belgium; the Leibniz-Institut für Europäische Geschichte, Germany; Sofiiski Universitet Sveti Kliment Ohridski, Bulgaria; the Stichting Refo500, Netherlands; the Theological University of Apeldoorn, Netherlands; the Universität Hamburg, Germany; and the Uniwersytet Warszawski, Poland. ReIReS received funding from the European Union's Horizon 2020 programme under Grant Agreement No. 730895 – https://reires.eu/ [Accessed 8 June 2021].
7. See UNESCO (2013). Quoted in Cannata et al. (2020: 14).
8. It is well known that until a few decades ago, before the spread of compulsory primary schooling and the advent of radio and television broadcasting systems, what are now indisputably primary national languages were secondary languages to a plethora of local languages or dialects, the real first languages – in particular – of oral communication. See Woolhiser (2005).
9. House of European History, "Mission and vision" (n.d.-a), https://historia-europa.ep.eu/en/mission-vision [Accessed 8 June 2021].
10. House of European History, "Permanent Exhibition" (n.d.-a), https://historia-europa.ep.eu/en/permanent-exhibition [Accessed 8 June 2021].

References

Braarvig, J. and Geller, M. J., eds. (2018). *Studies in Multilingualism, Lingua Franca and Lingua Sacra*. Berlin: Max Planck Institute for the History of Science.

Burke, P. (2004). *Languages and Communities in Early Modern Europe*. Cambridge and New York: Cambridge University Press.

Cannata, N., Sönmez, M. J.-M. and Gahtan, M. W. (2020a). Eurotales: A Museum of the Voices of Europe. In: N. Cannata, M. J.-M. Sönmez and M. W. Gahtan, eds., *Museums of Language and the Display of Intangible Cultural Heritage*. Milton Park, Abingdon, Oxon and New York: Routledge, pp. 206–218.

Cannata, N., Sönmez, M. J.-M. and Gahtan, M. W., eds. (2020b). *Museums of Language and the Display of Intangible Cultural Heritage*. Milton Park, Abingdon, Oxon and New York: Routledge.

Conn, S. (2010). *Do Museums Still Need Objects?*. Philadelphia, PA: University of Pennsylvania Press.

Council of Europe. (n.d.) Available at: https://www.coe.int/en/web/portal/home [Accessed 8 June 2021].

Council of the European Union. (2014). Conclusions on multilingualism and the development of language competences. Available at: https://www.consilium. europa.eu/uedocs/cms_data/docs/pressdata/en/educ/142692.pdf. [Accessed 08 June 2021].
Della Valle, V. and Patota, G. (2016). *Lezioni di lessicografia. Storie e cronache di vocabolari*. Rome: Carocci.
Dörnyei, Z. and Ushioda, E., eds. (2017). *Beyond Global English: Motivation to Learn Languages in a Multicultural World*. Special issue of *The Modern Language Journal*, 101(3), pp. 451–454.
European Commission. (2014). Education and Training: About Multilingualism Policy. Available at: https://ec.europa.eu/education/policies/multilingualism/about-multilingualism-policy_en [Accessed 08 June 2021].
European Commission. (2021). Education and Training: Linguistic Diversity. Available at: https://ec.europa.eu/education/policies/linguistic-diversity_en [Accessed 08 June 2021].
House of European History. (n.d.-a). Mission and Vision. Available at: https://historia-europa.ep.eu/en/mission-vision [Accessed 8 June 2021].
House of European History. (n.d.-b). Permanent Exhibition. Available at: https://historia-europa.ep.eu/en/permanent-exhibition [Accessed 8 June 2021].
Jenkins, J. (2007) *English as a Lingua Franca: Attitude and Identity*. Oxford: Oxford University Press.
Jenkins, J., ed. (2014). *English as a Lingua Franca in the International University. The Politics of Academic English Language Policy*. Milton Park, Abingdon, Oxon and New York: Routledge.
Kużelewska, E. (2020). Quo Vadis English? The Post-Brexit Position of English as a Working Language of the EU. *International Journal for the Semiotics of Law – Revue internationale de Sémiotique juridique* (October 2020). DOI:10.1007/s11196-020-09782-x
Meloni, M. G. and Oliva, A. M., eds. (2019). Religious culture and education in 20th and 21st Century Europe. Special issue of *RiMe. Rivista dell'Istituto di Storia dell'Europa Mediterranea*, 5/I n.s., pp. 1–117. Available at: http://rime.cnr.it/index.php/rime/issue/view/31 [Accessed 08 June 2021].
Research Infrastructure for Religious Studies. (n.d.) Available at: https://reires.eu/ [Accessed 8 June 2021].
Savelli, A. (2019). Online Resources for the History of Religion: A Look at National History Museums and at the House of European History. Special issue of *RiMe. Rivista dell'Istituto di Storia dell'Europa Mediterranea*, 5/I, pp. 89–110. Available at: http://rime.cnr.it/index.php/rime/issue/view/31 [Accessed 08 June 2021].
Scarino, A. (2010). Assessing Intercultural Capability in Learning Languages: A Renewed Understanding of Language, Culture, Learning, and the Nature of Assessment. *The Modern Language Journal*, 94(2), pp. 324–329.
UNESCO. (1991). *Draft Report of Commission II* (0000117961). Available at: https://unesdoc.unesco.org/ark:/48223/pf0000117961.page=38 [Accessed 08 June 2021].
UNESCO. (2013). Purpose of the Lists of Intangible Cultural Heritage and of the Register of Good Safeguarding Practices. Available at: https://ich.unesco.org/en/purpose-of-the-lists-00807 [Accessed 8 June 2021].

United Nations. (2007). International Mother Language Day. Available at: https://www.un.org/en/observances/mother-language-day [Accessed 08 June 2021].

Verga, M. (2017). Dal Consiglio d'Europa all'Unione: storia e cittadinanza europea. *Ricerche storiche,* 2, pp. 129–150.

Woolhiser, C. (2005). Political Borders and Dialect Divergence/Convergence. In: P Auer, F. Hinskens and P. Kerswill, eds., *Europe Dialect Change. Convergence and Divergence in European Languages.* Cambridge and New York: Cambridge University Press, pp. 236–262.

Wright, R. (2004). Latin and English as World Languages. *English Today,* 20(4), pp. 3–13.

Contributors

Vuk-Tadija Barbarić is a Research Associate at the Institute of Croatian Language and Linguistics, Zagreb. His main interests are textual criticism, historical sociolinguistics and the history of the Croatian language. In the last decade, his research has been focused on the oldest Croatian lectionaries. This particular research interest peaked in 2017 when his book *The Genesis and Linguistic Formation of Croatian Lectionaries* was published. He also co-authored two other books. In recent years, his attention has been drawn to historical orthography, which has led him to establish a project at the Institute that deals with Croatian historical orthography in Roman script.

Brian Bennett is Professor of Religious Studies at Niagara University, New York, United States. His research focuses on sanctified and vehicular languages, primarily Church Slavonic, Latin, and Esperanto, in Russia and beyond. He is the author of *Sacred Languages of the World: An Introduction* (Wiley 2018) and *Religion and Language in Post-Soviet Russia* (Routledge 2011).

Karen Bennett is Associate Professor in Translation at NOVA University, Lisbon, and a researcher with the Centre for English, Translation and Anglo-Portuguese Studies (CETAPS), where she coordinates the Translationality strand. She is general editor of the journal *Translation Matters* and a member of the editorial board of the Brill series *Approaches to Translation Studies*. Her recent publications include *Hybrid Englishes and the Challenges of and for Translation* (Routledge 2019) and a special issue on *International English and Translation* (*The Translator* 23.4), both co-edited with Rita Queiroz de Barros.

Joshua Brown is Senior Lecturer in Italian Studies at the Australian National University. His doctoral work focussed on the tuscanisation of merchant texts in late fourteenth-century Milan. His postdoctoral fellowship at Stockholm University looked at religious writing in late medieval Milan. He has research interests in historical sociolinguistics and digital humanities, particularly dialect contact and koineization in Renaissance Italy. His latest book is entitled *Early Evidence for Tuscanisation in the Letters of Milanese Merchants in the Datini Archive, Prato, 1396–1402* (Istituto Lombardo Accademia di Scienze e Lettere, 2017) and he is currently preparing an edited volume entitled *Languages of Renaissance Italy* (Brepols).

Angelo Cattaneo is a Researcher for the CNR (National Research Council of Italy) and a Foreign-Affiliated Researcher of the CHAM (Centre for the Humanities), NOVA FCSH, Lisbon. His research spans the thirteenth to the seventeenth centuries and focuses on the cultural construction of space (studying cosmography, cartography and travel literature); and the history of cross-cultural encounters at the interface of the European and Asian empires. He was the Co-Principal Investigator of the project *Interactions between Rivals. The Christian Mission and the Buddhist Sects in Japan (1549–1647)* and the Principal Investigator of the exploratory project *The Space of Languages. The Portuguese Language in the Early Modern World*. He is currently pursuing the history of the first contacts of world languages and cultures in early modernity.

Oliver Currie is a Lecturer in the Department of English and American Studies at the University of Ljubljana, Slovenia. He has research interests in historical linguistics (in particular syntactic variation and change), sociolinguistics, language contact and translation studies (in particular early modern Bible translations and the translation of folktales) with a focus on the Celtic languages, English and French. He did a BA in Modern and Medieval Languages and an MPhil Linguistics at the University of Cambridge and completed his PhD in Linguistics at the University of Ljubljana on the development of verb-initial word order in Early Modern Welsh.

Ivana Eterović is a Research Associate at the Faculty of Humanities and Social Sciences, University of Zagreb. She teaches at the undergraduate level in the area of Slavic philology and the history of the Croatian language in the Middle Ages and Early Modern Period. Her research interests include historical sociolinguistics, language contact (in particular multilingualism and diglossia), dialectology and minority languages. Her research has been focused mostly on Croatian literary language in the sixteenth century, especially early modern Bible translations written or printed in Glagolitic script.

Juan María Gómez Gómez is a Professor of Latin Philology at the University of Extremadura since 2003. His two main research interests are connected to the Classical Tradition, including the influence of the *Aeneid* on Spanish Literature between the sixteenth and eighteenth centuries and Linguistic Historiography, in particular, in Latin grammars from the sixteenth and seventeenth centuries.

Within this latest field, Juan María Gómez has published a critical edition of the 1572 *Syntax* of the Jesuit Manuel Álvares (Universidad de Extremadura, 2002) and a critical edition of the 1601 *Regia Art* of Juan Luis de la Cerda (Universidad de Extremadura, 2013).

Theo Hermans is Emeritus Professor in the Centre for Translation Studies, University College London (UCL). His monographs include *Translation in Systems* (St. Jerome Publishing, 1999; reissued in 2020 as a Routledge Translation Classic) and *The Conference of the Tongues* (2007). His main research interests concern the theory and history of translation.

Vicente Lledó-Guillem is Full Professor of Spanish at Hofstra University, New York, United States. His research focuses mainly on language ideology and the political and cultural history of the Spanish and Catalan languages. Apart from numerous articles on language and literature, he is the author of several monographs: *The Making of Catalan Linguistic Identity in Medieval and Early Modern Times* (Palgrave Macmillan 2018), which he himself translated into Spanish: *La formación de la identidad lingüística catalana (siglos XIII–XVII)* (Marcial Pons 2019). He published *Literatura o imperio: la construcción de las lenguas castellana y catalana en la España renacentista* (Juan de la Cuesta) in 2008.

Christina Märzhäuser is a Private Lecturer in Portuguese, Spanish and French linguistics at the Department of Romance Languages, LMU Munich, and is also affiliated with FLUC Coimbra and CEHUM, Universidade do Minho, Braga. She has lectured at the universities of Munich, Augsburg, Mannheim, Kassel, Erlangen (Germany), Praia (Cape Verde), Braga (Portugal), Vienna (Austria) and São Paulo (Brazil) from 2006 to 2020 and was visiting researcher at UC Berkeley in 2013. Her research focuses on bilingual education and heritage languages; creoles, language contact and multilingualism; language and music; nominal reference and the syntax–semantics interface. Her PhD was on the Capeverdean-Portuguese language contact in rap lyrics (FLUC Coimbra/LMU Munich, 2006–2009) and her Habilitation on Bare Noun constructions in French and Spanish (LMU Munich, 2009–2015).

Rogério Miguel Puga is Associate Professor at the Faculty of Social Sciences and Humanities (NOVA University, Lisbon). His research interests are Travel Writing, British Contemporary Fiction, Anglo-Portuguese Studies and History of the Portuguese and British Empires (India and the Far East).

Enrique Rodrigues-Moura is Full Professor at the Department of Romance Languages at the University of Bamberg. He received his

PhD in Romanic Philology at the Complutense University of Madrid and a Post-Doc-Award from the Calouste Gulbenkian Foundation to research at the University of Lisbon. His two main research interests related with this book are the Literatures and Cultures in Spanish and Portuguese of the sixteenth, seventeenth and eighteenth centuries (Botelho de Oliveira, Cervantes, Vieira, Saavedra Fajardo, F. Manuel de Melo, Costa Peixoto) and the theory and practice of textual criticism (*Fénix Renascida*, Cervantes, C. Castelo Branco, xPessoa, Botelho de Oliveira).

Eustaquio Sánchez Salor is Emeritus Professor at the University of Extremadura, having previously lectured at the University of La Laguna and University of Granada. One of his research lines is Humanism and the Latin Renaissance in Spain and Europe, with particular attention to the Grammar of the sixteenth and seventeenth centuries. He is the author of monographs such as *De las elegancias a las causas de la lengua: retórica y gramática del humanismo* (Alcañiz-Madrid, 2002) and *Las ediciones del Arte de Gramática de Nebrija, 1481–1700: Historia bibliográfica* (Mérida 2008). He has also investigated the connection between European Grammar and missionary Grammars.

Laetitia Sansonetti is Senior Lecturer in English (Translation Studies) at Université Paris Nanterre, France. Her recent publications include two co-edited volumes: *Auteurs-traducteurs* (Presses universitaires de Paris Nanterre, 2018) and *The Early Modern English Sonnet* (Manchester University Press, 2020). Her research bears on the reception of classical and Continental texts in early modern England, poetry and rhetoric, and questions of authorship and authority. Her current research project on translation and polyglossia in early modern England (https://tape1617.hypotheses.org/) is funded by a five-year grant from Institut Universitaire de France.

Delia Schipor is Associate Professor at the Faculty of Humanities, Sports and Educational Science, University of South-Eastern Norway. She teaches and supervises at the undergraduate and graduate levels in the areas of English linguistics, sociolinguistics, and didactics, as well as multilingualism and cultural studies. Her research interests include historical and present-day multilingualism and foreign language acquisition in a multilingual context. She has a doctoral degree in Literacy Studies with a thesis on multilingualism in documentary texts from nineteenth-century England. The main theoretical contribution of this project is the *multilingual event* framework, designed specifically for the study of multilingualism in written texts.

Index

Aeneas 4, 7, 55; *Aeneid* 15, 55, 134, 254; *see also* Roman, national origin myth

Africa/-n 15, 92, 186, 207–223; African language(s) 12, 13, 185, 207–223

Aldrete, Bernardo de 7, 10, 74–88, 116, 124, 127

Alembert, Jean le Rond de 10, 135

America/-n 3, 13, 119, 209, 213, 220, 224, 225, 226, 227, 229, 231, 232, 233, 235, 236, 237

Anderson, Benedict 2, 3, 14, 15

Arab 11, 186; Arabic (language) 3, 11, 15, 76, 93, 95, 96, 97, 101, 104, 105, 170, 173, 178, 184, 185, 186; 'Arabica' (script) 101

Aramaic 97, 100

Argentré, Bertrand de 56, 63–65

Asia/-n 11, 91, 96, 226, 254

Babel/-ian 7, 14, 56, 65, 74, 75, 77, 78, 79, 81, 82, 83, 84

Basque (language) 78, 96

Beauzée, Nicolas 10, 135

Belgium/-ian 90, 159, 227, 250; *belgica* 127

bible/ical 4, 6, 7, 8, 33, 40–52, 56, 58, 60, 61, 62, 67, 75, 91, 100, 153

bible translation 4, 6, 7, 40–52, 55–56, 58, 61, 62, 67, 91, 97, 98; Breton 67; Croatian 40–52; Dutch 91; Welsh 56, 58, 60–62, 67; *see also* Erasmus of Rotterdam, Erasmus's Bible; Luther's Bible; polyglot Bible; Vulgate

bilingual /-ism 43, 102, 149; bilingual editions 97, 99, 193, 194; *see also* dictionaries, bi- /trilingual; multilingual/-ism

Brazil/-ian 5, 12, 91, 93, 94, 207–223

Breton/Brittany 53–73; Breton (language) 4, 6, 7, 53, 54, 55, 56, 62–68, 69; *see also* bible translation; dictionaries; national origin myth, Breton

Britain/-ish/-on 7, 53, 55, 58, 59, 60, 62, 63, 64, 68, 69; Great Britain 224, 226, 230, 232, 235, 236; *see also* national origin myth, British

Brocense, El *see* Sánchez de las Brozas, Francisco

Burke, Peter 2, 3, 4, 9, 14, 85, 87, 131, 147, 170, 178, 248

Byzantium/Byzantine Empire 3, 146, 148; Byzantine 11, 41, 144, 160

Čakavian 6, 42–43, 45, 46, 48, 49

Canton/-ese 13, 224–241; Cantonese (language) 226, 230, 231, 234, 236

Cartesianism 123, 129; *see also* rationalism

Castile/-ian 15, 76, 78, 116, 125; Castilian language 3, 4, 7, 9, 10, 74–88, 114–124, 186; 'primitive Castilian' 7, 74, 78, 84; *see also* Spanish

Catalonia 76, 85; Catalan (language) 3, 78, 79, 83, 85, 178, 184

Catholic/-ism 7, 9, 53, 54, 55, 59, 60, 61, 65, 92, 94, 101, 102, 117, 129, 142, 143, 144, 152, 153, 195, 196, 210, 224

Catholic Reformation 151; *see also* Counter-Reformation

Celt/-ic 56, 64; Celtic (language) 65, 200

China/-ese 13, 93, 98, 103, 224–241; Chinese Empire 230, 238; Chinese (language) 98, 148, 224, 226, 228, 231, 232–234, 248; *see also* Canton/-ese

Index

Chinese Pidgin English (CPE) 5, 13, 224–241
church 3, 4, 7, 22, 54, 55, 56, 57, 59, 60, 62, 68, 69, 91, 101, 129, 142, 144, 145, 146, 151, 152, 153, 154, 155, 156, 158, 160, 209, 211; Calvinist church 91; Church of England 7, 55, 57, 59, 60, 61; Early British Church 7, 55, 59, 60, 61, 68, 69; Lutheran church 91; protestant churches 7, 55, 56, 57, 59; Orthodox (Russian) 142, 148, 151–155, 161; Roman (Catholic) Church 9, 41, 60, 129, 142, 151; Welsh Church 62
Church Slavonic 6, 11, 41–50, 143, 146, 147, 152, 154; Old Church Slavonic 6, 11, 41; Croatian Church Slavonic 6, 41–50
Cicero, Marcus Tullius 9, 113, 114, 121, 122, 124, 133, 134, 137, 139, 152
civil script (*grazhdanskii shrift*) 11, 42, 43, 46, 47, 49, 50, 101, 159, 160, 161
classical learning/civilization 9, 10, 60, 118, 147, 152, 156; classical languages 10, 95, 142; see also Greece/-k; Latin
codeswitching 2, 25
codify/-ication (linguistic) 4, 12, 14, 48, 65, 66, 68, 149, 173, 175
colonialism 12, 13, 95, 207–223, 224, 227, 231, 235, 236
commerce, language of see trading languages
Constantinople 3, 92, 94, 95
contact language/variety 13, 170, 172, 175, 179, 180, 184, 226, 232, 234, 236; see also language contact
contact zone 2, 5, 8, 89–108, 225
Counter-Reformation 90, 101, 151; see also Catholic Reformation
creole 172, 185, 187, 213; creolization 170, 180, 183, 187; see also Macau Creole Portuguese (MCP)
Croatia/-n 5, 6, 40–52; Croatian (language) 40–52; see also bible translation; Čakavian; Church Slavonic, Croatian Church Slavonic
Cyrillic 11, 42, 46, 47, 159, 160, 161

Defoe, Daniel 227, 234, 237
Dekker, Thomas 192, 198, 202, 203

dialect 3, 41, 42, 48, 49, 91, 131, 173, 175, 177, 179, 219, 228, 250; see also vernacular
dictionaries 65–66, 97, 120, 121–122, 126, 127, 137, 155, 169–189, 193, 200, 201, 202; bi- or trilingual 97, 122, 126, 155, 193; Breton 65–66; French 175; Italian 175, 193, 202; Latin 97, 121–122, 126, 127, 155, 175, 200; Spanish 122, 126, 175; see also glossaries
Dictionnaire de la langue franque ou petit mauresque 12, 169–189
diglossia/-c 6, 40, 41–50
Dutch 89–108, 159; Dutch Empire 90, 92, 95; Dutch (language) 8, 90, 91, 93, 94, 96, 97, 98, 99, 100, 101, 102, 103, 104, 105, 145, 157, 159, 203, 228; Dutch Republic 90, 92, 95; see also bible translation

East India Company (EIC): Dutch EIC 90; English/British EIC 93, 225, 231, 236, 237, 238; Swedish EIC 227, 228, 231
Eco, Umberto 4, 9, 11, 14, 15, 16, 76, 131, 140
Empire 3, 9, 11, 48, 76, 80, 81, 82, 83, 84, 85, 90, 92, 142, 145, 152, 156, 160, 219, 230, 238, 254; see also Byzantine Empire; Chinese Empire; colonialism; Dutch Empire; imperial; Ottoman Empire; Portuguese Empire; Roman Empire; Russian Empire; Spanish Empire
Encyclopédie 10, 135, 136; see also Alembert; Beauzée
England/-ish 5, 7, 12, 15, 21–39, 53–62, 63, 66, 68–69, 92, 94, 95, 111, 118, 129, 142, 151, 190–206, 224–241; English (language) 1, 4, 5, 6, 7, 12, 13, 14, 15, 21–39, 50, 53–62, 68–69, 94, 95, 97, 100, 101, 102, 103, 105, 111, 122, 129, 157, 190–206, 224–241, 242–245; see also East India Company, English; national origin myth, English
Enlightenment/-ed 112, 129, 130, 131, 135, 136, 137, 220; Enlightenment pedagogy 129–137
Erasmus of Rotterdam 46, 50, 114, 116–118, 125; Erasmus's Bible 46, 50

ethnic/-icity 63, 93, 207, 208, 210, 212–215, 216, 217, 218, 228, 235; multi-ethnic 93, 208
Europe/-ean 2–4, 5, 6, 8, 9, 10, 11, 12, 13, 14, 41, 46, 53, 56, 66, 68, 75, 84, 90, 91, 92, 93, 95, 96, 99, 100, 101, 105, 112, 122, 123, 129, 130, 131, 134, 135, 137, 142, 143, 144, 145, 146, 147, 148, 149, 150, 151, 152, 154, 156, 157, 159, 160, 175, 176, 195, 196, 208, 210, 213, 216, 218, 220, 224, 227, 228, 231, 237, 242–252

Florio, John 193, 194, 202
Folena, Gianfranco 45, 46, 50
fractal recursivity 75, 77, 84, 86
France/French 2, 7, 53–73, 76, 77, 78, 91, 92, 94, 95, 96, 97, 100, 102, 103, 130, 175, 176, 191, 196, 201, 202, 236; French (language) 3, 4, 5, 6, 8, 12, 21–39, 53–73, 76, 77, 78, 79, 83, 90, 91, 92, 93, 94, 95, 96, 97, 98, 99, 100, 101, 102, 103, 104, 105, 111, 116, 122, 125, 129, 143, 145, 148, 149, 150, 154, 156, 157, 160, 161, 175, 176, 178, 180, 182, 185, 191, 192, 194, 196, 197, 200, 203, 228, 244; *see also* dictionary, French; national origin myth, French
Franks 11, 63, 64, 186; Frankish (language) 11–12, 63, 169–199, *see also* Mediterranean Lingua Franca (MLF)

Galicia/-n 76, 77, 79; Galician (language) 77, 78, 79, 83
Gaul/-s 56, 58, 63–65, 68, 69, 132; Gaulish (language) 7, 56, 64–66; *see also* national origin myth, Gaulish/Celtic
Gbe (Fon) 12, 13, 208, 212, 219n; *see also* languages, African language(s)
gender 90, 208, 212, 216–218, 232; grammatical gender 194, 197
Genoa 130, 177; Genoese (language) 177, 178
Geoffrey of Monmouth 55, 58, 59, 60, 62, 63, 69
German/-y 2, 15, 56, 81, 92, 94, 97, 142, 148, 151, 250; German (language) 3, 46, 91, 94, 95, 96, 97, 99, 100, 101, 102, 103, 104, 105, 122, 143, 145, 148, 149, 150, 151, 154, 156, 157, 161, 244
Germanic 56, 66, 79, 82, 84, 203; *Germanica* 127
Glagolitic 40, 41, 42, 43, 44, 46, 47, 49, 50
glossaries 13, 98, 145, 175, 200, 207–223; *see also* dictionaries
glottonym 171, 173, 177; *see also* language naming
Gordin, Michael 15, 148, 149, 157, 159
Goth/-ic 76, 82; Gothic (language) 82, 83, 96; *see also* Visigoth/-ic
Grassi, Giacomo di 190, 191, 192, 200
Greece/-k 64, 80, 81, 134; Greek (language) 3, 14, 41, 80, 95, 96, 97, 100, 101, 104, 105, 111, 120, 133, 134, 142, 143, 144, 145, 146, 150, 151, 155, 156, 161, 178, 184, 186

Hebrew (language) 3, 14, 41, 91, 95, 97, 98, 100, 114, 142, 155, 156, 161
Hispania/-ic 7, 75, 76, 77, 78, 80, 81, 82–84, 123, 125, 132, 138; Hispanic (language) 78, 80, 82–84, 111, 112, 127, 186
Holland 90, 92, 96; *see also* Dutch; Low Countries; Netherlands
Horace 133, 138, 152
hybrid/-ity (linguistic) 1, 123, 176, 186; *see also* lingua franca, China Pidgin English (CPE); Mediterranean Lingua Franca (MLF); *sermo hispanolatinus*
humanism/-ist 9, 10, 100, 111, 112, 137, 146, 156, 201

Iberia /-n 3, 4, 7, 10, 14, 74, 75–79, 83, 84, 219; Iberian languages 3, 75–79, 83, 84, 219; *see also* Muslim occupation of Iberia
ideology (linguistic) 14, 56, 74, 79, 81, 84, 86, 255
imperial 11, 53, 57, 64, 68, 146, 147–151, 155–160, 161, 230, 233; *see also* colonialism; empire
Imperial Academy of Sciences (St Petersburg) 11, 143, 147–151, 160
India/-n 8, 11, 90, 91, 93, 96, 101, 119, 175, 225, 227, 231, 236, 237; Indian languages 119, 175; *see also* East India Company
Indies 93, 119, 125, 230, 238

Index

Indigenous: languages 53, 54, 120, 220, 247; peoples 59, 94, 95, 144, 212, 213, 220
intermediate language 93, 95, 98, 104, 105; *see also* indirect translation
interpreter /-ing 8, 75, 94, 95, 96, 98, 155, 228, 236
Ireland/-ish 9, 111, 117, 118, 119, 120, 122, 125
Italy/-ian 3, 9, 10, 12, 49, 91, 92, 94, 97, 102, 129–141, 146, 185, 190, 192, 193, 194, 195, 198, 199, 202, 250; Italian (language) 5, 12, 45, 46, 49, 92, 94, 95, 97, 100, 101, 102, 104, 105, 111, 116, 125, 127, 129–141, 145, 157, 170, 171, 175, 176, 177, 178, 179, 180, 181, 182, 184, 185, 186, 187, 190–206, 219, 244; Italianate 12, 190–206; *see also* dictionaries, Italian

Jansenism 129, 135, 137; *see also* Port Royal
Japan/-ese 93, 254; Japanese (language) 93, 96
jargon 5, 12, 157, 190–206, 228, 231; fencing 5, 12, 190–206
Jesuit 9, 12, 65, 94, 102, 111–128, 129, 130, 131, 134, 135, 136, 137, 139, 142, 151, 152, 161, 212, 255
Jew/-ish 91, 95, 98, 99, 177, 219, 232, 233; *see also* Hebrew
Jonson, Ben 192, 196, 197, 202, 203

Koiné 11
Kožičić Benja, Šimun 6, 40–46

Lagomarsini, Girolamo 10, 120–141
language *see* African langauge(s); Arabic; Aramaic; Basque; Breton; Čakavian; Cantonese; Castilian; Catalan; Celtic; Chinese; creole; Croatian; Dutch; English; French; Frankish; Galician; Gaulish; Gbe (Fon); Genoese; German; Gothic; Greek; Hebrew; Hispanic; Iberian languages, Indian languages, indigenous languages; intermediate language; Italian; Japanese; Latin; lingua franca; literary language; national language; Occitan; official language; perfect language; Persian; pidgin; Portuguese; prestige language; Provençal; Romance; sacred language; Sanskrit; Sicilian; Slavonic; Spanish; spoken/oral language; standard language; Swedish; Syriac; trading language; Turkish; Tupi; Tuscan; universal language, vehicular language; Venetian; *see also*
language contact 1, 3, 4, 8, 15, 53, 81, 84, 170, 172, 178, 179, 183, 184, 185, 186, 225; *see also* contact language/variety
language ideology *see* ideology (linguistic)
language learning/teaching 4, 95, 96, 111–128, 129–141, 152, 155, 202, 212, 219, 231, 236, 243, 244, 245; language manual 9–10, 118–122, 143, 194
language mixing 5, 11, 12, 76–77, 79, 83, 171, 172, 176, 184, 200–201, 228; *see also* hybrid/-ity; pidgin
language myths 3, 4, 5, 7, 11–12, 15, 53–73, 74–88, 169–189
language naming 171–175 *see also* glottonym
language philosophy 2, 12; *see also* ideology (linguistic)
language politics/policy 12, 212, 245
language status 3, 4, 6, 7, 15, 42, 43, 53–73, 91, 95, 147, 200, 224, 235, *see also* official language, prestige language, sacred language
Latin 3–11, 12, 14, 15, 21–39, 41–50, 53, 54, 56, 63, 65, 66, 68, 74, 75, 76, 77, 79, 80–86, 90, 91, 92, 94, 95, 96, 97, 98, 99, 100, 101, 102, 103, 104, 105, 111–128, 129–140, 142–166, 175, 177, 178, 184, 185, 191, 200, 201, 203, 244; Classical/Ciceronian Latin 9, 12, 111, 113, 116, 121, 122, 133, 134, 181, 191
Latinate script, *see* civil script
lingua franca 3, 4, 5, 6, 9, 10, 11, 14, 15, 41, 91, 92, 98, 100, 111, 121, 122, 131, 135, 136, 143, 145, 146, 160, 169–189, 192, 199, 201, 202, 226, 244, 245; *see also* China Pidgin English, Mediterranean Lingua Franca (MLF), Latin, *Lingua Geral da Mina* (LGM)
Lingua Geral da Mina (LGM) 5, 12, 13, 207–223

lingua sacra see sacred language
linguistic diversity 76, 79, 81, 89, 180, 242, 243, 246, 248, 249
linguistic essentialism 14, 74–88
linguistic hybridity see hybrid/-ity
linguistic purity 78, 83, 84, 114, 132, 196, 198
literary language 4, 6, 40–45, 46, 48, 49, 50, 147, 176
Low Countries 5, 8, 89–108; see also Belgium; Dutch Republic; Holland; Netherlands
Luther, Martin 46, 91; Luther's Bible 46; see also church, Lutheran church

Macao Pidgin Portuguese (MPP) 236, 237
Macau 5, 13, 98, 224, 225, 226, 227, 229, 231–236
Macau Creole Portuguese (MCP) 236
Maunoir, Julien 56, 65–68
Medieval/Scholastic Latin 9, 104, 116, 123; New/Neo Latin 9, 134, 146, 147, 152; Vulgar Latin 9, 15, 185; see also dictionaries, Latin
Mediterranean Lingua Franca (MLF) 5, 11–12, 13, 169–189
missionary/-ies 8, 41, 65, 94, 96, 119, 120, 139, 144, 224, 237
monolingual/-ism 2, 7, 14, 21, 35, 57, 62, 63, 74, 75, 76, 77, 79, 81, 82, 84, 89, 100; 'monolingual mindset' 2, 14
Moor/-ish 75, 76, 77, 79; see also Muslim
multilingual/-ism 2–3, 5, 6, 8, 12, 13, 14, 21–39, 40, 41, 68, 74–88, 89–108, 151, 154, 178, 191, 194, 196, 201, 203, 208, 212, 242–252; functional multilingualism 2, 6; individual multilingualism 2, 8, 89, 93–98; societal multilingualism 2, 8, 21, 40, 89, 90–93; textual/documentary multilingualism 6, 8, 26, 28–39, 89, 99–105
multilingual events 21–39
Muscovy 142, 144, 145, 156, 158, 160
Muslim 3, 77, 78, 82, 83, 93, 211; Muslim occupation of Iberia 77, 78, 82, 83; see also Moor/-ish
myth see language myths;

national origin myths
nation 2, 57, 58, 60, 61, 62, 63, 64, 66, 67, 120, 136, 175, 176; Breton-speaking nation 63; French nation 64, 67; Welsh-speaking nation 57, 58, 60, 61, 62; see also nation-state, national language
nationalism 2, 5, 11, 14, 54, 56, 61, 64, 68, 84, 175, 176, 232; linguistic nationalism 4, 14, 54, 68, 75, 76, 175, 176
national historical narrative, see national origin myths
national language 1, 2, 3, 4, 11, 12, 14, 44, 49, 54, 68, 69, 91, 147, 148, 150, 176, 242, 243, 245, 246, 250
national origin myths 4, 7, 15, 53–73; Breton 54, 56, 62–68, 69; British 55, 62; English 54, 55, 68; French 54, 55, 56, 63, 64–65, 68; Gaulish/Celtic 64; Roman 55, 64; Welsh 54, 55, 57–61, 68; see also language myths
nation-state 1, 3, 49, 68, 131, 172, 176
Netherlands 90, 91, 92, 94, 101, 102; see also Dutch Republic; Holland; Spanish Netherlands

Occitan 78, 85, 178
official language 21, 56, 57, 62, 67, 244
oral language see spoken/oral language
Orientalism/-ist 185, 224, 234, 235, 237
Orthodox/-y 142, 143, 144, 145, 151, 152, 153, 161
Ostler, Nicholas 15, 143, 147, 155, 202
Ottoman (Empire) 92, 94, 95

Peixoto, Antonio da Costa 13, 207–223
perfect language 4, 10, 131, 129–141
Persia/-n 96, 233; Persian (language) 3, 11, 96, 97
Peter the Great 11, 142, 143, 144, 146, 157, 159, 160
petit mauresque 12, 171; see also Frankish language; Mediterranean Lingua Franca(MLF)

philology/-ogical 3, 5, 40, 42, 44, 45, 48, 150, 173, 219
pidgin 5, 11, 12, 13, 170, 172, 183, 185, 186, 187; *see also* Chinese Pidgin English (CPE); Macao Pidgin Portuguese (MPP); Mediterranean Lingua Franca (MLF)
polyglot/-ssia 8, 89, 93, 94, 96, 97, 100, 145; polyglot bible 8, 100; *see also* multilingual/-ism
Port Royal 112, 123, 129, 130, *see also* Jansenism
Portugal/-uese 7, 13, 76, 77, 85, 93, 94, 122, 177, 208, 209, 210, 211, 212, 213, 218, 225, 226, 236; Portuguese Empire 210–212; Portuguese language 3, 8, 13, 77, 78, 79, 83, 90, 91, 92, 93, 94, 95, 96, 97, 98, 101, 105, 116, 122, 170, 178, 179, 184, 186, 207, 208, 209, 212, 214, 219, 220, 225, 226, 228, 229, 236, 237; *see also* Macao Pidgin Portuguese (MPP), Macau Creole Portuguese (MCP)
Pratt, Mary Louise 2, 8, 15, 89, 233; *see also* contact zone; linguistic utopia
prestige language 6, 11, 12, 41, 44, 46, 50, 56, 65, 91, 200
primitive Castilian, *see* Castilian
print/-ing (press/industry) 3, 5, 6, 7, 14, 44, 45, 47, 50, 67, 99, 145, 159, 201, 209; printed works 46, 47, 50, 61, 62, 92, 99, 100, 101, 102, 103, 104, 119, 120, 127, 130, 148, 157, 158, 181, 194, 209, 212, 218, 219
Protestant/-ism 6, 7, 46, 47, 50, 53, 54, 55, 56, 57, 58, 59–61, 67, 68, 90, 92, 94, 102, 125, 143, 151, 237; *see also* Reformation
Provençal 178, 179

Quintilian 113, 123

rationalism/-ist 4, 10, 111–112, 129, 130, 131, 156, 212, *see also* Cartesianism, Enlightenment
Reformation 4, 54, 55, 94, 146, 151; *see also* Counter-Reformation; Protestant/-ism
religion 6, 7, 8, 9, 12, 14, 24, 41, 53, 54, 55, 58, 59, 61, 62, 65, 67, 68, 69, 90, 94, 100, 101, 117, 129, 135, 143, 145, 146, 151–155, 160, 161, 207, 212, 217, 247–249; language of 6, 7, 8, 9, 12, 14, 24, 41, 54, 57, 62, 65, 67, 69, 100, 101, 145, 146, 151–155, 160, 161, 207; *see also* Catholicism; Muslim; Orthodox/-y; Protestant/-ism; sacred language
Renaissance 9, 43, 50, 123, 146
Roman/s 7, 9, 15, 27, 41, 44, 45, 60, 64, 66, 74, 79, 80–81, 82, 115, 116, 133, 134, 146, 151, 157, 155, 160; Roman Empire 9, 80, 81, 82; *see also* national origin myth, Roman
Roman Catholicism *see* Catholic/-ism; Church, Roman (Catholic) Church
Romance 9, 11, 50, 63, 64, 65, 69, 74, 76, 77, 78, 82–84, 122, 123, 124, 130, 169, 170, 173, 175, 176, 177, 178, 179, 180, 182, 184, 185, 186, 200
Rostrenen, Grégoire de 56, 65–68
Russia/-n 4, 10–11, 142–166; Russian Empire 11, 142, 145, 152, 156, 160; Russian (language) 47, 142–166

sacred language 6, 11, 15, 48, 144, 156, 160; *see also* religion, language of
Sánchez de las Brozas, Francisco 9, 111–128
Sanctius *see* Sánchez de las Brozas, Francisco
Sanskrit 11, 15, 96, 101
Saviolo, Vincentio 190–193, 194, 196
Scandinavia/-n 91, 145, 151; *see also* Sweden
Scholastic/-ism 4, 116, 123, 146, 153; *see also* Latin (scholastic)
science/-tific 8, 9, 10, 11, 15, 89, 100, 131, 135–136, 142, 145, 146, 147–151, 156, 160, 219, 246, 247, 249; science, language of 10, 15, 135–136, 145, 146, 147–151, 156, 159, 160; *see also* Imperial Academy of Sciences
script 6, 11, 27, 28, 35, 41, 42, 43, 46, 49, 50, 101, 159, 160; *see also* Arabica; civil script; Cyrillic; Glagolitic; Sanskrit; Slavonic
sermo hispanolatinus 5, 9, 111–128; *see also* hybrid/-ity; language mixing

Shakespeare, William 192, 194–196, 201–203
Sicilian (language) 178, 186
Silver, George 190, 192, 193, 196, 201
slave/-ry 12, 13, 93, 207–222, 227, 230
Slavic 41–47, 50, 144, 254; Slavic languages 41–47, 50, *see also* Glagolitic; Slavonic
Slavonic 6, 11, 41–50, 143, 144, 145, 146, 147, 150, 152, 154, 155, 156, 159, 160, 161; *see also* Church Slavonic
Society of Jesus 118–120, 130, 137, 151; *see also* Jesuit
Spain/Spanish 7, 8, 9, 74–88, 90–92, 94, 96, 98, 99, 101, 105, 111–128, 132, 175, 191, 196, 203, 256; Spanish Empire 76, 84; Spanish (language) 3, 8, 9, 12, 74, 84, 90, 91, 94–105, 111–113, 115–116, 122, 125, 129, 130, 137, 157, 175, 177–179, 185, 186, 192, 194, 195–197, 200, 202, 203, 244; *see also* Castilian; dictionaries, Spanish; Hispanic
Spanish Netherlands 90, 91, 92, 94, 101, 102
Spivak, Gayatri 13, 208, 216
spoken/oral language 5, 9, 21, 25, 63, 111–128, 171, 184, 250; *see also* vernacular
St Petersburg 11, 142–166; *see also* Imperial Academy of Sciences
standard/-ization (linguistic) 12, 44, 48, 62, 89, 93, 171, 175, 176, 177, 180, 182, 184, 186, 187, 226, 229, 230, 233, 234; standard language 44, 89, 171, 176, 184
Suebi 77, 79, 83
Swedish (language) 161; *see also* East India Company, Swedish
Syriac 97, 100

trading language 5, 11, 13, 91, 92, 169–189, 224–241
translanguaging 1, 2, 14
translation/-or 1, 4, 6, 7, 8, 13, 32, 33, 40, 41, 45, 46, 48, 50, 55, 56, 58, 61, 62, 67, 89–108, 111, 112, 114, 115, 116, 122, 134, 137, 138, 146, 148, 157, 176, 190, 191, 192, 193, 196, 199, 200, 201, 202, 207, 209, 213, 225, 227, 228, 229, 230, 231, 234, 236, 245; indirect translation 97, 104, 106; *see also* bible translation, interpreting
Tupi 12, 95
Turkish (language) 94, 95, 97, 173, 178; *see also* Ottoman Empire
Tuscany 129, 130, 137; Tuscan (language) 177, 180, 187, 253–254

Ukraine/ian 144, 151, 152, 156
universal language 4, 5, 9, 10, 135, 244
university 96, 97, 102, 117, 119, 120, 129, 150, 154, 242, 243, 246, 248; Leiden University 97; Leuven University 102; Moscow State University 150, 154; Salamanca University 111–120

vehicular language 135, 143, 146, 148, 158, 253; *see also* lingua franca
Venice/-etian 46, 50, 94, 95, 129, 143, 177; Venetian (language) 170, 178
vernacular 3, 4, 5, 6, 7, 9, 10, 15, 21, 29, 32, 33, 34, 35, 36, 37, 39, 42, 43, 44, 45, 46, 47, 48, 49, 50, 53, 54, 67, 68, 69, 95, 99, 100, 111, 112, 115, 117, 118, 121, 125, 129, 130, 131, 134, 135, 137, 144, 173, 175, 177, 179, 180, 201, 207
Virgil 15, 55, 133, 147, 152, *see also Aeneid*
Visigoth/-ic 77, 78, 79, 82–84
Vulgate 153

Wales/Welsh 7, 19, 53–73, 198; Welsh (language) 4, 6, 7, 53, 54, 55, 56, 57–62, 64, 66, 67, 68, 69, 96, 198, 254; *see also* national origin myth, Welsh